*Oracle Press*™

Oracle General Ledger Guide

Oracle
General Ledger
Guide

Melanie Anjele Cameron

New York   Chicago   San Francisco
Lisbon   London   Madrid   Mexico City   Milan
New Delhi   San Juan   Seoul   Singapore   Sydney   Toronto

The McGraw·Hill Companies

Cataloging-in-Publication Data is on file with the Library of Congress

McGraw-Hill books are available at special quantity discounts to use as premiums and sales promotions, or for use in corporate training programs. To contact a special sales representative, please visit the Contact Us page at www.mhprofessional.com.

Oracle General Ledger Guide

1234567890 DOC DOC 019

ISBN 978-0-07-162229-5
MHID   0-07-162229-2

Sponsoring Editor Lisa McClain	**Copy Editor** Robert Campbell	**Illustration** Apollo Publishing, Lyssa Wald
Editorial Supervisor Patty Mon	**Proofreader** Susie Elkind	**Art Director, Cover** Jeff Weeks
Project Editor LeeAnn Pickrell	**Indexer** Rebecca Plunkett	**Cover Designer** Pattie Lee
Acquisitions Coordinator Meghan Riley	**Production Supervisor** George Anderson	
Technical Editor Colin Terry	**Composition** Apollo Publishing	

For Bill, whose support and love made this book possible.

About the Author

Melanie Anjele Cameron has dedicated her career to improving business processes and business systems, especially in the areas of finance and accounting. Always a strong believer in the sharing of knowledge about computer systems and how to use them, she has been the chairperson for the AZOAUG, the Phoenix-area Oracle applications users group, for the past seven years, participating not only in scheduling the events but also as a lecturer. Her career has taken her from a transaction processing clerk to an executive during an IPO, as well as co-owner of her husband's business, giving her a well-rounded and in-depth knowledge of business, from detailed transactions to their broader impact on the business itself. Lucky to find an organization where this breadth of knowledge can be used to assist other companies, Melanie now manages the E-Business Suite practice at MSS Technologies, Inc. (www.MSSTech.com).

While participating in the high-tech world of business, Melanie keeps her feet firmly planted in the low-tech world of needlework, spending most of her nonworking hours knitting and creating pieces of art with a needle, including needlepoint and Japanese embroidery. This, combined with a love for good food and cooking, helps to keep the pressures of our high-tech society at bay. Melanie lives in Scottsdale, Arizona, with her husband, Bill, and two dogs, Josie and Yuki.

About the Technical Editor

Colin Terry is a Chartered Management Accountant who currently works as an independent consultant in the ERP software and associated applications arena. Relying on his accounting background, his primary area of expertise is financials applications, and most of his experience has involved the Oracle E-Business Suite. He does, however, have a strong understanding of much of the Oracle E-Business Suite product set and has had exposure to a number of other software applications, both COTS and proprietary.

Since originally transferring from the accounting function to information systems and technology some fifteen years ago, Colin's roles have encompassed business process design, applications configuration, training, test execution and management, data migration, and support. He has been engaged to work for companies in a wide range of industry sectors, including aerospace and defense, software publishing and distribution, and public transport. Colin is an active member of the UK Oracle User Group and currently sits on the committee of the Financials Special Interest Group.

Contents at a Glance

Contents

PART II
Subledger Accounting: Concepts and Setups

Acknowledgments

When acknowledging all the people involved in getting a book from concept to print, the list can be longer then the book itself! But there are always a few who stand out in the task, both directly and indirectly. My parents, by always instilling in me that I could accomplish anything, have to top that list. My Mom, a lifelong Teacher, is still a driving force behind my wanting to always learn more and find that ever-elusive answer to Why and then turning around and sharing the answer with anyone who wants to listen. My husband, in a much more subtle way, is always watching my back and looking out for me while I push forward in my endeavors.

Every technical author has two groups of people assisting to get the concept to market. The first is composed of the editors at their publisher, and Lisa McClain and her staff have been about as helpful and patient as any author can ask for. From late-night panic e-mails to re-explaining the formatting requirements yet again, these saints all deserve halos. Second are their technical editors. Colin Terry took the time to review and ensure that this book brought you not only accurate information, but also complete information in a logical order.

The drive to write came at an early age, starting around eighth grade, and never left me. It was the encouragement of both past and current mentors who have kindled that flame and given it the sparks it needed to move forward and never die. Becky Tipton is such a person, showing me that writing and work do not have to be mutually exclusive. Mike Hawksworth, owner of MSS Technologies, is another, always there to remind me that yes, you can reach for the stars and even get there. No book is written alone, for it is the experiences of the author's life that are combined to make it happen. Thank you, everyone, for these experiences.

Introduction

From being a user to an implementer, an executive to a clerk, I am a firm believer in utilizing business systems to achieve the wealth of information required to run businesses today. The systems that support corporations today are not the columnar ledgers of our ancestors. They are robust and provide in-depth insight into an organization—that is if you can figure out what they do and how to do it. As a user of Oracle E-Business Suite, I was often frustrated by the lack of information surrounding specific functionality or fields. I have spent hours or, in a few cases, years, acquiring the information I needed to incorporate a specific functionality into my company's processes so we could improve not only the information but also the timeframe the information was available in. The intent of this book is not to gloss over what a Ledger is or the new features Subledger Accounting provides; it is to give detailed insight into how to set up and process transactions in E-Business Suite to meet your company's specific business needs. During the processing steps, references back to setups are made so you know where options exist for processing to meet your specific needs. While functional users at all levels were my main focus when writing the book, support analysts and programmers will also greatly benefit from it. The setups are usually done by consultants, who then walk out the door with all the knowledge, and this book will assist in delivering some of that knowledge back to the company itself and just may prevent a customization or two for a functionality that already exists, just begging to be found and used.

This book, while designed to be read from cover to cover, is also self-inclusive for each section, allowing the reader to go directly to a particular section and not be referenced back to other areas for more information. For Oracle or industry-specific terms, a glossary at the back is included for rapid access. Besides being a step-by-step and field-by-field how-to guide, this book includes many business considerations to think about during an implementation, upgrade, and beyond.

PART
I

General Ledger: Concepts, Setups, and Processing

CHAPTER
1

Business Considerations
for New Implementations

n *enterprise resource planning (ERP)* system is the backbone of knowledge for any organization, sending and receiving information along its nerves to each corner of the company. As with all living organizations, it will continue to grow, in a fashion that is both controlled and uncontrolled, and will require care and feeding throughout its life cycle. That life has many stages, as do all lives, beginning with birth (implementation), moving into the terrible twos of post–go live, and taking on the wonder of a child in a new world, gathering and supplying information as it moves throughout its world. Once it passes puberty, it will continue to gather and process knowledge, but at some point, it becomes historical, living in the past and not quite keeping up with the current world. This uncontrolled growth can be tamed and shaped to the needs of an organization with a little care and feeding, which will take knowledge and understanding—not only of the system itself, but of an organization's information needs. This book is intended to assist with the stages of an ERP life cycle, providing the system knowledge required to shape its growth and control the data it processes and shares with the organization.

A new implementation of any system involves many decisions surrounding the project itself and the system setups. Some decisions, such as Ledgers, are specific to the Oracle E-Business Suite (EBS), while others, like testing, are software agnostic. Understanding what these decisions are can help to streamline the implementation and keep it contained. This chapter, designed more as a discussion guide than a how-to, talks about both system-specific and general implementation considerations and their impact on the project.

Chart of Accounts and Ledgers

One of your most important decisions will concern the Chart of Accounts and Ledgers. If you are integrating EBS modules with another General Ledger system, utilizing the Chart of Account format and numbering from that system can reduce cross-referencing requirements and reconciliation time between the two systems. If EBS will be your General Ledger, then taking the time to understand what data needs to be tracked on Financial Statements, and what data can be tracked in the submodules, such as Accounts Payable, is a critical first step. Ledgers control the General Ledger basic rules regarding calendars, currencies, accounting transactions from subledgers such as Payables, and the chart of accounts. In order to make valid decisions, you must first understand the options EBS offers for the Chart of Accounts and Ledger options.

Basics

Ledgers (known as Sets of Books in previous releases) are set up to group companies that share the same Chart of Accounts, Calendars, Currency, and aCcounting Methods. Previously called the 3 *C*'s of EBS, this phrase has changed to the 4 *C*'s in R12. (Yes, accounting starts with an A—these are programmers—what do you expect?) Accounting methods, set up as Subledger Accounting (SLA) processes in the subledgers, determine how transactions from each subledger, such as Payables, are accounted for in the General Ledger. Ledgers, which determine how transactions are grouped and processed, have Legal Entities assigned to them. Legal Entities, in general, correspond to your organization's legal, or tax, status. Each Legal Entity needs to be assigned a different tax identification number for reporting and to meet SEC and GAAP requirements. A Legal Entity can be assigned to only one Ledger.

The Chart of Accounts, called the General Ledger Key Flexfield in EBS, consists of the different segments that make up your account combination. Some of these segments, such as a segment for Plant number, have no significance in how the system behaves other than to store transactional data separated by plant. Other segments, such as the Balancing Segment, greatly impact how the system works, because all debits and credits associated with any value in the Balancing Segment must net to zero. EBS requires that a Balancing Segment and a Natural Account be assigned to every chart of accounts. A Cost Center, used to track departmental expenses, is only required when Oracle Assets is implemented. Optionally, Intercompany, Management, and Secondary Tracking segments, as well as other segments your business may require, can be added to make up the entire Accounting Flexfield. The legal requirements and business needs of these four things (Ledgers, Legal Entities, Segments to your Chart of Accounts, and Accounting Methods) determine how you will set up these basic components of your system.

Legal Entities

As seen in the accompanying illustration, starting at the top, the Legal Entity's main function is to combine multiple Ledgers for Tax Reporting. The formal definition of a Legal Entity is an entity that owns assets, records sales, and makes purchases. Ledgers, along with security rules for Balancing Segments and Data Access Sets, can restrict access and provide security within the General Ledger.

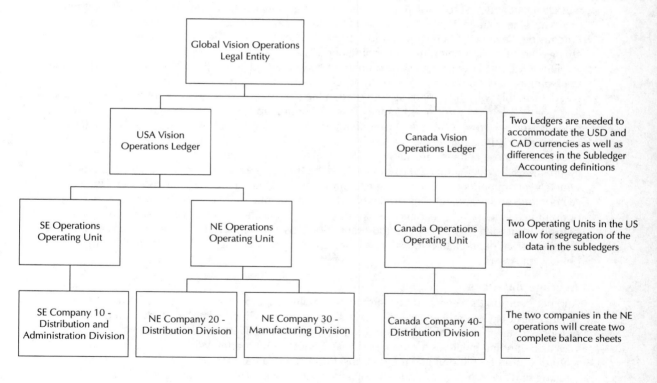

Within your Chart of Accounts, the Balancing Segment enables you to create Trial Balances for individual units of business, while the Management Segment assists in creating Management Reports for different units. The Balancing Segment's main function is to ensure all debits and credits entered to the same Balancing Segment value net to zero, while the Management Segment's main function is to enable Data Access Sets to be created to limit access to data within a specific ledger.

Operating Units

Operating Units do not affect the General Ledger setups per se, but they do control how subledgers segregate data, and while each Operating Unit can only be assigned to one Ledger, each Ledger can have multiple Operating Units.

Within EBS, you will see that many key setup decisions can be changed once transactions have been processed, but with varying degrees of difficulty. Some of these core decisions made at this early level cannot be changed, or only with a large amount of custom programming that is not supported by Oracle. For example, once an Operating Unit has been created and assigned to a Ledger, the assignments cannot be changed to a different Ledger. New Operating Units can be added to each Ledger, but the existing ones cannot be changed and assigned to a new Ledger. Keep this in mind when making decisions, and ensure you understand the impact of a changed decision both during an implementation and after the go live.

Calendars

Calendars in EBS relate to the fiscal year of an organization and control the Period, Quarter, and Year to Date balances stored in the tables, as well as when the Income and Expense accounts will clear out and post to Prior Year Retained Earnings. Once set, calendars are difficult, but not impossible, to change. When only some of the core financial modules are implemented, such as Purchasing, Payables, Receivables, and General Ledger, it is possible to create custom code to change the calendar beginning and ending periods.

EBS does not allow changing the number of periods associated with a calendar, but it is possible to create one-day dummy periods to "trick" EBS into behaving as if a fiscal year ends prior to the end date. In this way, the periods are still used in the system, but with no corresponding transactions. A last option, leaving the current Ledger as is and setting up a Secondary Ledger with a different calendar for reporting, is also an option that provides the least amount of risk, but also the least amount of functionality.

None of these changes are supported by Oracle except the last, but in reality all are made by companies who decide that the risk outweighs the time and expense of reimplementing, which is Oracle's recommended way of changing your calendar. When modules such as Assets, Projects Accounting, and Manufacturing are involved, reimplementation becomes the only reasonable option to change a fiscal year end. Looking at how periods are opened and closed in Assets helps us understand why. Asset periods cannot be closed without running depreciation and thus creating actual depreciation transactions for these periods, making them no longer "dummy" periods for Assets.

Average Balances

Another decision that needs to be made for an implementation is whether or not to use Average Balances in the General Ledger. EBS tracks specific actual balance data in tables for reporting purposes. They include Period, Quarter to Date, and Year to Date net debits and net credits, as well as Beginning balances for the Fiscal Year, Period, and Quarter. When the Average Balance feature is turned on, individual transactions are stored in a transactional table, allowing the tracking of daily transactions and creating average balances. The major things to be aware of when deciding if Average Balancing is going to be used relate to specific functions of EBS that will no longer be available once it is turned on. Budgetary Controls, which usually works in conjunction with Encumbrances to create controls on purchases and expenditures over a specific budgeted amount, cannot be used if Average Balances are turned on. Since you cannot enable or disable Average Balancing once the Ledger is saved, the decision to use it needs to be made before the setups are completed.

Chart of Accounts

The Chart of Accounts is also another area that requires a large amount of thought and foresight as to the number of segments set up and the size of each segment. The Chart of Accounts structure is difficult to change if you want to add a segment or change the length of a segment once you go live. You can change the display order of the segments, as well as the name of a segment, but this will not change how the segments are stored in the tables, nor can it change any functionality associated with the Flexfield Qualifiers assigned to each segment (e.g., you cannot change which segment is your Balancing Segment on the Chart of Accounts), with the exception that you can flag an existing segment as a Management Segment at a later date.

Oracle does not support any method of changing your Chart of Accounts once it is established. While a segment can be added or increased in size using SQL to directly update all the tables where the combinations and individual values exist, this option carries a high degree of risk and is unsupported. Also, any segment that was not set up as Right Justified, Zero Fill can technically be increased in size, but this will prevent use of some standard functionality, such as AutoSkip functionality in Forms. Because of this, it is not recommended that this option be used. For these reasons, it is a good idea if you think you need four characters in your natural account segment, to create it as a five-character segment to allow room for growth. And if you think you need four segments in your account structure (such as Balancing, Cost Center, Natural Account, and Intercompany), add a fifth called Undefined and default the value in as all zeros. This way, it can be used without risk in the future.

As you can see, these core decisions about Ledgers, Charts of Accounts, and Operating Units are difficult, are costly, and carry a high degree of risk to change, when they can be changed at all. Taking the time to create them with foresight into future business needs and growth will decrease your ERP cost of ownership in future years.

Business Process Reengineering

During most new implementations, the idea of reengineering the current business processes is discussed at least once and often multiple times during the implementation planning and project development. Sometimes it is dismissed as too costly or time consuming during an implementation, and sometimes the decision is made to use "Oracle's best practices" instead, without considering why some of the current processes are in place. Understanding, at least at a high level, what goes on in an organization, along with investigating the whys for these processes, often uncovers what can become costly implementation problems after go live, problems that would have been easier to address prior to starting the implementation. Let's take a look at these two scenarios separately.

First, let's explore implementations using current business processes, both manual and from the standpoint of an automated system. Business processes develop over time, for both valid business reasons and human reasons bearing no impact on the ultimate business goals. Valid business reasons, such as that all invoices must be approved by the requesting manager prior to payment to prevent payment for services in dispute or not delivered, are good controls that meet both the company's goals and many government requirements an organization may need to follow. Human reasons often arise from a person's belief that something is needed, rather than a specific business need. This could include a process entailing that all expense reports require CEO approval, which was implemented by a former controller because a CEO yelled at him or her for paying a $5,000 "employee appreciation" dinner for an employee terminated for fraud. This business process was implemented because of a poor business decision by an employee no longer at the company, with the sole purpose of preventing the CEO from yelling at him or her again. Setting controls within the system and an expense report approval policy can ease up on this use of a highly paid executive's time.

Choosing to use all of the best practices established by Oracle is not always a bad idea, but not understanding, for example, the steps taken today to complete a check run may increase the time needed to create that check run in EBS using the best practices. Reengineering the current process to meet the requirements for maximum benefits of the best practices is often needed. Let's review a scenario where the legacy system allowed only one group of suppliers to be included in a check run at one time, so the continuity of the grouping numbers was not important. In EBS Payables, these numbers are called Priorities, which can be run as a range as well as single numbers. EBS Best Practices is to run checks in groupings based on Priorities. This minor change, if not reengineered during the implementation and as a change made during the data conversions, could result in check runs continuing to take 1.5 days each week, as opposed to about 3.5 hours after a short reengineering of the numbering, so that certain groups can be combined into one check run.

When you look at any process, you need to understand a few basic questions: why do you do this, and is the data gained from doing it this way really used or required? I also have another favorite question for older companies with custom systems: do you do it this way because there was a system limitation that prevented it from being done another way, or is there a human limitation instead? (I mean human in the sense that "we always did it this way and it has to be continued because that is how everyone knows how to do it . . . .") Finding the answer to these questions is the only way to truly know if this process should be considered for a customization, and if so, if the cost of the customization can be regained in a reasonable time frame, or if the process can be retooled to use EBS-standard functionality.

Customizations

When the decision to create a custom process is made, ensure that the customization is created using Oracle's guidelines. Without taking the time to understand what can and cannot be upgraded, customizations become the albatross hanging around a company's neck when considering an upgrade, making a manageable project into a mountain that cannot always be climbed. There are many ways to include customizations in your system, leaving the door open for future upgrades, and these are well documented in much of Oracle's technical documentation.

Data Conversions

Data conversions make for some of the hardest decisions. What to convert? How much data? How far back? Should it be cleansed prior to conversions? After 15 years, I have found a formula that consistently works, taking cost, time, and user satisfaction into account. Let's take a look at some of the major decisions, breaking them down by subledgers.

Payables

In Payables, there are two options for open invoices: pay them out of the old system prior to conversion or convert them into EBS. This decision should be made on the basis of cash flow and how many transactions there are open in the system. Either way, if there are old, unresolved invoices, you should consider cleaning them up prior to conversion. Suppliers, at a minimum, will have to be converted for all open transactions that will be entered into EBS. But you will need to look at other suppliers for activity and usage to decide if they should be converted or not—converting a supplier that you have not done business with for three years will only increase the unused data in your new system.

Cleaning up active suppliers in the legacy system and inactivating unused addresses and suppliers according to a formula that makes sense for your company will help ensure that only relevant, accurate data is converted. Reviewing supplier data for accuracy prior to the conversions, where letters are sent out asking for confirmation of data in the legacy system or ZIP (short for *Zone Improvement Plan*) codes are validated with the post office, fits in well with an implementation project and helps to ensure the accuracy of converted data. Be sure this is decided upon and discussed at the beginning of the project, while there is still time to plan for it.

Receivables

Receivables will need to convert open transactions, and they must convert any customers related to these transactions. The decision to convert customers without open transactions will be based on your company's needs. Customers can always be added at a later time, but once they are in EBS, they cannot be deleted; only disabled.

Since customers are often considered part of a company's Business Intelligence, not bringing in enough customers can sometimes have a larger impact than bringing in too many. It is your organization's relationship with customer data that can help make this decision: if demographic analysis is performed going back five years, ensure there is five years of data either in your ERP or in a data warehouse to perform this analysis. On the other hand, if historical trends of customers have never been measured, then historical customer data may have no value in the new system. Another consideration for customers is accuracy of their address information. If the legacy system did not have address validation, and you will be using either EBS's tax engine (E-Business Tax) or a third-party tax program for sales tax, ensure the city, state, county, and ZIP code combinations are cleansed prior to conversions (how you combine these four segments depends on how you set up EBS to validate addresses and calculate tax; using all four segments of the address is most accurate, but your business needs may only require the city and state for accurate sales tax processing). This cleansing can often be done in Excel prior to conversions, or there are companies who specialize in this type of work.

General Ledger

General Ledger is a little easier for data conversions. You can import balances as far back as you need to go, but the first date needs to be decided early in the project, as you cannot add prior months once the calendar is set up and the first period is opened, and this is one of the very first things that will be set up in EBS. A mapping from the old chart of accounts to the new one will be needed no matter how far back you convert—for one thing, the accountants will probably need it for the first month or so. This can be loaded into a temporary table in the Oracle database or in Excel, depending on whether you are using an API or Web ADI to convert the balances.

In addition to determining how far back you want to import data, you must make two additional decisions: First, how to handle the transactions that will be generated with the subledger conversions, and second, how to handle foreign currency balances. When data is converted for the subledgers, such as Assets or open Payables transactions, they will result in General Ledger entries. These balances presumably already exist in the General Ledger and will result in duplicate entries and incorrect balances in these accounts. You have a few options as to how to handle this. Perhaps my least favorite is to "trick" the system by debiting and crediting the same account combination for each transaction. In other words, when a Payables invoice is converted, the expense distribution will have the exact same account number as the liability account, having no impact on the balances when the journal entries are created. The problem with this process is there is no record in EBS of where the transactions were originally coded, and it also results in incorrect entries if the transactions are voided or canceled. While this is not desirable during system conversions, it sometimes is useful when converting data during an acquisition or merger. Using a clearing account for the offsetting entry and moving the balance in the General Ledger helps with the cancellation issues.

A second option is to reduce the conversion amounts from the General Ledger balances being entered, and allow the subledger to create the entries for these transactions. Finally, the journal entries created from the subledger can be imported, posted, and reversed in the same period, leaving a zero impact on the General Ledger. If the last option is selected, ensure that *only* converted data is imported into the General Ledger, and that no new, nonlegacy transactions are included. No matter which option you select, it is important to reconcile the subledger and General Ledger in the legacy system, track the imported journal entries to ensure key accounts, such as Payables Liability or Asset accounts, create the same balances as the Ledger and legacy system, and make sure that the subledgers balance to the General Ledger after data conversions and prior to go live.

If you have accounts with foreign currency balances, you will need to decide which currency these balances will be converted in. Your options are to bring in the transactions in the foreign currency and to allow EBS to translate the data, or to convert the translated balances in the functional currency for the Ledger. Ensure that the currency exchange rates are set up as needed if the former option is selected. Since not all systems translate balances exactly the same, this may result in translated balances that are not the same as the legacy system. You may want to test this early on in the conversions to see the impact. The other option is to convert the data already translated, knowing that the original currency information will be lost for future translations or revaluations.

Fixed Assets

Fixed Assets has only one major decision for data conversions: are assets that are 100 percent depreciated going to be converted? Many companies are not diligent in retiring assets if they are fully depreciated and no longer in use, making their active asset listing larger than it needs to be. Conversion is a good time for cleanup, either by doing a fixed asset inventory or by making the decision that no zero-dollar assets will be converted or that only assets acquired after a specific date will be.

Manufacturing and Purchasing

Purchasing and Manufacturing will need all open purchase orders, on-hand quantities for inventory, and open work orders converted. Again, clean up any old purchase orders or work orders that are not valid prior to conversion. Item numbers should be converted for items with current open activity (requisitions, purchase orders, on-hand balances, or work orders), or that will be used again, or that have inventory against them.

Conversion Tools

There are three main ways data can be converted into EBS: via an API (application programmatic interface), which will require that the interface be programmed (usually in PL/SQL) for your data, or using Web ADI (Application Desktop Integrator), which is an interface between Excel and specific areas of EBS. ADI cannot be expanded to add functionality, so it is only an option for the areas where interfaces exist. Oracle is constantly adding interfaces to Web ADI, so you should check MetaLink to see what exists at the time of your conversions. Do not discount manual conversions as an option, as this can be a great training tool. Eight to ten hours of data entry is the round cutoff I use for manual conversion—much more than that and the accuracy usually suffers. One additional option is to use a keystroke mimicker tool, such as Data Loader, or a spreadsheet integrator. These tools enable you to take data from Excel and load it into any form in EBS. Remember to look at using Forms Personalizations to potentially change the form format, making keystroke mimickers more easily used on more forms. At all costs, avoid loading data directly into the EBS tables at the database level. Besides making your system unsupported, the data will bypass all the validations written into forms, APIs, and interfaces, potentially making garbage data the foundation for your new system.

With EBS, it is highly recommended that closed transactions never be converted in the subledgers. The APIs Oracle has written were designed for open transactions; they do not build all the links between transactional data, such as open invoices, and their resolution, such as paying the invoices. In order to load all transactions, you would have to load a Purchase Order and its corresponding receipts. Since the product relating to these receipts may no longer be in the company's warehouse, now the corresponding sales orders and shipments are needed. And this hypothetical company also uses lot control, so the proper lot numbers need to be recorded for each shipment. These shipments would create invoices in EBS automatically, with different numbers in the legacy system that would have to be matched to the proper payments…You can see how this quickly snowballs into a complicated web of transactions, often leaving the systems with bad data, or the company with a large programming bill that was probably not necessary. Keeping the legacy system up in inquiry mode through at least the next audit will satisfy most needs for legacy data, or alternatively, some companies create reports out of the legacy data to supply this data.

Accelerator Tools

When the decision is made to use the majority of Oracle's best practices with EBS, it opens the door to use Business Flow Accelerators as part of the implementation. This tool streamlines an implementation in two major ways: First, the installation of the software is streamlined because two instances, one for business flow review and training, and another as a clean installation for a production configuration, are installed at one time, reducing the DBA time needed to create these two instances. Second, the accelerators provide general, as well as industry-specific, tools to complete the setups required to make EBS run. When you answer the questions in these tools, specific key setups are generated and ready for testing, on the basis of best practice business flows. Additional setups can be added to configure the flows to your specific business needs. Accelerators decrease the configuration of the system by streamlining the setup processes as well as installation time, and they reduce the phase of a project where questionnaires are completed by the users and then converted into setup data by an experienced implementer. Now these two steps are combined into one, where the answers create the setups for you. The biggest benefit comes when the clients' needs closely meet the business flows in the accelerators.

Take the time to understand the key decisions that affect the implementation early on in the project, and make these decisions in light of future needs and growth of the company; then you will save time, costs, and headaches down the road. This portion of the implementation, when overlooked and underestimated, can limit the return on investment realized from using an integrated ERP system.

Testing

Testing is a problem with any implementation; it is time consuming, requires a much larger group of employees than the core implementation team, and often needs to be repeated more than one time. There are testing tools out there that record your business processes as keystrokes, allowing the test scripts to be rerun. For a large organization that is using a large footprint of the EBS functionality, these tools are a good option for decreasing the testing required. But it needs to be determined if your company has the bandwidth to do two implementations at the same time—these tools do not have tests programmed into them out of the box but require the tests to be recorded.

On a new implementation, never discount the value of manual, old-fashioned testing. Though time-consuming, it does actually serve additional purposes during a new implementation: Users can solidify any training they received, giving the company the starting point for creating superusers, or system experts, in each area. Also, for nervous employees who are concerned that EBS will not perform all the needed tasks to do their jobs, getting hands-on prior to the implementation can sometimes give them a higher comfort level (this does not always work—let's face it, there will always be those who will hate the new system, and no amount of use will change their minds). It is also often the first time users will get to see the new processes and really understand how they will work once the system is live, allowing them time to make any required changes for company-critical functions. Though subject matter experts will be involved in system selection, design, and customization requirements, this is often at a more conceptual level, with only core members of the team who are devoted 100 percent to the project having the time to be knee-deep in the workings of the system. Things often sound good on paper, and it is not until the actual users of the process get some hands-on that potential problems are ferreted out.

For testing in general, I use the Red Light, Yellow Light, Green Light process of categorizing business processes and their associated risks. Classifying your business application system's functionality and processes into these three categories allows intelligent testing, as opposed to blanket or blind testing. Red Light functions are the processes a company cannot live without. Functions should be classified using a global view of the company needs, not an individual user's perspective of his or her workload within the company. A user may believe a function is critical, such as exporting data, to make his or her job easier, and consider it Red Light. If that worker is able to perform his or her job duties with a reasonable workaround, the function is most likely not a Red Light.

Company-wide Red Light functions are processes critical to performing daily operations, as well as staying in compliance with any governing agencies. An example of a Red Light function is cutting checks in Accounts Payables. Not many companies can go without paying their bills for any period of time. These critical features will be tested with any and all patches, upgrades, and implementations.

Yellow Light functions are features that are highly important to a specific business application user or to the company but that will not be run for a period of time after the upgrade. These should be tested using one of two situations as a test case. Situation one is where time accommodates the testing. Situation two is a major upgrade, or an implementation, that affects most of the system's functionality. In this case more thorough testing is mandated, as the risk of problems is greater, but more time may pass before the processes are needed in the business cycle. An example of the flexibility of Yellow Light testing is 1099 reporting. If the upgrade or implementation is completed in June, testing can wait until the 1099 changes for that year come out from your software company. However, if it is the beginning of March and you have not yet filed for the previous year, you should make the tests prior to the production go live.

The Green Light category contains all the features that users like to use but don't really need to carry out their jobs, or that the company can function without. It also includes repetitive testing for different transaction types that use the same functions or forms. For example, if you test creating an invoice in Accounts Receivable and your system is set up to do 15 different invoice types, the probability is extremely high that if one works, they will all work. Therefore, you only need to test one type. This last statement is only applicable to an upgrade; on a new implementation, all setups do need to be tested for accuracy.

To ensure this type of testing is successful, an organization must adopt two critical mindsets. First, the saying "A successful go live is a nonevent" will have to come out of a project team's vocabulary. While this statement is always true, the support staff and system users must recognize that any issues found after go live for untested Yellow Light and Green Light items are not failures or issues with the go live. And second, support for the go live must include additional time post–go live to ensure all the issues are resolved in a reasonable manner. How these issues are resolved will become the determining factor of the success of the upgrade or patch.

During the testing process, there should be clearly defined test scripts (the format can vary, but at the least, it should have the task and the classification listed—adding navigation paths is extremely helpful for new implementations or changed functionality after an upgrade). Even with this, never discount the use of Free Style testing, where users play on the system, either randomly or by taking a stack of work from their desk and entering it into EBS. This can be extremely useful not in only testing, but also in helping the users learn the system. Just remember, when they find a problem from "free-style" testing, remember to classify the problem as a Red Light, Yellow Light, or Green Light problem to decide when and how it should be resolved.

While this method of testing is not applicable for custom development where there was no thorough in-house testing prior to receiving the upgrades, it works for large packaged programs, such as an ERP system. Taking the time near the beginning of the project to classify the functions will not only assist with the initial round of testing, but it will expedite any retesting required when a patch is applied or a setup changed, and it will significantly assist with any future testing after go live.

Consistency and Data Entry

One of the concepts most often missed during implementation is consistency of data input and usage. EBS, based on an Oracle database, sorts data according to a specific hierarchy—and that is not a straight alphabetical hierarchy. Lowercase will always be sorted prior to uppercase data—and EBS does not restrict cases during data entry in many places. For Suppliers, this becomes very evident when Smith comes before SAMS CAFÉ on a report. Using all uppercase for data entry and predetermined mixed case for setups can affect the readability of the system and reports. Case will also come into play when querying data: in Find forms, EBS does not consider case, but when using the Query by Example feature (View| Query By Example), the queries are case sensitive.

Another area for data consistency is naming conventions. In Payables, for example, supplier names are often inconsistent, leaving room for duplicate entries and payments. Setting conventions, like last name, first for persons, or Inc instead of Incorporated, as well as ST for Street, helps keep the data more consistent and leaves less room for errors.

The final topic is one you will actually hear repeated many times in the setups and processing sections of this book: Descriptions should not be optional! Entering more data into EBS, both for transactions and setups, reduces the number of times paper backup needs to be referred to as well as questions as to why something was done. Especially on setups, adding completed descriptions and keeping them up-to-date really helps three or five years down the road when the new CFO or CIO wants to know why something was done, and the information is now long gone, walked out with the employee that entered the data.

Training

Training, the final consideration in implementations or upgrades, is another subject that requires thought—more so than any other part of the upgrade. The way the users are trained can significantly impact the success of a project. I had a DBA tell me once that an implementation is successful if the system works as designed. I argued that no matter how well the system works, if the users are not comfortable with it and trained properly, and therefore do not use it to the fullest potential within the scope of the project, then the go live was not successful. Let's face it: the first month on a new system is the hardest; any process improvements are usually vitiated or reversed when the users do not know what keystrokes or mouse clicks to do, or do not understand the new business process. (I always say it takes longer to train the fingers than the brain—and until the fingers are trained, the system is cumbersome, as users fumble around to perform a task they could previously do in their sleep.) There are three main types of training: computer based, instructor led, and gained from a manual or written document. Three things should be considered when deciding which type—or combination of types—will be used.

First, how many users are you training? One or one thousand? It is significantly easier to hire a professional EBS trainer for a small core team than to take one thousand employees out of their jobs for a few days for instructor-led training. Second, to what extent will they be using the system? Entering a requisition in iProcurement is significantly easier than paying checks in a centralized Payables department. And finally, ask not only how individual users learn, but what is the corporate culture for learning? With superusers, it is a good idea to understand whether these users learn by reading, watching, or doing. These are the folks that need to know the system best after go live. For more casual users, a standard method is acceptable—such as computer-based training or required training materials that have to be read. If there are one thousand users entering requisitions into iProcurement, and 75 percent of them read the training materials and can fumble through their first requisition after go live, the rest can easily be assisted the first time they enter a requisition. It only takes about five minutes to walk a new user through the basics. Just ensure there is a help desk process in place to assist that user. A tool such as the User Productivity Kit (UPK), a means of recording procedures that integrates with EBS and can be saved under the help files in the system, can also assist with training casual users as well as new hires.

There are two chapters on setups in this book—and they occupy most of the book. Don't let this disproportionate coverage fool you; these chapters will define scope, explain business processes, and help you make informed setup decisions and implement the testing and training that will take the longest part of any implementation. The setups, once it is understood what the system can do and how to make it do that, are the easy part and take proportionately less time. The most critical part of the actual setups is not letting corporate culture override any recommendations made by an implementation partner: this is the biggest reason I see for dissatisfaction with an implementation due to setups—our partner told us not to do this, but we thought it was best, and now we are paying for it. As much as I enjoy being brought in as a consultant to fix these challenges, I would much prefer the implementation be done right the first time, and that phase 2 of a project be based on expanded scope and usage of the system.

The rest of the success factors are cultural. Did we define the project? Was there scope creep that extended the project into an unmanageable monster? Were the critical functions tested? Did we understand what EBS can do prior to making decisions about business processes and requirements? Did we train our key users properly? And did we step back after the project was complete to see what is next? Businesses are not static, and neither should the business systems running them be.

CHAPTER
2

Business Considerations
for Upgrades

ny time an EBS upgrade is considered that spans to a major release where the data concepts or technology are significantly different, there are decisions that need to be made early on in the project. R12 is such an upgrade. With new twists on old concepts (Ledgers vs. Sets of Books) and brand-new concepts (Subledger Accounting), not taking the time to review some key considerations is the foundation for failure.

Reimplement vs. Upgrade?

The first and ultimate business decision for companies considering an upgrade is the decision whether to upgrade or reimplement. An upgrade would involve taking the current EBS environment and upgrading it and all the data in it to the newer versions. A reimplementation involves installing the new version of EBS and performing setups and data conversions in the new version, leaving the old version to die a natural death. Every major release (10.7 to 11.0 or 11*i*, 11.0.*x* to 11*i*, and now any prior version to R12) has companies wondering which the better option is.

A good starting point is to understand what Oracle's plans are for your current release as well as for future releases. The current statement is that for 11.5.10, Oracle will provide all support except integration with new non-Oracle products, through November 2012. Accordingly, the more stable, older release, 11.5.10, may be a viable option for your organization when you are upgrading from an older version and the functionality in R12 will not benefit your business processes.

Some key changes in the core modules to R12 may make the more expensive upgrade to R12 worth the extra time and expense. Access to multiple Ledgers in the General Ledger is one of them, and the need to account for transactions in different ways is another. If your business processes are complicated and global enough that two representations are required for government and corporate reporting, this is a strong feature in R12 that is not as comprehensive in 11*i*.

Another major area for consideration is centralized and decentralized processes. R12 has done a nice job of allowing for both in the same organization and module. Prior to R12, EBS segregated all transactions for subledgers such as Receivables and Payables into separate organizations, requiring users to access each organization separately, making truly centralized processing cumbersome. Now, entries can be done into multiple operating units from the same responsibility without the segregation. Payment process also has a new centralized hub allowing payment processing and bank accounts to be combined for multiple organizations. Once you've decided on a version, consider a few significant points that can help make the decision whether to upgrade or reimplement a little clearer.

Instances

First, how many production instances are you running currently? If the answer is more than one, there are three upgrade options: 1) reimplement so that all the data will reside all in one instance, 2) continue with multiple instances and upgrade each one separately, or 3) upgrade one of the instances and use it as a basis for consolidating the other data into it by adding Ledgers and Operating Units as needed (in effect, reimplementing the other instances).

Current System Version

Besides the data in your system, the version of the current production system is critical to the amount of effort required to upgrade. Upgrade paths to R12 are always from 11.5.10. Any environment that is on an earlier version will need to be brought up to this level prior to proceeding. Though this can be done at the same time as the upgrade, it will increase the required downtime. Performing the upgrade over two or more weekends will require that each "stopping" point be tested to ensure accuracy and that the features of the system are still functioning. This can greatly increase the functional part of the upgrade from a testing and reconciliation standpoint.

Data and Setup Accuracy

Next, take a look at the data that resides in your system. Is it accurate, or do you have old garbage data, such as transactions or customers, that may be causing problems in analytical reports? Is there a large amount of data that will slow down the upgrade process? If the database is large enough to inhibit upgrading in a reasonable down period, usually about three days, purging and archiving data would be an option to eliminate this as a decision and speed up the upgrade, but would also extend the timeline due to the amount of planning and work involved in an archiving project, often needed to be performed by the same people involved in the upgrade project.

There are several upgrade diagnostics that can be used to check the current setups prior to upgrade. The tools ensure that there are no inconsistencies or inaccuracies in the setups based on the upgrade path Oracle supports. Using these tools can help guide some of the decisions required during the upgrade process, instead of leaving you to think it all needs to be done, or that none of it needs to be done. No one likes surprises during the first upgrade run.

Initial implementations tend to be fast paced and overwhelming for organizations. Decisions that were made about features that are not fully understood may have created an end result where after using the features, it is realized that the decision may not have been the best for the company's practices and needs. Changes in the company direction can also make a good decision no longer compatible with the new direction of the company. Depending on the setup change, reimplementing or engaging new features as part of the upgrade can give you the option to go back and make more informed decisions on key setup features. Also, changes in business needs, or mergers and acquisitions, can make setups no longer valid. This is one area where discussing your system "pain points" with an experienced but neutral business consultant can help guide you in what can be changed without a reimplementation, and when a reimplementation is the best option. These so-called system heath checks or assessments confirm your setups and procedures are in synch with each other, making suggestions on where updates need to be made to improve analysis and processing time.

Customizations

If you have any customizations in your system, ranging from reports to triggers to totally custom processes, take the time to review them with two main focuses. First, is the custom process still relevant to your current and anticipated business needs? Taking the time to upgrade a customization that is no longer required but still used out of habit is a costly practice. And second, with all the new functionality, there may now be standard functionality that can replace the customization. It is important that the persons performing this analysis are the ones who can think outside the box, and who really understand what is truly a business need, not just the process people are used to performing.

System Resources

One often overlooked part of an upgrade is the system/hardware resources that it requires. For some reason, it always seems to take a little more than you think it will. Doing a system assessment early on in the project will help prevent stoppages later, when the upgrade is going to slow or there is not enough space.

Considerations During the Project and Post-Production

A critical decision, for both upgrades and implementations, is deciding how new point releases or patches are going to be handled, both during the upgrade or implementation and after go live. Often, during the implementation process, new point releases or family packs are released, and these must be considered prior to making the decision whether to apply them or stay with the current patch levels for go live. Industry standard for upgrades are three passes through, but this number depends on the individual upgrade, and you need to be flexible.

The first pass is for the DBA team to create a recipe, if you will, that will be followed for the upgrade. No two instances in production are the same, and therefore no two upgrades have the same ingredient mix (as in specific patches to apply). A single patch difference in the current environment can lead to quite a different upgrade experience. The second pass is to confirm that the recipe produces the same result a second time; it involves both the DBA team to perform the upgrade, and the functional team to test the results at a high level. At this point, the developers will also get involved to determine if any updates are required to customize reports, interfaces to and from other systems, or if any customizations will need to be upgraded. The final pass is for unit testing. The time I listen to a DBA the most is after the second iteration—if the Lead DBA on the project says "I need another pass," never question him or her but work it into the project plan. A sure way to ask for problems during an upgrade is to fail to solidify the upgrade recipe and ensure consistent results—any deviations in any run will result in a new and untested recipe.

If the new releases or family packs come out during the first run, or problems are found by the functional team in the second run, then consider the releases, in terms of bugs that are fixed, functionality included, and how these relate to your specific company. If a lot of problems are found in accounts payable, and a new financial family pack comes out that fixes a lot of bugs, it would be wise to consider applying it. Releases that come out after the unit testing should usually only be considered if there were major issues unresolved at this time. This helps not only to keep the changes to the recipe in check, but also to minimize the amount of repeat testing that is needed.

After go live, you should devise a plan for any post-production issues discovered, as well as any noncritical issues found during testing that were not corrected prior to go live. Part of owning an integrated ERP system means continually improving the processes surrounding the system, integrating new functionality, or correcting existing problems. It is not a system where you can flip the on switch and never do any additional improvements or fixes to the system. It requires care and feeding, as do all business considerations that will grow with the life of the company.

When taking the upgrade approach, early on it should be decided how much of the new functionality will be engaged during this initial upgrade phase of the project. For a company to get the most out of its ERP system, the current processes need to be continually evaluated against the future needs of the business. Implementing a major ERP system is not a project with a beginning and an end—it is a journey that evolves over time. As long as your business needs are growing, so should your ERP system. Though each project, no matter how great or small, must have a beginning and an end, the projects themselves should never come to a halt, where the system stagnates and becomes stale. Continual analysis and changes will need to be made to meet the ever-demanding and changing business needs of the organization. An upgrade is just a small part of this life cycle, and it should be analyzed for scope and relevance. It will be important to keep a long-term plan in mind and continue the momentum of each phase of the project, ensuring the ultimate goal is always kept in sight.

Planning for the Upgrade

If the decision to upgrade has become the right one for your company, planning for downtime as well as balancing financial data becomes important. Any major upgrade will involve system downtime, depending on the upgrade path required as well as the amount of data being upgraded and system speed and resources. Normally, most of this downtime will be planned during nonbusiness hours, such as holidays and weekends. Sometimes, it encroaches on business hours. You should plan ahead for a few things. First, how will customer calls be handled to ensure the best customer service is still provided during any real or potential downtime during business hours? Creating a test instance that is inquiry only can help assist in answering customer questions. Any required updates to accounts will have to wait until after the system comes back up, so they will need to be tracked.

Cutting checks is another consideration that affects accounts payables. Ensure that all invoices that will need to be paid during and up to two days after the upgrade are paid out prior to bringing the system down. Having manual checks on hand, if the down time is longer than a weekend, is also helpful, but ensure that processes are in place to prevent duplicate invoice payments as well as to get these payments into payables. Any critical ERP transactions that cannot be halted during the upgrade will have to have manual processes and tracking to move this data into Production once it comes back up.

Balancing data in Production is often overlooked, and it can lead to surprises after the go live. Upgraded data may not transact properly or appear correctly on reports and forms. Ensuring that balancing reports are run prior to performing the upgrade, but after transaction processing has ceased, is critical to ensuring that key data upgrades correctly. Remember not only to do this during the production run, but in testing as well. You will want to be able to make sure that the balancing mechanism decided on actually does work. There are many reports that do change in R12, and ensuring that apples are being compared to apples is imperative.

Running a Payable Trial Balance and Aging pre- and postupgrade is a good balancing process for AP. In Receivables, running the Invoice Aging works well. Fixed Assets often uses the Reserve Detail reports, while Inventory uses the All Inventories Value report. Make sure prior to upgrading Production you have checked that there are compatible reports in the upgraded version to balance to. Also ensure that the reports run pre- and postupgrade are detailed, not summary, reports. Summary works fine if there are no problems, but these reports are not very helpful when the numbers do not tie out. The preupgrade reports should be saved outside of EBS to ensure there is no danger they will be overwritten during the upgrade.

It corresponds to best practices, and is often required, that all interfaces be cleared out prior to the upgrade, and often it is required that transactions from the submodules be posted to the general ledger prior to the upgrade. With the introduction of Subledger Accounting, this is even more important in R12. Both this and the balancing reports will often require user coordination and participation in the actual upgrade. A normal scenario would be for all general users to be locked out of the system, then for the upgrade functional team to manually clear out all interfaces and run balancing reports, which should be saved somewhere other than in the concurrent manager. This is the best time for the critical preupgrade support backup, which can be used to restore if anything goes wrong that prevents the systems from coming back up in a reasonable time frame. Once the upgrade is completed, then the users can run the new reports and ensure that everything balances.

As soon as the system is back up and balanced, having a few key users on hand to enter some production transactions is a great way of ensuring the next morning will go a little bit smoother—any major problems can be found and evaluated prior to the general users getting on the system. In addition to production, I always like to have two additional instances available, three if you have the resources.

First is the old version cloned from the backup just prior to go live. This is used to test any functionality that does not work in production. Knowing if a problem existed prior to upgrade can help lead to a solution faster, or at least tell you how critical it really is to business—numerous times, after researching a problem that a user insisted was caused by the upgrade, I have found that it never worked to begin with.

The second instance is the CRP instance. Again, for production issues that crop up as new, knowing if they existed in the test instance aids with the troubleshooting. Most often, if it can be confirmed that something worked in the testing phase of the upgrade, then there may have been something that changed during the production upgrade, or the issue may be data related (the data causing the problem may not have existed during the last test of the upgrade). To be honest, sometimes problems just happen, for no known reason.

Finally, get a clone of the newly upgraded production instance as quickly as possible. This will be used for troubleshooting and patching all production issues. If you only have room for one cloned instance, this is the one that is of the most importance.

R12 Specific Considerations

Realizing the amount of work involved in major upgrades where new functionality is introduced early on in the project, and planning for both the workload and decisions required, can make the upgrades less painful and more cost effective for any organization. And always remember that owning EBS is never a stagnant journey if you want to realize the potentials both of the system and for your company. It is a journey with beginnings and achievements and continual improvements, but not a lot of endings. Planning what is included in this project, and what will be done as part of the next project makes that journey a little more manageable.

When upgrading from a previous version, it is extremely important to understand the major setup differences between the two versions, as well as how these features and functions will be handled when converted from the old concepts and setups to the new ones. Table 2-1 outlines the key General Ledger concept changes between 11.5.10 and R12.

The functionality behind these new concepts and how to set them up is included in other sections of this book. Here, you'll learn the specifics relating to how your 11*i* instance will upgrade to R12 for these features.

11.5.10 Function	R12 Equivalent
Set of Books	Ledgers
MRC or Multiple Reporting Currencies	Reporting Currencies
Various Accounting Methods in Subledgers	SLA, or Subledger Accounting
GIS or Global Intercompany System	AGIS, or Advanced Global Intercompany System
Client ADI	WebADI and Report Manager
Reporting Set of Books	Reporting Currencies
Global Accounting Engine	SLA, or Subledger Accounting
Global Tax Engine	E-Business Tax
Automatic Tax Calculations	E-Business Tax
General Ledger Automatic Tax Calculation	E-Business Tax
Deferred expense (Global Descriptive Flexfields)	Multiperiod Accounting
Payables Reporting Entity (commonly used with 1099 reporting)	Part of Legal Entity functionality

TABLE 2-1 *General Ledger Key Concept Changes from 11i to R12*

Ledgers

Your existing EBS system already has Sets of Books set up—to varying degrees of use and functionality. How these setups look in 11*i* will determine how the new Ledgers will look in R12. There are many ways to use Sets of Books in 11*i*, and they all upgrade a little differently. If you have a Primary Set of Books set up for Multiple Reporting Currencies (MRC), this will become a Primary Ledger in R12, whereas MRC Reporting Sets of Books will become a Reporting Currency. Multiple Posting Sets of Books associated with the Global Accounting Engine will upgrade as Secondary Ledgers. Finally, Asset books will upgrade to Primary Ledgers for the Corporate Books, and the Tax Books associated with a Corporate book will then become Secondary Ledgers under that Primary Ledger.

Chart of Accounts

Besides understanding how the Ledgers will be created from Sets of Books, it is also important to understand how specific 11*i* functionality changed the upgrades. The Secondary Tracking segment and how it is used changes after the upgrade. In 11*i*, there were two separate check boxes, one for Revaluations, and a second for Closing and Translations. In R12, these are combined into one check box. The good news? The 11*i* functionality as it was set up still exists for upgraded Ledgers. The ability to track, or not to track, one of these processes with the Secondary Ledger is stored in a table and can continue to function as it did prior to the upgrade. On the flip side, this option is no longer tracked in a form and cannot be reviewed by users, nor can any new Ledgers be set up this way.

Primary and Reporting Ledgers, in R12, are always synchronized for setups other than currencies. This may not have been true for the MRC book and transactional books in 11*i*. EBS will maintain any differences in the setups of these books when the Ledgers are created, but this is again at the table level and not in the forms. Since these fields are synchronized in R12, updating one of the fields will cause the Reporting Ledger to have the same setup from that point forward. These fields include: Number of Future Enabled Periods, Rounding Difference Account, Encumbrance Reserve Account, Retained Earnings Account, Intercompany Balancing Rules, Enable Journal Tax, Journal Reversal Criteria Set, Require Budget Journals, Period End Rate Type, Period Average Rate Type, Translation Adjustment Account, Secondary Tracking Segment Option, Descriptive Flexfields (on the set of books and in R12, Ledger), and Suspense Accounts. As soon as one of these fields is updated after the upgrade, both the Reporting Currency and the Primary Ledger will have the same settings for that field.

The final field that has upgrade implications between the Reporting and Primary Ledgers is the Suspense Posting Flag. In 11*i*, these can be different, but not in R12. The Reporting Ledger will adopt the setting from the Primary Ledger, and it will utilize the suspense account on the Primary Ledger as well.

In 11*i*, Average Balances can be set at either the Primary or Reporting Set of Books. In R12, it is set only at the Primary Ledger and inherited for the Reporting Currencies. EBS will preserve the setting in a table for this, but it will need to be updated if this was set to Average for the Reporting Set of Books and not on the Primary Set of Books, as this inconsistency will cause an error when posting journal entries.

Translated Balances are upgraded as Balance Level Reporting Currencies in the Primary Ledger, and they can continue to be used by performing translations in R12. This process can only be used for upgraded, translated balances. Any new reporting currencies that are added in R12 must be added as reporting currencies under the Ledger and will be translated using the R12 methodology as set up in the Ledger.

Any inconsistencies in Reporting Sets of Books from Oracle's recommended setup can cause different results or errors during the upgrade. For example, Reporting Sets of Books that are not assigned to a Primary Set of Books will be upgraded as Primary Ledgers. And Reporting Sets of Books that are not constantly used between modules (such as being used in Accounts Payables but not Accounts Receivables) will cause upgrade errors. Reviewing all Reporting and Primary Set of Books setups prior to upgrade and making any adjustments needed to conform to Oracle's recommended setups will not be wasted time but will make the upgrade results more consistent and predictable.

Subledger Accounting

SLA will replace the accounting processes in Payables, Purchasing, Assets, Inventory, Projects, and Receivables. The standard setups for creating accounting that existed in 11*i* upgrade to one of the seeded Subledger Accounting Methods: Standard Accrual, Standard Cash, Encumbrance Accrual, Encumbrance Cash, or US Federal Accounting. The forms for accounting methods from 11*i* will still exist in R12 but are for reference (view) only, and you cannot update them. Any modifications needed to the accounting process will have to be completed in the new SLA forms and with its concepts. The SLA upgrade was only written to handle some of the more conventional and basic accounting setups, so ensure you review your setups and understand the results after the first upgrade. SLA setups may become mandatory if your accounting methods do not upgrade as expected, resulting in incorrect accounting transactions.

ADI Differences and FSG Reporting

In R12, the client version of ADI is no longer supported and Web ADI is introduced. In many places, Web ADI functionality is the same as the client version, such as for uploading journal entries or adding fixed assets, without the overhead costs of having to install and maintain the client version on the users' PCs. But there is one significant change that is causing some significant problems for some companies, and that is the replacement of the client ADI feature to publish FSGs (Financial Statement Generator reports) with the Report Manager. The Report Manager has the introduced functionality of creating a report repository where reports can be saved in directories and viewed by multiple users. It also takes a little longer to run the FSG reports using this new method. The drill-down feature is more robust but also requires more clicks of the mouse to see the detailed transactions. For heavy users of publishing FSGs in ADI and the drill-down feature, these changes will take some getting used to and are best introduced early on in the project.

Reviewing and understanding your current setups in these areas prior to the upgrade, and making adjustments to achieve the desired results, can actually reduce the project time, allowing the R12 features to be left as upgraded as opposed to having to implement them right away.

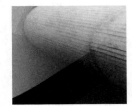

CHAPTER
3

Setup Considerations:
New Implementation
and Upgrades

BS, like all accounting systems, comes with a large range of features that are not required to set up and use, but can make the system more usable and accurate. Reviewing and understanding these features during an implementation or upgrade can lead to more accurate accounting with less manual intervention.

Chart of Accounts

Though your Chart of Accounts is perhaps one of the most important decisions that you can make, it is not an option that can be changed if you are upgrading. However, you *can* change the usage of Dynamic Insertion and Cross-Validation Rules, which directly affect the creation of the account combinations, making the system more accurate with less work. Dynamic Insertion allows EBS to automatically create account combinations when users enter them into the system. Dynamic Insertion is also a good option to use so that an accountant need not be paid to create account combinations every time one is needed.

Most companies have rules about which combinations should be allowed, and this is sometimes the reason given for not turning on Dynamic Insertion. Another feature, Cross-Validation Rules (CVR), tells EBS what combinations are valid and can be created, and which ones are not, preventing the users from creating them. A typical CVR for many organizations is that the department setting for balance sheet accounts must be 0. Reviewing the Cross-Validation Rules on a regular basis is a good idea to ensure they still meet your business needs. During normal monthly processing, Cross-Validation Rules should be reviewed for any account combination that was created and posted to in error and required a reclass—chances are a rule can probably be created to prevent this in the future.

Descriptive Flexfields

An option that is often unknown to users, and underutilized by programmers, is called Descriptive Flex Fields (DFF). These fields exist on many forms in EBS and can be customized to include data specific to your organization. You can identify DFFs on a form by two brackets ([]), and on HTML forms usually under Additional Information, and the field Context Value. These must always be set up prior to being used. Although I always recommend trying to use an existing field on a form to track data where it is reasonable (as these are more commonly found on seeded EBS reports, whereas DFF never are), DFF offers the flexibility of adding data that just does not fit into any existing field or all data to be defaulted based on other fields.

I also like to have developers use these fields, in conjunction with Value Sets, for data required on reports that may change at some point. This is so that the changes in the data will not require a programmer to make modifications. Updating the DFF and/or Value Set will automatically update the report definitions. A Value Set is really just a list of values that can be added to the system and maintained within the application. DFFs have multiple options when setting up for how data is entered, such as allowing the user to type in anything, only allowing data from a value set to be selected, or using a SQL statement to default data. You can also make the fields required or not required.

Journal Options

AutoReverse and AutoPost are two powerful features in EBS that can streamline work and reduce errors by taking the manual steps out of monthly processes. AutoReverse allows a scheduled concurrent request or opening a period to generate reversing entries when the journal is marked as Reverse, eliminating the problem of users forgetting to create the reversal. AutoPost is most effective when utilized to post journals from submodules, such as Accounts Payables. These journals should never be modified prior to posting to ensure system integrity between the modules is maintained, and to eliminate the extra manual step of posting.

Journal Approvals can be turned on to use Oracle's workflow features, sending notifications out to the proper person, who can then review and approve the journals prior to posting. This eliminates the manual process of obtaining journal signatures on paper. This feature can be turned on by Journal Source, so that entries created from submodules do not require approval, whereas journals created manually do. There are different options for how the approval process will work, such as directing the journal only to the person who can approve it, requiring the creator's supervisor to review it first, or having every person in an approval hierarchy review and approve the journal.

Calendars

When you reimplement or are doing a new implementation, deciding on the first period is critical—this is a decision that cannot be changed without creating a new Ledger. It is the creation of the accounting calendar that determines what the first period will be. The calendar is created and attached to a Ledger, and then the first period is opened. Once the period is opened, no periods prior to that point in time can be added to the calendar, or utilized with this Ledger. Make sure you go back far enough to accommodate any period over period comparison your organization requires. If you have changed your chart of accounts for the implementation, or at some point in the past, the legacy accounts will have to be mapped to get meaningful comparisons, and you should take this fact into consideration prior to deciding how many historical periods will be entered into EBS. Having a calendar set up for periods that eventually will not be used does not have an adverse effect on the system—but not going back far enough does.

Securing the General Ledger

One of the most common problems in any accounting system is people in Payables, Purchasing, and other modules outside the General Ledger using accounts that they should not be posting to, but that are valid and required in the General Ledger. One of the most common mistakes I have seen is purchase orders and invoices being posted against a specific fixed asset account, such as Automobiles, as opposed to the asset clearing accounts. Not only does this cause the General Ledger to be out of balance to the Asset subledger in EBS, but the transactions also will not be selected by Autocreate and transferred to Fixed Assets. Adding a Security Rule to prevent specific responsibilities from being able to post to these accounts resolves this problem. Security Rules, in a nutshell, secure the General Ledger data, restricting access to view or use specific account numbers. Unlike Data Access Sets, which are set up by Balancing and Management Segments, Security Rules can be set up for an individual account or range of accounts. This is also useful if you have one Ledger with multiple balancing segments—security rules can prevent some users from seeing or posting to other balancing segments.

One of the new options in R12 is the ability to secure specific setup information using Definition Access Sets. Previously, specific access to a setup screen could be secured with responsibilities, but this was for the form itself, not the data on the form. In R12, setup windows can be secured for data as well, assigning USE, VIEW, or MODIFY to users or responsibilities. In this way, users will either have the access to USE the setup to process transactions, VIEW the setup itself, or MODIFY the setup. Inherently, any time MODIFY is assigned, the user will also be given VIEW. When used, this security feature secures each specific setup on a screen, not the specific screen itself, allowing a user to view specific setups and not others. Table 3-1 shows the forms that can be secured, and what each type of security means to that form.

Definition	Use Access	View Access	Modify Access
Accounting Calendar	All users can use the calendar assigned to the Ledger they are in—making this not applicable.	View calendars.	Modify calendars.
AutoAllocation Workbench	Generate and Schedule AutoAllocation Sets.	View AutoAllocations Sets.	Modify AutoAllocation Sets.
AutoPost Criteria Set	Generate or schedule AutoPost Criteria Sets.	View AutoPost Criteria.	Modify AutoPost Criteria Sets.
Budget Formula	Calculate Budget Amounts from the Calculate Budget Amounts window.	View Budget Formulas.	Modify Budget Formulas.
Budget Organization	Use Budget Organizations when entering budget amounts or journals.	View Budget Organization setups.	Modify Budget Organization setups.
Chart of Accounts Mapping	Assign the mapping to Consolidation or a Ledger.	View Mappings.	Modify Mappings.
Consolidation Definition	Use Consolidation definitions to consolidation data in the Consolidation Transfer window as well as the Consolidation Set window.	View a consolidation definition.	Modify a consolidation definition.

TABLE 3-1 *General Ledger Setups That Can Be Secured with Definition Access Sets*

Definition	Use Access	View Access	Modify Access
Consolidation Sets	Use Consolidation Sets in the Transfer Consolidation DataSet window. A users must also have access to the Consolidation Definition included in the Consolidation Sets.	View Consolidation Sets.	Modify Consolidation Sets.
Elimination Sets	Generate Elimination Sets.	View Elimination Sets.	Modify Elimination Sets.
FSG Report	Submit FSG reports regardless of access to FSG components.	View FSG Report setup.	Modify FSG Report setup.
FSG Report Components	Assign FSG components to a FSG Report.	View FSG components in their respective definition windows.	Modify FSG components in their respective definition windows.
FSG Report Set	Submit the Report Set regardless of the privileges to the reports in the set.	View the Report Set.	Modify Report Sets.
Journal Reversal Criteria (AutoReversal)	N/A	View Journal Reversal Criteria.	Modify Journal Reversal Criteria.
Ledger Set	Use or assign Ledger Sets to Data Access Sets or another Ledger Set.	View Ledger Sets.	Modify Ledger Sets.
MassAllocation	Generate MassAllocations and assign them to AutoAllocation Sets.	View MassAllocations.	Modify MassAllocations.
MassBudget	Generate/schedule MassBudgets and assign them to AutoAllocation Sets.	View MassBudgets.	Modify MassBudgets.
Rate Type	Use or assign the rate type when entering journals, defining MassAllocations, or running Revaluations.	View Rate Type.	Modify Rate Types.

TABLE 3-1   *General Ledger Setups That Can Be Secured with Definition Access Sets* (continued)

Definition	Use Access	View Access	Modify Access
Recurring Journal	Generate Recurring Journals and assign them to AutoAllocation Sets.	View Recurring Journal definitions.	Modify Recurring Journal definitions.
Revaluation	Generate Revaluations and assign them to Request Sets.	View Revaluations.	Modify Revaluations.
Transaction Calendar	N/A	View Transaction Calendars.	Modify Transaction Calendars.

TABLE 3-1 *General Ledger Setups That Can Be Secured with Definition Access Sets* (continued)

As you can see, the Enable Security feature can add a needed layer of security to critical and noncritical setups, securing the application to a much greater level than was previously available.

Responsibilities are a key component in the security of EBS. At a high level, not only are Data Access Sets, Definition Access Sets, Ledger Sets, and Multi-Org Access Control assigned to responsibilities, they also restrict the forms (and functions) and concurrent processes that users can access. Ignoring this area and just assigning Superuser to everybody leaves a system at risk, while on the flip side, creating too many responsibilities can also make it confusing when assigning new users access to the system. Try to keep security and system access needed in check, creating role-based responsibilities. In any organization that is being audited or concerned about segregation of duties (which should be all companies for accounting processes), creating a simple matrix of the major conflicts, along with a second matrix of which responsibilities create these conflicts, assists not only in the audit, but also in assigning new users access to the system. A basic example of this is in Payables: the same person should not have access to three main functions—creating payments, creating or modifying suppliers, and entering or modifying invoices. Setting up three responsibilities and listing them as incompatible with each other assists in audits of the system and alerts the person assigning them that they should never be assigned to the same person.

Setting Up Access Sets

Creating security on setup windows is basically a three-step process: First, define the type of access (View, Modify, Use), and then assign the definition to a responsibility (or multiple responsibilities). The last step is to enable the security on the setup windows and assign a definition. Once this is done, access will be restricted by the security assigned. Because the restriction happens as soon as Security is enabled on a setup form, the first step is to assign unrestricted access to a superuser responsibility.

To set up the general security, first create an Access Set with just a DEFINITION ACCESS SET name and DESCRIPTION, which will be assigned to a superuser (full access) responsibility, granting full access to Modify and Use all setups in the system. By not selecting any Definition Type or Definition Name, you will allow full access to everything, as you can see in Figure 3-1.

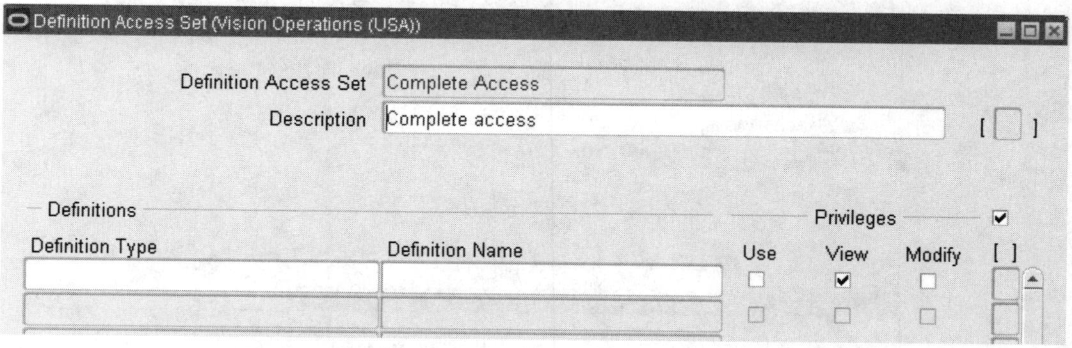

General Ledger Superuser | Setup | Financials | Definition Access Sets | Define

FIGURE 3-1 *Definition Access Set assigning full access to a user*

Next, assign this Access Set to a Superuser responsibility, as in Figure 3-2. Select the RESPONSIBILITY you want to assign the Definition Access Set to. Selecting AUTOASSIGN will cause this access set to be assigned to any setup where security is enabled. Select the DEFINITION ACCESS SETS from the list of values, and select the PRIVILEGES that it will have.

Now, under any security-controlled setup, such as Row Sets, you can set up the security by checking the ENABLE SECURITY check box and clicking ASSIGN ACCESS. The Definition Access Sets that are associated with your responsibility will appear and can be modified from this window for USE, VIEW, and MODIFY, as needed. Once these settings are saved, the Definition Name will be populated on the Definition Access Set window, showing that it is assigned to this definition, or Row Set name. Notice in Figure 3-3 that USE, VIEW, and MODIFY are available on all three levels—the Definition Access Set, the Assignment, and the actual setup window. This is hierarchical, and the lowest

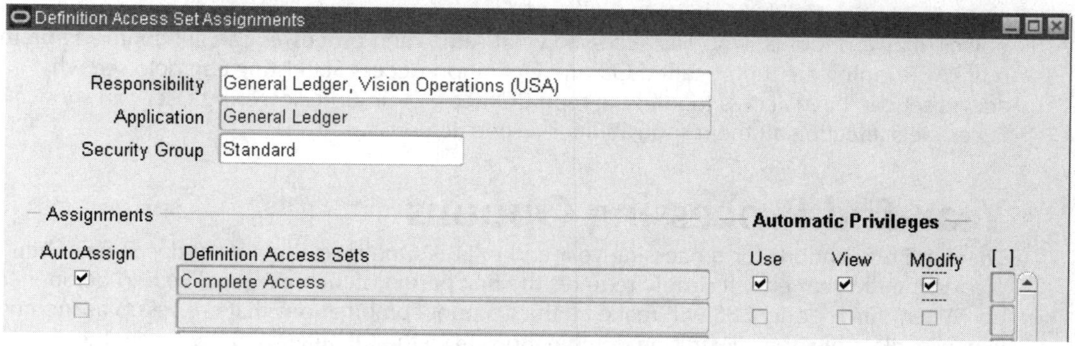

General Ledger Superuser | Setup | Financials | Definition Access Sets | Assign

FIGURE 3-2 *Assigning access to a responsibility*

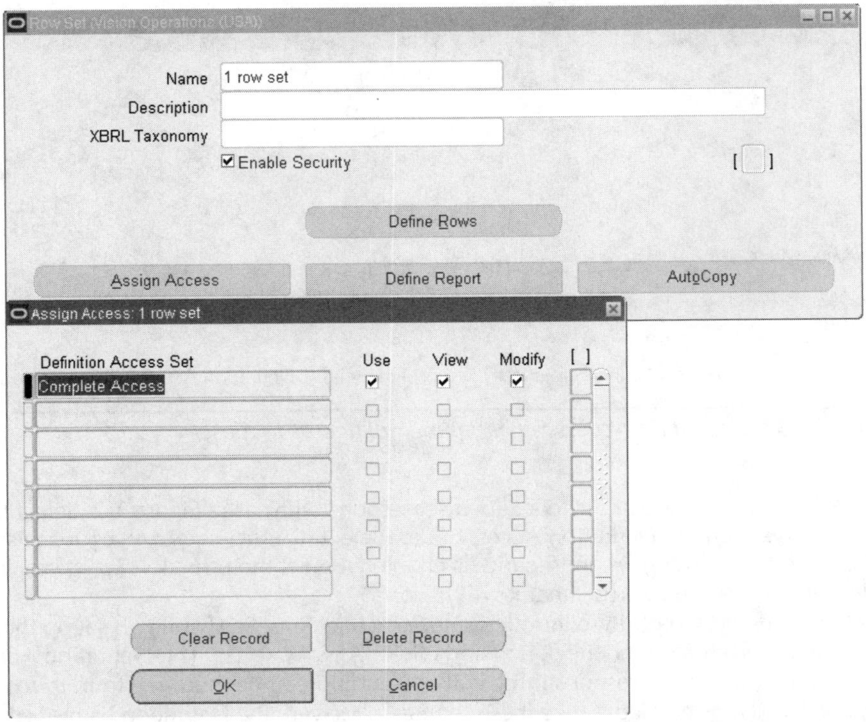

General Ledger Superuser | Reports | Define | Row Sets | Assign Access button

FIGURE 3-3 *Securing a setup window*

level, the actual setup window, will override all the others. The Set will default in for all Assignments and can be changed at this level as well to default onto the actual setups. As you can imagine, as powerful as this tool is, who has access to what setups and processes can get confusing pretty quickly. Running the report called Other – Definition Access Set Listing can help see what each access set can have access to, and the report Other – Definition Access by User can show all the access sets affecting all the responsibilities a specific user has.

Year-End Processing Options

There are two options for processing year end in EBS. One is so simple, yet deceiving when processing the year end. It simply requires the first period of the next fiscal year to be opened up. When this is done, EBS will make all the account combinations that are set up as Income or Expense (classifications default on combinations from the Qualifier of the value in the Accounting Flexfield) have a zero beginning balance, and move the cumulative net balance of these accounts for the year into the Retained Earnings account defined in the Ledger. This is deceptive because no journal entries are created—it just happens automatically. And as additional journals are posted in the prior fiscal year, the beginning balances are automatically adjusted.

The second takes a little more planning to use. There are two processes in EBS that can be used for closing the books at year end by creating journal entries: one for the balance sheet and one for the income statement accounts. Either one or both of the processes can be used at the end of the year. Oracle recommends that the last period and first period of the fiscal year be set up as adjusting periods when closing the books via Journal Entries. These adjusting periods are the periods the closing entries will be created in. Creating a Secondary Tracking segment in your chart of accounts can further segregate these closing entries, as they will all be posted in combinations using this special segment.

The adjustment periods allow for the posting periods to be closed prior to running the year-end processes, as well as to isolating the journals. Run Close Process – Create Balance Sheet Closing Journals to close out the Asset, Liability, and Owners Equity accounts for the year. The journal entry created with this process will need to be reversed in the first period of the next year to reinstate these balances. Close Process – Create Income Statement Closing Journals will zero out the Income and Expense accounts into Owners Equity, or the account that is specified when the request is run. This journal should not be reversed at the beginning of the next year. Both of these processes should be run only after the last journal entry for the year has been posted (including audit adjusting entries). If additional journals are required for the prior fiscal year, the journals generated by both of these processes will need to be reversed, and then the processes can be rerun. The Close Process concurrent requests will always select the balance in the accounts at the end of the year, not the net change since the last time it was run.

Taking time to review these setups and business decisions during upgrades or implementations can improve the overall benefits of the General Ledger system, reducing time spent on standard processing and increasing time spent on value-added tasks.

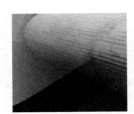

CHAPTER
4

General Ledger Setups and Maintenance: Step by Step

etups and the decisions surrounding them for any ERP or accounting system are critical not only to the success of the project, but also to the usability of the system. EBS is no exception. Taking the time to understand the setups and what they affect is time well spent not only during an implementation or upgrade, but also for any person trying to understand, is there a better way to use the system? As stated already, ERP implementations are not projects with beginnings and endings, but a journey that continues throughout the ever-changing landscape we call business.

Setup steps are broken down into two types: Required to use EBS and Optional, which means that they only need to be performed to use that specific functionality. The Required setups include, in this order:

1. Configure the Accounting Flexfield.
2. Configure the Accounting Calendar.
3. Configure the Accounting Setups (required fields of Legal Entity and Ledgers only).
4. Assign the Ledger profile and other required Profiles in System Administration.
5. Assign Data Access Sets, even if it is blanket access for everyone.
6. Open the first period.

All other setups are optional, depending on your specific business needs.

The Account Number

The Accounting Flexfield is the basis for your Chart of Accounts, and how transactions can be accounted in the system. When deciding the structure of your Chart of Accounts, be sure to allow room for growth, as it cannot be changed with any standard EBS functionality once it is defined. I tend to see two basic mistakes when designing the Accounting Flexfield: too complicated and not enough room for growth. The balance between the two takes time and consideration to figure out.

Having ten segments in the Chart of Accounts is complicated by any standard—what combinations are valid, when do I enter this field, what does it actually mean? There are times that a complicated Chart of Accounts is actually required; in these instances, ensure there are detailed Cross-Validation Rules in place to guide the users, and plan on a training process, both at go live and ongoing as new employees start using the system, to ensure they know how to use the Chart of Accounts. If the Chart of Accounts is too small, it will not allow the company the room it needs for growth, and not only will this inhibit the usability of the financial statements in the future, you may be looking at a reimplementation much sooner than you want.

There are two mandatory segment qualifiers in the Chart of Accounts: Balancing Segment and Natural Account. Cost Center is also required when Assests is implemented in EBS. Qualifiers give additional functionality to a segment. Three additional qualifiers are available, though they are not mandatory: Management, Intercompany, and Secondary Tracking. Details about each qualifier are shown in Table 4-1. It is a combination of segments with qualifiers and segments without that will make up a useful Chart of Accounts.

The Management segment, which is new in R12, is the only Flexfield Qualifier on the Chart of Accounts that can be activated after the Chart of Accounts has been defined and used. This is not done in the normal screen where qualifiers are added, but with a series of Concurrent Processes. First, run the request called Program – Prepare Journal Batches for Management Segment Upgrade. This request *cannot* be run when users are actively entering or posting journals. It takes and

Segment Qualifier	Description
Balancing Segment (Required)	All transactions within a Balancing Segment value must balance for Debits and Credits. Use a Balancing Segment value for each entity you want to obtain a Balance Sheet and Income Statement for. If only an Income statement is required, then it is not necessary to set up a balancing segment value for that entity.
Cost Center (Required when Assets is implemented)	Used to classify Departmental or Cost Center transactions for segregated Income Statements or Management Reports.
Natural Account (Required)	This is the core segment of your accounting Flexfield and is used to classify each transaction into accounts such as Revenue from Internet Sales or Cash. The Natural Account segment determines if an account combination is classified as an Asset, Liability, Owners Equity, Income, or Expense, and these classifications are used as part of the year-end process to determine which accounts roll into retained earnings, and which carry a balance forward into the next year.
Management (Optional)	Primarily used to restrict access, both Read and Write, with a Data Access Set. The Management segment will allow only specific data within a balancing segment to be viewed or updated by a group of users. The Management segment qualifier can be assigned to any segment of the account, except the Balancing segment and the Natural Account.
Intercompany (Optional)	This segment can help with intercompany and intracompany balancing by tracking all intercompany transactions in this segment.
Secondary Tracking (Optional)	Utilized by Revaluation, Transaction Gains/Losses, and Fiscal Close Journals to record cumulative translation adjustments, unrealized gains and losses, and fiscal close entries to retained earnings into a unique account combinations of balancing segment and secondary tracking segment.

TABLE 4-1   *Accounting Segment Qualifiers*

prepares these entries for adding a Management Segment. This process starts a second request, called Process Posted Journal Batches for Management Segment Upgrade, and prepares all journal entries for the selected Chart of Accounts for the actual upgrade. This process can be run during business hours and be rerun at any time, picking up where it left off. Do this by rerunning the Program – Prepare Journal Batches for Management Segment Upgrade, which will start the second program, picking up from the point it left off.

Once both processes complete successfully through to the end, the final process is run called Program – Complete Management Segment Upgrade, which finalizes all the transactions and adds the segment qualifier to the Chart of Accounts. This last process, again, cannot be run when journals are being posted or entered. This is the only way to add this qualifier to an existing chart that has been used, as just adding it to the Chart of Accounts does not update existing transactions in the General Ledger.

Setting Up the Accounting Flexfield

To set up your accounting Flexfield, first you query the seeded accounting Flexfield by using the flashlight on your toolbar and selecting General Ledger for the APPLICATION, and Accounting Flexfield for the FLEXFIELD TITLE. Ensure you do not select the GL Ledger Flexfield by mistake—this is a copy of the Accounting Flexfield that is updated when the Flexfield is compiled and the program Program – General Ledger Flexfield runs. EBS does this automatically when changes are saved. Changes should never be manually added to the GL Ledger Flexfield. The GL Ledger Flexfield was added in R12 to improve processing times for some of the more intensive processes, like FSG and Mass Allocations.

Reviewing Figure 4-1, make sure you set up a new STRUCTURE when implementing EBS and do not use the seeded one that queries up when you access the form. As in all places in EBS, modifying the seeded data runs the risk of losing your changes after patching or an upgrade. Setting up new setup data reduces this risk. Taking the time now to decide on a naming convention is also a good idea. As a rule, I use a two- or three-letter code for the company before all setups in the system names. Some DBAs are now recommending that an XX be added before that code, because as the Oracle family of products grows, the chance of your custom identifier being used is greater and greater. Oracle has stated that XX will not be used in the future.

The CODE is the system name for the accounting Flexfield and should use underscores instead of spaces, while the TITLE is the user name that will appear on most of the forms. An example of how to customize the CODE would be XXCFS_Accounting_Flexfield, where CFS is the three-digit code for the company. The TITLE may contain spaces, but naming the two consistently if possible (the TITLE with spaces and the CODE with underscores) makes troubleshooting and custom reporting easier. Add a DESCRIPTION of what this code will be used for. The VIEW NAME is not used by EBS for Accounting Flexfields.

FREEZE FLEXFIELD DEFINITION needs to be checked for this Flexfield to be active, but it will remain unchecked when you are doing work on the accounting structure. You cannot update any fields while this is checked. Once you are using EBS for production transactions, unfreezing Key Flexfields when users or processes are using the Flexfield can cause data integrity problems, so maintenance to the accounting Flexfield is always recommended during non-business hours. Checking CROSS-VALIDATE SEGMENTS will allow you to use the Cross-Validation Rules feature in EBS, and you should always use them when ALLOW DYNAMIC INSERTS is checked. Dynamic Insertion allows account combinations (combinations of your individual accounting segment values) to be generated by the system the first time it is used. If this is not turned on, each combination will have to be manually added prior to any transactions using it in any module.

Cross-Validation Rules are a set of guidelines that are input into EBS (see the next section for instructions on how to set these up) to ensure that no accounting combinations are created that violate the rules. A good example of a rule might be that Balance Sheet accounts cannot have a department code other than 0 associated with them, preventing departments from being assigned to Balance Sheet accounts. ENABLED allows the structure to be used in the application and should only be unchecked when the Flexfield is not in use, and FREEZE ROLLUP GROUPS are used with Summary accounts.

EBS has four main types of accounts that can be set up for each segment.

■ Posting or Budgeting accounts where all actual and budget transactions are posted to.

■ Parent accounts, which is a range of posting or budgeting accounts for reporting purposes. Parent accounts have no balances but are just listings of ranges of accounts.

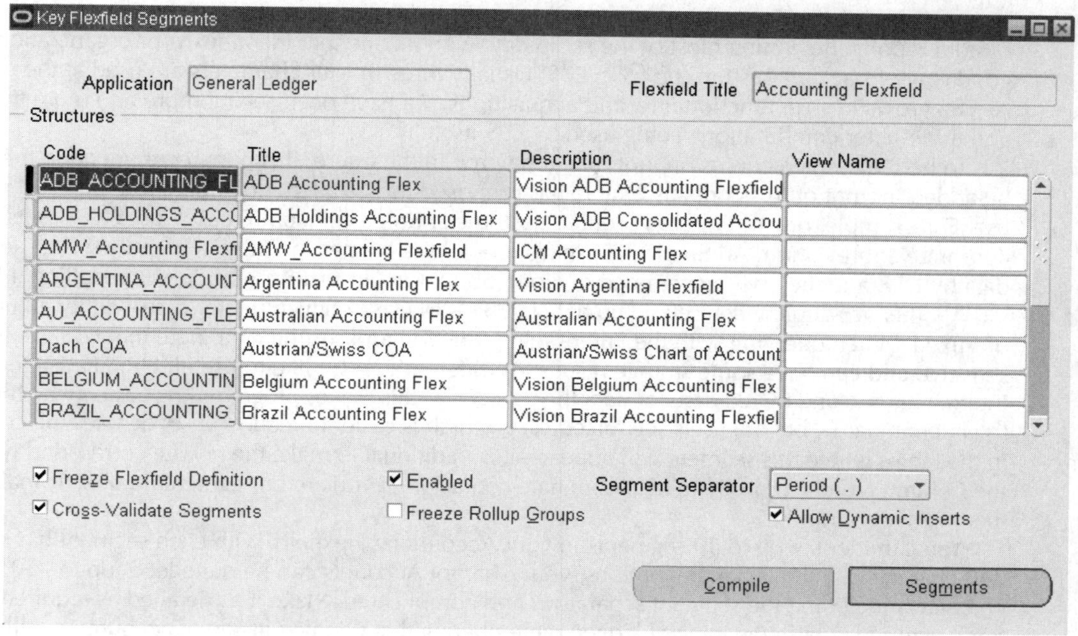

General Ledger Superuser | Setup | Financial | Flexfields | Key | Segments

FIGURE 4-1   *Setting up Accounting segments in the Accounting Flexfield*

- Statistical accounts, which work the same as posting and budget accounts, except that the currency will be STAT (Statistical), and journal entries do not have to have debits and credits that balance.

- Summary accounts.

Summary accounts work much like Parent accounts with one major difference. Parent accounts have no balances but are a shortcut to a grouping of accounts, whereas Summary accounts will actually have a balance associated with them. Summary accounts are most often used to improve performance of reporting, including FSG reporting, mass allocations, and to track Budgetary Controls. There is a tradeoff for this improved performance, which is decreased performance during journal entry posting.

The last field is the SEGMENT SEPERATOR, which determines what character will separate your segments when keying combinations or printing on reports. EBS comes with Period, Dash, and Pipe installed, and allows you to add additional custom characters. Remember to think about how people will do data entry when deciding on your segment separator—selecting a tilde, on the left side of many keyboards, will slow down data entry for numbers, which are still often done with a keypad.

Adding Segments to the Accounting Flexfield

Next, click SEGMENTS to create each segment as shown in Figure 4-2. The NUMBER is the order that your segments will appear on reports and in EBS forms. Leave no gaps in the numbering to prevent processing problems. NAME is the name of the segment, while PROMPT is what appears on data entry screens. Making the NAME and PROMPT consistent will help eliminate confusion when creating custom reports. Beginning most of the setup data with a code that identifies your organization is a good way of tracking custom setups in EBS. Usually three or four characters are used at the most. As EBS grows in size, functionality, and acquisitions, we have been seeing more and more two- and three-letter combinations being used by EBS itself.

To help eliminate confusion, not only today but in the future, it is now recommended that XX be added in front of this code, as Oracle has proposed this as a letter combination they will never use. For example, one of Oracle's profiled customers, Korea Telecom FreeTel, uses KTF as its corporate abbreviation. Adding XXKTF in front of all the Names in EBS will identify this as added data by KTF, and they will never need to worry about Oracle adding a module and calling it KTF.

Another good rule when setting up data in EBS is to use a convention for case—either all upper or mixed. When querying with the Enter Query function and sorting data, note that EBS is case sensitive and can have some strange results for different cases. I like to use all UPPERcase for internal names, and mixed case for data the user sees—this makes programming easier, which uses the internal name, but the users see mixed case, which is easier to read. COLUMN denotes the column in the tables where this segment will appear—it is traditional to make the NUMBER correspond with the Column Number, mostly to help eliminate confusion. If you are on segment number 1, make this segment Attribute 1.

You can identify up to 30 segments in your Accounting Flexfield, with each segment having 240 characters. With this many options, your Chart of Accounts can be quite long (up to 750 characters including the segment separator!) and complicated. Make it as detailed as required to track required data in the general ledger, remembering that people outside of accounting will most often be keying in this string (depending on which modules you use—for example, if you use iProcurement, most of your transactions will be entered by casual users who are not accountants). A lot of accounting data is often available outside of the General Ledger, especially if you are using many of the EBS subledgers, and you should give thought to whether this data can be reported on from the source, such as Inventory, as opposed to the end resting place, the General Ledger.

Creating a Value Set for the Accounting Flexfield

A VALUE SET needs to be set up for each segment in your account; it becomes the location where the valid values are stored for use. Figure 4-3 shows how the VALUE SET NAME is the name of the segment, usually prefixed with a unique code that identifies your company, often preceded with "XX" to ensure it is not a code that will be used by Oracle in future releases.

Click USAGES to see where Value Sets are used as far as Concurrent Program Parameters, Descriptive Flexfield Segments, or Key Flexfield Segments. This is useful information for determining where Value Sets are used, both seeded and custom sets. DESCRIPTION is a more detailed description of what this value set is used for. The LIST TYPE for the Accounting Flexfield will always be LIST OF VALUES, meaning that the user must enter (or select from a drop-down box) a value that is set up and active in this value set. Selecting NO SECURITY for the SECURITY TYPE will not add any security when creating combinations in your accounting Flexfields.

Securing Rules restrict access to specific account values for a responsibility. For example, iProcurement, Purchasing, and Payables can all be restricted from posting transactions to specific fixed asset accounts, such as Computer Equipment, preventing mispostings and problems because the asset clearing account was not used. Selecting NON-HIERARCHICAL SECURITY will allow Security rules to be set up, which will restrict the values users can have access to for entry and inquiry. Selecting HIERARCHICAL SECURITY works the same as Non-Hierarchical, except the rules are assigned at the parent level and cascade down to the child, as opposed to using account ranges.

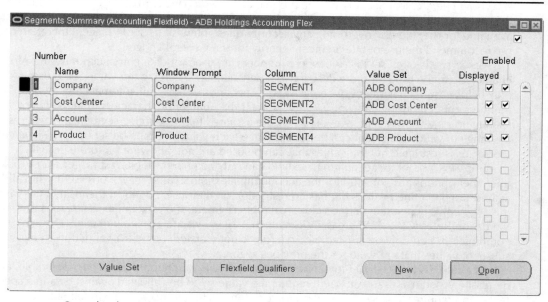

General Ledger Superuser | Setup | Financial | Flexfields | Key | Segments | Segments button

FIGURE 4-2   *Adding segments to the Accounting Flexfield*

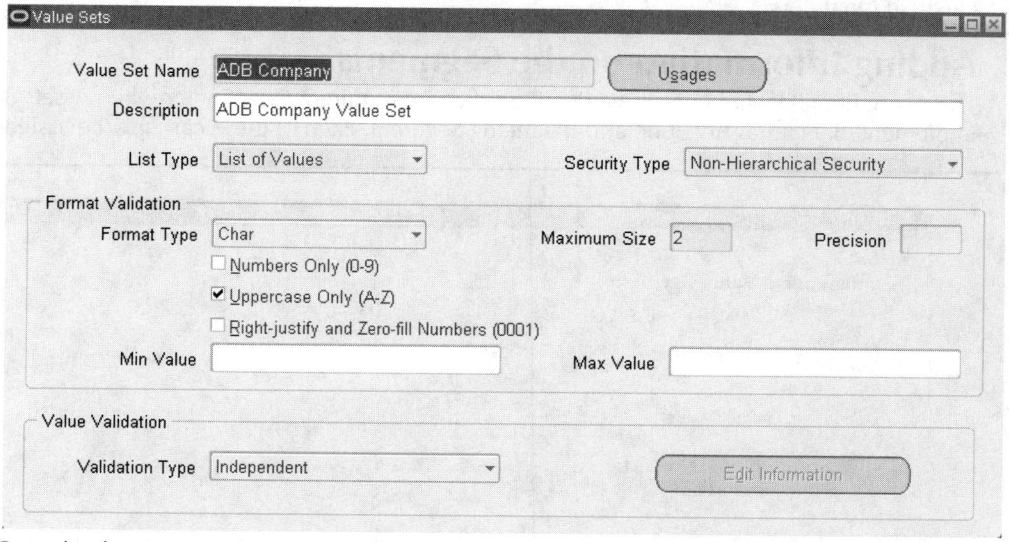

General Ledger Superuser | Setup | Financial | Flexfields | Key | Segments | Segments button | Value Set button

FIGURE 4-3   *Creating Value Sets used in the Account Numbers as well as many other places in EBS*

Using Hierarchical Security can be problematic. If you have a *T* parent value for all child values, you will probably need to assign this value for use. This would then render all children available for use, thereby overriding any security rules you wish to put in place. I therefore do not recommend the use of Hierarchical Security for the General Ledger.

FORMAT TYPE is often set to CHAR, where numbers are used for data entry accounts, and Alpha characters can be used for more descriptive parent accounts. Forcing the Value Set to use UPPERCASE ONLY helps ensure consistency, whereas RIGHT-JUSTIFY and ZERO-FILL will automatically zero fill any numbers entered during data entry. MAXIMUM SIZE is the number of characters in the segment, and usually no MINIMUM VALUES or MAXIMUM VALUES are assigned for Accounting segments, which restricts the range of valid values that can be set up. Since each value needs to be set up, usually access to the setups is restricted but the values that can be used are not, allowing for future growth.

VALIDATION TYPE for an accounting Flexfield can only be DEPENDENT, INDEPENDENT, or TABLE VALIDATION (the other options are not valid for the accounting Flexfield's value sets). INDEPENDENT will validate against the predefined values but has no restriction on their use. DEPENDENT means that the value of this segment is dependent on the value in another segment; it offers similar validations as Cross-Validation Rules (CVRs). Whereas CVRs state that all values are available in every segment, but combinations can only be created where a rule is not violated, DEPENDENT validation creates a subset of values that are valid for the previous segment.

As a rule, CVRs are easier to maintain than DEPENDENT validation and, where applicable, are more often used. TABLE VALIDATION will require the value set to be validated against data in a specific table, and requires SQL to be added on the Edit Information form, which will tell EBS how and were to validate the data. This is commonly used with the accounting Flexfield value sets when the data must be validated against a custom table that houses the accounts from a nonrelated system.

Click EDIT INFORMATION to select the segment you want to make this segment DEPENDENT on. When you actually enter the values, the dependencies will show up as shown in Figure 4-4. Close the Edit Information and Value Set form to get back to the Segments Summary form to set up the Flexfield Qualifiers.

Adding Information on the Segments

The Accounting Flexfield has three qualifiers that are required: Cost Center when Assets is implemented, Natural Account, and Balancing Segment. Each of these can only be assigned

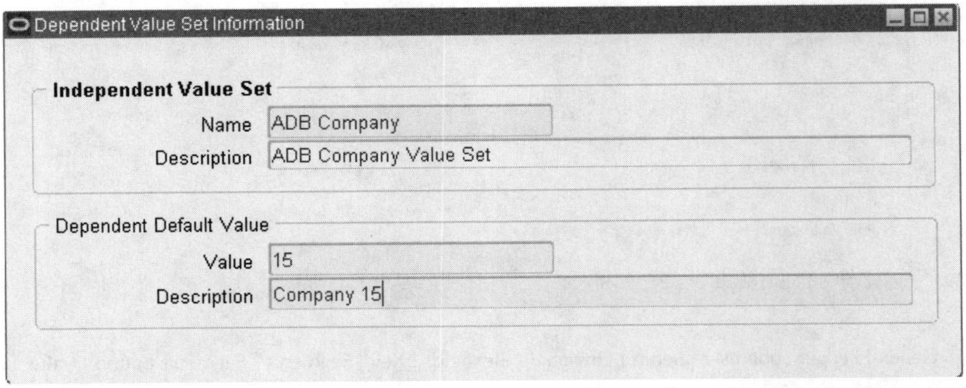

General Ledger Superuser | Setup | Financial | Flexfields | Key | Segments | Value Set button | Edit Information button

FIGURE 4-4 *Adding dependency information to the segments*

to one segment within an Accounting Flexfield. Optionally, an Intercompany segment can be defined for tracking intercompany balances. Management segments are used to identify combinations as part of a specific management segment for reporting, and a Secondary Tracking segment is used with revaluations, translations, and year-end processing to more uniquely identify these transactions. Use care when adding these qualifiers, shown in Figure 4-5, as they are important to key General Ledger functionality, such as year-end processing (Natural Account determines which accounts will be cleared into retained earnings, and which will roll the balance forward) or to creating balanced journal entries (Balancing Segment), and they cannot be changed once the accounting Flexfield is used.

Referring to Figure 4-6, back on the Segments window, ensure all segments of your Accounting Flexfield are ENABLED and DISPLAYED, and select OPEN to complete the setups for each segment. The NAME, DESCRIPTION, COLUMN, and NUMBER will default from the previous page and cannot be changed on this form. Ensure ENABLED and DISPLAYED are still checked as well. INDEXED will default to checked, ensuring that this segment is picked up with the Program – Optimizer concurrent request and indexed for faster transaction processing and reporting. The Optimizer program will gather statistics and create indexes for your Accounting Flexfield, making reports and such processes as interfaces run faster. The VALUE SET and DESCRIPTION will default in from the previous page as well.

Adding a DEFAULT TYPE and a DEFAULT VALUE will cause all Accounting Flexfield forms to default the DEFAULT VALUE in so that users do not have to key the data (but they can change it). This is very effective in Future Value segments, where they will always default to zero for now, and this default can be removed later on when the segment is used. REQUIRED needs to be checked for all Accounting segments, because EBS does not support having null, or no data, in an account combination string. SECURITY ENABLED will determine if this segment will use Security Rules.

Security Rules can restrict the values a specific responsibility has access to. The DISPLAY SIZE will default from the value set, whereas the DESCRIPTION SIZE will determine how much of the value's description will appear on the forms and can be modified. CONCATENATED DESCRIPTION SIZE is used on reports when this segment is concatenated with the other segments, allowing a smaller portion of each segment's description to appear on the report—this is really for space saving on the report, especially ones that are not written in XML using Oracle's BI Publisher. PROMPTS are what the users will see in both the LIST OF VALUES and WINDOW in EBS.

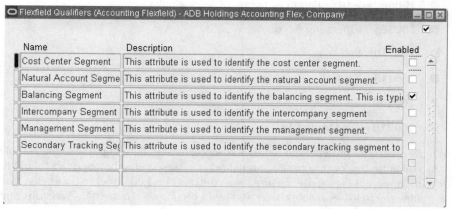

General Ledger Superuser | Setup | Financial | Flexfields | Key | Segments | Flexfield Qualifiers button

FIGURE 4-5 *Flexfield qualifiers*

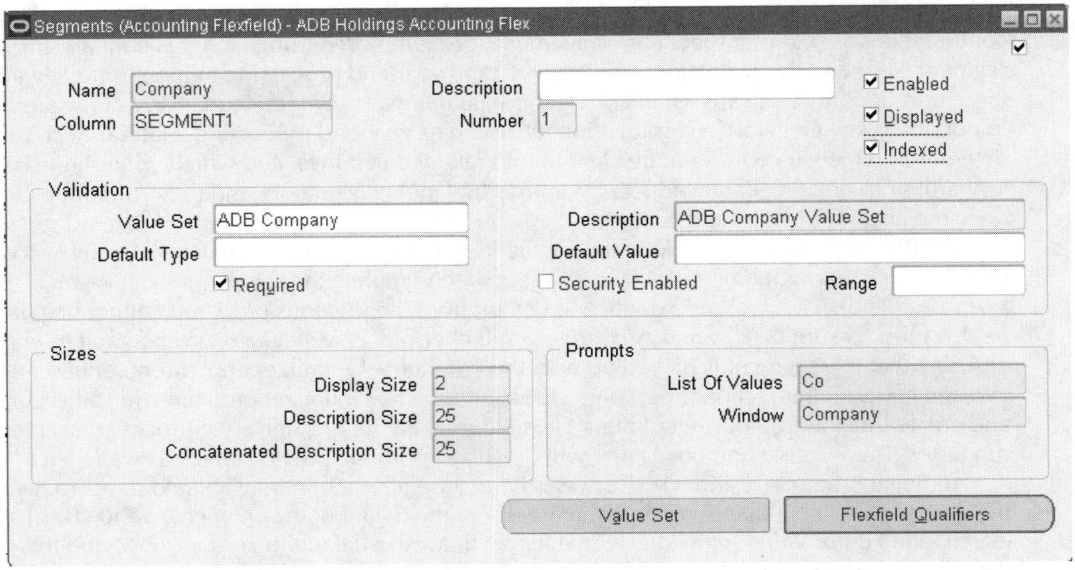

General Ledger Superuser | Setup | Financial | Flexfields | Key | Segments | Open button

FIGURE 4-6 *Additional segment information*

Adding and Maintaining Values for Your Accounting Segments

Once the Flexfield structure is set up, values will need to be created prior to using them in a combination. When assigning values to each segment, ensure you leave room for future growth (due to either increased business lines or acquisitions). A sample of growth would be as follows:

- **100000** Cash – Parent Account

- **100105** Operating Account

- **100110** Petty Cash

- **100115** Payroll

- **100200** Short Term Investments – Parent Account

- **100210** Six-Month CD

This leaves room for growth both within the accounts already set up and at the end of each section.

As you enter the form to create and maintain values, a Find box appears to find the accounting Flexfield, as seen in Figure 4-7. Ensure KEY FLEXFIELD is checked under FIND VALUES BY (these selections will change the fields available). APPLICATION will be GENERAL LEDGER (older versions upgraded in specific paths may still show ORACLE GENERAL LEDGER). The TITLE will always be ACCOUNTING FLEXFIELD. Select the STRUCTURE you want to load values in for (it will have the same NAME as the one you set up in the preceding step), and select the SEGMENT for which you want to load the values.

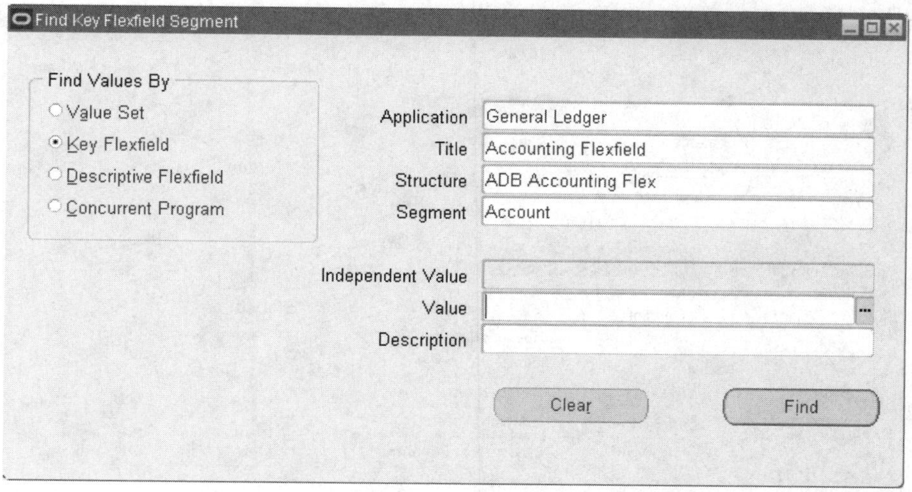

General Ledger Superuser | Setup | Financial | Flexfields | Key | Values

FIGURE 4-7   *Querying up the Accounting Flexfield to add or modify segments*

As seen in Figure 4-8, the VALUE represents the actual account number you want to set up. EBS will populate the TRANSLATED VALUE for you, and this cannot be updated unless your database is set up for multiple languages and this field was made Translatable. If set up, this field will represent the translation for the VALUE you entered. When designing the Chart of Accounts numbering methodology, using alpha characters for parents and numbers for posting accounts often helps to eliminate confusion if an account is postable or not. Using numbers for the postable accounts can increase data entry speed for most accountants, who are often faster at ten-key than alpha characters.

Add the DESCRIPTION that will show on posting screens and reports. For a value to be available for use, check the ENABLED box. Although FROM dates are not required, they are useful in seeing when an account was first intended for use, can allow accounts to be set up for future use without risk or additional maintenance required on that future date, and can be helpful in troubleshooting transactions that are stuck because the account had been end-dated or disabled (entering a FROM date prior to the date of the transaction will often resolve posting problems that are not resolved just by reactivating the account).

The TO date is the last general ledger date (not system or physical date) that a value can be used, and is helpful in ending accounts as of the fiscal year end ahead of time. It is good practice to End Date values rather than to Disable accounts by unchecking the ENABLED box, as EBS has had problems in the past with disabled accounts that are used on setup forms disappearing from the form and causing errors and confusion.

Checking the PARENT account will allow you to add child ranges, and also to make this account unavailable to post transactions to. Enter a ROLLUP GROUP if this is a summary account (see Chapter 8 for details on setting up Summary Accounts), and a LEVEL value for your specific company's purpose to see what level of reporting this falls on. This field is informational data only in EBS, and is not used to create actual hierarchies or build levels into the accounting structure. It is included to allow users to see what level of the hierarchy this value falls into if there are multiple levels. The Qualifiers data is different for each segment qualifier that was set up.

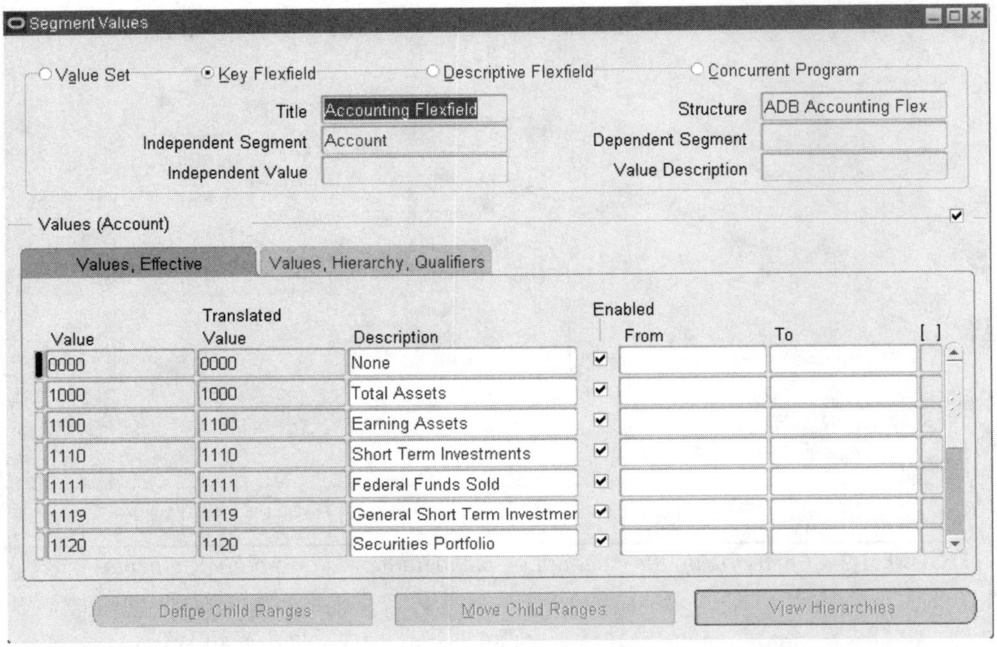

General Ledger Superuser | Setup | Financial| Flexfields | Key | Values | Find button

FIGURE 4-8   *Adding or maintaining Accounting values*

Figure 4-9 shows the Qualifiers for the Natural Account. For all segments, ALLOW BUDGETING and ALLOW POSTING will default to NO for parent accounts, or YES for posting accounts. These can be changed to meet your company's needs with one limited restriction: Parent accounts should never ALLOW POSTING.

For the natural account, ACCOUNT TYPE is available and has two main purposes: to classify accounts as Assets, Liabilities, Owners Equity, Revenue, or Expense (Budgetary CR and DR are available for encumbrances), as well as to determine which accounts will roll into Prior Year Retained Earnings at the end of a fiscal year. It is very important to ensure the ACCOUNT TYPE is set up correctly, as there is an in-depth process required to correct accounts that were set up incorrectly. THIRD PARTY CONTROL ACCOUNT will need to be CUSTOMER, SUPPLIER, or YES to use the Third Party Balance feature. This feature will prevent manual transactions from being allowed to use this segment, and any combinations created with it, only allowing journal entries created in the subledgers. This will prevent manual mispostings to the account and make reconciliations easier between the subledger and the General Ledger.

Selecting CUSTOMER restricts journals to subledgers where the application is identified as CUSTOMER or ANY, and the same goes for SUPPLIERS. Selecting either CUSTOMER or SUPPLIER will restrict posting to these accounts and prevent mispostings. For example, a common posting error is to create a manual journal entry to the payables liability account in the general ledger, which throws this account out of balance with the subledger. Setting up the payables liability account as Suppliers will restrict entries to the account to only entries from Payables. RECONCILE needs to be set to YES to use the feature of Reconciling accounts, usually for VAT transactions or clearing accounts.

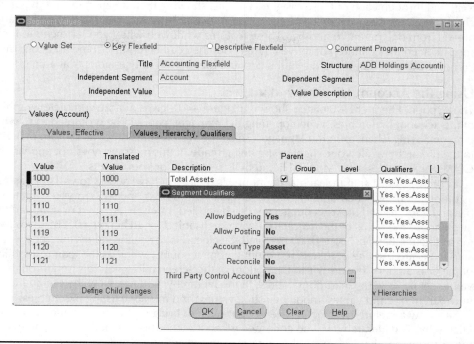

FIGURE 4-9 *Adding value-specific qualifier data*

Viewing and Maintaining Account Hierarchies for Parent/Child Relationships

Parent/child relationships can greatly reduce some of the maintenance involved in such EBS features as FSGs and MassAllocations, but the logic of the relationships must be established and the accuracy maintained. That said, maintaining the hierarchy relationships is often much faster in the long run than maintaining the FSGs or writing complicated MassAllocations without the hierarchy in place. See Chapters 5 and 6 for more information on how parent/child relationships can help with each area.

Using the Values Form

If a value is set up as a Parent account, you will need to assign Child accounts to the parent. These accounts can be added from the Key Values form as well as from the Account Hierarchy Manager. On the Key Values window (Setup | Financials | Flexfields | Key | Values), there are three buttons pertaining to Parent/Child relationships. DEFINE CHILD VALUES allows you to add an account or a range of accounts to a parent. Both Parent and Child accounts can be made a child of other accounts. After selecting the To and From accounts, select either PARENT VALUES ONLY or CHILD VALUES ONLY under the INCLUDE field.

Child values will ignore any parents in the range of accounts and create the relationship with only the child values under this parent. If PARENT VALUE is selected, then their Hierarchy, or assigned children, now becomes available, as the relationship was created with the parent instead of the child accounts. The VIEW HIERARCHIES button allows you to move up and down the tree of the hierarchy for this parent, starting at the top, which is the parent itself, with other parents assigned to it, and through each of these assigned parents, showing their assignments (both parent and child accounts). The MOVE CHILD VALUES button is available for any child and allows a range to be moved from one parent to another. These features work well when you just need to look up a specific account's children or move a range, but they can be cumbersome and confusing and do not show a complete picture of the account hierarchy—only fragments at a time.

Using the Account Hierarchy Manager

The Account Hierarchy Manager, shown in Figure 4-10, gives a more complete, graphical view of the account hierarchies. When opening the manager, you will be prompted as to whether you Plan on Saving Changes in the Manager. Selecting Yes prevents other users from making changes to the hierarchy while your changes are being made. If this message does not appear, the profile GL AHM: Allow Users to Modify Hierarchy is set to No for your access.

When you first sign in, each accounting Flexfield you have access to will appear, as well as the segments for each one. Highlight the CHART OF ACCOUNT and SEGMENT you want to see the hierarchy for. TO and FROM accounts can also be added for either a parent or child, and you can also choose the status of the accounts (enabled, disabled, or all accounts). EBS gives two options for sorting the data: by VALUE or by DESCRIPTION. Select FIND to see the values that meet your criteria. Two icons are used here: folders represent Parent accounts, whereas the icon resembling a sheet of paper is a child. The arrows at the bottom of the screen allow you to scroll through all of the values set up in your Chart of Accounts. In the hierarchy, you can view the hierarchies, create new parent or child values, modify existing values, and modify existing hierarchies.

To view a hierarchy, select a Parent, right-click to bring up the context menu, and select View Hierarchy. The hierarchy will be collapsed when it comes up—click the plus icon to the left of the account, and it will expand the hierarchy. To see additional data on each account, click the parent again and a new screen opens up to show specific data about each account.

To create new parent values, select the folder with a green plus sign from the icons. To create a new child, select the paper with a green plus sign. The following fields can be added here: VALUE, DESCRIPTION, EFFECTIVE DATES, determining if it is ENABLED, and an ACCOUNT TYPE. For Parents only, ROLLUP GROUPS and a RANGE can be added. For Children only, BUDGETING and POSTING ALLOWED can be selected.

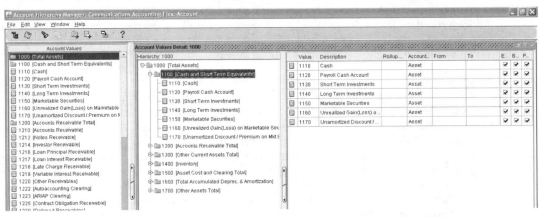

General Ledger Superuser | Setup | Accounts | Manager

FIGURE 4-10 *Viewing and maintaining parent/child relationships in the Account Manager*

To modify an existing value, right-click the value and select View Attributes. DESCRIPTION, EFFECTIVE DATES, BUDGETING ALLOWED, and POSTING ALLOWED fields can all be updated. Once any updates or additions are completed to the hierarchies and accounts, use the yellow diskette icon to save any changes made in the hierarchy manager prior to closing.

You can change existing Hierarchies by REMOVING an account or by modifying the range associated with a parent; these ranges can be deleted or modified, or else you can create a new range. The last feature is the ability to export the hierarchy into a delimited file. To use this feature, right-click the hierarchy window you want to export. (All data in this window will export, not just the parent you are on). You will be prompted for the character you want to delineate the file with (the comma is a common choice), and the directory and filename you want to save the file under. EBS then saves the file. Since this is not a graphical version of your hierarchy, but just the actual account listings, with child accounts indented, it is a little more difficult to read than the Hierarchy Manager, but it can be manipulated using such tools as Excel.

Account Maintenance

Once account segments and combinations are created, ongoing maintenance has to be done to accommodate changing business needs. Accounts will be disabled over time, sometimes requiring balances to be moved from one combination to another, and rules set up and maintained.

Performing Balance Maintenance Associated with Disabled Accounts

As part of the normal cycle of doing business and accounting, how things are reported changes, and new accounts are set up and old ones are no longer used. Part of this cycle may include transferring balances from one account combination to another. Although journal entries do work, EBS offers a feature to move not only balances, but the actual journal entries themselves, preventing the double account research when performing reconciliations and analysis. Figure 4-11 shows the account maintenance form.

Select the REQUEST TYPE of MOVE/MERGE to move journals and merge account transactions and balances. Add a REQUEST NAME and DESCRIPTION, and select the LEDGER this request pertains to. Under ACCOUNTS, enter a unique LINE number. The SOURCE is the account you are moving the transactions from, and the TARGET is where they are moving to. Select PREVALIDATE to see a report of all the transactions that will move; it is a good idea to review this report to ensure this is what you want to do. Once you have validated that data, requery the REQUEST and select SUBMIT. This will start a concurrent process that will move the transactions and reflect the new account. The REVERSE button can be used to reverse any REQUEST that has been SUBMITTED in error and therefore reverse the move of the transactions. The SEGMENT VALUES button will take you to the screen where segments are created and maintained.

This form can also be used to create account combinations based on another value as well. For example, you can create all the combinations for a new department 110, based off all the combinations that are active for department 105. This feature is most useful when Dynamic Insertion is not turned on, when account combinations are being imported via an interface that requires that the combination already exist, or for faster processing.

Account Combination Maintenance

Although Dynamic Insertion allows EBS to create account combinations automatically, you may still need to do some maintenance in the combinations screen. Adding an alternative account for processing subledger transactions for a disabled account is one example.

Figure 4-12 shows the ENABLED box, which determines if this combination is available for use. Use caution if you uncheck this box—if this combination was used on a setup form in EBS,

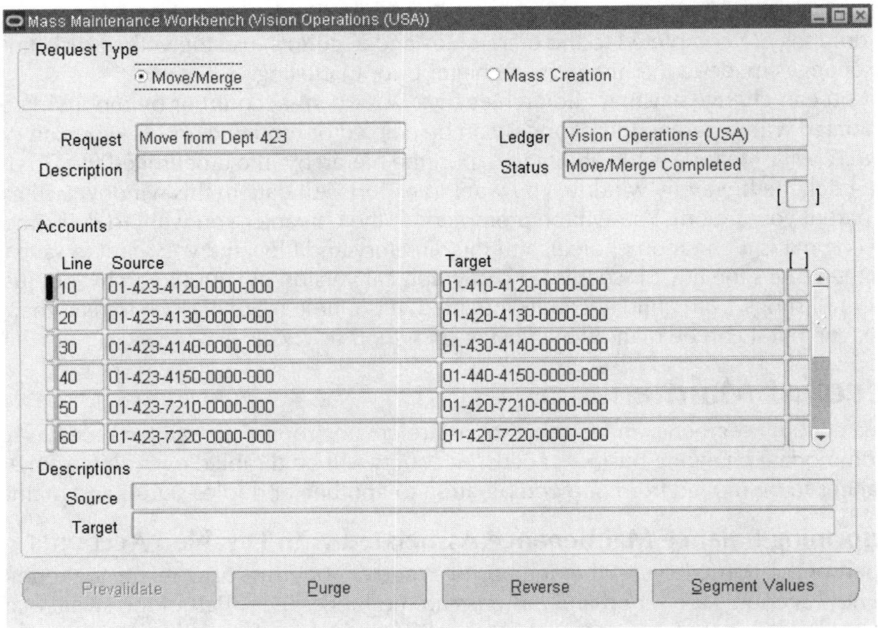

General Ledger Superuser | Setup | Other | Mass Maintenance

FIGURE 4-11 *Moving balances out of accounts no longer used*

unchecking the ENABLED box has in the past caused the account number to disappear from the setup form. Adding a TO date is the recommended way to disable an account combination. PRESERVED will prevent this account from being updated when the PROGRAM – INHERIT SEGMENT VALUE ATTRIBUTES (see Chapter 10 for more information on this program) is run. The TYPE will default in from the TYPE assigned to the natural account value; it cannot be updated in this form. If a natural account is set up with the wrong TYPE, and a combination is created, Oracle provides SQL scripts to correct the combination type (see "Correcting Accounts Set Up Incorrectly" later in the chapter for more information).

Using EFFECTIVE DATES enables you to create combinations ahead of time or to disable them for a future date. The ALLOW POSTING check box determines if this combination can be posted to with a journal entry or used by the subledgers, whereas ALLOW BUDGETING determines if budgets can be entered against it. For an account combination to be used, all the values of each segment must be active, they must have a qualifier of Postable, the combination must be enabled with no end date, and ALLOW POSTING must be checked. The ALTERNATE ACCOUNT field is used when a combination has been disabled or end-dated or ALLOW POSTING has been unchecked. For journals being imported via the Journal Import interface when the inactive account is on one of the journal lines, the ALTERNATE ACCOUNT will be used by EBS instead when creating the journal entry. This is a powerful tool in coordinating the timing of disabling combinations when transactions are being fed into the General Ledger from subledgers and feeder systems. Checking the RECONCILE box will allow reconciliations to be performed on this combination.

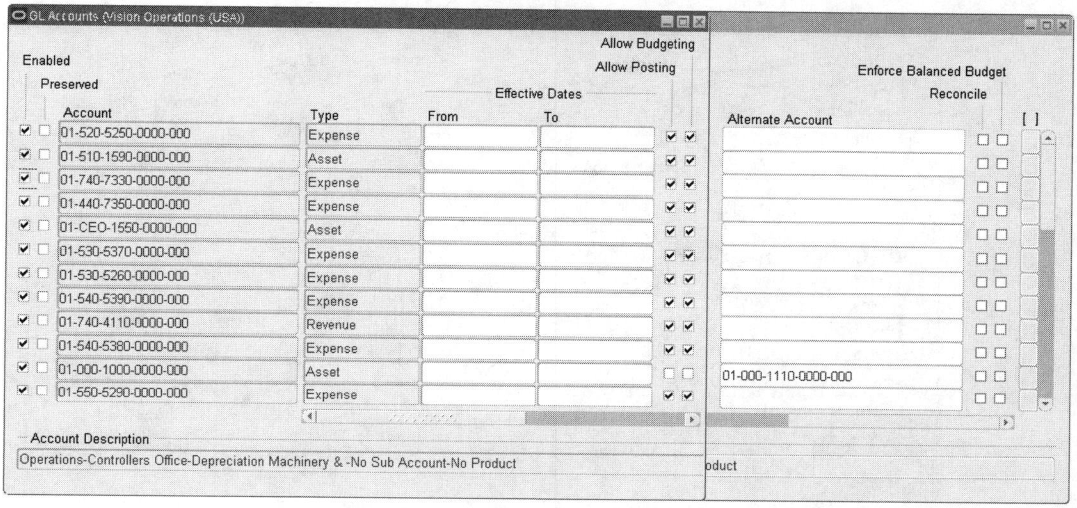

General Ledger Superuser | Setup | Accounts | Combinations

FIGURE 4-12   *Account combination maintenance*

Account Aliases

EBS has the ability to set up aliases (usually words) for account combinations or portions of the combination. The alias allows the users to select all or part of a combination by typing in a word such as CASH as opposed to keying the entire accounting combination, as shown in Figure 4-14. This feature is particularly useful when the accounting string is long, as it can reduce keypunching as well as error, though it does require some setup.

Query the General Ledger APPLICATION and select the FLEXFIELD TITLE you want to add an alias to. Select ENABLED, and add the MAX ALIAS SIZE to set a limit on the alias name, as well as the PROMPT, which is seen by the users when entering the alias on a form. In Figure 4-13, the ALIAS is the name the user will enter instead of the actual account combination. The TEMPLATE determines which segments will default in for this ALIAS, and what the defaults will be. Notice that on the Cash alias in the example, the Cost Center is not completed, allowing the user to add a cost center when using the alias. The ALIAS DESCRIPTION is the description that appears on the Alias form. Under the ALIASES, EFFECTIVE tab, the aliases can be ENABLED and given a FROM and TO date.

Recompile your Flexfield to engage the alias on the forms, by going into the Key Flexfield Segments screen (Setup | Financials | Flexfields | Key | Segments), querying the accounting Flexfield and clicking COMPILE. Once this is set up, the alias pop-up box will appear when users encounter a form where an account combination is available to be entered. Once this is turned on, it will appear on all forms. This option may not
be appropriate for all Key Flexfields or all users.

Setting the profile option called Flexfields: Shorthand Entry (System Administrator | Profile | System) can help control the alias usage. This profile can be set at multiple levels, from user on up to application, allowing the pop-ups to be controlled. Selecting Not Enabled will turn the alias feature off, even if an alias is enabled. New Entries Only will limit the alias to most forms for the

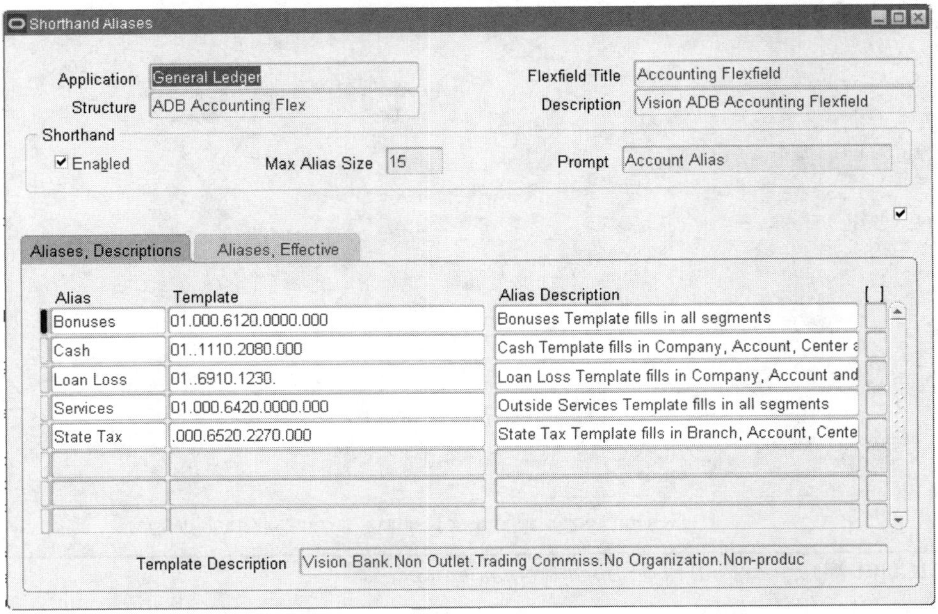

General Ledger Superuser | Setup | Financials | Flexfields | Key | Aliases

FIGURE 4-13 *Account aliases setup*

Flexfield where a new record is created, whereas Query and New Entry will use the alias when new records are created or in query screens. All Entries will use the alias for creating new records or updating existing records, and should not be confused with Always, which will use the alias for creation, update, and querying data. This feature works with form data entry, such as journal entries, but not with web forms such as iProcurement, as the pop-up for the alias does not appear on HTML forms.

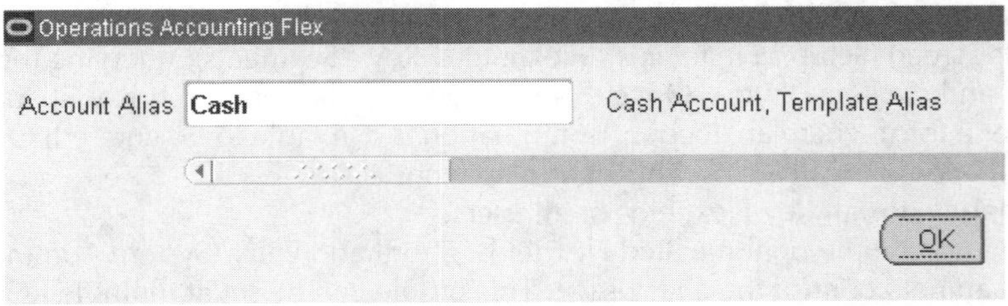

FIGURE 4-14 *Alias pop-up box on data entry forms*

Setting Up Rules for Valid Account Combinations

Cross-Validation Rules (CVRs) are used to prevent inaccurate combinations from being created in EBS, and are essential in preventing mispostings when Dynamic Insertion is turned on. With Dynamic Insertion, account combinations are created on the fly when a user enters a new combination in any module. While decreasing setup work to enable the combinations, this can also sometimes create invalid combinations, causing inaccurate analysis and the need for reclass entries at the end of the month. Cross-Validation Rules can be created to stop these combinations from being created in the first place, eliminating the need for the reclasses.

The rules are not static in most places but require constant review and revisions, so keep that in mind when designing the rules. As with many accounting processes and EBS setups, these rules can quickly get complicated. Keeping the setups simple, creating a larger number of simple rules as opposed to a smaller number of complicated rules, helps with the maintenance. An example of this is an organization with multiple companies set up as balancing segments, each of which have unique departments reporting to them. Instead of creating one Cross-Validation Rule for all the invalid combinations, create one rule for each company.

To create a Cross-Validation Rule, enter the window (Setup | Financials | Flexfields | Key | Rules) using a find box where the Accounting Flexfield is queried up. Select the Accounting Flexfield, and click FIND. General Ledger will appear in the APPLICATION, and Accounting Flexfield in the FLEXFIELD TITLE, and the STRUCTURE that was selected in the Find box. To begin entering the Cross-Validation Rule, enter a NAME for this rule. Using a naming convention, including some sort of numbering logic, will help when troubleshooting violations of the rules later on. In this example, CVR1 is the NAME of the rule, and that same number is also used in the error message so that the rule can be easily queried up and reviewed for maintenance or research. Add a DESCRIPTION for the rule. Including the segment value the rule pertains to in the DESCRIPTION also assists in maintenance, so you can easily query all the rules that pertain to a specific value. Ensure the ENABLED box is checked for the rule to be active.

The ERROR MESSAGE is the message the users will see when they enter a combination that violates the rule. Making these messages as simple and descriptive as possible will help to reduce the calls to support or accounting when violations are made. An example of a good error message is "Department 1 is invalid with company 50—please select department 2 or 4 for company 50." An example of an error message that might lead to questions is "Please enter a valid department/company combination"—it is unclear what a valid combination is from this message. Including the rule number included in the name will assist in troubleshooting problems with the CVR setups, easily identifying the actual rule that is causing the error. The ERROR SEGMENT, when populated, will take the cursor back to the segment where the violation most likely occurred and can reduce some confusion as well as keystrokes for the user. FROM and TO dates can be added so that rules can be set up or disabled ahead of time.

Cross-Validation Rules can quickly get complicated. I am a strong supporter of the KISS camp when creating these rules—Keep it simple . . . silly! The two rules described in the example could have been created as only one rule, but breaking the Dos and Don'ts into separate rules as shown in Figure 4-15 makes them a lot easier to follow and troubleshoot. TYPE is always INCLUDE or EXCLUDE. Most rules should be written to include the entire universe, and then exclude a specific portion of the universe. Including only a portion will make everything that falls outside that universe invalid, so always include everything.

FROM and TO are the value ranges to either include or exclude. Adding only the segment value that the rule pertains to in the INCLUDE values makes it a little bit more readable. Make sure you include the entire universe of that segment. In this rule, the first line reads "Include every combination with companies 00–ZZ and all departments 000–ZZZ." The fields where there are no ranges filled in actually include all values—leaving them blank helps readers to understand more quickly that this rule pertains to the department and company segments of the account number. The second line reads "Exclude departments 300–999 for company 00, making all departments less than 300 invalid with company 00."

Setting Up Rules When Combinations Already Exist An important thing to remember is that CVRs only prevent new combinations from being created. They do not disable any existing combinations that were created prior to creating the rule. Run the concurrent process called Cross-Validation Rule Violation Report, found in System Administrator. This report can be run to review or disable all the combinations that violate all the active CVRs in your system. Combinations can also be disabled manually in the General Ledger | Setup | Accounts | Combinations form.

Correcting Accounts Set Up Incorrectly

From time to time, it is inevitable that a natural account value will be set up with the wrong account type. This account type is added to each combination whenever one is created, and is used by EBS, among other things, to clear out balances in income and expense accounts to retained earnings at the beginning of each fiscal year. If an account combination is set up as an expense in error, the balance will zero out when the first of the fiscal year is reached. Correcting

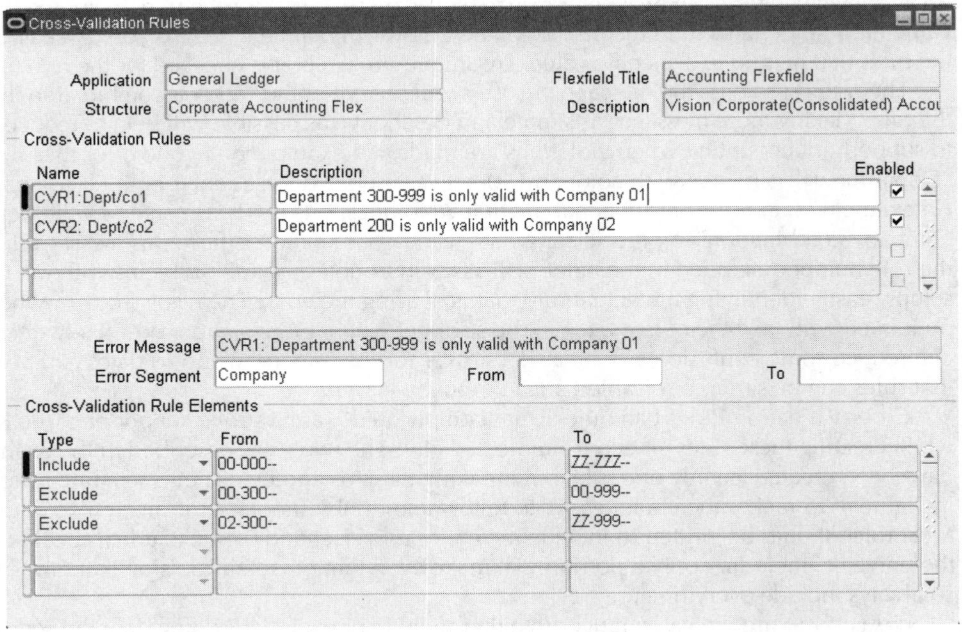

General Ledger Superuser | Setup | Financials | Flexfields | Key | Rules

FIGURE 4-15 *Adding rules for valid account combinations*

the account type on the value that was set up wrong will not totally resolve the problem—it will only fix the problem for combinations created after the change, not for any combinations that already exist. Several steps are required to identify the problem accounts and fix them.

1. Identify all the combinations that are incorrect. There is a diagnostic script that comes with EBS Diagnostics that will detect all misclassified accounts. It is a good preventive measure to run this on a regular basis, or at the very least prior to year end. Once the accounts are identified, there are several steps to fixing them, which will require the assistance of your DBA or support analyst.

2. Run a detailed trial balance for the last of the prior fiscal year and check if there was a balance in the account combinations in question. If not, then proceed to step 4.

3. If the account has a balance in it, then reopen the last period in each fiscal year with a balance and create and post a journal entry to reverse the balance. If this problem has been going on for many years, this needs to be done for each fiscal year that ended with a balance. The goal here is to create a zero balance in the accounts with problems for each fiscal year end.

4. After confirming that the accounts have zero balances, you can correct the account segment values and combinations.

    a. To correct the segment values, query the value (Setup | Financials | Flexfields | Key | Values) and change the qualifier.

    b. Combinations need to be updated via SQL in the tables. The table that needs to be updated is gl_code_combinations. As of this book, there were no published sql updates for R12 on MetaLink (Oracle's support site), so please log a Service Request to obtain the R12 scripts.

5. After confirming the combinations now have the correct qualifier, reverse and post the reversals of the journals created in step 3.

6. Close the periods.

After completing these steps, the balances should roll properly at the end of each fiscal year end.

Custom Segments for Tracking Additional Data (Optional)

A powerful feature in EBS is the ability to add custom fields on many of the forms. This information is tracked in the tables in the Attribute columns. On many forms, square brackets ([]) appear at different spots on the forms. These brackets denote that a Descriptive Flexfield (DFF) is available, which can be enabled and set up. DFF setups look exactly like the Key Flexfield used for creating your account number, and you can refer to "The Account Number" for a good overview of how to set them up. (You choose GL Superuser | Setup | Financials | Descriptive | Segments.) Perhaps the hardest part of setting up DFF is finding out the DFF name that appears on the form and table you want to use. The easiest way to see all the DFFs on a specific form is to use the Examine feature, shown in Figure 4-16. This feature requires either that the user enter the APPS password or that the profile called Utilities: Diagnostics be set to Yes (this can be set for just a few key users, as it can be set at the user level).

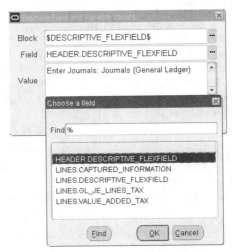

From the toolbar: Help | Diagnostics | Examine

FIGURE 4-16 *Finding Descriptive Flexfield names for a specific form*

Select $DESCRIPTIVE_FLEXFIELD$ from the list of values on the BLOCK field, and then select the list of values for FIELD. All the DFFs for this form will appear. Be aware that DFFs do not appear on any seeded EBS reports but will need to be added for reporting.

Some of the key features of DFFs are that they can be either required or optional, unlike Key Flexfields, and can default data in according to other information about the record. DFFs use value sets or table validation, just like KFFs, and can also allow any record to be entered without validation.

Calendars (Required)

The next step in setting up the General Ledger is defining Periods and Calendars. Period Types relate to how many periods are associated with each year. Although you can set up calendars with multiple period types for custom reporting purposes or subledger usage, only one period type can be associated with each Ledger. EBS comes with Month, Quarter, and Year periods already set up, but additional ones can be added. The one most commonly used is Month, either having 12 periods or 13 periods, which includes an adjustment period.

Calendar Types

Referring to Figure 4-17, assign a Name in the PERIOD TYPE. This field must be unique and is case sensitive. Try to avoid setting up multiple PERIOD TYPES called something similar, like MONTH, Month, Months, etc. This is confusing when it comes time to set up calendars. Add the PERIODS PER YEAR for this Type, including any adjusting periods you want included in the calendar. Adjusting periods are used by the General Ledger only and not any of the subledgers. They can be used to post Adjusting or Audit journal entries, for revaluation journals for foreign currencies, and for year-end closing journals. Though not required, it can be helpful to segregate these entries. The

YEAR TYPE determines how the period name will default when used to set up a calendar, though this default can be overridden. If FISCAL is selected, then the last two digits of the period name will default to the fiscal year. If CALENDAR is selected, then the last two digits will default to the From date that period pertains to, or to the calendar year. Setting this correctly can reduce the amount of time it takes to add periods to the calendar. Add a DESCRIPTION to identify why this type was set up. Some Period Types come seeded with EBS, and if they are appropriate for your calendar, new ones do not need to be added.

Calendars

Once the Types are defined, they can be used to set up a calendar, as seen in Figure 4-18. Give the CALENDAR a name and a DESCRIPTION. Select ENABLE SECURITY if you want to secure access to this calendar setup using Access Sets. Enter the PREFIX, usually the month this period pertains to. This will be used with the last two digits of the YEAR if FISCAL was selected as the YEAR TYPE on the Period Types, or with the last two digits of the FROM date if Calendar was selected to create the NAME. TYPE is the Period Type set up in the previous step. If the calendar is set up with multiple TYPES, only one will be available in the General Ledger, based on which one is assigned to the Ledger setups. The additional types can be used in custom reporting or other subledgers but are not required to obtain Year to Date or Quarter to Date balances.

QUARTER relates to the quarter of the fiscal year this month is in, and NUM refers to the period number for this month. You must set up the Calendar with the same number of defined periods as identified on the PERIOD TYPES, though some of these periods can be Adjusting. FROM is the first date of the period, and TO is the last date. The NAME will default in based on the PREFIX and YEAR TYPE that was assigned to the period TYPE. Selecting ADUSTING defines that period as an adjusting period, which is the only type of period that can have overlapping dates with other periods.

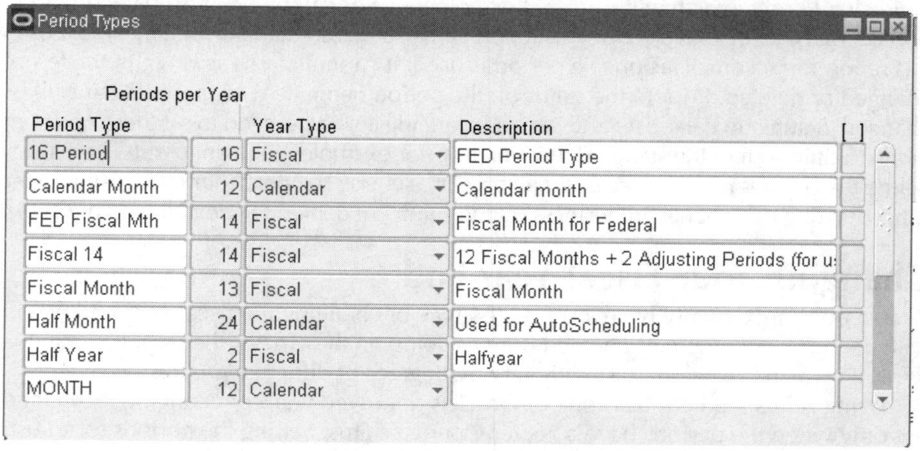

General Ledger Superuser | Setup | Financials | Calendars | Types

FIGURE 4-17   *Calendar types*

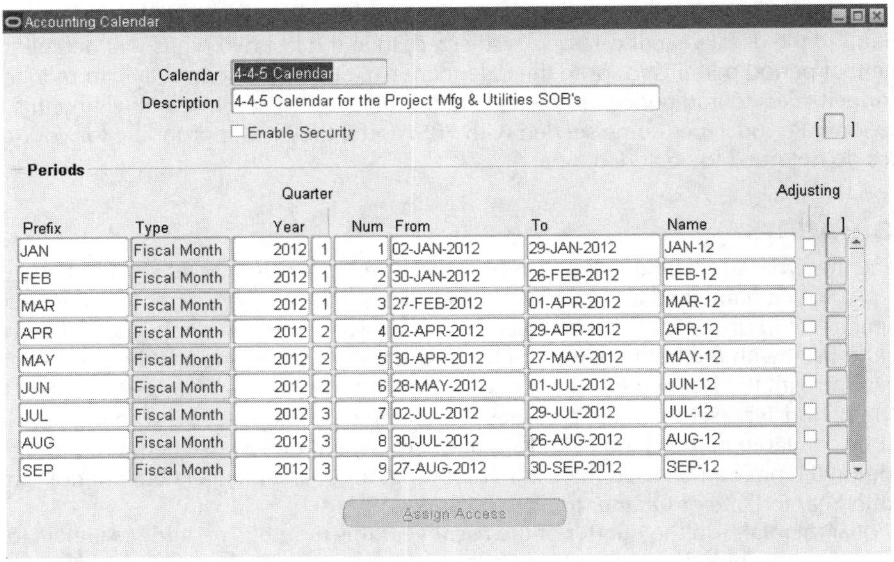

Prefix	Type	Year	Num	From	To	Name	Adjusting
JAN	Fiscal Month	2012	1	1	02-JAN-2012	29-JAN-2012	JAN-12	☐
FEB	Fiscal Month	2012	1	2	30-JAN-2012	26-FEB-2012	FEB-12	☐
MAR	Fiscal Month	2012	1	3	27-FEB-2012	01-APR-2012	MAR-12	☐
APR	Fiscal Month	2012	2	4	02-APR-2012	29-APR-2012	APR-12	☐
MAY	Fiscal Month	2012	2	5	30-APR-2012	27-MAY-2012	MAY-12	☐
JUN	Fiscal Month	2012	2	6	28-MAY-2012	01-JUL-2012	JUN-12	☐
JUL	Fiscal Month	2012	3	7	02-JUL-2012	29-JUL-2012	JUL-12	☐
AUG	Fiscal Month	2012	3	8	30-JUL-2012	26-AUG-2012	AUG-12	☐
SEP	Fiscal Month	2012	3	9	27-AUG-2012	30-SEP-2012	SEP-12	☐

General Ledger Superuser | Setup | Financials | Calendars | Accounting

FIGURE 4-18 *Setting up accounting calendars*

Validating Calendars

When you navigate away from the calendar form, a message will prompt you if you want to validate the Current calendar or All calendars. Select Current if that is the only calendar you made changes to, and All if you made changes to more than one. EBS will run a report called Other – Calendar Validation Report, which will valdiate that no periods or dates were missed (a common mistake is to skip February 29 in a leap year). This report can also be run manually at any time. Ensure you review this report for accuracy, as once a period is used, it cannot (easily and with Oracle's blessing) be changed or deleted. Prior to the status on the period being OPEN or FUTURE, it can still be deleted or changed. Setting up calendars is always a balancing act—you need to set them up far enough in the future to utilize all of the standard functionality (for example, you cannot run fixed asset forecasting before the periods for the forecast time frame are set up), but not so far into the future that if a change is needed due to a change in business options, you are denied the flexibility to make that change.

Changing Your Fiscal Year End

Oracle does not actually have a supported way of changing the fiscal year end of a calendar, and with the number of mergers and acquisitions going on these days, that is becoming more commonly done. There are a few options, with varying degrees of difficulty and results.

Using Adjusting Periods is one of Oracle's approved ways of changing the calendar year end, but only when the periods have a Never Opened status. Setting the periods to Adjusting will make them ignored by the subledgers but allow all the periods defined in the period type to be used. For example, if your current fiscal year is set to end in November and has no adjusting periods, but you need to change it to May, you can enter six adjusting periods with the date of May 31 to use up the balance of the periods. Then define the first period as June 1 for the new fiscal year.

This does cause a few reporting problems if you want historical data based on the new periods, depending on the change you made. Quarter to date information for the current period will be May–July for the first quarter but January–March for the prior year. This can be resolved by creating FSG reports for the first year of comparative reporting, but you do need to consider the point prior to using this option. If the reporting is either not important or can be resolved with FSGs, then this is a lower-cost solution than creating a new Ledger and transferring the data or creating a secondary Ledger with the new calendar, which are Oracle's other supported solutions to changing the calendar.

Special Calendars for Average Balance Calculations

Transaction Calendars are used in conjunction with Average Balances in EBS; they define the days of the week that are business days, so the average balances can be calculated (Setup | Financials | Calendars | Transaction).

Currencies (Optional)

EBS has two main features for foreign currencies: the ability to record transactions in currencies other than the Ledger currency, and the ability to perform a remeasurement of the balances into foreign currencies. Both may require either adding or enabling the additional currencies, as well as conversion rates.

Rate Types can be added in the Currency Rate Types form (Setup | Financials | Currencies | Rates | Types) if you just want to set up a simple rate type, for instance, Daily, where only the RATE TYPE, DESCRIPTION, and optionally ENABLING SECURITY are required. If you want to add a Rate Type where a Pivot Currency is to be used, then use Setup | Financials | Currencies | Currency Rate Manager | Rate Types. Pivot Currencies, or Cross-Rates Rules, will allow you to load rates for specific currency conversions, and have EBS create rates based on a pivot currency. This is most commonly used in the European Union countries for conversions for the Euro and any local currencies, where the Euro is set up as your Pivot Currency. For example, if you load the rate for USD to Euro and Euro to Francs, if the Euro is your pivot currency, EBS can calculate Francs to USD for you.

Enter a name in the RATE TYPE and add a DESCRIPTION for that type. The next fields, seen in Figure 4-19, are used in conjunction with Enterprise Planning and Budgeting, and have no effects on the rest of EBS, including the General Ledger. Enter the main currency you want to Pivot off in PIVOT CURRENCY (usually the EURO), and any additional currencies for conversions by clicking ADD ANOTHER ROW. Rates can be entered either within the HTML form or with Web ADI. To enter daily rates via EBS in the HTML form, select CREATE DAILY RATES in the RATES tab. Enter the FROM and TO currency, the START DATE, and optionally the END DATE. Select the RATE TYPE and enter the RATE. EBS will calculate the INVERSE RATE.

Use the HISTORICAL RATE tab to enter Historical Rates. This will take you back to a form in the apps, shown in Figure 4-20. Select the LEDGER from the list of values. The FUNCTIONAL CURRENCY will default in from the Ledger. Enter the TARGET CURRENCY. To assign rates account by account, enter the PERIOD, ACCOUNT, and RATE. CREDIT AMOUNT is used to enter a historical amount for this specific account. When translations are run, the CREDIT AMOUNT will be used as the account balance. For USAGE, you can select Standard or Average (used for average balances only), and the RATE TYPE will default in as historical.

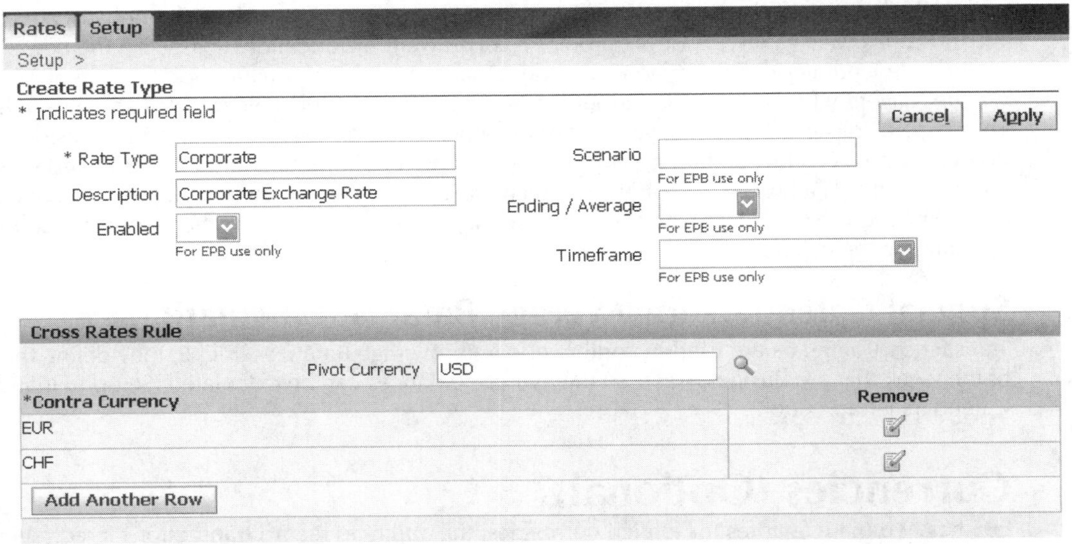

Rates	Setup

Setup >

Create Rate Type

* Indicates required field   Cancel | Apply

* Rate Type	Corporate	Scenario	
Description	Corporate Exchange Rate		For EPB use only
Enabled		Ending / Average	
	For EPB use only		For EPB use only
		Timeframe	
			For EPB use only

Cross Rates Rule

Pivot Currency USD

*Contra Currency	Remove
EUR	
CHF	

Add Another Row

General Ledger Superuser | Setup | Currencies | Currency Rate Manager | Daily Rates | Create Rates button

FIGURE 4-19 *Currency and Pivot Currency setups*

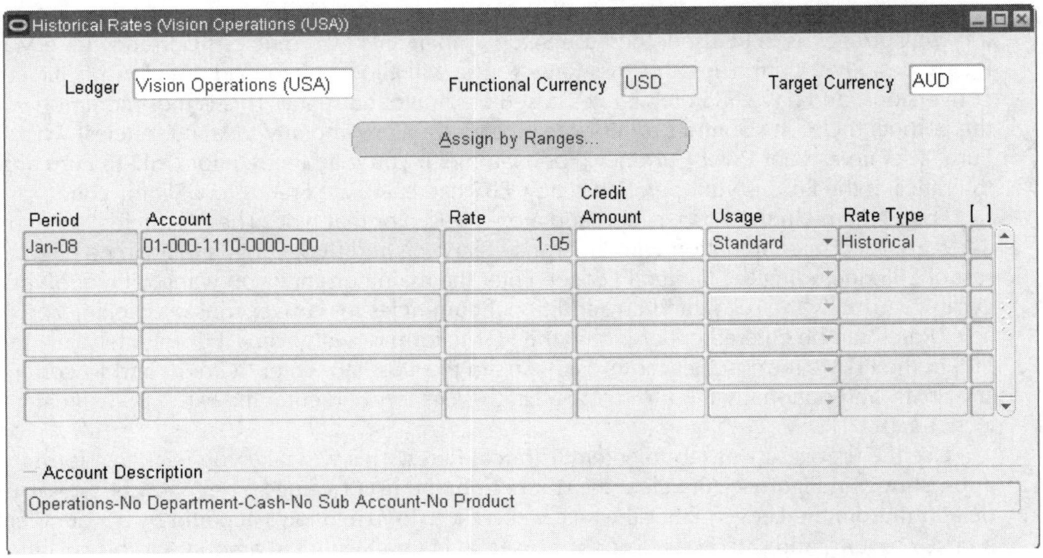

Historical Rates (Vision Operations (USA))

| Ledger | Vision Operations (USA) | Functional Currency | USD | Target Currency | AUD |

Assign by Ranges...

Period	Account	Rate	Credit Amount	Usage	Rate Type	[ ]
Jan-08	01-000-1110-0000-000	1.05		Standard	Historical	

Account Description

Operations-No Department-Cash-No Sub Account-No Product

General Ledger Superuser | Setup | Currencies | Currency Rate Manager | Rates | Historical Rates | Create Historical Rates button

FIGURE 4-20 *Historical rates*

Journal Controls

There are several criteria you can set up and modify that will control your Journals in the General Ledger.

Journal Sources

Journal Sources identify the source of the journal entries. EBS comes with a large number of journal sources already seeded, which are used by the subledgers that integrate into the General Ledger, as well as Manual for journals keyed directly into the GL, and Spreadsheet, used for journal entries loaded from Web ADI (Application Desktop Wizard, also known as Journal Wizard). Additional sources can be added for journals imported from third-party systems or for any type of transaction.

For Sources that came seeded with EBS, the SOURCE and SOURCE KEY should not be updated. Use Figure 4-21 to add a new Source, by entering a meaningful name in the SOURCE field. SOURCE KEY is an alternative name that can be assigned to a specific source or groups of sources, making the names consistent across instances and/or languages. This field is ignored if the IMPORT USING KEY box is not checked. Add a DESCRIPTION, including more details on the source of the journal entry.

IMPORT JOURNAL REFERENCES is required if you want to use the drill-down functionality on journal and account inquiry screens, and it should be checked for most of the EBS-seeded SOURCES. This functionality allows users to drill down on a summarized entry created from a subledger, like Payables, to see the invoices or payments that originated the journal entry. For third-party journal entries, drill-down can only be used if the transactions are first run through Subledger Accounting.

FREEZE JOURNALS will prevent users from changing a journal after it has been successfully imported, and this setting is recommended for all EBS subledgers, such as Payables or Assets. This will prevent the journals in the General Ledger from getting out of synch with the source transactions in the subledgers, as these transactions usually cannot be re-created once the creation process was successfully completed.

There are times that a manual update is needed on an imported journal entry from the subledgers, such as changing a period. This check box can be unchecked to make these changes, but it should be rechecked as soon as it is completed, and in busy systems, it is best to do this during non-peak accounting hours.

REQUIRE JOURNAL APPROVAL tells EBS if this journal will require an approval prior to posting. In order for Journal Approvals to be enforced, the LEDGER must also have ENABLE JOURNAL APPROVAL turned on.

The EFFECTIVE DATE RULE appears only if Average Balancing is enabled in this ledger, and it allows the system to decide if Journal Entries that are imported for closed periods should ROLL to the next open period, FAIL, or import with the date as sent over from the source and not be allowed to be posted until the period is opened.

Journal Categories

Journal Categories are another way of segregating journal entries, and when combined with Sources, it can make finding all the journals that pertain to specific transactions, such as Accruals or Payments, much easier. Commonly I see only one category used for Manual journals, until after the first month or quarter end, when reconciliations or research takes place, when a category policy is devised. Adding this during the implementation instead can greatly reduce research during that first month.

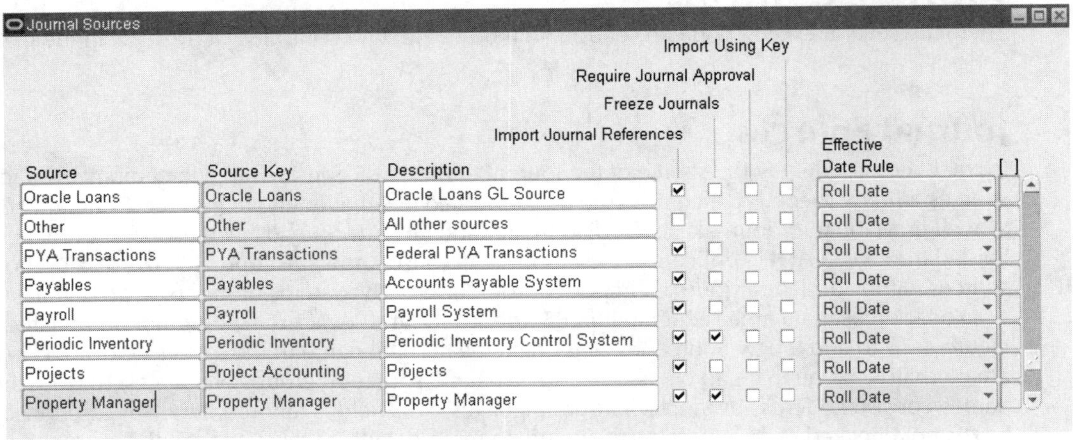

General Ledger Superuser | Setup | Journal | Sources

FIGURE 4-21 *Journal sources*

Changing a CATEGORY name for transactions that come over from submodules may cause some problems with imports, and the existing data should be left alone. New CATEGORIES can be added for Manual or imported journals from third-party systems. Figure 4-22 shows how the CATEGORY KEY defaults in from the CATEGORY but can be changed for consistent data between instances, languages, and third-party systems. As with SOURCE KEY, this requires IMPORT USING KEY to be selected on the source to be used. When this is selected, both the CATEGORY and SOURCE KEYS will be used, as opposed to the SOURCE and CATEGORY during imports. The DESCRIPTION will assist in understanding why this is used or added. Categories that come seeded with EBS cannot be deleted or disabled, nor can the CATEGORY KEY be changed. Manually added categories can be modified or deleted at any time.

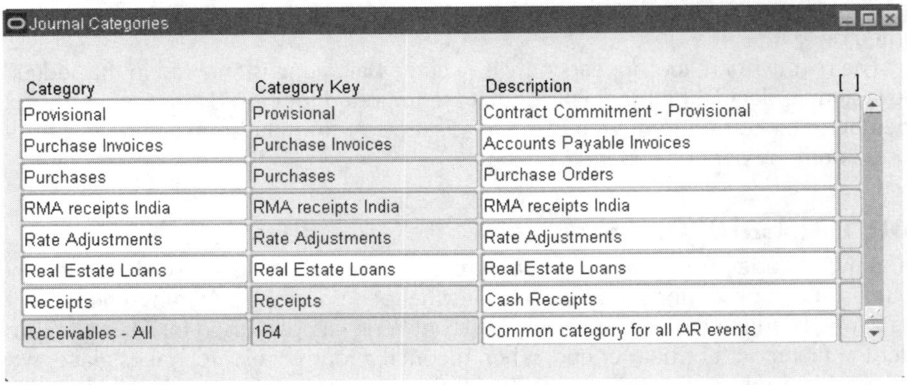

General Ledger Superuser | Setup | Journal | Categories

FIGURE 4-22 *Journal categories*

Enabling Automatic Posting and Reversals

AutoPost and AutoReverse can reduce the manual work involved in closing the month. AutoReverse sets up criteria for generating reversing journal entries automatically each month, and AutoPost can post journals automatically upon import or approval, preventing any changes to them prior to posting as well as reducing the time spent manually posting all the journals.

AutoReverse

Journal entries are reversed for a few main reasons: either a journal was posted in error or posted incorrectly, or an accrual needs to be reversed when the actual expenses are recognized. AutoReverse is most useful for reversals of accruals, and when you know what month it needs to be reversed in. The AutoReverse feature in EBS will select all the journal entries that were entered with the reverse period field completed, and it matches the period AutoReverse is being run for, creating reversing journal entries for review and posting. This process can be run (or scheduled) at any time with a concurrent request, or the system can be set up to run this whenever a period is opened, generating any reversing entries for that period.

To set up AutoReverse, refer to Figure 4-23 and enter the name in the CRITERIA SET. As a maximum of one CRITERIA SET can be assigned to each LEDGER, either naming the sets consistent with the LEDGERS or neutral so that they can be assigned to multiple LEDGERS is a good naming convention. Add a DESCRIPTION for what it will be used for. If you have multiple LEDGERS, selecting ENABLE SECURITY will prevent others from accessing a specific autoreversal rule that does not pertain to them. At this point the data needs to be saved, which will populate all the Categories in the system for this set.

Now, select each category you want to set up AutoReverse for, and enter the REVERSAL PERIOD to default as Next period or Next nonadjusting period, Next day (for average balance ledgers), or Same Period, or else use No Default to require the users to identify the period. If No Default is selected, then the users will have to add a reversing period when they enter the journal entry. For any of the other options, EBS will populate the reversing period for ALL journal entries entered for that category based on the setups. Add a specific default REVERSAL DATE if Next Day was selected for the period for Average Balance ledgers.

EBS gives the choice of reversing journal entries by either switching the DR and CR or Changing the Sign as the METHOD. While most accountants like to see reversing entries with the debits and credits switched instead of negative debits and positive credits, utilizing the Change Sign feature is very helpful when creating financial statements where you want to know all the debit or all the credit transactions in a specific account (such as in Asset Gains or Losses on a Cash Flow statement). A reversing entry with the debits and credits switched can throw off the feature EBS provides in allowing users to select total debits on FSGs.

The settings up to this point can be made even if AutoReverse is not going to be used, to default reversing information in journals when they are entered and manually reversed. Select AUTOREVERSE if you want these reversing entries to be generated when Program – Automatic Reversal is run. Select AUTOPOST REVERSAL to automatically post the generated reversing journals when Program – Automatic Posting is run. Once an AutoReverse Criteria Set is saved, it can be assigned to specific Ledgers in the Ledger Option Setups. Even when AutoReverse is not used, the Method is used for any journals that are reversed manually—this will become the default for the Journal Entry form, allowing the users to change it if needed.

There is one profile option, GL: Launch AutoReverse After Open Period, that determines if the autoreverse process will automatically generate reversing entries when a period is open. Reversing journal entries with the opening of a period or at any point during the month, the concurrent request called Program – Automatic Reversal will generate journal entries for any posted journal

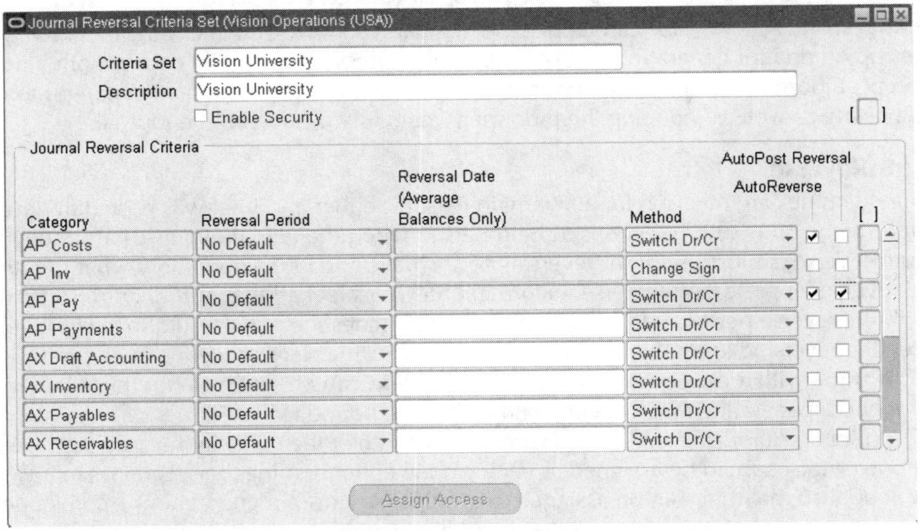

General Ledger Superuser | Setup | Journal | AutoReverse

FIGURE 4-23 *Setting up AutoReverse rules*

set up to reverse in the selected period. It is important to know that only posted journals can be reversed in EBS.

AutoPost

Automatic posting of approved (if required) journal entries not only helps save a few manual steps by the accountants, but it can also ensure that once a journal entry is approved, it is posted in the system. AutoPost is set up at the source and category levels, allowing some level of control over what journals are automatically posted and which are not. At the very least, it is a good idea to set up subledger journals to post automatically to streamline the process and ensure there are no changes to them. AutoPost follows the same rules as posting, so journals must be approved, if required, and the period must be open as well.

AutoPost Criteria Sets set up journal entries, based on the Sources and Categories, to be posted by EBS when Program – Automatic Posting is run. If multiple Ledgers have the same Chart of Accounts, then a Ledger Set can be created for them and AutoPost can be set up to post all the journals for the Ledgers assigned to the set. As shown in Figure 4-24, assign a name to the CRITERIA SET, adding a DESCRIPTION. Select ENABLED for the criteria to be used, and select ENABLE SECURITY to restrict access to this set. The POSTING SUBMISSION OPTIONS setting determines if all your criteria sets are submitted at the same time (SUBMIT ALL PRIORITIES IN ORDER), or if only a specific number are submitted at the same time, based on the NUMBER OF PRIORITIES entered. This will decrease system load on the concurrent manager and can be useful if autoposting is happening throughout the business day on systems with a large load.

The way this works is that if the NUMBER OF PRIORITIES is set to 2, EBS will only post the first two PRIORITIES that have journals, bypassing any priorities that have journals available for posting. The next time AutoPost is run, it runs the next two PRIORITIES, and so on until it reaches PRIORITY 99, where it starts again. Make sure that if you use this option, you run the concurrent request often enough that all the priorities are processed in a reasonable period of time. Checking SUBMIT ALL PRIORITIES IN ORDER will submit all eligible batches for posting, in the order of their priority. The FROM and TO dates determine what criteria of journal entries, based on effective dates, are available for AutoPost; they serve as a second control to opening and closing periods. Reducing the time frame here will not prevent manual journal postings, but it will prevent postings from happening automatically too far in the past and too far in the future.

Enter the PRIORITY for this posting, which can be repeated for several of the lines entered. Select the LEDGER / LEDGER SET this autoposting pertains to, along with the SOURCE, and either a specific CATEGORY or ALL categories. The BALANCE TYPE will define the types of balances that will be posted, just as the PERIOD limits or posts all periods. Once it is defined, you can submit this set to run, or schedule it for recurring runs at a specific time each day. AutoPost will only select approved (if journal approval is turned on for that source) journals in open periods for posting.

Journal Approvals

Journal Approvals can be enabled for some or all of your General Ledger journal sources. This is a nice feature to replace manual journal approvals, but it is important to understand that EBS does not track who actually approved the journal entry, only that it was approved. For auditing purposes,

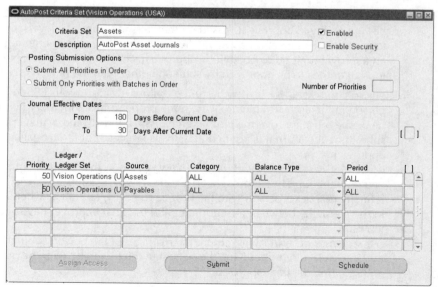

General Ledger Superuser | Setup | Journal | AutoPost

FIGURE 4-24   *AutoPost setup*

this takes a little explaining, and usually proof that the approval limits and processes are tightly controlled in EBS. Once the decision to enable Journal Approvals has been made, the following setups must be completed to use the feature:

1. SET UP THE LEDGER TO REQUIRE APPROVALS. Under General Ledger Superuser | Setup | Financials | Accounting Manager Setup | Accounting Setups, query the Ledger you want to turn on Approvals for. Select Update Accounting Options, and then click the Update tab next to the first Setup Step. The name of this step will actually be the name of your Ledger, so it is different for each ledger. On the second page, Ledger Options, the section for Journal Processing has a box that controls Journal Approvals. Select ENABLE JOURNAL APPROVAL to use approvals for this Ledger.

2. SELECT WHICH JOURNAL SOURCES WILL REQUIRE APPROVALS. (General Ledger | Setup | Journal | Sources). Check Journal Approval for every source you want Journal Approvals to be used for.

3. MODIFY THE APPROVAL WORKFLOW TO SET THE PERFORMERS FOR THE NOTIFY SYSTEM ADMINISTRATOR — NO APPROVER AND NO APPROVER MANAGER. Without completing this step, when any journal entry is submitted where an approver is not in the employee's hierarchy or there is no manager set up for a person in the hierarchy, the workflow will error out with a No Performer error. Setting these performers will send notifications to the system administrator of the actual error, with the journal name and employee with the problem, so that it can be resolved. See Oracle's Workflow Guide for instructions on how to set an approver.

4. SET PROFILES OPTIONS FOR APPROVALS. There are two profile options associated with approvals that need to be set in the System Administrator | Profile | System at the Site, Application, or Responsibility level.

    a. JOURNALS: ALLOW PREPARER APPROVAL determines if the person submitting the journal entry has the ability to approve it, based on that person's approval levels, or if it is required to go to the next level for approval. Yes will allow any person entering a journal with an approval limit set to potentially approve his or her own journal. No requires all journal entries to be approved by someone other than the person entering it.

    b. JOURNALS: FIND APPROVER METHOD has three options. GO DIRECT tells EBS to find the first person in the approval hierarchy with the proper limits and notify that person that he or she must approve the journal entry. As a courtesy, the manager of the person submitting the journal is notified that it was created, but the manager cannot approve it.
        GO UP MANAGEMENT CHAIN will require every person in the hierarchy of the person who entered the journal to approve it. The journal will become approved for posting after it finally reaches a person with the proper authority, as well as when all the people in the hierarchy between the submitter and the final approver have approved the journal.
        ONE STOP THEN GO DIRECT will require the manager of the person submitting the journal to approve it prior to notifying the person in the hierarchy with the proper authority and securing the final approval.

5. SET UP EMPLOYEE HIERARCHIES AND APPROVAL LIMITS. Human Resources does not need to be implemented to use the Employee form to set up employee hierarchies in EBS, but it does need to have employees set up. When HR is partially installed, a modified employee form is available for use in a limited fashion (less required fields than when HR is implemented).

It is the Employee form that creates the hierarchies for journal approvals. Oracle Approvals Manager (AME) is still not available for Journal Approval hierarchies, as it is in many other areas of EBS. This means that approval hierarchies are still limited to strict employee-supervisor hierarchies (General Ledger | Setup | Employees | Enter). Use the Enter Employee form to create the supervisor hierarchy. To access this form, the Profile Option HR: User Type will need to be set to HR User for the responsibility being used. If you still cannot access this form once this profile is set, read the message carefully—if it tells you the HR is fully installed, someone at one time selected this at the database level in error as Fully Installed. Contact Oracle Support to receive a script that will reset this to Partially Installed.

Enter the LAST NAME and FIRST NAME of the employee, and click MORE. The Assignments tab will allow a SUPERVISOR to be added to the employee. In this way, Approval Hierarchies are created for journal approvals. Once the hierarchy is created, then approval limits will need to be set for specific employees.

6. Next, set up the actual approval limits for people with final approval authority, using Figure 4-25 as a guide. It is important to understand that not all employees need to be set up with approval limits to use the EBS features of Going Up Management Chain or One Stop. Only people who have an actual approval dollar amount need to be set up on this form.

Select the LEDGER this approval limit pertains to. If someone has journal approval authority in more than one ledger, that person will need to be set up multiple times. Select the CURRENCY this limit pertains to, which allows control of journal approvals at both the Ledger and Currency levels. Select the EMPLOYEE from the list of values, and enter an AUTHORIZATION LIMIT. Journal approval limits are determined by the largest line item on a journal entry, not the total debits or credits of that journal. The theory behind journal approvals is that each person should be set up to be authorized to approve a risk of up to a specific dollar amount for a given account, not the total of a journal entry.

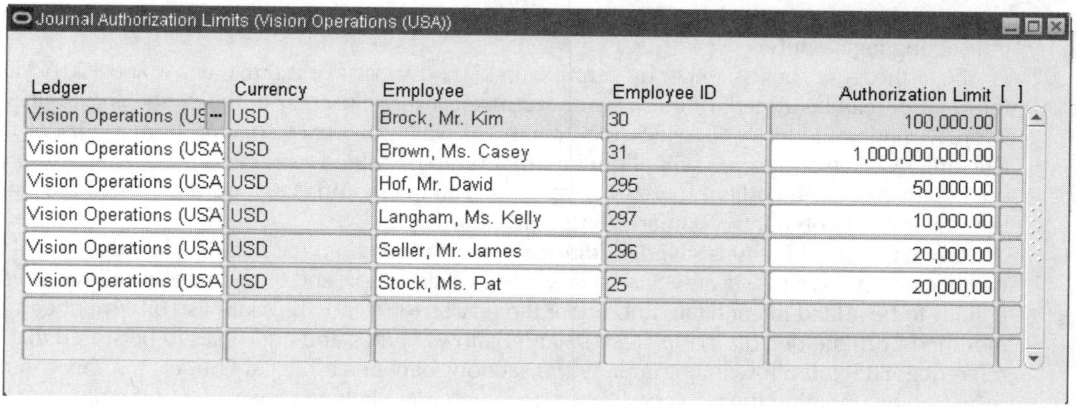

Ledger	Currency	Employee	Employee ID	Authorization Limit [ ]
Vision Operations (US⋯	USD	Brock, Mr. Kim	30	100,000.00
Vision Operations (USA)	USD	Brown, Ms. Casey	31	1,000,000,000.00
Vision Operations (USA)	USD	Hof, Mr. David	295	50,000.00
Vision Operations (USA)	USD	Langham, Ms. Kelly	297	10,000.00
Vision Operations (USA)	USD	Seller, Mr. James	296	20,000.00
Vision Operations (USA)	USD	Stock, Ms. Pat	25	20,000.00

General Ledger Superuser | Setup | Employees | Limits

FIGURE 4-25 *Setting journal approval limits*

Ledger and Legal Entity Setups (Required)

EBS uses three main concepts for setting up the core of the General Ledger: Legal Entities, Ledgers, and Accounting Methods (also called Subledger Accounting). Legal Entities define the legal aspects of a company (such as address and tax identification numbers). In R12, Ledgers must have at least one Legal Entity but can also have multiple legal entities assigned to them. Legal Entities are defined as legal enterprises that enter into business transactions with other legal entities and are usually governed at some level by the local governments and tax authorities of the entity. Ledgers are defined by four main aspects in R12 (instead of three in R11*i*). Currency, Chart of Accounts, Calendar, and aCcounting Methods have been added. Accounting Methods (also called Subledger Accounting) creates the accounting rules for transactions from subledgers before sending them to the General Ledger.

Legal Entities are required in specific instances, such as when transactions are fed into the General Ledger from subledgers. Where the GL is used as a standalone or with non-EBS feeders, or where it is a reporting ledger, Legal Entities are not required. Setting up a Legal Entity allows you to assign Tax ID numbers and addresses that EBS uses for specific reporting, such as 1099s and payroll. In EBS, Legal Entities own the following data and transactions: Accounting structures; both balancing segments and ledgers; eTax Tax Rules; Bank Accounts; Payables and Receivables invoices; and finally, Inter- and Intracompany relationships, accounts, and processing rules. Keeping these in mind when structuring your legal entities in EBS will help them to closely mirror your actual Legal structures.

Setting Up Legal Entities (Conditionally Required)

To create a legal entity as shown in Figure 4-26, select the TERRITORY from the list of values, and enter the LEGAL ENTITY NAME. Assign an ORGANIZATION NAME, which can be the same or different as the LEGAL ENTITY NAME, and a unique value for the LEGAL ENTITY IDENTIFIER. Creating the IDENTIFIER similar to the NAME, where the spaces are replaced with underscores, will make identification easier for troubleshooting and development. The EIN/TIN is utilized on some reports, such as 1099 reporting. Selecting YES for the TRANSACTING ENTITY will allow transactions in any subledger to be created; selecting NO identifies this as a Registration against another Legal Entity in a specific region and does not allow transactions in EBS; it denotes the legal requirement of a registration against the transacting legal entity.

Enter the LEGAL ADDRESS, either by SELECTING an EXISTING ADDRESS or CREATING a NEW ADDRESS. Additional information can be added for the PLACE OF REGISTRATION, INCEPTION DATE of the entity, and NAICS 1997 (North American Industry Classification System), as well as a TYPE OF COMPANY from the list of values. Clicking SAVE AND ADD DETAILS will allow information to be added for REGISTRATIONS, ESTABLISHMENTS, CONTACT INFORMATION, and INTERCOMPANY EXCEPTIONS. The intercompany is required if you are using the Advanced Global Intercompany System (AGIS).

Once the Legal Entity is saved, additional information can be added. By default, a Legal Entity will become its own REGISTRATION and ESTABLISHMENT. Clicking NEXT and then CREATE will allow additional entities to be added to each tab, and under the ESTABLISHMENT tab, the Main Establishment can be modified from the default. CONTACT INFORMATION allows names and addresses to be stored for reference. EBS will allow intercompany transactions between all Legal Entities, but this can be restricted by updating the INTERCOMPANY EXCEPTION tab and clicking UPDATE to add the name of the legal entity with which intercompany transactions cannot be performed.

If you found the Legal Entity Configurator to set up your Legal Entity (a responsibility called Legal Entity Manager), be aware that the last tab to set up, BALANCING SEGMENT, does not appear here

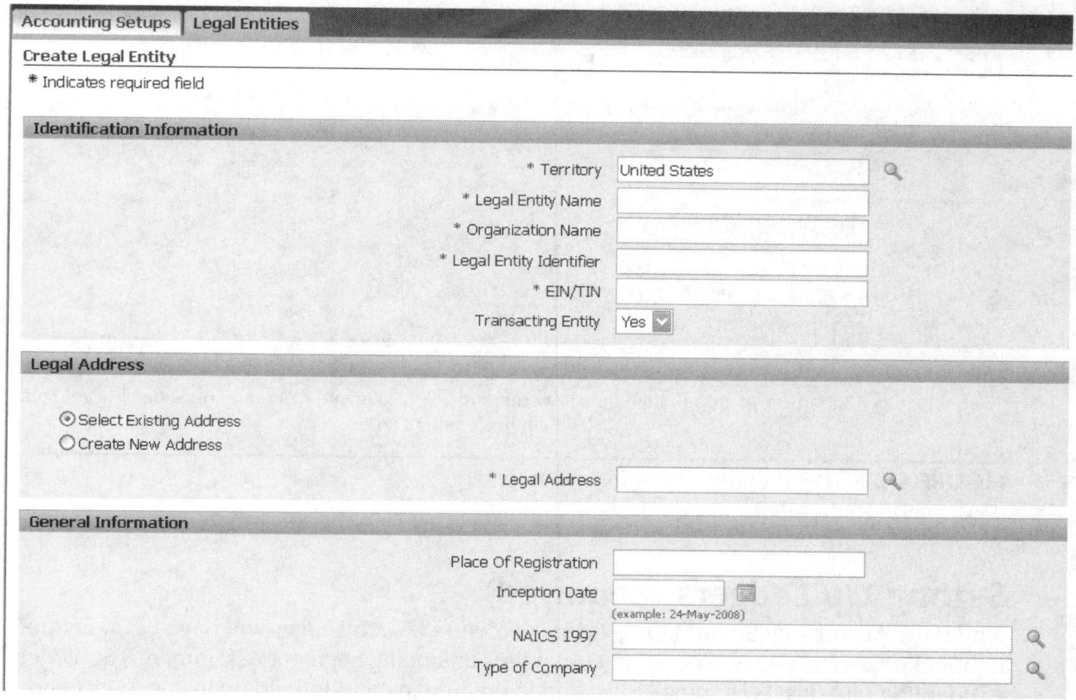

General Ledger Superuser | Setup | Financials | Accounting Setup Manager | Accounting Setups | Legal Entity tab | Create Legal Entity

FIGURE 4-26 *Legal entities*

but can only be accessed from the Accounting Setup Manager. Balancing Segments is shown in Figure 4-27.

Balancing Segments are required if the Advanced Global Intercompany System (AGIS) is going to be used. The setups here are a little backward. Once you have set up the legal entity, you must first assign it to a Ledger, where the Accounting Value Set is assigned. Then you can go back and the VALUE SET will default to the Legal Entity. To add multiple Accounting Value Sets to a Legal Entities, add Secondary Ledgers to the Primary Ledger with a different Chart of Accounts. Selecting ADD BALANCING SEGMENT will allow segments to be added to this Legal Entity (based on the values in a specific Value Set), and doing so will restrict transactions in this legal entity to only the added balancing segments.

A Balancing Segment Value for a specific value set can only be assigned to one Legal Entity at any time. If this data is updated after the legal entity or accounting setups are complete, ensure the General Ledger Accounting Setup Program runs successfully. You may have to assign this program to your responsibility prior to being able to running it. Typically, it will kick off automatically, but some screens do not trigger the report to run. Ensure you have added at least one balancing segment to your legal entity prior to setting up your Ledgers.

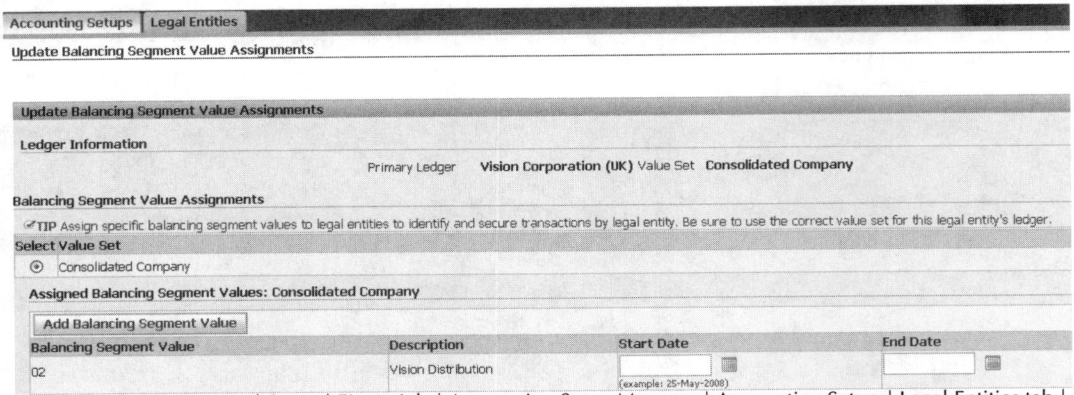

General Ledger Superuser | Setup | Financials | Accounting Setup Manager | Accounting Setups| Legal Entities tab | Balancing Segment tab

FIGURE 4-27 *Legal entity balancing segments*

Setting Up Ledgers (Required)

Under the Accounting Setups tab, Ledgers are defined. Each Ledger will have Legal Entities, Journal Processing setups, Reporting currencies, Balancing Segment Assignments, Subledger Accounting Options, Operating Units, and Intercompany and Intracompany accounts and rules, as well as Sequencing setups. If any of the data in each of these areas is different for a legal entity, a new, secondary Ledger can be set up to accommodate the differences. A new primary Ledger does not need to be added just to accommodate differences in local government reporting and reporting to a parent—a secondary Ledger can be added to accommodate this.

Ledgers (Required)

The first step is to create your Ledger, and then you go back and enter the additional information for each screen. After clicking CREATE ACCOUNTING SETUPS, you can add Legal Entities to this Ledger. Legal Entities are not required when EBS is only to be used for a basic General Ledger, but it is required if any of the subledgers will be used or any of the Legal Entity features will be used, such as Intercompany Accounting. You can add one or more legal entities to a Ledger. Since each Legal Entity had Balancing Segments assigned to it, and each Balancing Segment cannot be assigned to more than one Legal Entity, it ultimately becomes the Balancing Segment that determines which Legal Entity has ownership over transactions and data. To complete the Primary Ledger information shown in Figure 4-28, select NEXT to get this screen.

Enter the NAME for the Primary Ledger, and select a CHART OF ACCOUNTS that this ledger will use from the list of values. Add the ACCOUNTING CALENDAR and the primary CURRENCY for this Ledger. Select the SUBLEDGER ACCOUNTING METHOD for all submodules for this Ledger. EBS comes with several seeded methods, such as Cash and Accrual. Additional Methods can be added by clicking OPEN SUBLEDGER ACCOUNTING METHODS, and they will need to be assigned to the submodules you want to use them for.

Select ADD REPORTING CURRENCY to add additional reporting currencies for this primary Ledger. Reporting Currencies allow transactions to be tracked not only in the primary CURRENCY for this

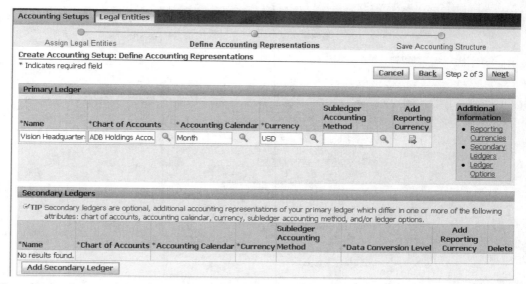

FIGURE 4-28   *Setting up Ledgers – Accounting Representations (Required)*

Ledger, but for the additional currencies that are set up here. Using Reporting Currencies can create all transactions associated to this Ledger in all EBS subledgers in both currencies, allowing a large number of seeded reports to be run in either currency. Reporting currencies can be added at a later date, if needed, and are also added automatically by the system if a translation is run for a reporting currency that does not exist (see Chapter 9 for more information).

Under Secondary Ledgers, click ADD SECONDARY LEDGER to complete the setups for the secondary ledger. This ledger is used to track the same transactions with different criteria than the primary ledger, such as a different Chart of Accounts, currency, or calendar, or else different Subledger Accounting Methods. The only additional field on Secondary Ledgers is DATA CONVERSION LEVEL, where you decide whether the data will be converted into the secondary ledger at the Journal, Balance, or Adjustments Only level. Ensure you review and confirm that all your information on the Primary and Secondary Ledgers is correct prior to saving your setups, as most of this information (all required fields) cannot be changed once it is saved. Now additional data can be completed for the Ledger. The way this section is outlined is that you query your ledger and select UPDATE ACCOUNTING OPTIONS.

Modifying Ledger Setups and Adding Additional Information

The LEDGER and SHORT NAME can be updated from here, as can the DESCRIPTION. The data shown in bold in Figure 4-29 is informational and cannot be updated once the Ledger is saved. These fields include CURRENCY, CHART OF ACCOUNTS, ACCOUNTING CALENDAR, and the PERIOD TYPE associated with it, and once the first period has been opened, any prior periods cannot be used or added to the calendar.

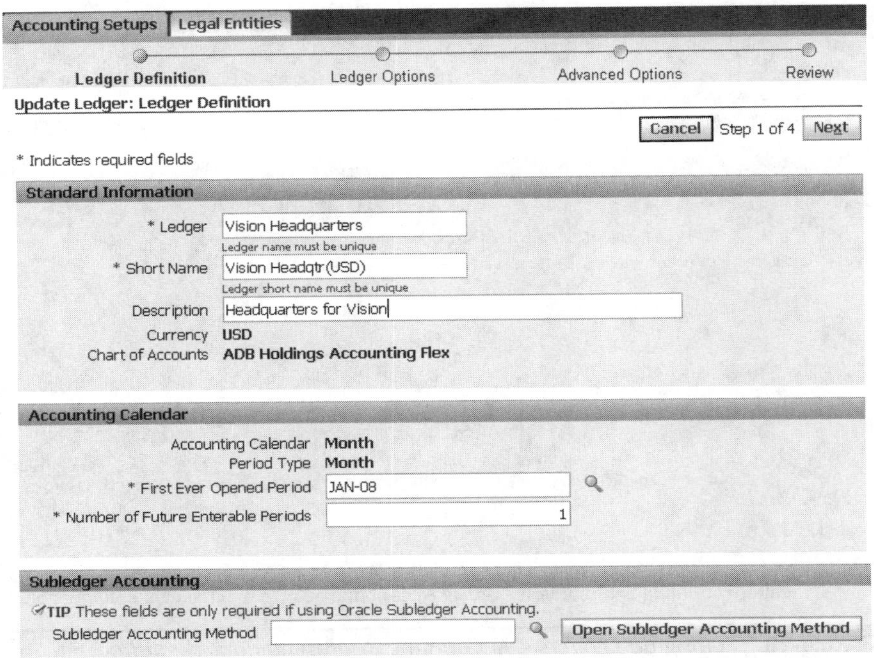

General Ledger Superuser | Setup | Financials | Accounting Setup Manager | Accounting Setups | Accounting Setups tab |
first setup step, which is the name of the Ledger

FIGURE 4-29 *Additional Ledger information*

It is important to make sure all the information was accurate prior to saving the Ledger initially, as it cannot be changed and will require setting up a new Ledger if any of it is incorrect. Add the NUMBER OF FUTURE ENTERABLE PERIODS suitable for your organization. A future period not only allows the entering of journal entries, but also the generation of Reversing, Recurring, and Mass Allocation Journals, or future-dated invoices in Payables (such as a recurring invoice generated for the next period). But Future periods will not allow these transactions to be posted to the General Ledger.

The only real caution in using future periods is that once a period has a status of FUTURE-ENTRY (periods in this status will correspond to the last period opened plus the NUMBER OF FUTURE ENTERABLE PERIODS set up here), that period of the calendar can no longer be modified in any way. Periods can be deleted from a calendar prior to that point. (For example, you forgot leap year when setting up the calendar and missed seeing the error on the calendar validation report. The period can be deleted and reentered or modified up to the point it has a STATUS of FUTURE-ENTRY, after which it cannot be deleted or modified.)

The SUBLEDGER ACCOUNT METHOD, which assigns the accounting rules to subledger transactions, can be changed, and clicking the OPEN SUBLEDGER ACCOUNTING METHOD will take you to the form to set up subledger methods. The SUBLEDGER ACCOUNTING METHOD OWNER will default in based on the METHOD selected. ORACLE means it is a seeded method, and USER means it was created by a user. Select the JOURNAL ENTRY LANGUAGE, which determines what language any Lookup Values will appear in when entering transactions, and optionally add an ENTERED CURRENCY BALANCING ACCOUNT, which is used when journal entries get entered in multiple currencies to balance any small conversion differences. EBS requires that the Debits and Credits for each currency balance, and any variances, are posted to this account (usually pennies). Select USE CASH BASIS ACCOUNTING to account for the invoices in both the Project costing and billing module and the General Ledger when the payables invoice is paid as opposed to when it was entered; this should be selected along with a cash basis SUBLEDGER ACCOUNTING METHOD. Selecting this will create debits to expense and credits to cash, and not generate an Accounts Payable liability account transaction. Selecting BALANCE SUBLEDGER ENTRIES BY LEDGER CURRENCY will balance any subledger journal entry by both currency and balancing segment. If this is not enabled, then unbalanced transactions will error out in the General Ledger interface.

Next, the YEAR END tab is completed, as shown in Figure 4-30, where the RETAINED EARNINGS account will be used during the year-end processing to record cumulative retained earnings. Suspense Posting is a feature that will balance any journal entry that is unbalanced to a SUSPENSE ACCOUNT; it is enabled when an account is entered here. This is the default SUSPENSE ACCOUNT EBS will use—you can set up module- and category-specific accounts in the General Ledger | Setup | Accounts | Suspense form. ROUNDING DIFFERENCES TRACKING ACCOUNT is utilized when currency conversions are performed. If this account is not populated, then EBS will add any rounding differences into the largest line of the journal entries created in the General Ledger. For journals coming over from subledgers, journals will error out if this account is not populated and the journal is out of balance due to conversion rounding.

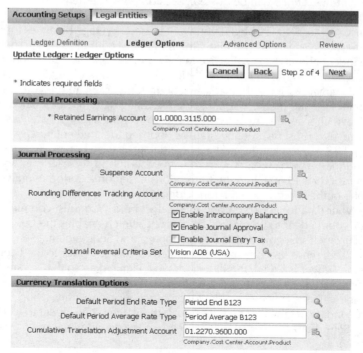

General Ledger Superuser | Setup | Financials | Accounting Setup Manager | Accounting Setups | Accounting Setups tab | page 2

FIGURE 4-30 *Year-End, Journal, and Currency options*

When you are using multiple balancing segments in your ledger, EBS will create a rounding difference account combination for each balancing segment, with the rest of the segments based on the account entered here. ENABLE INTRACOMPANY BALANCING will balance any journal entry created where the balancing segments all belong to the same Ledger. The Intracompany balancing rules will need to be defined if you select this option (see "Intracompany Setups" later in this chapter for more information). ENABLE JOURNAL APPROVAL will require all journal sources that have Journal Approval selected to be approved prior to posting. ENABLE JOURNAL ENTRY TAX allows tax codes to be added to journal lines, and tax calculated on these lines (you must also set up the tax codes General Ledger | Setup | Tax | Tax Options).

Select the JOURNAL REVERSAL CRITERIA SET from the list of values to use the AutoReverse feature. The AutoReverse settings that were made earlier will appear in this list. If currency translations are to be performed, select a DEFAULT PERIOD END RATE TYPE and the DEFAULT PERIOD AVERAGE RATE TYPE. Enter the CUMULATIVE TRANSLATION ADJUSTMENT ACCOUNT where EBS will record the cumulative adjustment for translations. Once this account is used in a translation, it cannot be updated.

Selecting ENABLE JOURNAL RECONCILIATION, as shown in Figure 4-31, will enable the account reconciliation feature in EBS and allow you to reconcile the accounting segments or combinations either manually or with a report. This feature is most often used with VAT or clearing accounts. ENABLE BUDGETARY CONTROL turns on budgetary controls; this setting is used most often in Government agencies, where the expenses are fixed for a given year based on the approved budget and cannot be exceeded. The REQUIRE BUDGET JOURNALS will require journal entries for all budgets, not just funded budgets. The RESERVE FOR ENCUMBRANCE ACCOUNT is the account where any out-of-balance encumbrance transactions will be posted. The company segment of this account will be overridden to the balancing segment on the out-of-balance transaction.

Set AVERAGE BALANCES to Enabled if you want to track average balances for your ledger, and AVERAGE BALANCE CONSOLIDATIONS will allow the updates to both the standard and average balances to be done independently. Basically, this feature allows you to create standard journal entries and average journal entries independently in consolidated books; it is only applicable for a consolidated Ledger. Assign a NET INCOME ACCOUNT number to capture your net income on the average balances. Enter the TRANSACTION CALANDAR that will be used for calculating your average balances. Next, choose the RATE TYPE to be used converting average balances (USER is not a valid rate type here, as it must be a defined rate as opposed to a rate entered by the user at time of transaction). EBS will track translated average balances based on your selections of MAINTAIN END OF DAY AMOUNT, MAINTAIN QUARTER AVERAGE TO DATE AMOUNT, and MAINTAIN YEAR AVERAGE TO DATE AMOUNT. The default for EBS is to maintain the translations based on a Period Average to Date amount. Selecting one of these settings will be in addition to this.

Review your data for accuracy, and then select DONE. You must complete three more screens after this for your Ledger to be marked as COMPLETE, which enables the Ledger to be used. They are Reporting Currencies, Segment Value Assignments, and Sequencing. Even if these features are not going to be used, these sections must be marked as COMPLETE prior to the Ledger being ready for use. Once the Ledger is saved, it will lock down specific data so that it cannot be changed. The following data cannot be updated: Currency, Chart of Accounts, Accounting Calendar, Period Type, Average Balance Processing, Net Income Account, and Transaction Calendar. Also, the Track by Secondary Segment cannot be updated once the status is set to Complete. Once the Accounting Setups tab is saved, the Setup Step for the accounting options will default to the Ledger Name.

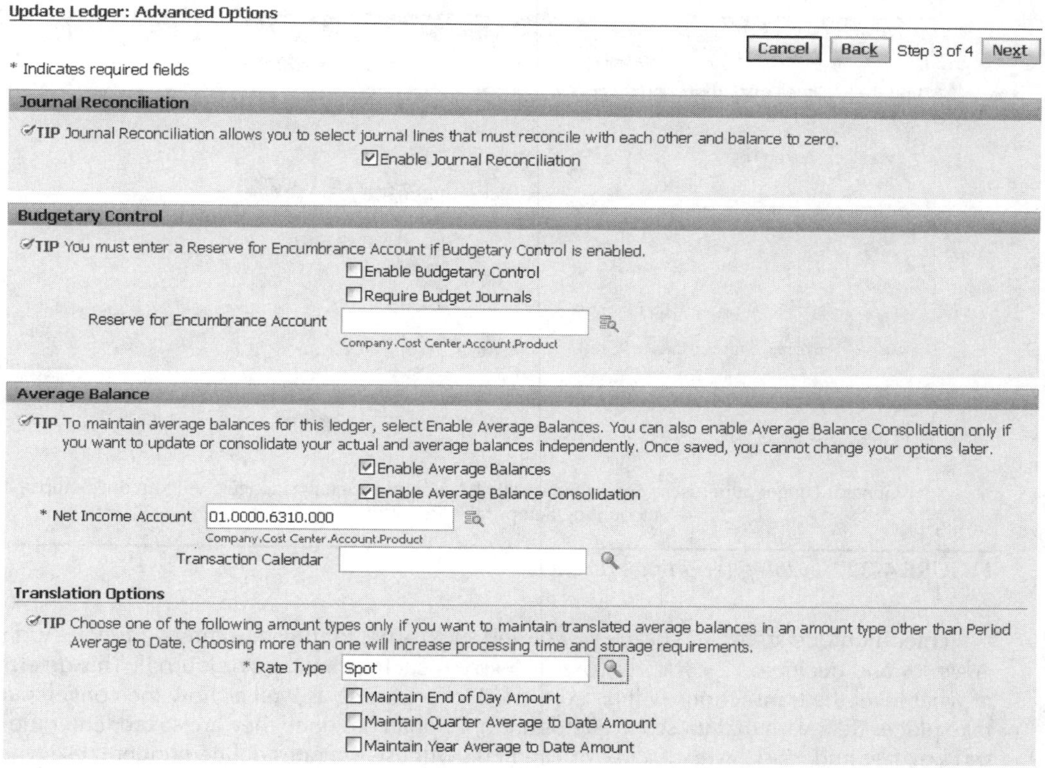

Update Ledger: Advanced Options

Cancel | Back | Step 3 of 4 | Next

* Indicates required fields

Journal Reconciliation

☑TIP Journal Reconciliation allows you to select journal lines that must reconcile with each other and balance to zero.

☑ Enable Journal Reconciliation

Budgetary Control

☑TIP You must enter a Reserve for Encumbrance Account if Budgetary Control is enabled.

☐ Enable Budgetary Control
☐ Require Budget Journals

Reserve for Encumbrance Account [   ] 🔍
Company.Cost Center.Account.Product

Average Balance

☑TIP To maintain average balances for this ledger, select Enable Average Balances. You can also enable Average Balance Consolidation only if you want to update or consolidate your actual and average balances independently. Once saved, you cannot change your options later.

☑ Enable Average Balances
☑ Enable Average Balance Consolidation

* Net Income Account [01.0000.6310.000] 🔍
Company.Cost Center.Account.Product

Transaction Calendar [   ] 🔍

Translation Options

☑TIP Choose one of the following amount types only if you want to maintain translated average balances in an amount type other than Period Average to Date. Choosing more than one will increase processing time and storage requirements.

* Rate Type [Spot] 🔍

☐ Maintain End of Day Amount
☐ Maintain Quarter Average to Date Amount
☐ Maintain Year Average to Date Amount

General Ledger Superuser | Setup | Financials | Accounting Setup Manager | Accounting Setups|
Accounting Setups tab | page 3

FIGURE 4-31   *Reconciliation, budgetary controls, and average balancing*

Reporting Currencies

Additional Reporting Currencies can be added to Ledgers, as seen in Figure 4-32, where transactions will be automatically created in the selected currencies from all modules. It is no longer necessary to add additional reporting books or secondary Ledgers to use this feature.

There are several options for the level of detail maintained for reporting currencies. The option of Balance Level Reporting Currencies allows you to track your balances in more than one currency at a high level for the balances only; it will require running a process for the reporting currency balances to be created. The other options are Detail, which translates journal entries in the reporting currency when the journal is posted, and Subledger, which creates the foreign currency transactions when the subledger accounting is performed. The Status of this page becomes important, as a Ledger can only become completed if the status of Reporting Currencies is either Not Started or Complete, and the simple act of clicking into this page can change the status to Started.

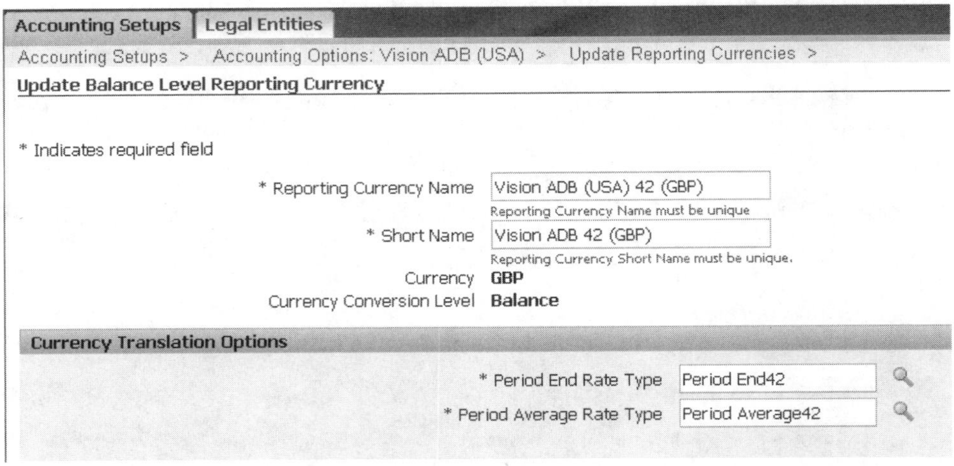

General Ledger Superuser | Setup| Financials | Accounting Setup Manager | Accounting Setups | Accounting Setups tab | Reporting Currencies

FIGURE 4-32 *Adding reporting currencies*

Enter a unique REPORTING CURRENCY NAME and SHORT NAME for this reporting currency. Add the CURRENCY and decide on a CURRENCY CONVERSION LEVEL, such as Balance or Journal. This determines at what level the transactions will be converted for reporting as well as how the conversions will take place. Be aware that these two fields are not updatable once they are saved. Enter the PERIOD END RATE TYPE and PERIOD AVERAGE RATE TYPE, and EBS will use the rates defined under these types to complete the conversions. Using this feature requires that the Rate Type selected is maintained at all times. See Chapter 9 to better understand currency handling in EBS.

Company Assignments

In conjunction with the Legal Entity Balancing Segment Value (which defaults in from the Legal Entity setups), you can add values that will be valid for this ledger, but that are only associated to, not part of, the legal entity assigned to this Ledger. Often, these segments represent adjustment entries. If you cannot add segment values to the Ledger, double-check and ensure at least one segment has been added to the Legal Entities. (Look at the top portion of the form in Figure 4-33 and you will see the Legal entity segments.) Once segments have been added to Legal Entities, they cannot be deleted, only end-dated. Balancing Segments added to only the Ledger and not the Legal Entity can be removed.

Sequential Numbering

Sequential Numbering is assigned in the application for better tracking or legal and government requirements. R12 has changed sequencing slightly from earlier releases. Sequences are broken down into two separate categories: Accounting and Reporting. Accounting sequences are assigned when journals are posted in the General Ledger or when journals are created in Subledger Accounting. Reporting sequences are assigned when a period is closed, for either manual journals or journals created in the subledger.

These sequences are based on an accounting event (such as Posting, Accounting, or GL Period Close) and the controlling entity (such as GL Journal Entry or Subledger Journal Entry). Reporting

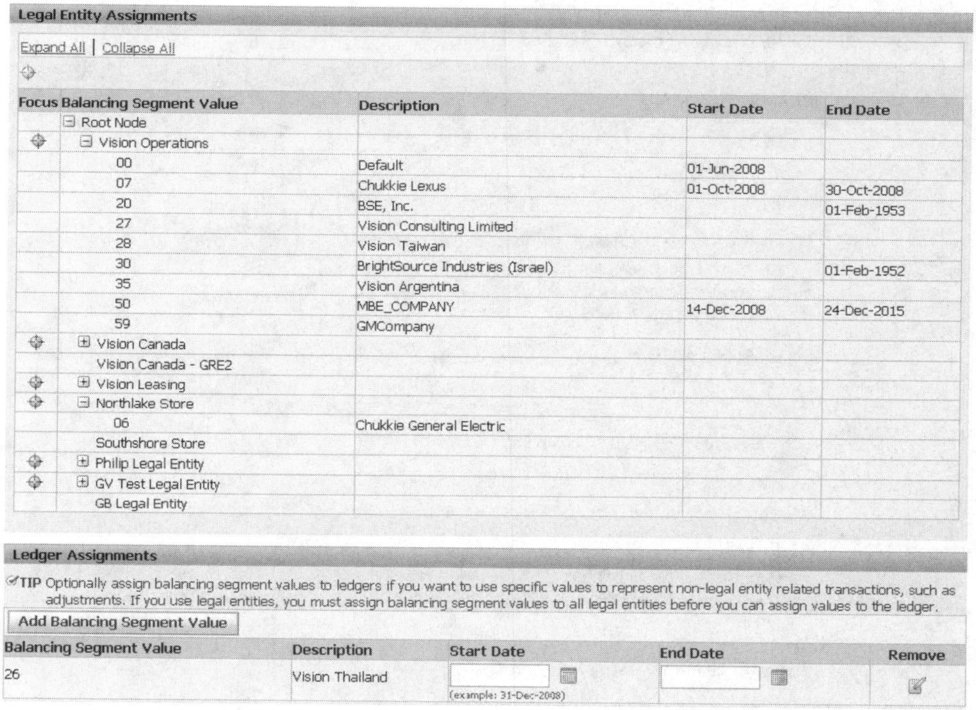

Legal Entity Assignments

Expand All | Collapse All

Focus	Balancing Segment Value	Description	Start Date	End Date
	Root Node			
	Vision Operations			
	00	Default	01-Jun-2008	
	07	Chukkie Lexus	01-Oct-2008	30-Oct-2008
	20	BSE, Inc.		01-Feb-1953
	27	Vision Consulting Limited		
	28	Vision Taiwan		
	30	BrightSource Industries (Israel)		01-Feb-1952
	35	Vision Argentina		
	50	MBE_COMPANY	14-Dec-2008	24-Dec-2015
	59	GMCompany		
	Vision Canada			
	Vision Canada - GRE2			
	Vision Leasing			
	Northlake Store			
	06	Chukkie General Electric		
	Southshore Store			
	Philip Legal Entity			
	GV Test Legal Entity			
	GB Legal Entity			

Ledger Assignments

☑ TIP Optionally assign balancing segment values to ledgers if you want to use specific values to represent non-legal entity related transactions, such as adjustments. If you use legal entities, you must assign balancing segment values to all legal entities before you can assign values to the ledger.

Add Balancing Segment Value

Balancing Segment Value	Description	Start Date	End Date	Remove
26	Vision Thailand	(example: 31-Dec-2008)		

General Ledger Superuser | Setup | Financials | Accounting Setup Manager | Accounting Setups | Accounting Setups tab | Balancing Segment Value Assignments

FIGURE 4-33 *Company assignments*

Sequences help to ensure gapless sequence numbers based on the period being closed and the transaction dates. The profile Sequential Numbering relates to document sequencing and must be set to Partially Used or Always Used to use any of the sequential numbering types, depending on how Sequencing is set up. Partially Used should be selected when some of the transactions will have sequences assigned to them. Always Used will cause all transactions to be assigned a sequence, preventing any transactions from being entered where sequences are not set up.

To set up Reporting and Accounting sequences as seen in Figure 4-34, click SEQUENCING UPDATE. Under the Add Sequencing Context, confirm your LEDGER NAME, and then add SEQUENCE EVENT–SEQUENCE ENTITY. These options are based on Events, which appear before the dash, and Entities, which appear after the dash. As mentioned, Events determine when the sequence is applied, and Entity determines whether the General Ledger or subledger owns the transaction. Options for SEQUENCE EVENT-SEQUENCE ENTITY include GL PERIOD CLOSE, which is available for both GL JOURNAL ENTRIES and SUBLEDGER JOURNAL ENTRIES and will create the reporting sequences for manual journals or subledger journals. These sequences appear under the Reporting Sequence field on the journal entry form. The final options are POSTING – GL JOURNAL ENTRY, which creates sequences when the journal is posted, and ACCOUNTING – SUBLEDGER JOURNAL ENTRY, which creates sequences when the Subledger Accounting process creates a subledger journal entry. Click CREATE to add the Sequencing Context NAME that uniquely identifies this sequence. The Context information will default from the previous page and cannot be updated here.

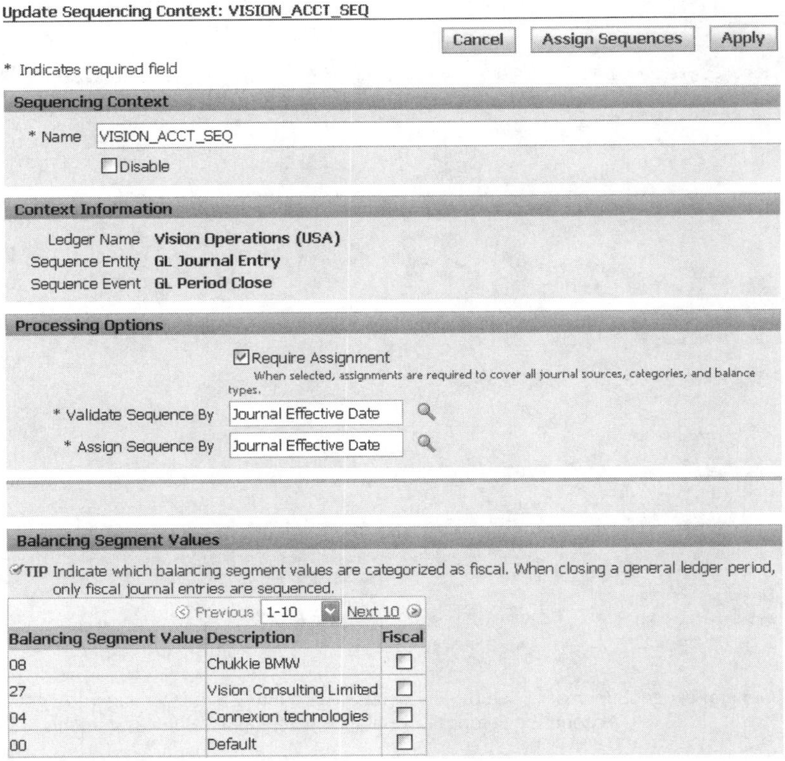

Update Sequencing Context: VISION_ACCT_SEQ

[Cancel] [Assign Sequences] [Apply]

* Indicates required field

Sequencing Context

* Name   VISION_ACCT_SEQ

☐ Disable

Context Information

Ledger Name   **Vision Operations (USA)**
Sequence Entity   **GL Journal Entry**
Sequence Event   **GL Period Close**

Processing Options

☑ Require Assignment
When selected, assignments are required to cover all journal sources, categories, and balance types.

* Validate Sequence By   Journal Effective Date   🔍
* Assign Sequence By   Journal Effective Date   🔍

Balancing Segment Values

☑ TIP Indicate which balancing segment values are categorized as fiscal. When closing a general ledger period, only fiscal journal entries are sequenced.

Ⓢ Previous [1-10 ▾] Next 10 Ⓢ

Balancing Segment Value	Description	Fiscal
08	Chukkie BMW	☐
27	Vision Consulting Limited	☐
04	Connexion technologies	☐
00	Default	☐

General Ledger Superuser | Setup| Financials | Accounting Setup Manager | Accounting Setups | Accounting Setups tab | Sequencing

FIGURE 4-34   *Adding accounting and reporting sequences*

Selecting REQUIRE ASSIGNMENT will cause sequencing to be set up to cover all Sources, Categories, and Balance Types. This is a good selection when the Sequential Numbering profile was set to Always Used to prevent a setup from being missed and causing errors for the users. The other Processing Options will allow you to assign different sequences to different journal sources. VALIDATE SEQUENCE BY determines the date used when determining if the journal should be sequenced, and ASSIGN SEQUENCE BY determines the date used to assign the sequential numbers. Click ASSIGN SEQUENCES to determine which sequences get assigned to which categories (or assign one sequence to all categories). Under the Balancing Segment Values section, select the balancing segments that you want to record sequences for on journal entries. Any segment not selected will not have any sequences assigned.

Select ASSIGN SEQUENCES to complete the setups. Existing sequences can be assigned to specific combinations of BALANCE TYPE, JOURNAL SOURCE, and JOURNAL CATEGORIES. If you need to create a new sequence, click CREATE SEQUENCE, and add a NAME for the sequence and a DESCRIPTION. Sequences can have multiple versions, so assign a NAME to the version, then select a START DATE, and supply the first number the sequence should use. Additional Versions can be added, but they cannot have overlapping effective dates. The END DATE should remain blank until the sequence is no longer going to be used. Select APPLY to continue with the assignments. Enter a START DATE, and leave the END DATE blank.

The combinations of BALANCE TYPE, JOURNAL SOURCE, and JOURNAL CATEGORY can be set up individually (for instance, Actual, Manual, Adjustments) to assign different sequences to each combination, or selecting ALL will assign a sequence to any combinations not assigned as a separate line item. Multiple sequences can be assigned to each Ledger, creating comprehensive sequences for all transactions.

Now that all the required setups are completed, requery your ledger and confirm that the status on these sections are all Complete (green check under status) or Never Started (blue square), even if data was not added for the Sequences or Balancing segment Value Assignments. Completing the Ledger will trigger the concurrent process called General Ledger Accounting Setup Program, which validates the setups for inconsistencies and also creates a default Data Access Set for this Ledger and Reporting currencies. This Ledger is now ready for use.

Required Profile Options

When a responsibility is set up in EBS, it gets assigned to a Ledger; this is a required step prior to using the responsibilities. This is done in System Administrator (Setup | Profile | System). Check the box by Responsibility and select the responsibility name from the list of values that you want to assign this Ledger to. In the Profile box, select GL: LEDGER NAME and click FIND. Select the proper Ledger under the Responsibility section. Sometimes, this is set at the Site level, which means if this step is *not* completed, the responsibility will default to the value at the site level, which may not be correct if you have more than one Ledger.

Inter- and Intracompany Setups

Setting up the Intercompany accounts and Intracompany balancing rules for a Ledger will allow journal entries to be created for different balancing segment, without having to enter the balancing transactions manually. Intercompany accounts are used when the balancing segments (the Company segment of the account number) on the journal entry are assigned to two different legal entities. When EBS adds the balancing account numbers, it is usually set up as Intercompany Payables and Receivables accounts. Intracompany balancing rules, on the other hand, are used when the balancing segments are both assigned to the same Legal Entity, and are defined as Debit and Credit offsets. Make sure that the option to BALANCE SUBLEDGER ENTRIES BY LEDGER CURRENCY is selected on the Ledger setups (under the Subledger Accounting section) to use intercompany balancing. Selecting the ENABLE INTRACOMPANY BALANCING, under the Journal Processing section, allows the Intracompany balancing to be used.

Intercompany Accounts

Intercompany setups can be created for any Legal Entity assigned to the Ledger and any other Legal Entity in the system. Once the relationship is defined, then the Payables and Receivables accounts can be added.

To create the relationships shown in Figure 4-35, select the DEFINE RELATIONSHIPS link next to the Legal Entity you are setting up the intercompany balancing for. This is where you add the balancing segments that will have a relationship with the current legal entity. From the list of values, select the TRANSACTING BALANCING SEGMENT VALUE—what appears in this list is all the balancing segments for the Transacting Legal Entity, and the list is limited to the balancing segments assigned to the legal entity you are currently in. Then select the TRADING PARTNER LEGAL ENTITY they will be doing business with—this will be a different legal entity than the Transacting Legal Entity. (If you want to set up

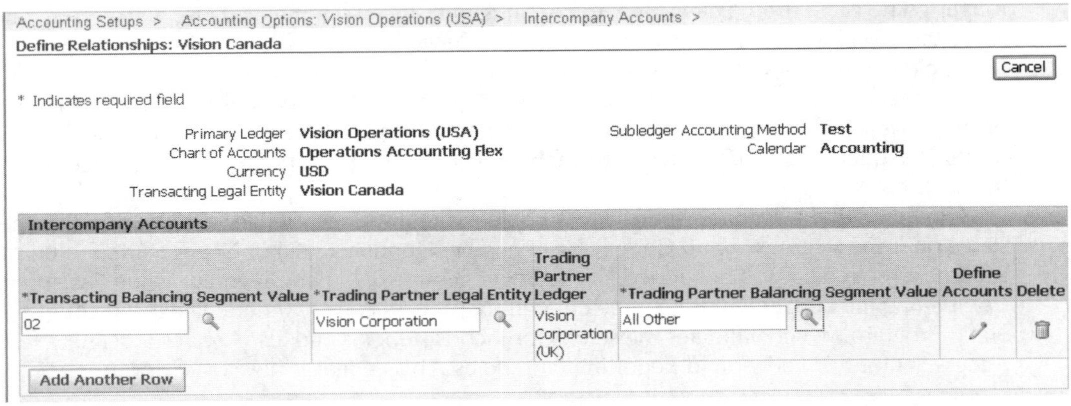

General Ledger Superuser | Setup | Financials | Accounting Setup Manager | Accounting Setups | Accounting Setups tab | Intercompany Accounts | Define Relationships

FIGURE 4-35   *Intercompany relationships*

a relationship between two balancing segments in the same Legal Entity, use the Intracompany Balancing Rules form instead.) The Trading Partner Ledger will default to the Primary Ledger associated with the Trading Partner Legal Entity that was selected.

Add the TRADING PARTNER BALANCING SEGMENT VALUE this rule is valid for. Every relationship can be set up for not only a specific balancing segment code, but also for All Others, which will default this rule in for any undefined balancing segments. To define a generic rule for all balancing segments between these two trading partners, select ALL ACCOUNTS under the TRANSACTING BALANCING SEGMENT VALUE and the TRADING PARTNER BALANCING SEGMENT VALUE. If there are no balancing segments available in the list, then none have been assigned to the Ledger.

Select DEFINE ACCOUNTS to add the Payables and Receivables accounts. This will make the rule applicable to any balancing segment for each ledger. Add specific ACCOUNT numbers for both the Intercompany Payables and Receivables accounts, and add a START DATE for this rule. Rules can only be DELETED prior to being used. Once journals have used the rules to create intercompany transactions, use the END DATE to disable this rule. If there is more than one rule defined for a given period, the rule with the USE FOR BALANCING selected will be used, shown in Figure 4-36.

Intracompany Setups

Intracompany accounts can be set up for a specific journal entry SOURCE and CATEGORY, defining catch-all rules for any undefined balancing segments or sources and categories, or different rules for each segment.

When setting up an Intracompany account, first select the Legal Entity name you want to create Intracompany accounts for. Only the Legal Entities assigned to this Ledger are available. Intracompany rules can be set up for a specific source and category (or group of categories, such as Payables – All), or a generic rule for all journals. Click CREATE RULE to add a new rule, referring to Figure 4-37 as a reference for the set. Select the SOURCE for the rule: a SOURCE of Other will become the default for any source that is not defined; Other should be set up even if specific rules are set up for specific sources, to prevent errors from happening during subledger accounting and journal creation. Select the specific journal CATEGORY, or a grouping of CATEGORIES (denoted by the word ALL at the end of the Category name, such as Payables – All—this denotes all payables categories), or select Other to identify any CATEGORY under this SOURCE. To disable a rule, change the STATUS to Disabled.

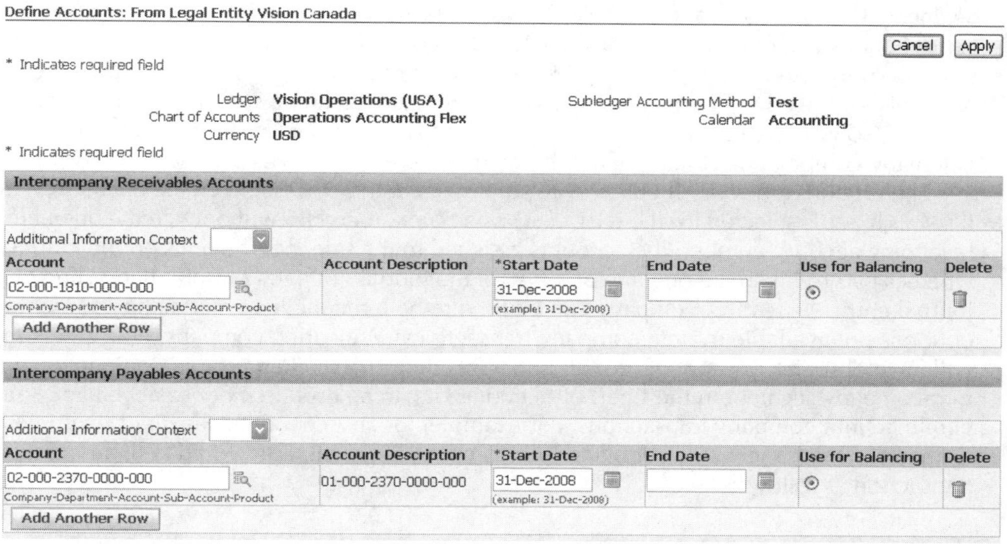

Define Accounts: From Legal Entity Vision Canada

Cancel   Apply

* Indicates required field

Ledger **Vision Operations (USA)**   Subledger Accounting Method **Test**
Chart of Accounts **Operations Accounting Flex**   Calendar **Accounting**
Currency **USD**

* Indicates required field

Intercompany Receivables Accounts

Additional Information Context

Account	Account Description	*Start Date	End Date	Use for Balancing	Delete
02-000-1810-0000-000		31-Dec-2008		⦿	🗑
Company-Department-Account-Sub-Account-Product		(example: 31-Dec-2008)			

Add Another Row

Intercompany Payables Accounts

Additional Information Context

Account	Account Description	*Start Date	End Date	Use for Balancing	Delete
02-000-2370-0000-000	01-000-2370-0000-000	31-Dec-2008		⦿	🗑
Company-Department-Account-Sub-Account-Product		(example: 31-Dec-2008)			

Add Another Row

General Ledger Superuser | Setup | Financials | Accounting Setup Manager | Accounting Setups | Accounting Setups tab | Intercompany Accounts | Define Relationships | Define Accounts

FIGURE 4-36 *Intercompany accounts*

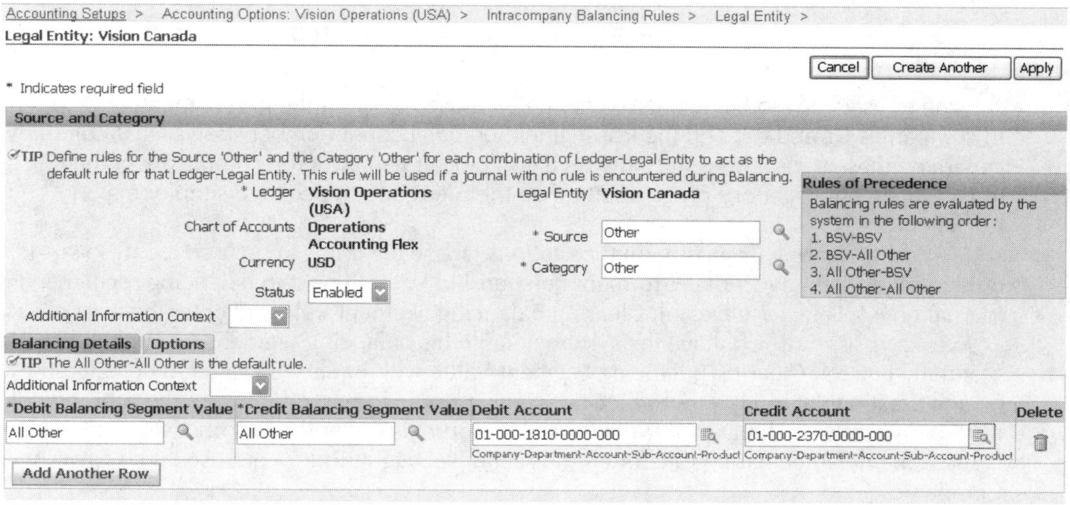

Accounting Setups > Accounting Options: Vision Operations (USA) > Intracompany Balancing Rules > Legal Entity >
Legal Entity: Vision Canada

Cancel   Create Another   Apply

* Indicates required field

Source and Category

☑ TIP Define rules for the Source 'Other' and the Category 'Other' for each combination of Ledger-Legal Entity to act as the default rule for that Ledger-Legal Entity. This rule will be used if a journal with no rule is encountered during Balancing.

* Ledger **Vision Operations (USA)**   Legal Entity **Vision Canada**
Chart of Accounts **Operations Accounting Flex**
                                                        * Source Other
Currency **USD**   * Category Other
Status Enabled

Additional Information Context

Rules of Precedence
Balancing rules are evaluated by the system in the following order:
1. BSV-BSV
2. BSV-All Other
3. All Other-BSV
4. All Other-All Other

Balancing Details   **Options**
☑ TIP The All Other-All Other is the default rule.

Additional Information Context

*Debit Balancing Segment Value	*Credit Balancing Segment Value	Debit Account	Credit Account	Delete
All Other	All Other	01-000-1810-0000-000	01-000-2370-0000-000	🗑
		Company-Department-Account-Sub-Account-Product	Company-Department-Account-Sub-Account-Product	

Add Another Row

General Ledger Superuser | Setup | Financials | Accounting Setup Manager | Accounting Setups | Accounting Setups tab | Intracompany Accounts | Define Rules

FIGURE 4-37 *Intracompany rules*

For each Source and Category combination, you can set up different rules for each balancing segment. This is by DEBIT and CREDIT BALANCING SEGMENTS, so if the Debit is set to 01 and the Credit is set to 02, this will only cover Debits to 01, not Credits to 01—a separate rule must be set up for that. ALL OTHER denotes any segment value that is not otherwise set up. Add the DEBIT and CREDIT accounts for the transaction. As many rules as are needed can be set up, but ensure you add the CATEGORY, SOURCE, DEBIT BALANCING SEGMENT VALUE, and CREDIT BALANCING SEGMENT VALUE of All Other to catch any combinations that may not be set up.

The Options tab will tell EBS how to summarize transactions and create balancing lines. If SUMMARY NET is selected for the LEVEL of SUMMARIZATION, then EBS will only create one line per balancing account number (the accounts assigned to the rule, not the lines on the journal entry), whereas DETAIL will create one line or entry on the journal for each out-of-balance line on the journal entry. A Clearing Company can be used to help reconcile intracompany transactions (this option is not available for intercompany transactions). A clearing company, typically company 99, will have offsetting transactions for all unbalanced journals. Often used in conjunction with an Intracompany segment in the Chart of Accounts, it can be used to more easily balance and eliminate intracompany transactions. For example, for an Accounting Flexfield set up with Company, Department, Account, and Intracompany Segment, EBS would treat an intracompany transaction as follows:

Debit 01.100.502000.00   100

                         Credit 02.100.401000.00   100

Lines added by the Intracompany Balancing Rules with a Clearing Account:

Debit 99.100.102000.01   100

                         Credit 99.100.202000.02   100

Debit 02.100.102000.99   100

                         Credit 01.100.102000.99   100

The transactions to balancing segment 99 are used to offset the intracompany transactions in companies 01 and 02, and the last segment of the account number shows what company generated these transactions. It is always a good idea to analyze the complexity of the intracompany transactions prior to setting up the rules, and to decide if simpler may not be better.

To add a Clearing Company on the Options tab, select if it is to be used for ALL JOURNALS, or only journals that have a many-to-many relationship (more than two balancing segments on one journal entry). Select the Default Clearing Balancing Segment Rule and enter the DEFAULT CLEARING BALANCING SEGMENT VALUE to have the system default this balancing segment in for all transactions. A Manually Entered Clearing Balancing Segment Value will require the value to be entered by the person creating the journal (not practical when importing transactions from the submodules or a third-party system). The Default Rule is used for journals under the ALL OTHER segment values and is set as the default clearing rule for all transactions. Default Rule is not used with Clearing Companies.

Secondary Ledgers (Optional)

Secondary Ledgers can be added to a primary Ledger to track the same transactions, but reflecting them with one or more of the following differences: Chart of Accounts, Calendar, Currency, and Subledger Accounting Method. Transactions are processed in the Primary Ledger and replicated in the Secondary Ledger(s) using the different rules assigned to the Secondary Ledger. This allows for multiple currency reporting where other differences exist, such as Accounting Methods where the Reporting Currency feature will not work, statutory or tax reporting differences, and consolidation differences. Data is transferred differently from the Subledger, depending on the Data Conversion level that is selected when setting up the secondary ledger. For example, BALANCE level will use the consolidations feature to get data from the primary to the secondary ledger (see Chapter 7), whereas ADJUSTMENTS ONLY and JOURNAL will have the journal entries created when they are posted in the Primary Ledger. SUBLEDGER journals are created when the Subledger Accounting processes are run for the Primary Ledger.

In order to use Primary and Secondary Ledgers in two different currencies, daily rates must be maintained at all times. For different calendars, the Effective Date of a journal entry is used to determine the new period in the Secondary Ledger. The Chart of Accounts Mapping is used to map accounts from one Chart of Accounts in the Primary Ledger to a different Chart of Accounts in the Secondary Ledger. This mapping must be set up when the primary and secondary ledgers have two different Charts of Accounts, but it can also be used when the Charts of Accounts are the same to reflect different rollups or accountings for journal entries not created from the subledgers (Manual journals). The subledger journal entries can be created differently by using a different subledger accounting. When using the Adjustments Only option, then the Chart of Accounts, Calendar, and Currencies in the Secondary Ledger must match those in the Primary Ledger.

An additional note on currencies: If you want to track a primary currency and a second reporting currency, and that is the only change, then a Secondary Ledger does not need to be set up. Add the reporting currency to the Primary Ledger under Reporting Currencies, and select when the data is transferred and how it will be translated. This will maintain both currencies in the Primary Ledger and allow reporting on them.

To define a Secondary Ledger, click ADD SECONDARY LEDGER from the Ledger form and the form in Figure 4-38 will open. Add a NAME for the Secondary Ledger, and select the CHART OF ACCOUNTS, ACCOUNTING CALENDAR, and CURRENCY that are to be associated with the ledger—these can be different than in the Primary Ledger. The SUBLEDGER ACCOUNTING METHOD can optionally be added when data from the subledger will be accounted in the Secondary Ledger differently, and requires the DATA CONVERSION LEVEL to be Subledger or Adjustments Only if one is selected.

SUBLEDGER will transfer all Subledger and General Ledger data into the secondary ledger, both when the subledger accounting process is run and when the journals that are not created in the subledgers are posted. ADJUSTMENTS ONLY will transfer only Adjusting journal entries from the General Ledger or from the subledger accounting program. This is an incomplete picture of the ledger transactions, but it does allow for viewing and analysis of the adjusting entries.

Leaving the SUBLEDGER ACCOUNTING METHOD option blank defaults it to the Accounting Method of the Primary Ledger. The other DATA CONVERSION LEVELS of JOURNAL or BALANCE are only available if the accounting method is not changed. JOURNAL will transfer all journals to the secondary ledger, based on the Source and Category, whereas BALANCE will transfer only balances, using EBS's consolidation feature. The DATA CONVERSION LEVEL determines what level of detail that is transferred to the Secondary Ledger. Once a Secondary Ledger is added, it cannot be deleted, but clicking the DISABLE CONVERSION option will stop all future data from transferring to the ledger. Once conversions are disabled, they cannot be reenabled.

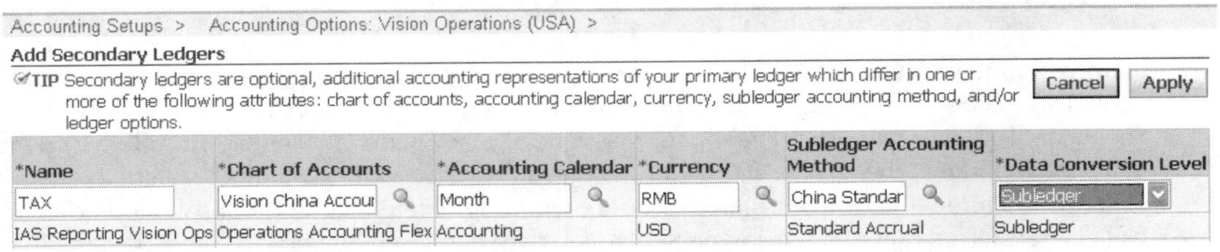

Accounting Setups > Accounting Options: Vision Operations (USA) >

Add Secondary Ledgers

☑TIP Secondary ledgers are optional, additional accounting representations of your primary ledger which differ in one or more of the following attributes: chart of accounts, accounting calendar, currency, subledger accounting method, and/or ledger options.

[Cancel] [Apply]

*Name	*Chart of Accounts	*Accounting Calendar	*Currency	Subledger Accounting Method	*Data Conversion Level
TAX	Vision China Accour 🔍	Month 🔍	RMB 🔍	China Standar 🔍	Subledger ▼
IAS Reporting Vision Ops	Operations Accounting Flex	Accounting	USD	Standard Accrual	Subledger

General Ledger Superuser | Setup | Financials | Accounting Setup Manager | Accounting Setups

FIGURE 4-38 *Secondary Ledger*

Additional Secondary Ledger Setup Options

The same setup options available in Primary Ledgers, such as Ledger Options and Currencies, can also be set up for the Secondary Ledger. These options can be seen for each Secondary Ledger by clicking SHOW under Details. HIDE will hide the Ledger options for that Ledger. You can only see one set of Secondary Ledger options at a time (if you have more than one Secondary Ledger defined).

The only additional option is Primary to Secondary Ledger Mapping (see Figure 4-39). This is used to set up the Journal Conversion rules, which are used when the data conversion levels were set to Subledger or Journal. Select if journals will be posted automatically (this is just related to the posting; the data conversion rules determine how the journals are created in the Secondary Ledger) under the POST JOURNAL AUTOMATICALLY FROM SOURCE LEDGER option, and also select if the Journal Creator will be the same as for the Primary Ledger, or if the creator will become the person who posts the journal entry in the Secondary Ledger. When RETAIN JOURNAL CREATOR FROM PRIMARY LEDGER is set to No, the person posting the journal will become the creator.

When setting up the Journal Source and Category Conversions, it is important to understand how these work when Subledger was selected as the DATA CONVERSION LEVEL. This selection will cause all EBS subledger transactions imported to the Primary Ledger to automatically create the journal in the Secondary Ledger, using any subledger accounting methods selected on the Secondary Ledger (if none were selected, then the Primary Ledger accounting methods are used by default). If these sources are set up under the Journal Source and Category Conversion as "Yes, Transfer Journals to this Secondary Ledger," then the journal entries will be duplicated in the Secondary Ledger (once from a journal entry and once from the subledger accounting process). This is because they are created when the subledger accounting is run, and again when they are posted in the Primary Ledger.

EBS will default a few settings under the Journal Source and Category Conversion section. A SOURCE and CATEGORY of Other will be set to transfer all undefined journals to the Secondary Ledger. And any journal created by Revaluations or Mass Maintenance (or a reversal of a Mass Maintenance) will be set up *not* to transfer to the Secondary Ledger. Any revaluations that need to be run on the Secondary Ledger should be created in that ledger, not transferred from the Primary Ledger. These will basically ensure that *all* journals are transferred to the Secondary Ledger that belong there, but any additional sources can be added.

If these additional sources and categories are set to NO for Transfer Journals to This Secondary Ledger, then this will override the default of OTHER and not transfer the data. OTHER can be changed to NO for transferring data, and each individual source and category combination can be set up for the transfer. The basic rule is that if most of the sources are going to be transferred, set OTHER to YES and add the exceptions set to NO. If most of the sources are *not* going to be transferred to the subledger, then set OTHER to NO and add only the sources that will be transferred.

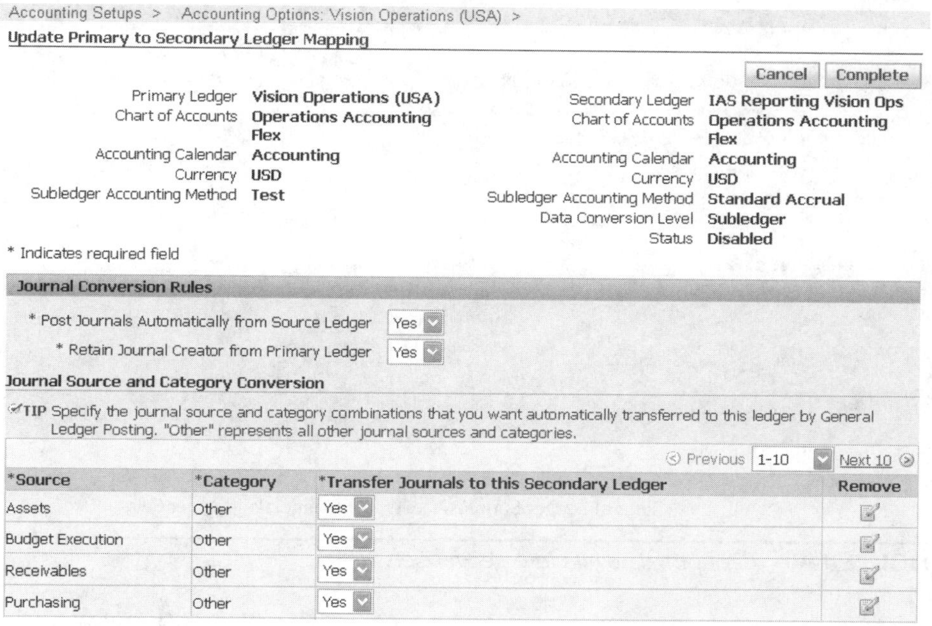

FIGURE 4-39   *Secondary Ledger journal transfer rules*

Restricting and Grouping Data (Optional)

One of the new features in R12 is the ability to both restrict Ledgers and provide access to multiple Ledgers from the same responsibilities. This is completed with the creation and assignment of Ledger Sets.

Ledger Sets to Group Ledger Access

Ledger Sets, which are optional, are used to group Primary and Secondary Ledgers, and reporting currencies within these Ledgers. The purpose of the groupings is to allow Periods to be opened or closed for all the Ledgers within a grouping at the same time, or to enable recurring journals that create transactions across Ledgers to be generated, or to run FSG reports across this set of Ledgers. Ledger Sets can only combine ledgers that have the same Chart of Accounts and calendars. Individual Ledgers, as well as Ledger Sets, can then be added to an Access Set, which grants full or limited access to a specific responsibility.

To set up a Ledger Set, refer to Figure 4-40 and assign the LEDGER SET a name, which is used by the users, and a SHORT NAME, stored in the tables and used by EBS and programmers. Add a DESCRIPTION to explain what this set is for. Ledger Sets are limited to the same CHART OF ACCOUNTS and CALENDAR and PERIOD TYPE within the calendar, which are required to be assigned to each set. The DEFAULT LEDGER is the ledger that will default in on any form, though it can be changed on the form to any other ledger in the set. Add either a LEDGER, or a LEDGER SET from the list of values to add to the set

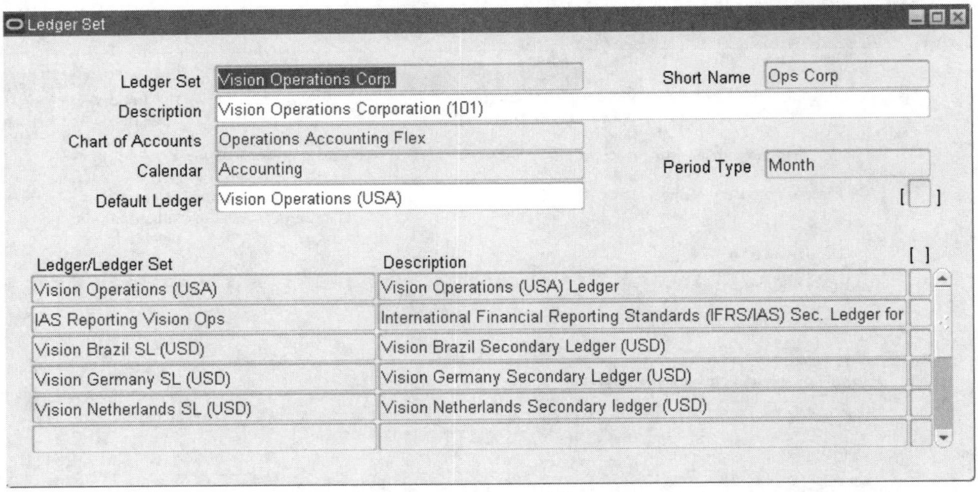

General Ledger Superuser | Setup | Financials | Ledger Sets

FIGURE 4-40   *Grouping Ledgers into Ledger Sets*

you are creating. If a Ledger Set is selected here, all ledgers assigned to that set will now be available to the ledger set you are creating. The DESCRIPTION will default in. Security Enabled is not available in some versions of this setup to secure the setups.

Data Access Sets

Data Access Sets can be used to restrict data in Ledgers that have the same Chart of Accounts and calendar. Data can be restricted by either balancing segment or management segment, or unrestricted for that Ledger or Ledger Set, and can allow read or read and write access. The Default Data Access Sets that were created with the General Ledger Accounting Setup program, which ran when the Ledger setups were completed, are found here and cannot be modified or deleted. At the very least, it is this automatically created data access set that must be used to grant unrestricted access to all data. Additional Access Sets can be created as needed to restrict data.

Give a name for the DATA ACCESS SET, and add a DESCRIPTION. Select the CHART OF ACCOUNTS, CALENDAR, and PERIOD TYPE that this set will be valid for, and assign the ACCESS SET TYPE. Shown in Figure 4-41, this determines whether the person will have access to all the Ledgers assigned to this set, called Full Ledger Access, or only specific balancing or management segment values. Selecting a DEFAULT LEDGER will default this ledger on the forms for the users.

Select either a LEDGER or a LEDGER SET to be assigned to this Access Set. If a Ledger Set is selected from the list of values, then all the Ledgers assigned to this Ledger Set will be available in this

Access Set. If a Default Ledger is assigned to the access set but not selected below as a Ledger assigned to this Access Set, then it will automatically default into the set when it is saved. It will always default in as Read and Write. If you want the Default Ledger to be Read Only, ensure you manually add it to the Access Set and assign the appropriate Privilege. Also, if a Ledger Set is assigned to an Access Set, and then a Ledger within that Ledger Set that is assigned separately with a different PRIVILEGE, then the PRIVILEGE of the Set will override that of the Ledger, potentially granting access the user should not have. Use care when assigning both Ledgers and Ledger Sets within the same Access Set to prevent this from happening.

If Balancing or Management Segment Values were selected in the ACCESS SET TYPE, the VALUES section of the form becomes updatable. Select ALL to assign this access to ALL the Balancing or Management segments in this Ledger or Ledger Set. Uncheck ALL to add a SPECIFIC value to grant this access to. Parent Accounts can be used here as well, limiting access to the child segments assigned to the Parent. Select the PRIVILEGE of Read Only for querying data and not creating transactions, or READ and WRITE for creating transactions.

Once the Data Access Set is defined or created by saving a Ledger, it needs to be assigned to a responsibility in System Administrator (System Administrator | Profile | System). Check Responsibility and select the responsibility name from the list of values that you want to assign this Access Set to. In the Profile box, select GL: Data Access Set from the list of values and click FIND. Under the Responsibility column, select the Data Access Set for this responsibility. This is a required profile and must be set prior to using General Ledger.

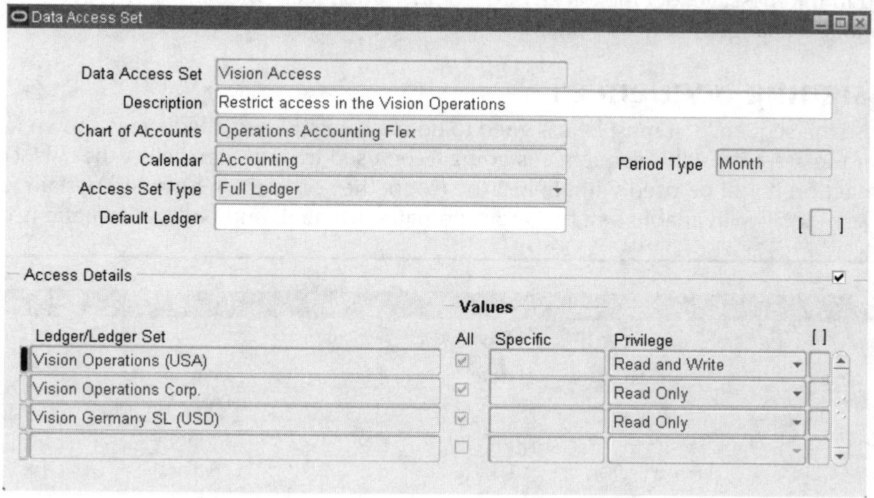

General Ledger Superuser | Setup | Financials | Data Access Sets

FIGURE 4-41 *Creating new data access sets*

Document Sequences: Additional Setups (Required If Using Sequencing)

Document Sequences assign sequences to specific documents within each module of EBS. Setups require three steps. First, the profile option Sequential Numbering must get set. The default value for this is Not Used. Second, to use document sequencing, it must be set for either Partially Used, where EBS requires sequences only when one is set up, or Always Used, where every document must be assigned a sequence in order to be saved. Third, sequences then need to be both defined and assigned to the category and ledger they will be used with.

Defining Sequences

To set up a sequence as shown in Figure 4-42, assign a NAME to the sequence, and select the APPLICATION it pertains to. Sequences can be assigned to more than one category as well as more than one Ledger, but each category can only have one active sequence. Enter the EFFECTIVE dates, where the FROM date is required, but the TO date should be left blank for active sequences. There are three TYPES a sequence can be set up as: Automatic, where EBS assigns the sequence number for you; Manual, causing the user to assign the number; and Gapless. Gapless will ensure there are no gaps in the sequence numbers.

Since these numbers are cached in the EBS memory in chunks, some are lost from time to time if they are not used once issued to memory. Gapless will only issue the current number being used to memory at any time, preventing this problem, but does come with a cost of speed. Checking MESSAGE will cause a pop-up box to appear whenever the users save a transaction and a sequence is assigned, and will have both the sequence number assigned as well as the sequence used in the message. Set the INITIAL VALUE for the sequence. Once these are saved, a sequence cannot be changed, only end dated.

Assigning Sequences

To use the sequence, it must be assigned to both a category and a ledger, as shown in Figure 4-43. Enter the APPLICATION this sequence is going to be used in, and then select the CATEGORY for the transaction it will be used with. Select the LEDGER the sequence setups will pertain to, and select the METHOD. The available METHODS are Automatic, Manual, and Null. Automatic is used when the

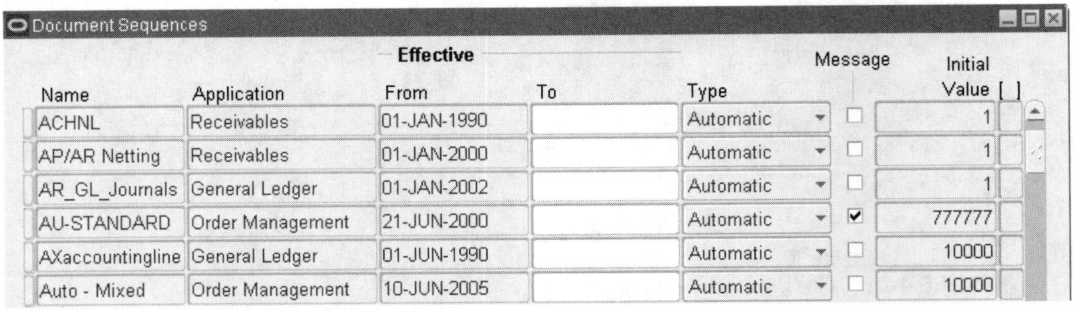

Name	Application	Effective		Type	Message	Initial Value [ ]
		From	To			
ACHNL	Receivables	01-JAN-1990		Automatic	☐	1
AP/AR Netting	Receivables	01-JAN-2000		Automatic	☐	1
AR_GL_Journals	General Ledger	01-JAN-2002		Automatic	☐	1
AU-STANDARD	Order Management	21-JUN-2000		Automatic	☑	777777
AXaccountingline	General Ledger	01-JUN-1990		Automatic	☐	10000
Auto - Mixed	Order Management	10-JUN-2005		Automatic	☐	10000

General Ledger Superuser | Setup | Financials | Sequences | Document | Define

FIGURE 4-42   *Setting up document sequences*

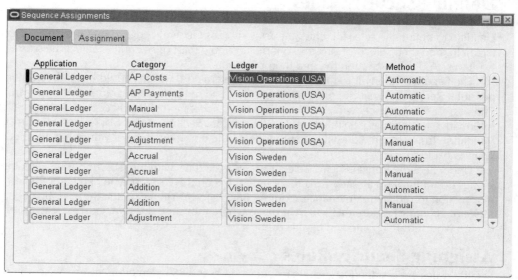

General Ledger Superuser | Setup | Financials | Sequences | Document | Assign

FIGURE 4-43   *Assigning document sequences*

document is entered into EBS via an API or Intraface table, signifying that the transaction was automatically created. In the case of journal entries, Automatic would be used when the journal is imported via the Journal Import program, including journal entries uploaded from Web ADI. Manual is used when the document is entered with a form, such as the Enter Journal form. Null will use this sequence for both Manually and Automatically created transactions. Under the Assignment tab, START and END DATES are assigned, as well as the actual SEQUENCE name. Each Category can only be assigned one active sequence at a time, but sequences can be assigned to multiple categories at the same time.

Additional Security

Security Rules can be added to your Chart of Accounts to limit access to specific accounts or ranges, by application and responsibility. This used to be the only way to prevent users from accessing certain accounts in the General Ledger, but now Data Access Sets can also restrict data by balancing segment or management segments. Although Security Rules can perform the same function as Data Access Sets, they are also used to restrict specific account segment values, such as Natural Account, to help prevent mispostings. Inquiry and reports are also limited by Security Rules, preventing users from seeing balances and transactions in these accounts.

An example of where I like to use these is in Purchasing and Payables, restricting access in these subledgers from the specific asset accounts, only allowing postings to the asset clearing accounts. This prevents the inevitable misposting caused by helpful users who want to post their requisitions to the fixed asset account for computer equipment instead of the asset clearing account, causing assets to be inaccurate and this transaction not to get sent over to Oracle Fixed Assets.

Defining Security Rules

When entering the Define Security Rules form shown in Figure 4-44, you must select what Key Flexfield to define the rules for. Enter the APPLICATION as General Ledger, enter the TITLE as Accounting Flexfield, and then select the STRUCTURE name for your Chart of Accounts. Select the SEGMENT you want to set up the restriction for, and then click FIND.

   The Security Rule will require a NAME and a DESCRIPTION, which should be as descriptive as possible. Remember security rules can be assigned to multiple applications and responsibilities. The MESSAGE is what users will see when they try to access a restricted account, so make it as informative for them as possible to reduce confusion. Security Rules work much like Cross-Validation Rules in that you will want to Include the entire universe of values before selecting what to exclude.

   Under Security Rule Elements, select the TYPE as INCLUDE, with the FROM and TO all encompassing. Values do not have to already exist to include them on this form, so you can enter the last number in a section to reduce maintenance required on this form. Then exclude the specific account or range of accounts. Again, this can be a range where the value does not exist. Select ASSIGN to decide who should be affected by this rule.

Assigning Security Rules

Security rules are assigned to specific responsibilities in EBS by entering the APPLICATION a given rule pertains to (see Figure 4-45). The APPLICATION is actually the one that is assigned to the responsibility you want this rule to affect, which may be a custom application or one that does not make sense if

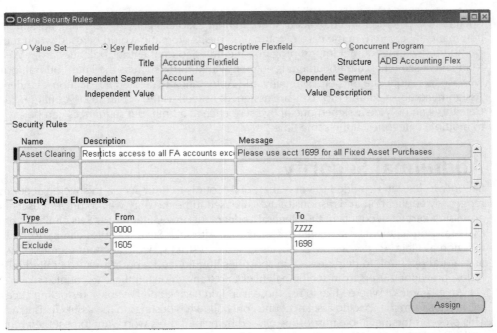

General Ledger Superuser | Setup | Financials | Flexfields | Key | Security | Define

FIGURE 4-44   *Defining security rules*

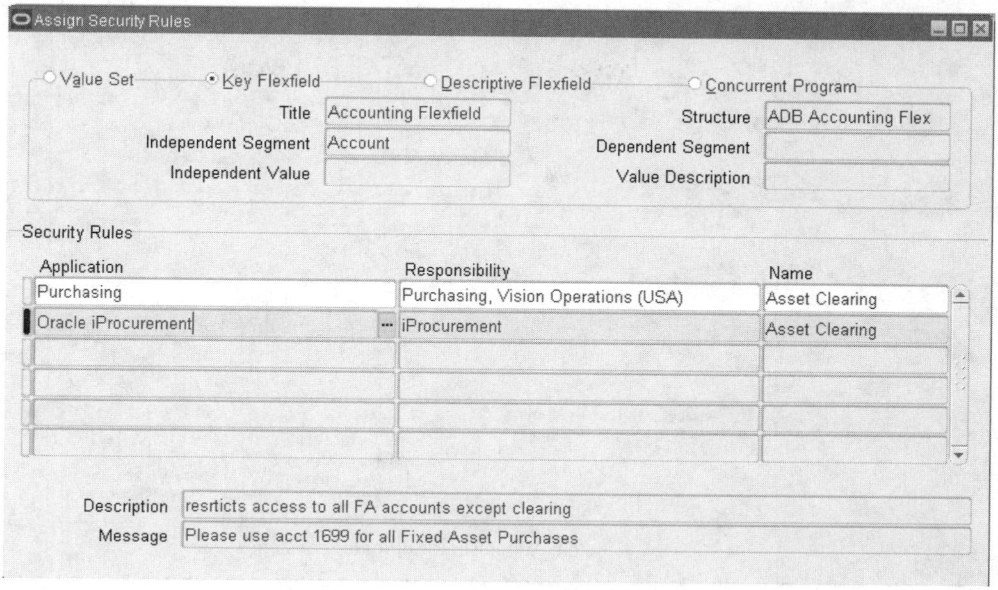

General Ledger Superuser | Setup | Financials | Flexfields | Key | Security | Assign, or Define | Assign button

FIGURE 4-45 *Assigning security rules*

the responsibilities are custom and not the seeded ones. (Responsibilities can be assigned to any application when they are created, which is why a Payables responsibility can be assigned to the Purchasing application.) Then select the RESPONSIBILITY from the list of values, and assign the NAME of the rule you want to use. Once this is saved, it will require that users sign out of the system for it to take effect.

General Ledger Profile Options

There are several Profile options available for the functionality in the General Ledger. Some are required, and some are not, and many come seeded with the application with a value. Of the 6,626 (okay, I had insomnia one night and counted profiles instead of sheep), very few are actually set with each implementation. That is not to say you should not be aware of what is available and what they control.

Profiles can be set at different levels, shown in Figure 4-46. At the highest level, Site, the profiles set here will affect all applications installed. The Application level pertains to only a specific application, such as General Ledger or Payables. Responsibility will restrict this setting to this responsibility only, whereas Server will restrict the control of the settings to a specific EBS server. Organization is used for anything for a specific Organization, and finally, User is valid only for that User. The hierarchy of these levels always goes from User at the top, then Organization, Server, Responsibility, Application, and Site at the bottom. When some profiles are not set, or when the system / profile is installed, there is a default setting. These are noted for each profile. Table 4-2 details the profiles that affect General Ledger processing.

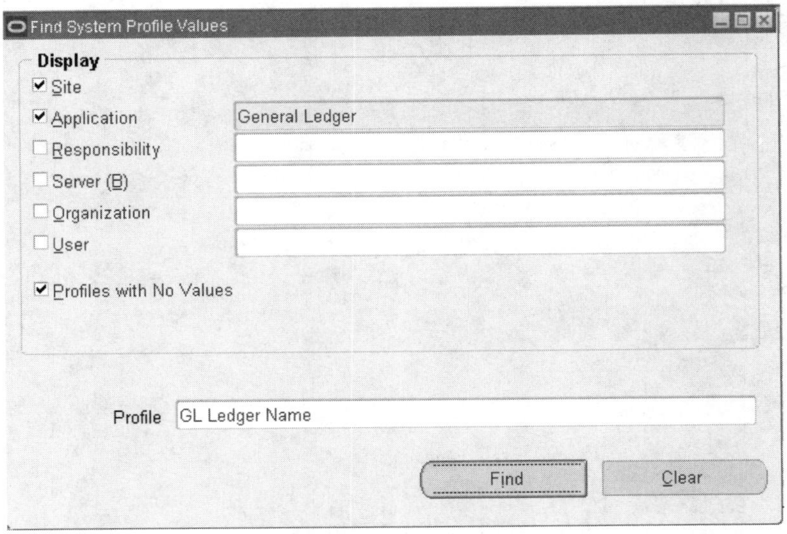

System Administrator | Profiles | System

FIGURE 4-46 *Setting profiles*

Profile	Description
MO: OPERATING UNIT	Operating Units are assigned to transactions created and stored in subledgers, such as Payables, Receivables, and Purchasing. Drill-down functionality for the General Ledger does not look at any of the OPERATING UNIT profiles, but it allows access to all Operating Units with transactions in the General Ledger. The only profile used by the General Ledger for operating units is mo: operating unit. This profile controls which Tax setups are used in EBTAX, EBS's Tax Engine. The Tax Codes are derived by this profile. There is no default for this profile.
MO: SECURITY PROFILE	This profile groups Operating Units to allow access to more than one organization from the same responsibility. When the profile SLA: ENABLE SUBLEDGER TRANSACTION SECURITY is set to Yes, drill-down functionality in the General Ledger will show only transactions that are in the organizations assigned to the group in the MO: SECURITY PROFILE. The SLA: ENABLE SECURITY profile is set to No, MO: SECURITY PROFILE is ignored during drill-downs, and all transactions are displayed. There is no default for this profile.

TABLE 4-2 *Profiles That Affect General Ledger Processing*

Profile	**Description**
FLEXFIELD: OPEN KEY WINDOW	This profile will cause the Accounting Flexfield to automatically open when the user hits the field, instead of when the list of values is selected. It will open on all forms, even if the account number is already populated. This defaults to No.
BUDGETARY CONTROL GROUP	This profile only needs to be set when Budgetary Controls are turned on for a Ledger and a control group is going to be used. Select the group you want to control the funds at. This has no default.
DAILY RATES WINDOW: ENFORCE INVERSE RELATIONSHIP DURING ENTRY	Controls if the Inverse, or reverse, rate is calculated by EBS. If this is set to Yes, EBS will calculate conversion rates from USD to EUR, for example, when EUR to USD is entered. If it is set to No, then the inverse rate will need to be manually entered and updated. This defaults to No.
ENTER JOURNALS: VALIDATE REFERENCE DATE	Determines if a reference date entered on a journal entry falls within an open or future-enabled period. Yes validates the reference, and No does not. This profile was designed for compliance with Italian Libro Giornale rules, but it can be used for any other reason where the reference date needs to be validated in this manner. This defaults to No.
FSG: ACCOUNTING FLEXFIELD	This determines the Flexfield used by FSGs when creating FSG definitions and running reports. The default for this profile is Accounting Flexfield.
FSG: ALLOW PORTRAIT PRINT STYLE	FSG reports that are 80 characters or fewer can be printed either Portrait or Landscape. This profile will determine which one. Yes will print 80-character reports portrait, whereas selecting No will print them landscape. The default for this is Yes.
FSG: ENABLE SEARCH OPTIMIZATION	This profile will use a process called FSG Performance Enhancements to increase the speed of reports containing a large number of Parent accounts. Selecting Yes will use the Performance Enhancements, whereas No will run these normal. No is the default.
FSG: ENFORCE SEGMENT VALUE SECURITY	When you set up Security Rules and assign them to specific responsibilities, you have the option of also applying these rules to FSGs. This will prevent users from entering transactions against a specific GL account, but it will allow them to run reports for these values. Selecting Yes will enforce these rules for FSGs, but No will allow the users to access this data. When the Security rules are enforced, they are only effective for independent segments; these rules never are applied to dependent segments. Be aware that the default is No for this profile, making Security Rules ineffective for FSG reporting.

TABLE 4-2   *Profiles That Affect General Ledger Processing* (continued)

Profile	Description
FSG: EXPAND PARENT VALUE	This is used with Summary accounts only (not straight parent/child account hierarchies). When looking at a rollup group, parents will be expanded for their child ranges only if the parent does not belong to any rollup group. If a parent does belong to a rollup group, then the child ranges will not be expanded when this profile is set to Yes. Selecting No will cause EBS to use the summary flag associated with the FSG Flexfield assignment on either the Row or Column set. When the Summary flag is set to Yes, the rows are not expanded for parent values. When the summary flag is not selected, then the range is expanded into the child values. The default for this is No.
FSG: MESSAGE DETAIL	If an FSG encounters an error when running, the log files will show the error message details based on this profile. When it is set to No, there are no error messages in the log, making troubleshooting difficult. Minimal, the default, will contain only error-specific messages. A Normal selection will show the error messages as well as all File and Function names. Full gives the most detailed messages; it shows memory figures, timings, and SQL statements, as well as all the other messages. This is useful for unresolved problems or extremely slow-running reports but is not needed for all reports. Changing this at the user level and rerunning the reports is a good option for this type of troubleshooting. The default is Minimal, which is enough information to resolve the most common FSG errors.
GL: ARCHIVE JOURNAL IMPORT DATA	Normally, once journals are imported in the Intraface tables successfully, the data is purged periodically, based on the source programming and selections when running the import. Once it is purged, it is lost for any research in the future. This profile will cause this data to be archived from the GL_interface table into the GL_Interface_history table. This happens when the profile is set to Yes. Since the archiving happens during the Journal Import process itself, it will cause imports to run slower than when this option is not selected. Data is archived when this profile is set to Yes. The default is No for this option.
GL: AUTOALLOCATION ROLLBACK ALLOWED	Selecting Yes here will allow AutoAllocation Batches to be rolled back in the general ledger. This defaults to Yes.
GL: DATA ACCESS SET	This profile assigns the data access set that a specific responsibility can access, limiting Ledgers, Ledger Sets, and balancing or management segments. This profile has no default and is required.

TABLE 4-2 *Profiles That Affect General Ledger Processing* (continued)

Profile	Description
GL: DEBUG MODE	Log files, in general, are limited in the data that is recorded in them. By selecting Yes for Debug mode, more detailed error messages are added to the log file. This works for many of the General Ledger processes, including Journal Import, Posting, Translations, etc. Use FSG: Message Detail will assist with problem solving if an FSG report errors out. This defaults to No.
GL: INCOME STATEMENT ACCOUNTS REVALUATION RULE	When using Revaluations, this profile determines if PTD or YTD balances for the income statement will be revalued. This defaults to YTD.
GL: JOURNAL REVIEW REQUIRED	Similar to Journal Entry Approvals, this profile determines if reviews are required prior to posting for AutoAllocations. There are no dollar limits on this review. This defaults to No.
GL: LAUNCH AUTOREVERSE AFTER OPEN PERIOD	When this is set to Yes, the AutoReverse program will be launched when a period is opened. If this is not set and AutoReverse is used, it will have to be manually launched for the period. The default is Yes.
GL: NUMBER OF ACCOUNTS IN MEMORY	This profile will improve the speed of MassAllocations and MassBudgets by using more memory. If this is set above the default of 2500, be sure to run the concurrent request Program – Optimizer for both indexes and Statistics prior to running the Mass Processes. The higher this value is set, the faster these processes will run, using more memory. This defaults to 2500.
GL: NUMBER OF FORMULAS TO VALIDATE FOR EACH MASSALLOCATION BATCH	This profile is only effective when average balances are enabled; it determines how many formulas are validated for errors prior to actually creating the MassAllocation process. This process will randomly select formulas for validation, causing an error in the program if an error is found. Any errors not found during this prevalidation process will cause an error during the MassAllocation process. The default is 5.
GL: NUMBER OF FORMULAS TO VALIDATE FOR EACH RECURRING JOURNAL BATCH	As in the MassAllocation validation profile, this will again prevalidate a set number of formulas when average balance is enabled. This defaults to 5.
GL: NUMBER OF PURGE WORKERS	Workers are the number of processes that run at the same time. The higher the number, the faster the purge process will run, but it will also take more system resources. There is no default.

TABLE 4-2 *Profiles That Affect General Ledger Processing* (continued)

Profile	Description
GL: NUMBER OF RECORDS TO PROCESS AT ONCE	Designed to improve the performance of processing MassAllocations, MassBudgets, and Journal Import via the Journal Intraface, the higher the number of records that are processed at the same time, the faster the performance, but it will use more memory. This feature requires that the concurrent process Program – Optimizer be run after setting the profile. This will default to 1000.
GL: OWNERS EQUITY TRANSLATION RULE	When performing translations, this profile will determine if Owners Equity is translated for each PTD value, using the historical rate set for the period-average rate, or YTD, which uses the period-end rate. This defaults to PTD.
GL: ACCOUNT ANALYSIS REPORT: ENABLE SEGMENT VALUE SECURITY ON BEGINNING/ ENDING BALANCES	When running any of the Account Analysis reports, EBS gives the option of having Security Rules apply to the beginning and ending balances. Setting this profile to No will cause the beginning and ending balances to include all account combinations within the report ranges, whereas the period activity will only include transactions for any segments this responsibility has access to and is not secured. Selecting Yes will enforce the security rules for both the balances and the activity. This will default to No. Note that this selection may cause the report to foot incorrectly (beginning balance plus period activity may not equal ending balance).
GL AHM: ALLOW USERS TO MODIFY HIERARCHY	This profile allows users to have access to the Account Hierarchy Manager, without having the ability to modify or save updates. Setting this profile to Yes at any level will give that level access to save changes, whereas No will prevent this. This defaults to No.
GL AUTOALLOCATION: CONTINUE TO NEXT STEP IF NO JOURNAL CREATED	Step-Down allocations usually build off the previous allocation. Not having an allocation generated for a step (i.e., there is no journal batch generated) can make the rest of the allocation calculations unneeded. No will prevent Step-Down allocations from continuing once an allocation is reached that has no output or journals created. Yes will allow the allocation calculations to continue after a step results in no journal entries. If your allocations are written to build on the previous allocation or a balance in all steps, selecting No will save processing time. This will default to No.

TABLE 4-2 *Profiles That Affect General Ledger Processing* (continued)

Profile	Description
GL CONSOLIDATION: PRESERVE JOURNAL BATCHING	During consolidations, the option to retain specific journal header data is available, as opposed to using the naming conventions for consolidations that EBS uses. Selecting Yes will cause the following data to be changed during the consolidation process. Batch Name will have 50 characters of the originating batch name, as well as the same Batch ID. Journal Name will have 25 characters of the originating journal along with the journal ID. Journals will stay grouped as the same batches as in the subsidiary Ledger, along with descriptions, and journal categories. If No is selected, then EBS will use its naming conventions to rename the batches and journals, add Consolidation descriptions, and change the category to Consolidation. This defaults to No.
GL CONSOLIDATION: PRESERVE JOURNAL EFFECTIVE DATE	Utilized when the GL Consolidation: Preserve Journal Batching is set to Yes, this profile will cause the Effective Dates of the journal entries to retain the effective date from the subsidiary ledger after consolidations when they use the same calendars. Selecting No will cause the effective date to be based on the target calendar, and will default in to the last day of the period. This defaults to No.
GL CONSOLIDATION: CROSS INSTANCE WORKFLOW NOTIFICATION CONTACT	EBS can transfer data across instances between databases that are linked. When the transfers are made, a user can be notified of the transfer results. To use this feature, set this profile in the instance that is the source of the data by entering an EBS employee name. Ensure that the name selected has a valid e-mail address on the Employee screen. This has no default.
GL CONSOLIDATION: SEPARATE ROWS FOR DEBIT AND CREDIT ACCOUNT BALANCES IN CONSOLIDATION JOURNAL	Working with the Consolidation and Elimination processes in EBS, this profile controls if one line is generated for both the debit and credit transaction against the same account, or if two lines are generated on the journal entry, one for the debit and one for the credit. This does not control if the journal data is summarized or posted in detail. This defaults to No, creating only one line for both the debits and credits.
GL DAILY RATES: CROSS RATES OVERRIDE	Many setups are done to default rate information in during processing. Depending on how this is set, EBS can be instructed to allow rates defaulted in to be overridden by a user (System-Generated Rate Overrides), or allow a rate entered by a user to be overridden by a system rate (User-Entered Rate Overrides). Selecting No Override means that where a system rate is defaulted, the user cannot enter a rate, and the system will not change any rates entered by a user. This will default to User Entered Rate Overrides.

TABLE 4-2 *Profiles That Affect General Ledger Processing* (continued)

Profile	Description
GL JOURNAL IMPORT	Separate Journals by Accounting Date. When importing journal entries, EBS can either create a separate journal entry for every accounting date on the transactions or post all transactions with different accounting dates that fall within the same period onto one journal entry. No will create one journal entry for each period. Yes should be selected if you are using Average Balances. This defaults to No.
GL: LEDGER ID	This will default in the ID based on the Ledger name assigned in the GL: Ledger Name profile.
GL: LEDGER NAME	This Required profile needs to be populated based on the Ledgers available in the list of values. For subledger transactions, this controls the Ledger ID that is associated with each transaction. Populating this field will default the proper Ledger ID for the profile GL: LEDGER ID, which cannot be changed except by selecting a new GL: LEDGER NAME, as well as GL: DATA ACCESS SET. This will default to the generic access set to everything for this Ledger that is created when the Ledger is saved.
GL REVALUATION: USER PRIMARY CURRENCY FROM SOURCE LEDGER TO CREATE ENTRIES IN REPORTING CURRENCY	Determines if the Primary Currency or Entered Currency is used during revaluations. This defaults to No, which means the Entered Currency will be used.
GL REVALUATION: DAYS TO ROLL FORWARD DAILY RATES	In order to perform Revaluations, this profile provides a rate for the date it is being run for. If no rate is defined, EBS gives the option of using a prior periods rate. This profile controls how many days back EBS will go to find that rate. If this profile is set to 5, for example, EBS will look back five days for a rate to use for processing the revaluation. If a rate is found, then the Revaluation concurrent request completes with a warning, showing the rate used on the Exception report. If no rate is found, the process will error out. This defaults to zero.
GL REVALUATION: TRACKING BY COST CENTER	Unrealized Gains and Losses are recorded in the General Ledger during the Revaluation processing. Select a No here and the gains and losses are only recorded for each balancing segment. Selecting Yes will cause the gains and losses to be recorded by both balancing segment and cost center, based on the accounts that are originating the gain or loss. This defaults to No.

TABLE 4-2   *Profiles That Affect General Ledger Processing* (continued)

Profile	Description
GL REVALUATION: USE PRIMARY CURRENCY FROM SOURCE LEDGER TO CREATE ENTRIES IN REPORTING CURRENCY	Revaluations can come out different when transactions are created in multiple currencies, depending on whether the revaluation is done from the Entered currency for a transaction or the Reporting currency for the Ledger that owns the transaction. Selecting Yes for this profile will create revaluations to be created off the reporting currency, whereas No will use the transaction's entered currency. Remember, if No is selected, Rates must be entered for the Entered currencies to the currencies they are being revaluated into, as well as the Ledger currency. The default is No for this option.
GL REVALUATION: VALIDATE GAIN/LOSS ACCOUNTS	This determines if the Gain/Loss Accounts are validated during the processing, preventing errors. This defaults to Yes.
GL SUMMARIZATION: NUMBER OF DELETE WORKERS	When running the Summarization processes for Summary Accounts (Add/Delete Summary Accounts and Program – Maintain Summary Templates), they can take a long period of time to complete, especially if there are a lot of accounts or a complicated hierarchy for the summarization. Running the Program – Optimizer is the first step to improve performance. The second is to assign more workers to the process. Workers basically determine how many concurrent system resources Oracle will use to complete this task—the more workers, the more resources are going to be used for the summarization programs and the less for the rest of the system. This defaults to 3.
GL SUMMARIZATION: ACCOUNTS PROCESSED AT A TIME PER DELETED WORKER	After the number of workers is assigned to this process (GL SUMMARIZATION: NUMBER OF DELETE WORKERS), the number of accounts processed by each worker is the last way to improve the summarization processes. This defaults to 5000 per worker.
GL SUMMARIZATION: ROWS DELETED PER COMMIT	Again, this profile is designed to improve the summarization process. This time, it is specific to Deleting a summary template. Instead of increasing the speed of the processing, setting the number of rows deleted per commit will affect whether this process can roll back if an error is encountered. The larger the number, the more records that will not be saved and will have to be reprocessed if an error is encountered. The lower the number, the fewer records that will have to be reprocessed. This defaults to 5000.

TABLE 4-2   *Profiles That Affect General Ledger Processing* (continued)

Profile	Description
GL TRANSLATION: REVENUE/EXPENSE TRANSLATION RULE	Determines if PTD balances or YTD balances are translated during translations. This will default to PTD.
JOURNALS: ALLOW MULTIPLE EXCHANGE RATES	When entering a foreign currency Journal Entry, the Exchange Rate is entered at the top of the journal and will default all lines to this rate. If this profile is set to Yes, a user can override the converted amount, in effect changing the rate for that line. This defaults to No.
JOURNALS: ALLOW NONBUSINESS DATE TRANSACTIONS	If Average Balancing is used, the balances are based on a Transactional Calendar, which identifies which days are business days, or normal workdays. This same calendar is used by such modules as Manufacturing. If a day is not designated as a working day, then typically transactions cannot be performed on that day until that is changed. Selecting Yes for this profile will allow transactions on nonbusiness days. This defaults to No.
JOURNALS: ALLOW PREPARER APPROVAL	If Approvals are required for any or all journal entries, this profile determines if the person who creates the journal entry in EBS can also approve it, based on that person's approval authority. Selecting Yes for this profile will cause EBS to look at the creators' approval limits, and if the journal falls within their limits, it will allow them to approve their own entries. When set to No, it will require someone in the creators' hierarchy to approve it. This will default to No.
JOURNALS: FIND APPROVER METHOD	After JOURNALS: ALLOW PREPARER APPROVAL, this is the other profile that controls who can approve a journal entry. There are three options here: Go Up Management Chain will cause every person in the hierarchy to approve this journal entry between the person who entered it and the final person with the proper approval authority. Go Direct will only require one person to approve a journal—the one with the proper authority in the hierarchy. And One Stop Then Go Direct will be a two-person approval for journals, where the immediate supervisor of the person entering it is required to approve it, as well as the first person in the approval hierarchy with the proper approval authority. This will default to Go Up Management Chain.
JOURNALS: DEFAULT CATEGORY	Manual journal entries afford the ability to select a large number of categories. This profile will cause one specific category to default on to all manual journal entries. This is useful if different categories are not used by your organization, or if each department has its own, as well as its own responsibility. This has no default.

TABLE 4-2 *Profiles That Affect General Ledger Processing* (continued)

Profile	Description
JOURNALS: DISPLAY INVERSE RATE	Specifically for the journal entry form, this determines if an inverse, or reverse, rate is displayed when entering a foreign currency journal entry. Yes will show the conversion rate from the Ledger to the Transaction, whereas No will only display the rate from the Transaction to the Ledger currency. This will default to No.
JOURNALS: ENABLE PRIOR PERIOD NOTIFICATION	There are no controls in EBS to prevent a journal entry from being entered for a prior period—this is a normal part of accounting life. But this situation can sometimes get confusing if an accountant is entering transactions for multiple periods, and it can cause unintentional mistakes. Selecting Yes for this profile will cause a pop-up box informing users they are about to enter a journal for the prior period, helping to ensure they really want to do this. This defaults to No.
JOURNALS: MIX STATISTICAL AND MONETARY	This profile determines if a journal entry can have a dollar amount, such as USD, and statistical entries on the same journal. Yes will allow this, whereas No will require a separate journal entry for each monetary amount. This defaults to No.
JOURNALS: OVERRIDE REVERSAL METHOD	Reversing Journal Entries can be generated either by Switching the Debits and Credits or by Reversing the sign (creating negative debits and positive credits). The default for each category is assigned when AutoReverse is set up (even if AutoReverse is not used). Enter Yes for this profile to allow users to override that default. No prevents users from changing the reversal method. This defaults to No.
USE PERFORMANCE MODULE	The concurrent process Program – Optimizer was designed to create indexes and gather statistical data on the General Ledger tables. This data improves the performance of many of the resource-intensive processes, such as Posting, Summarization, MassAllocations, Consolidations, Year End processing, Budget assignments, and Historical Rate Assignments. This profile determines if these processes will use the statistical data collected when running the Optimizer. This defaults to Yes; it is recommended that it not be changed unless by a request from Oracle Support. Doing so will decrease performance of these processes.

TABLE 4-2 *Profiles That Affect General Ledger Processing* (continued)

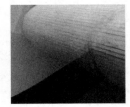

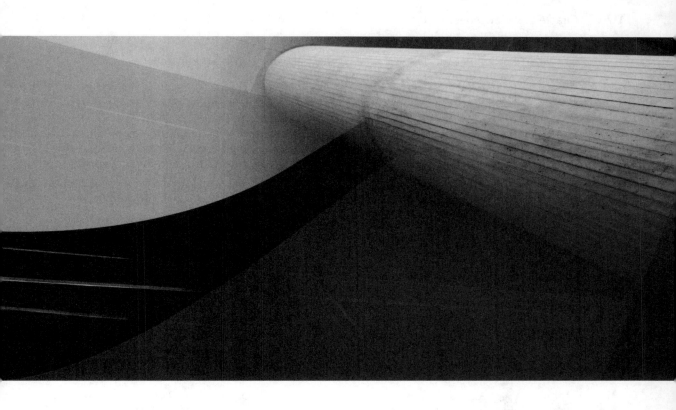

CHAPTER
5

Transaction Processing
and Flows

he General Ledger is the final resting place of all financial transactions created within an organization, from within EBS as well as other systems. EBS has predefined flows for creating journal entries from subledgers, such as Payables and Assets, and also allows manual journal entries directly into the General Ledger, or you can use tools such as Application Desktop Integrators (ADIs). APIs, or Application Programmatic Interfaces, allow automated creation of transactions from non-EBS systems, leaving each company with many options on how to create accurate and complete financial systems. Understanding these options is the first step to creating processing procedures that are best suited to your organization.

Subledger Transaction Flows

General Ledger is the core of all Enterprise Resource Planning (ERP) systems, and the end result of all subledger data. The flow of the core subledgers into the general ledger is depicted in the Transaction flow image. The following diagram will help you understand this flow and how transactions appear in the General Ledger, which is an important part of automating the month-end close. Let's look at each process area at a high level next.

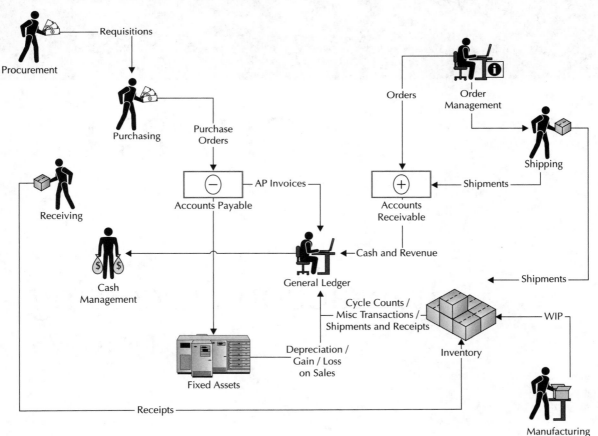

Procure to Pay

Transactions begin the procure-to-pay cycle as requisitions. How requisitions generate the account number depends on how the workflow is set up (customized at most locations), usually on some combination of item or category, dollar amount (for assets), and employee assignments. Requisitions are then turned into Purchase Orders, defaulting the accounting from the Requisition. The orders are received, creating receiving and accrual transactions, where the accounting is dependent on whether they were for expense or inventory items. Invoices in Accounts Payables are matched to the receipts or purchase orders, relieving the accruals and booking the inventory or expense transactions and creating the liability to the company. Once the invoice is paid, the liability is relieved and cash is reduced.

Any invoice that was distributed against the asset clearing account will transfer the data to Fixed Assets, where the clearing account will be relieved and the asset entry created in accordance with the category assigned to the asset. Monthly, depreciation will run, recording accumulated depreciation and depreciation expense, as well as any asset transfers, and gains or losses recorded on the retirement of an asset.

Order to Cash

Orders are entered, either beginning the manufacturing process or reserving items already in inventory. Once the products are ready, they are shipped against the order, relieving inventory and recording cost of good sold. The shipment interacts with Accounts Receivables, where an invoice is generated, recording a Receivable and a Revenue transaction. Once payment is received for the invoice, the Receivable is relieved and cash is recorded.

Though this is an oversimplified vision of business according to Oracle, it does help at a high level as you attempt to understand all the transactions that are created by subledgers.

Journal Entries

You can create Journal Entries in the General Ledger (GL) by importing them from both subledgers as well as third-party systems via the import interface; by manually entering them directly into the GL; by using Web ADI to create a journal or convert a text file to an ADI journal, or by generating allocations, reversing journals, or recurring journals. The ultimate goal is to reduce the manually created journal entries and increase the accuracy of all automated journals. Automated journals include any imported journals from third-party systems and subledgers, and journals created by the EBS process for allocations, reversing entries, and recurring entries.

There has always been a long-standing debate in the accounting area: should imported journal entries be corrected in the source subledgers (such as in Payables) or manually as an adjusting journal entry directly in the General Ledger? There are two sides to this argument. Way back in the good old days when the grass was greener and the air was fresher—oops, sorry, I just dated myself. But realistically, only about ten years ago, changing a transaction in a source module such as Payables was a complicated process. When an invoice was matched to purchase orders and receipts, first the invoice needed to be unmatched to the purchase order, then the receipt needed to be reversed, then the purchase order corrected and reapproved, then the receipt performed again, and finally, the invoice rematched to the PO, correcting the distribution.

This process was a very valid reason for not making the corrections in the subledgers—it was long and time consuming and involved quite a few users. But today, correcting a distribution is very easy in payables, requiring minimal work. So this will lead to the second argument. It is always easier to just make a journal entry than to talk to users in another department and train them on the correct way to perform transactions so that the accounting is accurate, something most non-accountants care very little about. For one-off fixes, the journal entry approach works fine—but if a company's accountants are spending days reclassifying transactions from upstream every month, the problems need to be fixed at the source.

For payables, where most of the problems occur, that means looking into one of three areas. First, is this a user training issue for the persons creating the requisitions, which default the accounting onto invoices? Second, should the defaults for the requisitions be different than what they are currently set up to do? (For example, should item ABC be hitting the expense account for supplies instead of shop expenses as a default?) And finally, if this transaction was not matched to a Purchase Order, does the person assigning the coding to the invoice need some guidance? Once the area that is causing the problem is identified, it can be resolved either with a system setup change or by providing some training to the users.

Importing Journals from Third-Party Sources or Subledgers

Besides creating journal entries directly into the General Ledger, EBS also allows journals to be imported from both third-party sources and subledgers, such as Payables or Assets.

Journals from Third Parties

To import data from a third-party system, the data must get populated into the GL_Interface table using an API (application programming interface) written in PL/SQL. To import a text file using ADI, you must first map the fields on the text file to the ADI template. Once the data is populated in the interface table, you can import it, which will perform additional validations on the journal, including that the account string is accurate and not disabled. The general flow for importing third-party journal entries is to run a custom process that populates the journal entry interface table, and then run the Journal Import process. If there are any errors, you can fix them in the Journal Correction screen and reimport them. Once they import, you can optionally have them approved prior to being posted.

You can use the Journal Import window, shown in Figure 5-1, to import journals from third-party systems as well as reimport any errored entries after they have been corrected. Select the SOURCE for the journal from the list of values. EBS does come with all the subledgers as sources, and additional ones should be added for third-party journal entries. If any journals exist in the interface for that source, the LEDGER will have a list of values for you to select from (limited by access for your responsibility). If there is no LEDGER in the list of values, it means that there are no journals in the interface for the selected SOURCE and the LEDGERS your responsibility has access to, though data may exist for other Ledgers. The value for SELECTION CRITERIA is dictated from the journal that you are trying to import; usually, data coming from third-party systems will have No Group IDs. If Specific Group ID was selected, click the list of values under SPECIFIC VALUE to see a listing of the group IDs available for import for the selected SOURCE and LEDGER. If no list of values comes up, then the data in the interface does not have a Group ID.

Under Run Options, selecting POST ERRORS TO SUSPENSE will automatically post any errors found for the account numbers to the suspense account assigned in the Ledger setups. This can only be used if the Ledger was set up to allow suspense posting—if it was not, selecting POST ERRORS TO SUSPENSE will cause the import to fail if the journals are out of balance, but will import any balanced journals. If this option is not selected, then errors will cause the import to fail and allow the user to correct the problem prior to rerunning the import.

Selecting CREATE SUMMARY JOURNALS will summarize the journal entry to have only one amount for all transactions for a specific GL account combination and signage (debit or credit), making

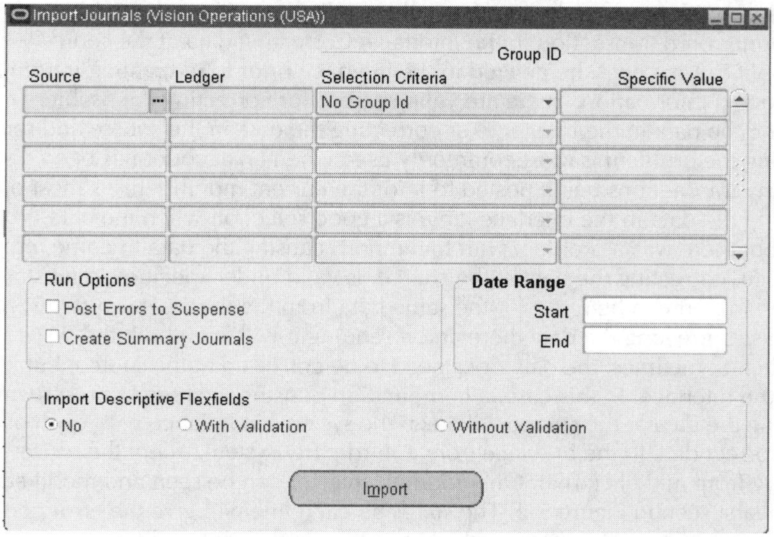

General Ledger Superuser | Journals | Import | Run

FIGURE 5-1   *Journal import*

the account analysis easier to read. Drill-downs (literally, drilling down on a journal to the submodule source transactions) are still available with the summary feature to review detailed transaction-level information, and this information is available on specific reports as well.

Entering a DATE RANGE will limit the data that the import will consider. Using a START date will limit the data to only transactions with a GL Date after that time. Usually, leaving this blank is the good idea to ensure there are no old transactions in the interface that might be causing an out of balance in the General Ledger. Lines that have a GL date in a prior period that is closed will error out, letting you know they are in there and need to be addressed. Entering an END date will prevent transactions after a certain period of time from being selected, and can be useful during the month-end close. IMPORT DESCRIPTIVE FLEXFIELDS determines how EBS will handle Descriptive Flexfields on individual transactions. If you created SUMMARY JOURNALS, then always set this option to NO, as Descriptive Flexfields cannot be imported for summary data. If detailed journals were brought in, the Descriptive Flexfield data can optionally be imported as well, either WITH or WITHOUT VALIDATION.

Once you click the IMPORT button, a concurrent request will be kicked off. This process will end in a Warning if there were any journal entries with import errors. These errors can result from such things as invalid account numbers, periods not being opened, or unbalanced journal entries. The errors can be seen in the report by clicking the View Output button in the concurrent manager. If a journal entry errors out during import, take a look at the error code on the report, along with the data that errored out. Drawing on this information, you can decide if the error should be resolved by correcting the problem, updating the interface data, or deleting the import and correcting it at the source. Correcting the problem works well when an account has been disabled or end-dated, and an alternative account has not been assigned.

Updating the interface can be done on the EBS screen that allows updates to be made to transactions with errors in the interface tables—this form can only update journals with errors, not any unerrored transaction in the interface. Correcting data at the source will require that the errored-out journal entry be deleted in the interface prior to re-creating it from the source with the corrected information. There are valid reasons for correcting the problem causing the error, correcting the data in the interface, or correcting the data in the source and reimporting it. Correcting the problem is most commonly used when an account has been disabled but still has third-party transactions being posted to it for the current month. This is most often a timing issue. Correcting the data in the interface table is a good selection when the data is correct in the source system but there was a problem with the import, causing the data to come into EBS incorrect. The last choice, correcting the data at the source, is valid under specific circumstances. The first is when the import can be rerun for the same data from the third-party systems; not all systems allow this. Correcting the data there and resending it will keep both the systems in synch with each other. Sometimes, the data does need to be corrected at the source, but it cannot be resent over to the interface. In this case, a combination of using the correction screens in EBS and correcting the data at the source will keep the systems in balance with each other.

To correct data in the interface from a third-party system, query the SOURCE where the journal is coming from and click FIND. Only journals in error can be seen and modified on the screen that appears, seen in Figure 5-2. The STATUS on each line will give the error code for the line. The Journal Import report (it was created when the Journal Import process was run) will provide

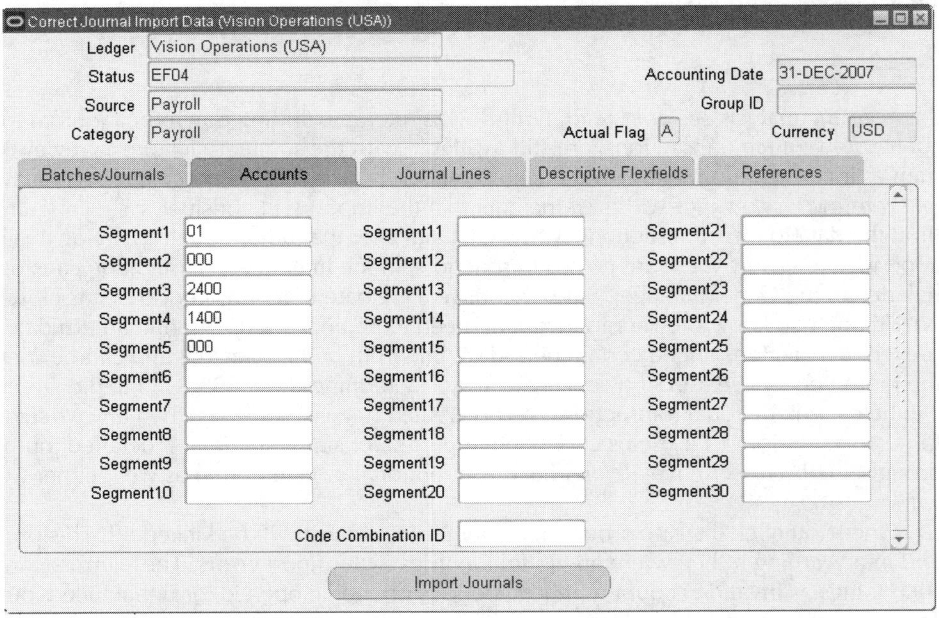

General Ledger Superuser | Journals | Import | Correct

FIGURE 5-2 *Journal import correction*

detailed information on the error codes, as well as what specific data is incorrect on this report. EF04, in this example, states that Detailed Posting is not allowed for the specified account. To correct this error in the interface, go to the ACCOUNTS tab and enter a valid, active account combination that allows posting. This error could also be corrected by resolving the problem that caused the error; in this case, that would mean making account 01-000-2400-1400-0000 allow detailed posting or adding an Alternate Account on the Account Combinations form. This works for disabled or end-dated accounts. See Chapter 4 for details on how to do this.

Journals from EBS Subledgers

Journals being created for subledgers, such as Payables, are imported from the seeded Payables responsibility and not the General Ledger. A profile option, SLA: Disable Journal Import, dictates how these journals are created. This comes seeded as YES and should, as a rule, always remain Yes. This profile determines that the journal import process is controlled at the subledger as opposed to the General Ledger, causing errors to roll back to the subledger. Changing this to No makes the subledger journal creation process a two-step process, where the subledger pushes the data, and the General Ledger pulls the data, leaving problem transactions in the General Ledger interface tables with no way to correct the data at the source (this is how R11*i* worked for journal imports). Leaving this profile set to Yes will cause any errors to roll back to the subledger, allowing the problems to be resolved at the source instead of the General Ledger.

You can run the Create Accounting process in three different modes in the subledger. Draft mode creates a draft representation of the data for reviewing and reporting within the subledger. This is not transferred to the General Ledger using this mode, allowing any changes to the source data (such as the distribution lines) or Accounting rules to result in a change to the accounting data next time the create accounting process is run. Final mode marks the transactions as available to transfer to the General Ledger, as part of either the same request or a separate request. And Final Post makes the transactions accounted, transferred, and posted to the General Ledger. If data is transferred over as Final or Final Post, any entries that do not pass the journal import validation, such as an inactive account number, will be rolled back, or reversed, from the interface, allowing the transactions to be updated in the subledger where the error occurred.

To find the invoice with a problem takes a combination of reports. The Journal Import report will tell you what account combinations are a problem, and running the Journal Entries report for unposted items in the subledger and then searching for that account combination will reveal the invoice number. This invoice can now be queried and the incorrect line be discarded and a correct distribution entered.

Journal Maintenance for Period and Currency

Once a journal has been successfully imported, no matter what the source was for the entry (including Manual), both the Period and Currency for the journal entry can be maintained prior to posting as long as the source is unfrozen (Setup | Journal | Sources). From the Journal Entry screen (Journals | Entry), query the journal in question. Click Review Journal. If this journal has not been posted, and the source is set up to allow changes, the Change Period button is available. From here, a new Effective Date and Period can be entered for this journal. Click Change Currency to enter a new currency for the journal entry, as well as an exchange rate. Remember, this does not change the amounts on the journal, just the currency these amounts are entered for.

Manual Journal Entries

Manual Journal Entries can be either entered directly into EBS or uploaded from an Excel interface called Web ADI or Journal Wizard (these are both the same thing). Any journal in EBS has both a batch and at least one journal associated with it, though it is not required to manually create the batch—EBS will automatically enter it for you if one is not entered. Batches allow you to group more than one journal entry together. When Payables Journal Entries are imported from Account Payables, one batch is created, with multiple journal entries associated with it, separating journals for transactions like Purchasing Invoices from the journal entry for Payments. If a batch is not entered for manual journals, EBS creates one by assigning the Journal Name, along with the Date and Time it was created, to the Batch Name. Whereas Batch Names, which are case sensitive, do have to be unique within the same period, Journal Names are not.

To create a batch manually with the journal entry, click the NEW BATCH from the Journal Find form (refer to Figure 5-3). Enter a unique BATCH name for this period, and select any Open or Future-Entry-enabled PERIOD from the list of values. You can only create journal entries for periods that are currently OPEN, or marked as FUTURE-ENTRY. Periods become Future-Entry based on how many future periods were assigned in the Ledger. Future-Entry periods allow for invoices or journals to be entered, but they cannot be posted until the actual period is opened. Add a DESCRIPTION to explain what this batch is for. The BATCH TYPE will default to Actual for manual journals but can also be set to Budget, as discussed in Chapter 8. Then select the JOURNAL TYPE of Standard or Average. Optionally add a CONTROL TOTAL to balance the batch's net debits or net credits to. Once one is added, EBS will not allow an out-of-balance batch to be posted. A warning is given when the journal is saved, "There is a Control Total violation in this journal batch. Do you still want to save this batch?" This warning will still allow the journals and batch to be saved, but the out of balance will have to be corrected before the journal entries can be posted. EBS will create BATCH TOTALS, keeping a running total of the total debits and total credits in both the ENTERED and ACCOUNTED currencies for this batch. The STATUS reflects if this batch is Posted or Approved, or else the status of the Funds Checking for budgetary-controlled Ledgers. DETAILS give the date CREATED, the date POSTED, and the person who posted the batch. Click JOURNALS to enter the individual journals associated with this batch.

To start entering a journal without manually creating a batch, click the NEW JOURNAL button from the Find Journal screen (Journals | Enter). On the screen shown in Figure 5-4, enter a JOURNAL name, which can be used later to query this journal, along with a DESCRIPTION for why it was done. The JOURNAL names do not have to be unique. The DESCRIPTION will become the default for the journal lines DESCRIPTION but can be overridden on each line with more detailed or accurate information. The LEDGER will default in from the setups if this responsibility only has access to one Ledger or was assigned a default Ledger, or else it can be selected from the list of values if it has access to more than one. Select a CATEGORY from the list of values that best describes this journal entry. Some of the categories are utilized by EBS for journals imported from the subledgers—though these can be used on manual journal entries as well, it is easier during submodular reconciliations (especially when they do not balance) to have these used by the subledgers only and not manual journal entries. Additionally, categories can be added for journals interfaced from third-party systems, or to better describe your business.

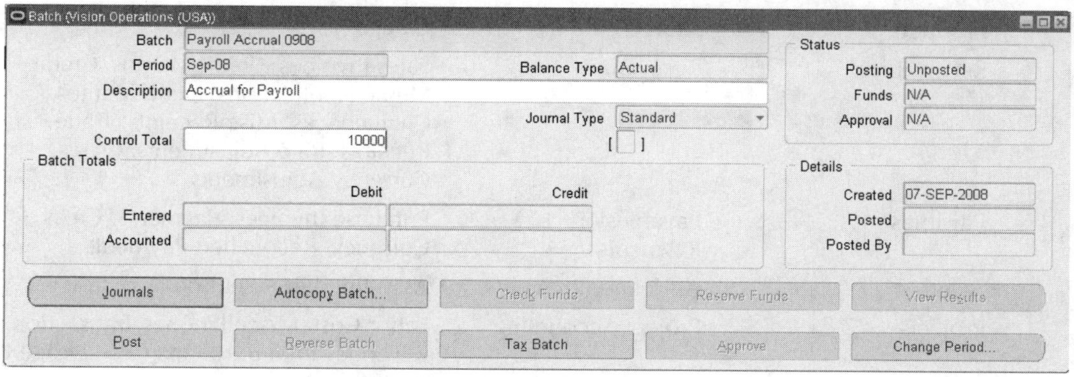

General Ledger Superuser | Journals | Enter | New Batch button

FIGURE 5-3 *Manual journal batches*

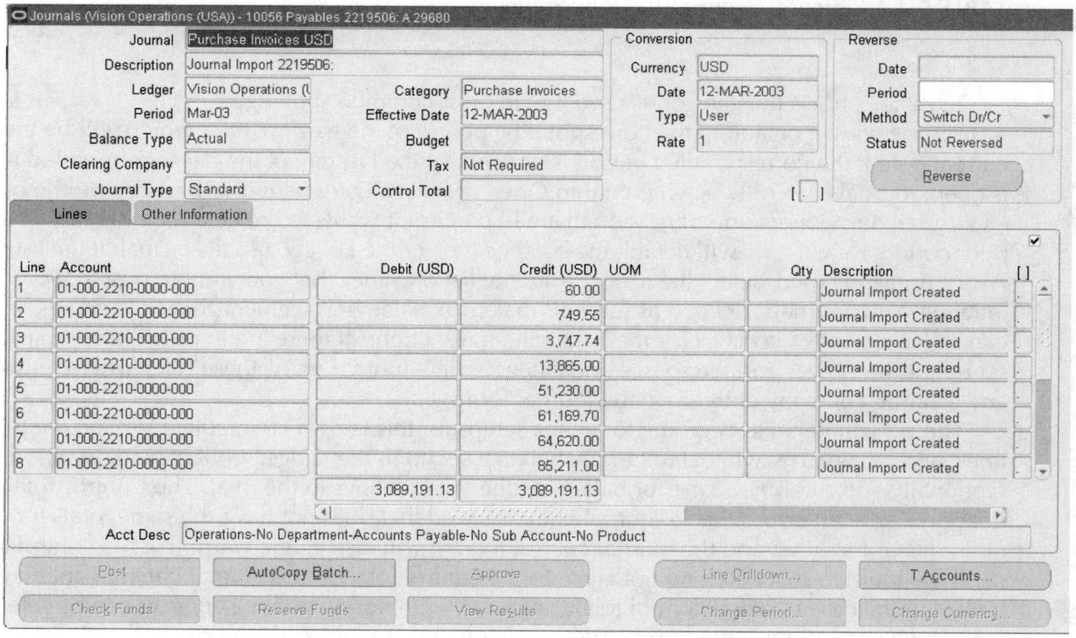

General Ledger Superuser | Journals | Enter | New Journal button | Journals

FIGURE 5-4 *Manual journal entries*

Product	Source	Category
Receivables	Receivables	Sales Invoices, Credit Memos, Credit Memo Applications, Debit Memos, Chargebacks, Misc Receipts, Trade Receipts, Rate Adjustments, Cross-Currency Adjustments
Payables	Payables or Payments	Purchase Invoices, Payments, Cross Currency, Reconciled Payments
Assets	As defined in Assets	As defined in Asset Book Controls
Projects	Project Accounting	Labor Cost, Miscellaneous Transaction, Revenue, Total Burdened Cost, Usage Cost
Purchasing	Purchasing or Periodic Inventory	Receiving, Accrual
Inventory	Inventory	MTL, WIP

TABLE 5-1   *Journal Categories Used by Subledgers*

Table 5-1 shows the categories used by the most common subledgers in EBS.

The PERIOD will default to the corresponding period of the EFFECTIVE DATE, which will be the current date if the corresponding period is opened, or the last day of the latest prior period that is open. Journals can only be entered into Open or Future-Entry periods. There is a profile option JOURNAL: ENABLE PRIOR PERIOD NOTIFICATION that will confirm it wants to create a journal entry in a prior period. BALANCE TYPE will default the balance type of the Ledger, usually Actual. If the BALANCE TYPE of Budget is used, select the BUDGET from the list of values that you want to post to. For intracompany journals, defined as journals that cross balancing segments but not Ledgers, you can select a CLEARING COMPANY for the balancing transactions. If there are Intracompany Rules set up for the Ledger and the source and category on a journal entry, these rules will override any clearing company entered on the journal form.

The TAX will default according to the tax setups for this Ledger to calculate VAT on the journal lines, and JOURNAL TYPE will default to the balance set up in the Ledger, either Standard or Average. Optionally add a CONTROL TOTAL for balancing the entered lines to the total. The Control Total will not only cause an error when a journal entry is saved that does not have the same totals for debits or credits or for either and the journal control total, it will also give a warning if the control totals of all the journals in a batch do not agree to the control total on the journal batch (if entered). Unlike in the case of batch control totals, a journal with out-of-balance controls can be selected for posting but will error out during the posting process, requiring the journal to balance prior to posting.

CONVERSIONS are used for foreign currency journals, where the CURRENCY being entered is something other than the base currency for the ledger, or will be STAT for statistical journals. STAT currency is used to post statistical transactions, like headcount or square footage, in the Ledger. This data can then in turn be used for Allocations and Recurring journals, or on financial reporting (FSGs). An effective DATE for the conversions will be required. Selecting the TYPE will either default in the RATE from the currency setups or allow the user to enter a RATE at this time. REVERSE allows the user to select the PERIOD the reversal should happen in, and is the main indicator that a journal is a reversing entry. If REVERSE is not entered here, the AutoReverse feature will not pick up this journal entry and AutoReverse it as part of the automated processing. The DATE will populate when the journal is reversed, and will reflect the date the reversal is actually performed. Select the reversal METHOD of Switch DR/CR, most commonly used for accruals reversed in the subsequent period, or Change Sign, used for reversing a journal in the same period. STATUS will update to Reversed when the reversal is processed, either manually with the Reverse button, or via the AutoReverse process. EBS prevents journals from having a reversing entry generated if the initiating journal has not yet been posted.

The number entered on the LINE dictates the order the journal lines appear, and it is recommended these numbers be consecutive with no gaps to reduce the chance of errors when processing. Enter the ACCOUNT combination, and DEBIT or CREDIT amounts. UOM and QTY are defaulted in for transactions from subledgers, such as inventory. DESCRIPTION will default from the DESCRIPTION entered above on the journal header and can be overridden for each line. If the account is set up to be reconciled, you can add a RECONCILIATION REFERENCE to the journal line to assist with this reconciliation. The OTHER INFORMATION tab provides additional information EBS adds to the journal, such as POSTING STATUS, SEQUENCING, and SOURCE.

Once a journal entry is saved, EBS checks to see if approvals are required, based on the journal SOURCE. It will not allow the journal to be posted if approvals are required. Clicking APPROVE will start the process by routing the journal to the appropriate person for approval. Once the approval process begins, the journal cannot be posted, changed, or deleted until it is either approved or rejected. Once approved, it can be posted; any changes made after it was approved will require another approval. Both approved and rejected journal entries can be deleted. Approval limits are determined by the largest line item on a journal entry, not the total debits or credits on the journal entry. Once the Journal is Approved, the user can either UNAPPROVE it for changes (which will require reapproval) or deletion, or POST it. Journals can be posted one by one from the Journal Entry screen or posted via the Post screen. Both Posting and Approving a single journal in a batch will result in the entire batch being posted or approved, as these processes are at the BATCH level, not the JOURNAL level.

Attachments

Many screens in EBS allow attachments, such as files or additional information, to be added to the data saved on a page; Journal Entries is one of them. When adding information in the form of an attachment, you will not see this information on any seeded report. From the Journal Entry screen, select the paperclip icon, which will open the Attachments form as seen in Figure 5-5. Here, add a SEQENCE number, which determines the order that attachments are seen on this form if more than one attachment is entered for this journal entry. Enter the CATEGORY of JOURNAL or OTHER to indicate if the actual journal is attached, or only information relating to the journal. A DESCRIPTION and TITLE can be assigned to the attachment; these are very useful if you are going to publish this attachment to the document catalog. Select the check box next to MAY BE CHANGED to allow the attachment to be changed, but this will not prevent it from being deleted. For uploading a file, go to the SOURCE tab and select the DATA TYPE of FILE, which will open a web browser so that you can browse to the file you want to upload into EBS. After the attachment is saved, it can be PUBLISHED TO CATALOG, which will make it available to attach to other documents. To attach a catalog item, click DOCUMENT CATALOG and fill in the Find data to search for a specific document, preview it, and then select ATTACH to attach it. Once an attachment is saved, the paperclip will now have a little piece of paper in it, showing that this journal has an attachment. Click the paperclip and then OPEN DOCUMENT to see the attachment. Besides attaching a file, you can also associate comments and a web address as an attachment for future reference.

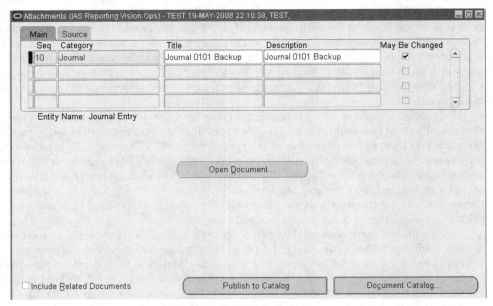

Click the paperclip on the toolbar

FIGURE 5-5   *Attaching additional information in EBS*

Journal Wizard–Web ADI

Journal Wizard is a part of the functionality available in Web ADI. Web ADI is an integrator into EBS that enables you to enter transactions in an Excel environment, or to upload data from a CSV file using predefined templates. Web ADI has around 150 integrators, and new ones are continually released. Web ADI was available in two forms in prior releases: both as Web ADI and as ADI, a client version of the product that was installed on the user's PC. The client version of ADI no longer exists in R12 and has been replaced with the Journal Wizard for uploading journal entries and the Report Manager for running reports. This section is going to address the Journal Wizard and how journal entries can be created with it, whereas the Report Wizard will be covered in Chapter 6.

The Journal Wizard uses templates, or layouts, to determine what fields appear on the Excel file and are available to use for upload. EBS comes with four predefined templates: Functional Actual, Foreign Actual, Budget, and Encumbrance. All of these come as either a single version, where header data is tracked one time for the entry, or multiple, where this same data is tracked at the line level, allowing it to be changed to create more than one journal entry. This header data includes such fields as Ledger, Category, Source, Currency, Dates and Descriptions. These templates can be modified to add additional fields and hide nonrequired fields.

Launch the Journal Wizard from Journals | Launch Journal Wizard, and select the LAYOUT from the list; the Layout, or template, will determine the fields available when entering a journal entry. Web ADI can be used to upload data directly from a text file by changing the CONTENT of text, and will be described next. After you select CREATE DOCUMENT, a process will start that opens Excel and sets up the template. This download process can take a few seconds to complete.

Some of the fields, called Context Data, will be populated and cannot be changed. These include Database, Data Access Set, Balance Type, and Chart of Accounts. Any time one of the fields does need to be changed, then a new spreadsheet needs to be created, using the correct responsibility or instance (in the case of Database) to default the data in.

An asterisk (*) will appear before any fields that are required in EBS. There are four basic types of fields: List-Text, List-Date, Text, and Number. List-Text and List-Date both refer to fields where the data is validated and a list of values is available. The list of values can be opened up by either selecting Oracle| List of Values from the Excel toolbar or double-clicking the field. When lists are available, it is a good idea to use them, as this data will be validated against the lists when the journal is uploaded. Selecting the data from the list will reduce the number of problems during the validation phases.

TIP
If a journal entry will not load due to an error message, and the data in question is a field that is validated by EBS, such as account number, but was not created using the list of values, reenter the data using the list of values as opposed to typing it in. This will usually resolve the errors.

Journal spreadsheets, when first created, have a limited number of rows for the journal. To add more rows, the spreadsheet must be Unprotected first. In Excel, select Tools | Protection | Unprotect Sheet from the menu. This will allow more rows to be added to the body of the ADI Journal. While journal data can be copied from one ADI template to another, the entire spreadsheet, including the headings, cannot be. This is because the macros downloaded with the Journal Wizard do not get copied, losing the links to EBS. Table 5-2 lists all the Journal Wizard fields with a description of each one.

Journal Wizard Field Name	Description
Ledger	Selects the Ledger Name from the list.
Database	Defaults to the database associated with the users responsibility and cannot be changed.
Category	Selects the category that pertains to the journal entry.
Data Access Set	Defaults in from the user's responsibility.
Source	Selects the Source for the journal entry. EBS comes with Spreadsheet as one of the seeded sources.
Currency	Selects the Currency for this journal entry.
Accounting Date	This date is used by EBS to determine the period this journal is for.

TABLE 5-2 *Journal Wizard Fields*

Journal Wizard Field Name	Description
Group ID	Group ID is used by the journal import program to group journals with the same Source, Category, and Group ID. If a journal is uploaded and there is some incorrect data, the Group ID can be changed so that the corrected journal will not add on to the incorrect data in the interface. Use the concurrent process Program – Delete Journal Import Data to delete any spreadsheet journal entries that loaded into the interface with errors. Because this program has the ability to delete all journals from the interface, keeping the source for the Web ADI journals as well as any third-party journals assists when deleting the data.
Journal Description	Populates the Journal description field in EBS.
Journal Name	Populates the Journal Name field in EBS.
Upl	Upload flag—can be used to determine if a line is uploaded or not into EBS. There is a feature that allows all lines to be uploaded, which ignores this flag. The flag populates when data is typed into any field on that line.
Balance Type	Defaults in from the template and cannot be changed.
Co-Dpt-Acct-Sub-Prd	These fields represent the account segments for the Chart of Accounts associated with the Data Access Set.
Debit/Credit	Amount associated with the line transactions. Though both of the columns can be populated, only one is required.
Chart of Accounts	Defaults in from the Data Access Set associated with the user's responsibility.
Line Description	Enters a description for each line.
Additional Line information	These are unique to each EBS environment.

TABLE 5-2   *Journal Wizard Fields* (continued)

Once the journal is complete, select ORACLE | UPLOAD from the Excel menu, and the upload box seen in Figure 5-6 will appear. Select if you want ALL ROWS (with journal data) or only FLAGGED ROWS to be uploaded. Ensure you select ALL ROWS if there are no UPL flags on the spreadsheet. (This usually happens when the same sheet is used month after month, just updating the amounts and the dates.) Selecting VALIDATE BEFORE UPLOAD will validate the account numbers and other mandatory fields prior to uploading the journal and importing it into the interface, making it easier to correct and eliminating having to delete the journal from the Journal Import interface.

ADI journal entries work just like journals created in third-party systems, requiring a Push into the interface from ADI and a Pull from the interface to the General Ledger. Unlike third-party system

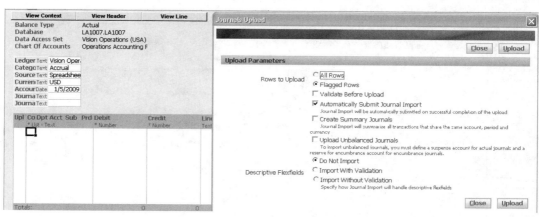

General Ledger Superuser | Journals | Launch Journal Wizard

FIGURE 5-6   *Journal Wizard in Excel*

journal entries, an API does not need to be written, as ADI works as that interface. AUTOMATICALLY SUBMIT JOURNAL IMPORT will complete the Push and Pull all in one step, eliminating the need to import this journal manually. CREATE SUMMARY JOURNAL will group all the lines with the same account number onto one summarized line in EBS (the spreadsheet will not be updated). UPLOAD UNBALANCED JOURNALS will send journals that do not balance to the interface and, if suspense posting is turned on, will balance the journal with the suspense account. If Suspense is not turned on, after the journal is uploaded, it will have to be balanced prior to importing.

The upload will process through and tell you how many lines were validated and how many (if any) had errors. A green smiley face in the MESSAGES area denotes that the lines were uploaded successfully, while a red frowny face shows which line has a problem and why. If there is an error on one line, no lines will be uploaded into EBS. Once uploaded, these journals can be routed for approval if required and posted just like any other journal entry.

Journal Wizard also has the ability to upload journals from a text file. In the Content field, select Text file, and additional fields will appear. When uploading a Text file, the file must be in a specific order, one that matches the MAPPING that is selected. Referring to Figure 5-7, enter the LOCAL FILENAME by clicking BROWSE and selecting the file. Select the format of the file under TEXT FILE DELIMITER. Checking IGNORE CONSECUTIVE DELIMITERS will cause blank fields to be ignored, as well as any time two delimiters are in a row. When deciding how to format the text file, keep in mind the data you are uploading; if a comma or semicolon is selected, then ensure there are none of these in the actual data, causing a false delimiter. (Commas in numbers are not a problem as long as they are for formatting only and not actually saved in the source data.) Determine which line the data begins on, and enter that under START IMPORTING AT LINE NUMBER. This feature allows for headers on a file.

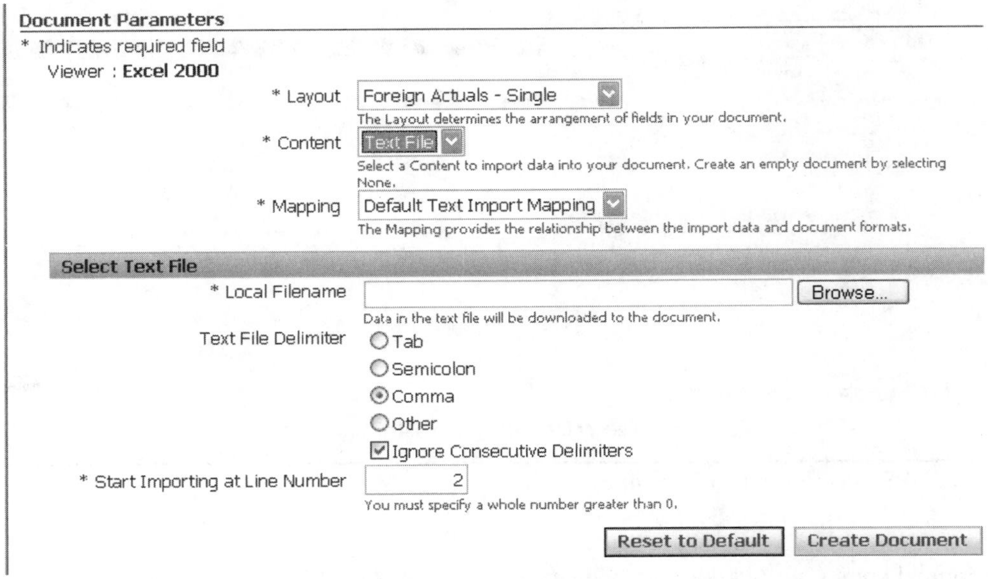

General Ledger Superuser | Journals | Launch Journal Wizard | content = TEXT

FIGURE 5-7 *Journal Wizard, file upload*

Deleting Journal Entries from the Journal Interface

Journals uploaded either via ADI or from a third party can be deleted if they error in the interface tables during upload. This is done by running the concurrent request called Program – Delete Journal Import Data. Enter the SOURCE, REQUEST ID, LEDGER, and GROUP ID from the list of values. Only journals already pushed into the interface table but not yet successfully imported can be deleted. Remember, after a journal entry is deleted, it can not be reimported into the General Ledger without putting the data back into the interface tables.

Posting Journals

Once journals are approved (if required) and ready for posting, navigate to the posting screen to select a specific journal batch, or multiple batches, for posting manually. If AutoPost is enabled in EBS, then this step does not need to be done for any sources that are using AutoPost. The request called Program – Automatic Posting should be scheduled to run at set intervals. When it runs, it will post all journals whose sources are set up for AutoPost and are approved (if required) and balanced. To post a journal from the Post screen, go to Journals | Post, and a find screen will come up, allowing you to query all unposted journals or narrow it down to a specific period or batch. Only unposted journals will appear on this screen.

Once the form is opened, select a single or several journals by clicking the box to the left of the name. Some of the journals may appear as light gray and the box cannot be checked; this indicates that the journal is not in a postable status. Look at the BATCH STATUS at the bottom of the form (see Figure 5-8 as a reference), and the reason will appear in the box next to it. Once journals are selected, click POST to start the concurrent process, which will perform a final validation on the data on the journal. This process ensures that the account combinations entered on the journals are still valid combinations, and that the selected journal is balanced, both for debits and credits as well as control totals. Monitor your concurrent request to ensure there are no errors during the posting process, such as accounts that have been disabled since the journal was created. When a journal batch posts with an error, the concurrent request will complete with a status of Warning. Error reasons can be seen on both the Posting Report in the concurrent manager and under BATCH INFORMATION – BATCH STATUS on the posting form. The Posting process will add any intercompany lines required based on the inter- and intracompany setups on the Ledger.

Once the journal is successfully posted, it will drop off the Post screen. Any batches that appear on the Post screen without debits or credits are batches that do not contain any journals. These happen for a few reasons: Someone enters a Journal Batch, never adds a Journal Entry under it, but does save the batch record, or else a Journal is deleted without the batch being deleted. A user causes this when he or she does not delete the Batch as well as the journal when prompted during the deletion process. Journals with their batches can be deleted from EBS in only two statuses: unapproved and never posted. Monitoring the Post screen should be part of the month-end process, ensuring there are no unposted transactions, and all invalid transactions (both batches and journals) are deleted or corrected and posted. To delete a Batch or Journal, highlight the line and click REVIEW BATCH. If the Journal has been approved, click the UNAPPROVE button on the batch, and then select the DELETE button on the toolbar (the icon with a red *x*) and save the record. A prompt will pop up asking if you want to delete only the journal, or the entire batch. Select Batch when all the journals within the batch—even if there is only one—are to be deleted so that there are no batches hanging out without journals. A journal batch that is pending approval cannot be deleted until it is rejected by the approver.

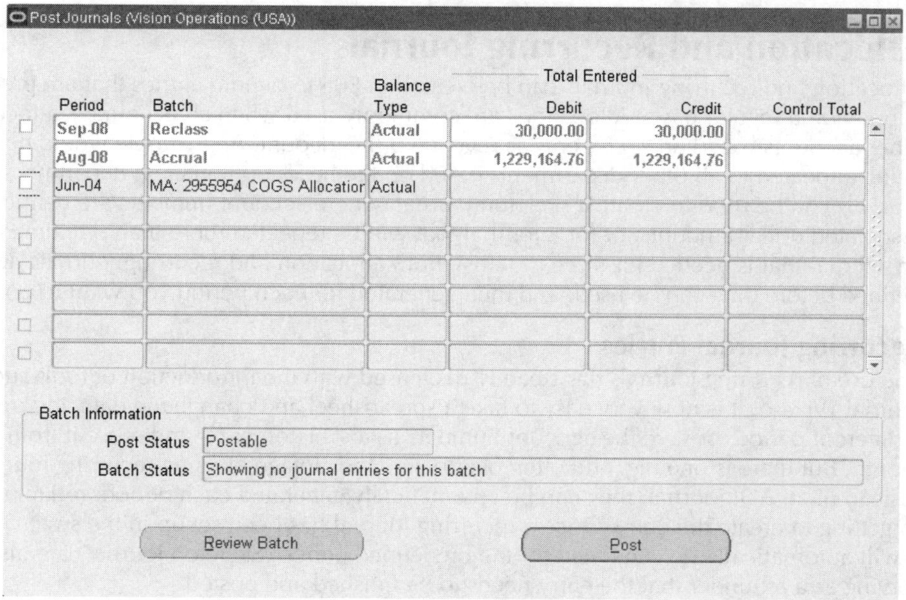

General Ledger Superuser | Journals | Post

FIGURE 5-8 *Group posting of journal entries*

When entering an encumbrance journal, note that it follows basically the same rules as other journals but is entered from a different form and has one additional field (General Ledger Superuser | Journal | Encumbrance). The BALANCE TYPE will default to Encumbrance, and then you select the ENCUMBRANCE TYPE from the list of values. The rest of the fields are the same as for regular journals. These manual encumbrance journal entries will relieve an encumbrance that is outstanding.

Reversing Journal Entries

After a journal entry has been posted, it can be reversed. Reversing a journal actually creates a new journal entry, based on the information on the original entry, and can either be manually generated or created with the EBS AutoReverse feature. When a journal was entered, a PERIOD could have been added under the Reverse section of the journal. It is the populating of this field that tells EBS that this journal requires a reversing entry, based on the METHOD entered below the period.

Traditionally, when an entry is reversed, the debits and credits are switched. This works well for accruals, but not as well for same-month corrections. The Reverse feature can also be used in the same month to reverse a journal entered in error or against the wrong accounts. Using the Method of Change Sign will cause any debits on the initial journal to be negative debits, and credits to be positive credits, ensuring that the total debits or credits for the period are still accurate. These balances for debits or credits can be used for FSGs, especially when creating cash flow statements. Once a PERIOD is added to a journal under the Reverse section, and the journal entry is posted, the reversing entry can be created either by clicking the Reverse button on the journal or by running the concurrent process called Program – Automatic Reversal, which will select all journals ready for reversal and generate the new journal entries. This program can also be set to run whenever a period is opened, creating all the available reversing journals for the period when it is opened.

Allocation and Recurring Journals

Allocation and recurring journals can be created in EBS to handle entries that are predefined and happen on a regular basis. Allocations are commonly used when an account is allocated out to other accounts based on such items as revenue or headcount. An example would be HR salaries being allocated to all other departments based on the headcount in each department. Recurring journals can be used to create a skeleton journal, where account numbers are defined with no associated dollar amounts, or for a journal that will be repeated more than one time (such as an accrual that is needed for three months). Both allocation and recurring journals need to be defined before they can be used, and then generated for each period you want to post them in.

Recurring Journal Entries

The use of recurring journals has steadily decreased with the introduction of tools such as the Journal Wizard. It is now very easy to take a spreadsheet and change the data and upload it for a different period, or save the account numbers as a skeleton entry and reuse it from month to month. But there is one big, and often overlooked, advantage of using recurring journal entries instead of an ADI journal: they can be automatically generated each period, reducing the risk of forgetting to create the entry. Once a recurring journal has been set up in the system for accruals, it will automatically be generated for the predefined period. Skeleton journals are also generated, serving as a reminder that the entry needs to be finished and posted.

Using Figure 5-9 as a reference to create a recurring journal entry, note that it will need to be defined prior to use. But unlike a regular journal entry, EBS will not create the batch for you. To define the batch, add a BATCH name and a DESCRIPTION. Select the RECURRING BATCH TYPE as SINGLE or MULTIPLE LEDGERS to identify if the transactions will cross Ledgers (Multiple) or not (Single). Select the LEDGER if the RECURRING BATCH TYPE is SINGLE. This field is not used if Multiple Ledgers was selected. The responsibility you are in must have access to a specific LEDGER in order to create a recurring journal for it. Select ENABLE SECURITY to restrict access to this recurring journal to a specific access set. If ENABLE SECURITY is selected, click ASSIGN ACCESS to select which sets should have access to this recurring journal. LAST EXECUTED PERIOD and DATE will be populated by EBS when this recurring journal is generated each month. Enter the JOURNAL name, and select the LEDGER, CURRENCY, and CATEGORY for this journal. Assigning EFFECTIVE DATES will limit what periods or how long this journal can be generated for, and can be used as a forced review in a set time period. Select the LINES button to enter detailed line information.

Enter the LINE number for this line. The lines will be generated in the order of the line numbers. LINE number 9999 is a reserved number, used as the offset line on all recurring journals; line 9999 will be used to balance all the debits and credits entered on all the other lines, and will become their offset. If you have ten lines with a net debit of $200,000, then line 9999 will be for 200,000 CR. If the lines all net out to zero, then line 9999 will have a zero balance. While line 9999 is not required, it does prevent unbalanced entries when the journals are generated. By breaking your recurring journals into smaller, simpler batches, as opposed to one large one, you can usually make effective use of line 9999. Enter the ACCOUNT for this line, and add a LINE DESCRIPTION. The FORMULA section is how the balance for this line will be determined. If you leave it blank, you have a skeleton journal that will generate a journal with only account combinations and no amounts, so they will have to be added after it is generated.

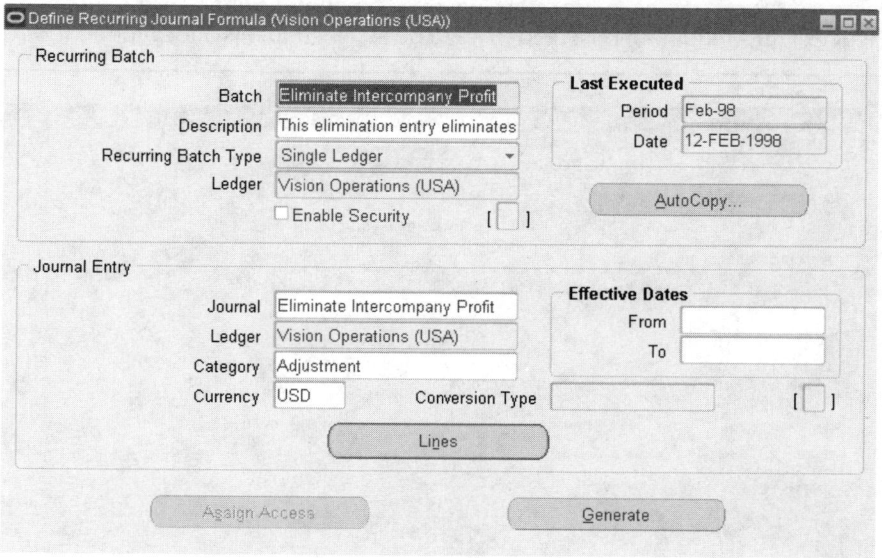

General Ledger Superuser | Journals | Define | Recurring

FIGURE 5-9   *Recurring journal definitions*

To create a recurring journal, enter either a single line with an amount or a formula to generate the amounts. In the example shown in Figure 5-10, it takes 0.15 times the PTD Actual balance in account 01-000-1410-0000-000, times 0.1. STEP is the order in which the calculation will be performed. OPERATOR is what will be done with the data on this line and is limited to the list of values. AMOUNT can be entered, or an ACCOUNT number, but not both on the same line. For ACCOUNTS, select the BALANCE TYPE of ACTUAL or BUDGET and AMOUNT TYPE to determine if Year, Quarter, or Period to Date balances are selected. The balance sign of this line (debit or credit) will be determined by the outcome of the calculation; if it is a positive, it will be a debit. If the calculation comes out as a negative, it will credit this account. The offset will be to the account identified by line 9999. When entering LINE 9999, no FORMULA is entered, just the account NUMBER. Once the Recurring entry is saved, it will need to be GENERATED prior to use; it can either be GENERATED at this time or scheduled for set times in the future. When generating a recurring journal, EBS will prompt you for the period you want to generate it for. Once the journal is generated, it can be reviewed for accuracy, approved, and posted just like any other journal.

Allocation Journal Entries

Allocations are usually used to move the balance in one account to another, or to create journals based on balances in specific accounts. Journal entries created with Statistical (STAT) currencies are particularly helpful with allocations. Often, amounts are reclassified, or allocated, based on headcount or square footage, which can be booked as Stat journals. Like recurring journals, allocations need to be defined prior to generating them, including the Batch. Referencing Figure 5-11, enter a BATCH name and DESCRIPTION, and then click FORMULAS. Enter the NAME for this journal (multiple journals can be created in each batch), and select a CATEGORY that will be assigned when the journal is generated. Add a DESCRIPTION as well as selecting the CURRENCY. Selecting CONVERTED AMOUNTS will allocate both entered and converted transactions for the accounts being allocated. Select CALCULATED AMOUNTS to use only Converted amounts for the allocation (not the Entered currencies); this requires a CONVERSION TYPE to be assigned to this allocation.

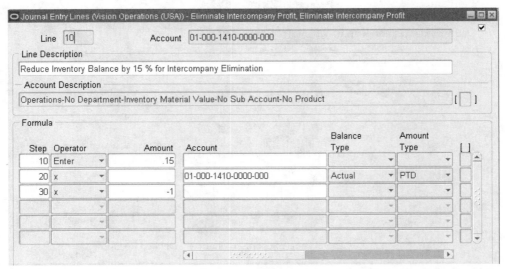

General Ledger Superuser | Journals | Define | Recurring | Lines button

FIGURE 5-10   *Recurring journal definitions – lines*

FULL COST POOL ALLOCATION will look at the balances in the target accounts and determine the incremental difference between the allocation being generated and the allocation that already exists in the target accounts. This option works well when the Target accounts only have transactions from this allocation in them. If they have balances from other sources, it can cause a problem using the FULL COST POOL ALLOCATION because EBS will use the balance (from all sources) in the target account to determine the incremental difference between what the target account balance currently is and what it should be after the allocation.

The lines marked A, B, and C are actually the formulas for creating the allocation, whereas the T and O are the Target and Offset accounts for the journal. Walking through the example in Figure 5-11, this allocation is taking the value in the statistical account 01-401-5110-0000-000 (headcount for this department as a percentage of total headcount for manufacturing) times the Period to Date balance in the parent account 01-DB3-COGS-0000-000 divided by 1 (in other words, allocate cost of goods sold by multiplying the headcount percentage in department 401 times the total cost of goods sold total). The outcome of this formula is posted to 01-401-5110-0000-000 (a debit if it is a positive number, and a credit if the outcome of the formula is negative), and the offset to the entry is 01-510-5110-0000-000. Enter an AMOUNT or ACCOUNT number on the first line. For ACCOUNT, the pop-up box will also have TYPE. This determines how EBS will process through the account numbers, especially for a parent or summary account. Constant is always used for nonparent accounts or Summary accounts. Summing is used with Parent accounts and will add up all the values in the child accounts prior to performing the calculation. Looping, also used with parent accounts, will complete the calculations defined in the formula for each child account assigned to the parent.

In the example, Row B is looping for the department, as is the Target account for the department. EBS will loop through all the children assigned to the parent 401 and create an allocation for each individual department. If these were set up as summing, it would summarize all the balances in department 401 and would require a single account as the Target. Select the LEDGER, CURRENCY, and CURRENCY TYPE to determine what balances the allocations are calculated from. TOTAL is used for Actual and Budget balances as well as Ledgers with multiple currencies or having balances in a foreign currency. STAT will pick up only statistical balances, while ENTERED will use only transactions where the entered currency equals the LEDGER CURRENCY.

Add the AMOUNT TYPE to determine what balance in the account is used for the allocation, as well as the RELATIVE PERIOD. This will tell EBS which period's data to select, based on the month the allocation is run. Enter TARGET and OFFSET account numbers, which represent the actual accounts the journal entry will debit and credit. Parent accounts can be used in either of these places. EBS determines if the TARGET receives a debit or a credit based on the outcome of the formula—this can help decide if an account should be the target or the offset. As seen, allocations can be used to allocate out entire accounts, or portions of the balances, based on other account transactions or statistical data stored as journal entries in EBS.

Once the journal allocation formula is saved, it needs to be generated to see a journal entry. Since these allocations are complicated to write, I recommend that you create them in a test instance, generate them, and validate them for accuracy before you move them to production.

Allocation Workbench

The Allocation Workbench (General Ledger Superuser | Journal | Autoallocation | Workbench) allows you to combine recurring and allocating journals into sets, where they can be generated together or in a specific order, and monitored to ensure they are run each month end. Each set is assigned a contact (which is the person or department who should be notified about any problems with the allocations) and also determines how the steps are run: Step Down, meaning

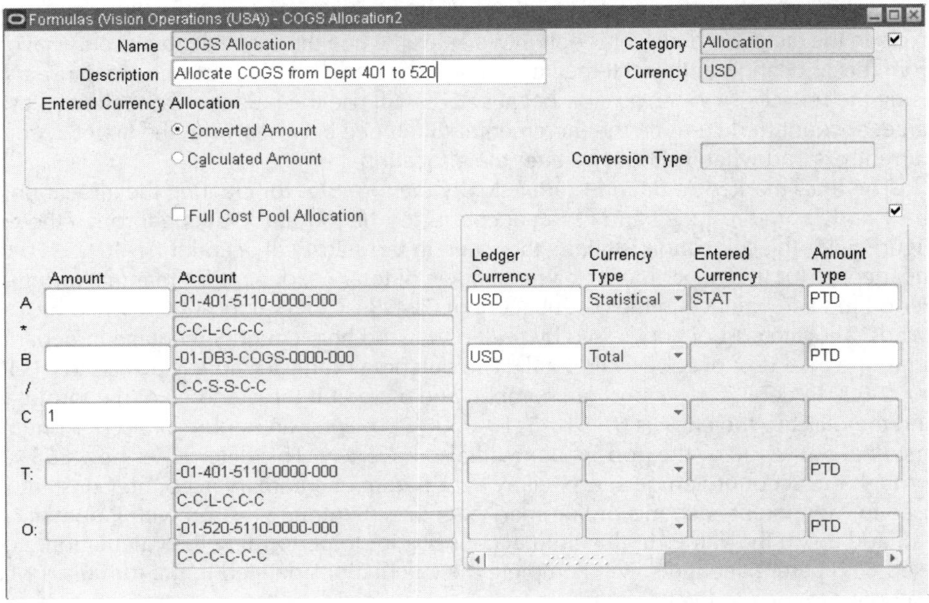

General Ledger Superuser | Journals | Define | Allocations | Formulas button

FIGURE 5-11 *Allocation journal definitions*

complete the previous step prior to performing the next step, or Parallel, which runs all the steps at one time, depending on system resources. Step Down should be used if the same account is used in multiple steps and each step requires the prior one to be posted to ensure the balance is accurate.

Account Reconciliations

EBS has the ability to set up either natural account segments or account combinations as reconcilable, and is used to help reconcile zero balance accounts, such as VAT or Clearing accounts. Once a natural account is flagged as RECONCILE = YES in the qualifiers, or a combination itself is flagged as Reconcile, this feature can be used. Transactions can be either manually reconciled using the reconciliation form seen in Figure 5-12 or automatically reconciled using the Reconciliation – Automatic Reconciliation concurrent request, which will reconcile the transactions based on account number and reference; balancing segment and reference; balancing segment and natural account with a blank reference; or balancing segment, natural account, and reference. This report can be run without updates so that the data can be reviewed prior to updating the transactions as reconciled.

To manually reconcile accounts, enter the LEDGER and CURRENCY you want to RECONCILE, along with the PERIOD. All additional information on this form is not required but can help reduce the number of transactions that will be queried for reconciliation. Select the SEARCH button to see the available transactions. The results can be seen in Figure 5-13.

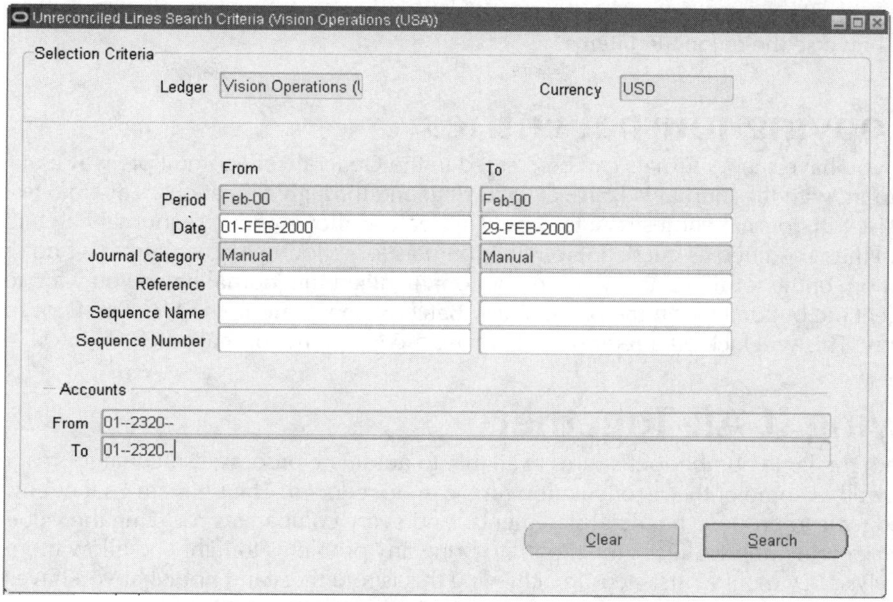

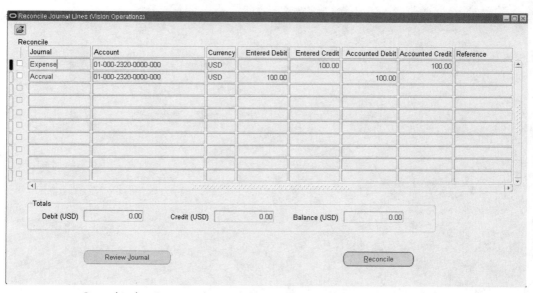

General Ledger Superuser | Journals | Reconciliation | Reconcile

FIGURE 5-12 *Automated reconciliations*

General Ledger Superuser | Journals | Reconciliation | Reconcile | Search button

FIGURE 5-13 *Account reconciliation lines*

Select the items that offset each other with the RECONCILE check box, and select RECONCILE. To unreconcile, go to Journals | Reconciliation | Reverse and enter either an ID or DATE RANGE and EBS will reverse the reconciled items.

Copying Journal Entries

As you have seen, journals can be created in the General Ledger multiple ways: manually, by import, with the Journal Wizard, as recurring, and through allocations. The final feature in EBS to assist with journal entries is AutoCopy. This feature allows an entire journal batch to be copied and then modified as needed. From the Journals form (Journal | Enter, enter a find criterion), the bottom of the form has an AutoCopy button; highlight the journal batch you want to copy and select the button. Assign the batch a new Batch Name, Period, and Effective Date for the journal entry. This will kick off a request that creates a copy of the journal batch.

Tying It All Together

With the large number of features available to automate processes, manual journal entry creation as well as some of the reconciliation time can be reduced. The ultimate goal of any General Ledger is to produce financial statements. And every company is realizing the value of having these earlier and earlier in the month to bring any problems to light and allow more time for analysis. One of the first steps in achieving this is to understand not what you have to do in the Ledger, but what the General Ledger package can do for you.

CHAPTER
6

Financial Statement
Generator

he Financial Statement Generator, or FSG, is EBS's tool for writing financial statements without having to engage a programmer every time a change is needed to a financial statement. FSGs can only be used to report on data that is housed in the General Ledger, and not other modules. When written correctly, FSGs can provide financial reports that do not need to be modified each time an account is added to the General Ledger, for actual and budget data. This section will provide in-depth details for each step needed to create an FSG.

FSG Overview

When working with FSGs, perhaps the most important thing to remember is the FSG functionality is old. While some features, such as BI Publisher or Content Sets, are newer, the core functionality has not changed in the 15 years I have been writing them. This means that the majority of older installs (implemented prior to 11*i*) had one-off patches that greatly affected the way FSGs behave. The contents of a report created three years ago that is copied or mimicked for a new report— well, they just might give different results when set up the same. Research will show the new report is behaving as Oracle documentation explains it should but the old report is not. So why does it happen? One word...Patches. The older version was created prior to a patch to resolve a problem but still behaves the old way, whereas the patch affects all new reports, so they behave differently. This is important to know because changing a working report just to be consistent with documentation breaks it more often than not in older installs of EBS. So unless you are planning a major overhaul of your FSGs and are willing to rewrite a working FSG, leave the working ones alone and modify the newly created FSG that is not working.

Prior to learning how to write an FSG, it is best to first understand what the components of a report are and what they control, as shown in the accompanying image. Each report is composed of up to five components: Row Sets, Column Sets, Content Sets, Order, and Display Sets. Row and Column Sets are the only two required components, and they represent where most of the time is spent building and maintaining a report.

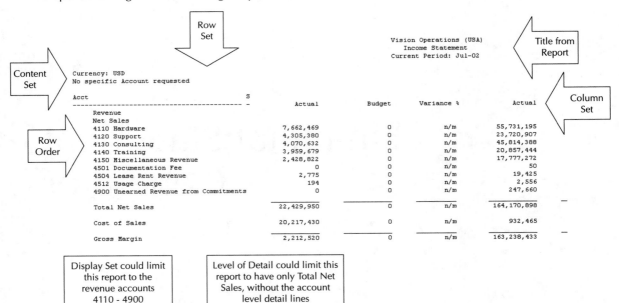

Looking at this image, we are going to address each component in relation to a traditional income statement. The Row Set represents not only the row titles down the left-hand side of the page, but also the account numbers or calculations pertaining to each row. The Column Set determines what data is represented, such as Actual or Budget, as well as the period of time it is represented for, including Year to Date or Period to Date balances. Calculations are also available to create Variance columns.

Content Sets allow such data as Companies or Departments to be grouped, or contained, on specific tabs of the report. For example, a report contains all three balancing segments in an organization. A Content Set can be created to "contain" company 1 on the first sheet, company 2 on the second, company 3 on the third, and a total of the three companies on the last page of the report.

Order helps to enhance the readability of detailed reports by determining how much of the account number is shown, and if descriptions are shown, for each line of the statement. And finally, Display Sets are used to only include or exclude specific rows or columns on a given report, allowing the Row and Column Sets to be used for multiple purposes.

Report Overview

The final step in an FSG is to create the actual Report, shown in Figure 6-1, which links all these components together. REPORT is the name of the FSG that will be selected when running the report, and it must be unique. TITLE will print at the top of the report; making the REPORT and the TITLE consistent will make it easier for the person running the report: when they are looking at a printed copy of the report, they will not have to guess which report it really is in EBS. DESCRIPTION is the detailed description of what is included on this report. Select ENABLE SECURITY if you want to limit access to the definition of this report—it is important to understand that this does not limit access to running the report, only the definition of the report. The REQUIRED COMPONENTS, consisting of ROW SETS and COLUMN SETS, and OPTIONAL COMPONENTS all need to be defined prior to selecting them on a report.

ROW SET determines the rows that appear down the left side of the report. ROW SETS can control the calculations and accounts on a given row as well as the titles that appear. COLUMN SET determines the columns that appear across the top of a report. Column Sets typically control the period of time assigned to a given column as well as the titles across the top. ACCOUNTS and CALCULATIONS can also be assigned to a Column Set.

About now you are thinking, if Row Sets assign accounts and calculations to rows and Column Sets assign accounts and calculations to columns, and columns and rows intersect on my report, which will be used? In general, for a standard income statement or balance sheet, your Row Sets identify the account ranges for each row, and the calculations for totaling groups of rows. Column Sets are used for calculations to add or subtract columns to create variances. The precedence on an FSG is that a Column Set will override a Row Set unless you tell it otherwise.

Notice that Row and Column Sets are the only two required fields when creating a report; the OPTIONAL COMPONENTS will allow the data to be shown, limited, or displayed in a specific way. CONTENT SET further determines the account ranges that appear on a report and will override any accounts that are defined in Row and Column Sets. These are most often used to restrict an FSG to specific companies or departments, or to have specific departments summarized on different pages of the report. ROW ORDER will determine how the account names and numbers of the detailed listing of accounts will appear on your report. DISPLAY SET allows you to hide specific rows or columns on one report while allowing them to print on another report without creating entirely new Row or Column Sets.

SEGMENT OVERRIDE is similar to a CONTENT SET in that you can limit the report to a specific segment value's data only. It works differently from Content Sets in that there is no To or From field, so

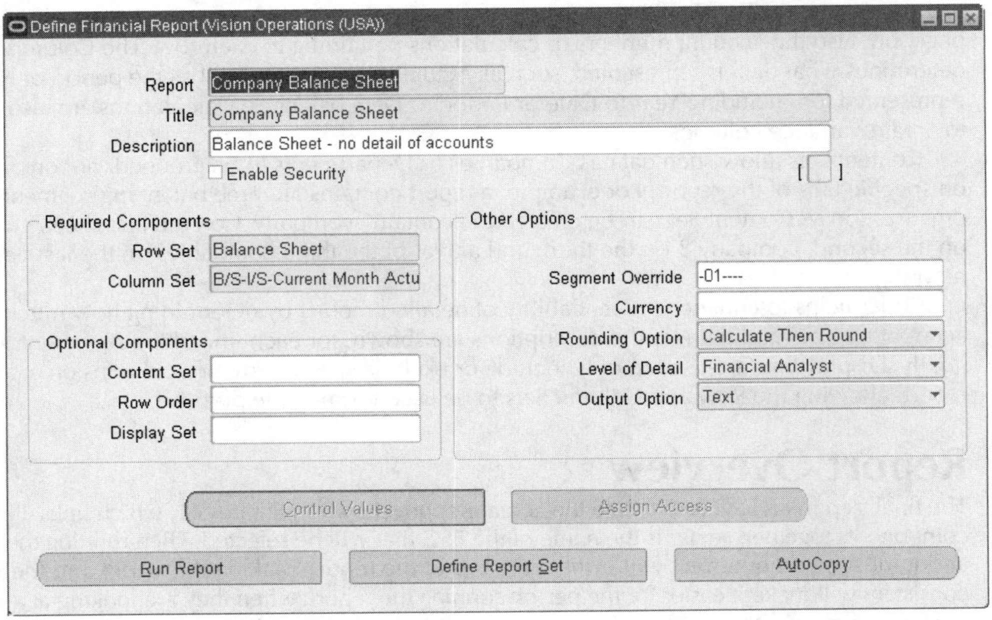

General Ledger Superuser | Reports | Define | Report

FIGURE 6-1   *Final Step, Report*

only one value can be selected for each segment. Also, Segment Override cannot print different companies on different pages as a Content Set can. CURRENCY will restrict this report to a specific currency if you are using multiple currencies in your General Ledger.

This is one important change in R12 from 11*i*: the CURRENCY at the Report level or when entered when the report is being run can only equal a currency assigned to the Ledger in R12, whereas 11*i* allowed currencies that were not assigned to the Set of Books, such as STAT. If you want to create a report in STAT or any other currency not assigned to the Primary Ledger, add this currency on the Row Set or the Column Set, not to the report itself or when running it. When FSGs are upgraded from a prior release of EBS, they will need to be modified for this change prior to running and getting accurate data. (Currencies defined at the Report level that are not included in the Primary Ledger will display a blank field.) If a currency is entered, it will default to your reporting currency for the Ledger.

ROUNDING OPTION can affect the way a report calculates data, causing an out-of-balance condition when compared to the actual total of the column. Calculate then Round is the default and usually works best. This will add the column or row up prior to rounding the sum. LEVEL OF DETAIL allows one report to be used for several levels of management, providing more and more detail as you go lower. Row Sets and Column Sets will also have the Level of Detail identifier. When using the Level of Detail on a report, it will include the level you select as well as all the levels above it. EBS comes with three defined levels: Financial Analyst, Supervisor, and Controller.

For example, if you select Financial Analyst, it will include all the rows marked as Financial Analyst and Supervisor. The highest level, Controller, usually contains the least detailed data, with Supervisor in the middle and Financial Analyst at the lowest level containing the most data. If you leave the LEVEL OF DETAIL blank on a report but include it on the Row or Column Sets, EBS will assume it is Financial Analyst and select all the rows. OUTPUT OPTION controls the output format of the FSG when it is run. Where you run the report will also control the output format and will override what is on the report.

Row Definitions

Row Sets are used to define the Row data on your reports. Typically, you define your row titles, account ranges, and calculations here. For example, on a traditional income statement, your Row Set would have Revenue, Cost of Goods Sold, Gross Margin, whereas a Column Set would have PTD, QTD, and YTD defined. Both the Column Sets and Row Sets have very similar fields, but some fields are more traditionally completed on one component as opposed to the other. This allows flexibility in creating reports and the format they follow. All the examples will be given in terms of a traditional income statement, with a note as to which fields are available on both columns and rows.

Using Figure 6-2 as a reference, note that the NAME must be a unique name for each Row Set. Make this as descriptive as possible of the data in the Row Set. Adding things like BS for Balance Sheet or IS for Income Statement to the name groups them together and makes them easier to find. DESCRIPTION is not required but should be completed to help identify what data is tracked and why it was created—remember to update this when the data in the Row Set changes.

XBRL TAXONOMY will enable electronic filing, with data tagging standards for financial reports. The Extensible Business Reporting Language is similar to XML and will be required for SEC and other reporting for all companies by 2010 (some companies are already required to report using XBRL). EBS comes with the XBRL functionality already installed and can be added to any financial report. It comes with a large dictionary of tags to select from, but it also allows additional tags to be loaded into the database. To use it on this specific report, select XBRL TAXONOMY, which will allow the tags to be added to each line of this Row Set. ENABLE SECURITY will restrict access to this Row Set definition but not reports using this Row Set. Click DEFINE ROWS to define the rows for your report.

Figure 6-3 shows the Lines for the Row Set. The LINE NUMBER determines the order your rows will print on your report.

TIP

Do not number your lines 1, 2, 3. When you need to go back and add a row in the beginning of your report, you will need to renumber all your rows. This can be tedious, especially since you will have to renumber a row and save it before you can use an existing number on a different row. Instead, number your lines 10, 20, 30 or 100, 200, 300 (depending on the complexity of your report and company), which leaves you room to add lines later on.

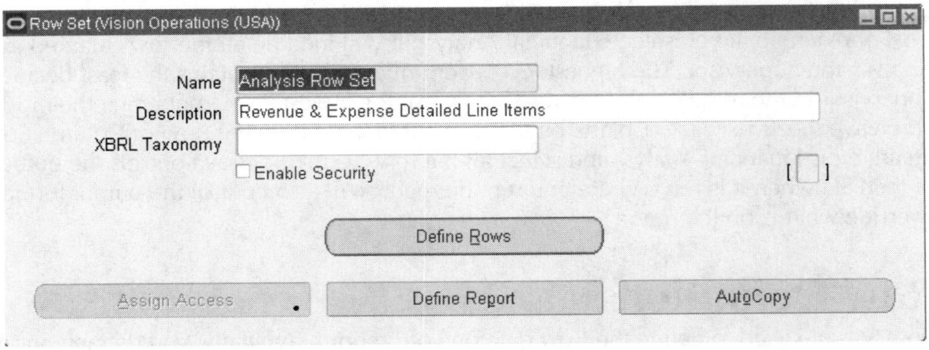

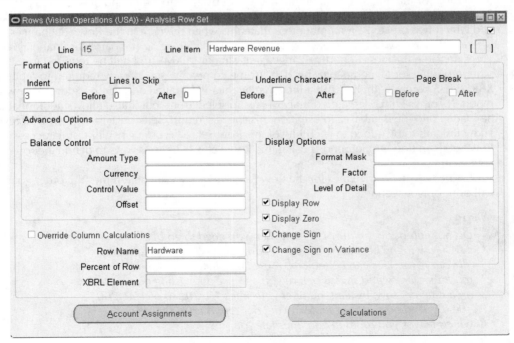

General Ledger Superuser | Reports | Define | Row Set

FIGURE 6-2 *Row Sets*

LINE ITEM is the name that will appear in the left column of your report—in essence, the row headings on your report. You can easily create headers for groups of rows on a report by creating a row with just a Line Number and Line Item, with no accounts or calculations. What will print is just the data in the Line Item. FORMAT OPTIONS are some of the formatting available to you when

General Ledger Superuser | Reports | Define | Row Set | Define Rows

FIGURE 6-3 *Row Lines*

creating reports; additional formatting can be added with Templates in BI Publisher (previously known as XML Publisher). INDENT determines how many spaces you want the Line Item to indent before it prints. LINES TO SKIP is how many rows to skip before and after this row, whereas UNDERLINE CHARACTER is the character (such as _____ and =======) you want to print before or after this row. PAGE BREAK will force a Page Break before or after this row.

Setting up the LINES TO SKIP and PAGE BREAK consistently before or after rows (use one, not both in a Row Set) makes the report easier to maintain, just as adding the UNDERLINE CHARACTER, both before and after, to the row the underline belongs to (such as by specifying that the total row, but not the last row of the details, will have the underline characters before and after) will mean less maintenance when new rows are added. ADVANCED OPTIONS are not required but can help make reports more readable and more detailed, and Row Sets easier to maintain.

BALANCE CONTROLS are traditionally added to a Column Set and will be discussed in the section "Column Definitions."

OVERRIDE COLUMN CALCULATIONS allows Row settings to override the Column Sets. The override is limited to the following fields: AMOUNT TYPES, OFFSET, CONTROL VALUES, FORMAT, FACTOR, DISPLAY ZERO, and LEVEL OF DETAIL. A good example of how this is used is for Format. If you are creating an income statement, where each column has a format of $9,999,999, and one of the rows is Cost of Goods Sold as a % of Gross Margin, you can add a format mask to the row for %99.99 and have that override the column format mask.

ROW NAME is given to a row to be used in calculations instead of the Line Number.

TIP

Using Row Names in Calculations makes seeing what your calculation is doing much easier. Naming your row the same as a Line Item, or a shortened version of that, lets you easily identify the row in a calculation. For example, if your calculation is to Add Line 10 + 20, it is easier to understand what the calculation is doing by creating a calculation that will Add Revenue + COGS. Though I do recommend using Row Names in calculations, sometimes when doing complex calculations involving rows that themselves include calculations, using Row Names instead of Line Numbers may cause inaccurate calculations. This only happens when you are adding rows that also contain calculations, in which case the Line Number should be used.

The setting PERCENT OF ROW works in tandem with the Percent of Column in order to create a column that represents the percentage of a total, such as As a Percent of Revenue. In the Column, enter the column name or number you are using as the basis for your percentage calculation in the PERCENT OF COLUMN field. In the Row, enter the row number or name that is the Total Row (that is, the one that equals 100%—usually a calculated row adding all the other rows up, such as Total Revenue) for each row that you want to calculate a percentage on.

XBRL ELEMENT field is only available if you populated the XBRL Taxonomy on the previous page. You can select the proper element from the dictionary that is in EBS to represent this row's data.

Display Options are used for additional formatting options, such as FORMAT MASK, which formats the number output in the proper format when publishing without using a template (more on templates later). Traditionally, this is set up on the Column Set because an entire column will have the same FORMAT MASK. If it is set on the Row Sets, it would need to be set for every individual row. FACTOR determines to what point the numbers will round to, such as Millions, Billions, Thousands, Units (which does not actually round at all), or Percentiles.

LEVEL OF DETAIL is a very powerful tool in reducing the number of FSGs you create and maintain in your organization. It allows you to create one Row Set with different levels of detail for different levels of management. The Highest level, Controller, typically has the least amount of detail, and the lowest level, Financial Analyst, contains the most detailed data. Create one FSG with detailed lines that have account numbers assigned to them and summary lines that are calculations, and then assign different Levels of Details to these lines to control which lines appear on the report. Only the line with the level you selected or lower will appear on that report. One report can now be created and maintained for all levels of management, reducing time to maintain the reports as well as ensuring that reports going to different people actually have the same data.

DISPLAY ROW controls if a row is displayed on a report. Since the calculations available on an FSG are basic math functions, gathering account balances in a row that is not displayed, and then using them in calculations is a way to create more complex computations. DISPLAY ZERO controls if a row is displayed when there is no value for that row; this is particularly useful on detailed reports where every account is displayed on the report. DISPLAY ZERO can also be a powerful tool to add Proofing rows to your report or to add rows for clearing accounts to bring attention to them when they do not zero out.

An example would be to add a row for Assets – Liabilities – Owners Equity = zero, based on the rows on your report. If this row shows up with a number other than zero, rest assured that your balance sheet does not balance, and you need to look at this *prior* to doing anything else with the report (like giving it to the CFO). The usual culprit? Someone added an account that is not being picked up on a balance sheet row. CHANGE SIGN flips the sign of the account or calculation, allowing Revenue to appear as a positive. CHANGE SIGN ON VARIANCE flips the sign on Variance calculations to allow for variances that are intuitive and make sense (for example, an overage on Revenue is a Positive variance, but an overage on Expenses is a Negative variance).

You can use each defined row as a Header row, which is just a header on the report with no underlying data, or else you can add Account Assignments or Calculations. You cannot do both calculations and account assignments on the same row, which is why having rows that do not display is a necessary feature.

Account Assignments, as seen in Figure 6-4, allow you to add and subtract specific accounts, ranges of accounts, and parent accounts to create either a detailed listing of each account or a total on the report. It also controls the way these accounts display on your report. SIGN has only two options—PLUS or MINUS—and determines if you want to add or subtract the accounts. The ACCOUNTS and DISPLAY fields are the most time-consuming part of setting up and maintaining your Row Sets. Think about how your reporting is structured and try to be consistent when creating multiple Row Sets.

Some basic things to know when adding accounts: Leaving a segment blank is the same as saying from 000–ZZZ but takes less work and is more easily read. Basically, you will get all the available values for that segment. Putting in a range of values will limit EBS to that specific range for the segment. Using a Parent Account will bring in all the amounts for the Child accounts of that parent. And putting a Parent or Range of accounts on one row and then subtracting a specific account out on the next row will in effect remove it from the balance on the row. This works well if you are only displaying the total of the accounts. If you are actually printing out the detailed accounts (as described next), then adding in an account only to subtract it back out has the effect of making the account appear twice on the report—both the addition and the subtraction appear. In this case, it is better either to list the account ranges accurately so that the account is not included or to create a parent that includes the correct accounts.

As a rule, many lines on financial statements are reused from statement to statement with the same account numbers, such as Revenue or Cost of Goods Sold. Using Parent Accounts can

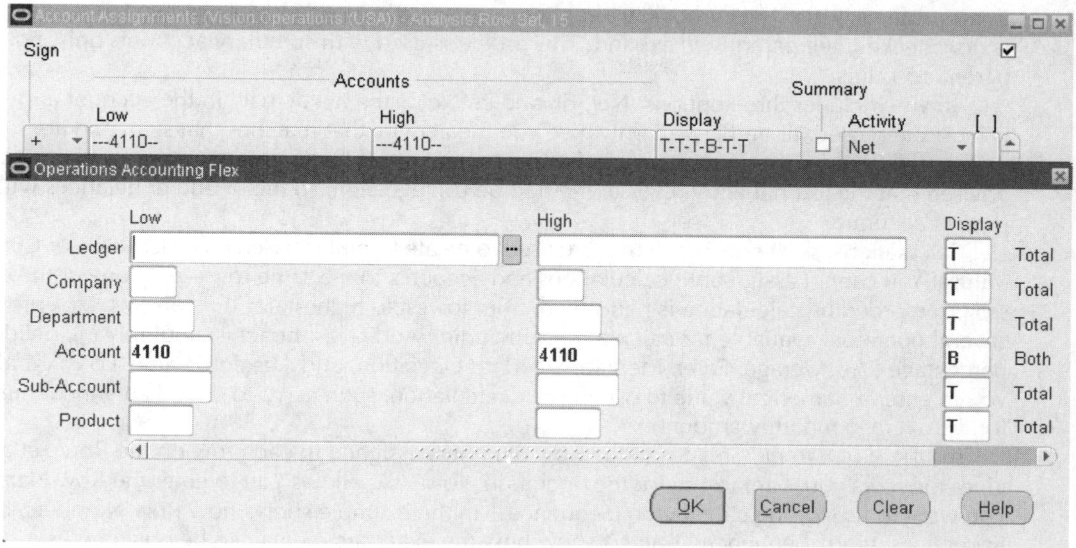

General Ledger Superuser | Reports | Define | Row Set | Define Rows | Account Assignments

FIGURE 6-4   *Adding account ranges to rows*

greatly reduce maintenance required on FSGs because you can maintain a parent, and all your FSGs that use the parent will automatically be updated for the change. If you need to use Ranges, for whatever reason, I recommend making a cheat sheet of the ranges (for instance, Revenue is always Range 4000–4999) so that the same range is used for Revenue on every report that has Revenue. Make sure your ranges are large enough to allow room for growth. This way, when you add an account within the range, you will know that the reports using this range will not need to be maintained, and conversely, you will know that when you add an account outside the range, all your reports will need to be maintained.

LEDGER allows you to select the specific Ledger or a range of Ledgers you want the data to come from, as long as they share the same calendar and Chart of Accounts. When selecting from different Ledgers, the ACTIVITY must be set to NET. DISPLAY determines how the accounts are displayed on a report. The options are all the accounts in a range listed separately (EXPAND), TOTAL only, or BOTH, which displays all the accounts with a total at the end. This option works extremely well when creating detail and summary reports using the Display Option: the rows that have the accounts assigned to them use Detail, which shows all the detailed accounts, and are assigned Supervisor. An additional row is then added, with a calculation, adding the above detail rows, and is assigned Controller. The report created with the Level of Detail of Controller will only have totals, whereas the report created with the Level of Detail of Supervisor will show both the detail and total rows. This allows the same row set to create two different reports, and ensures that they both balance, and updating one report also updates the other.

Only the rows with accounts will need to be maintained, and both reports will always be the same. SUMMARY is a flag that works in conjunction with the Profile Option FSG: Expand Parent Value. When this profile is set to Yes, the profile will override the flag and all accounts belonging to rollup groups will *not* be expanded. All parents *not* belonging to a rollup group *will* be expanded. If this profile is set to No (or not set), then the parent will not expand for any accounts. When it is *not* checked, the parent *will* expand. This profile is used with summary accounts only, not parent accounts.

ACTIVITY includes three options: Net, dr, and cr. Net is the net activity in the account and is most often used. dr and cr will only give you the activity that matches that sign, and are commonly used for such reports as Cash Flow statements. If the cr and dr options are used, it is advised that the journal entry reversal method be Change Sign, so the dr and cr balances will remain accurate.

Calculations, shown in Figure 6-5, are used to create formulas based off other Rows or Constant Values. You cannot assign both calculations and accounts to the same row—only one or the other. SEQ is the order the calculation is performed, from lowest to highest, for this row. OPERATOR provides several operators available for calculations, including Add (+), subtract (-), multiply (*), divide (/), percentage (%), Average, Enter, Median, Standard Deviation, and Absolute Value. CONSTANT allows you to enter a numerical value to use in your calculation, such as 12 to divide an annual number for the average monthly amount.

SEQUENCE: LOW to HIGH relates to the Row Numbers assigned to each row on the Row Set and gives the rows you want to use for the operation. ROW NAME allows you to enter the Row Name you want to use for the calculation. Sequence 1 in the example shows how Row Numbers, or Sequences, work. Sequences 2 and 3 show how the exact same data can be obtained using Row Names. As you can see, Row Names make it easier to see what the calculation is doing, whereas using Row Numbers would require you to go back and see what data is included in Rows 10–19. The names take a little longer to write and maintain but make the Row Sets much easier to read.

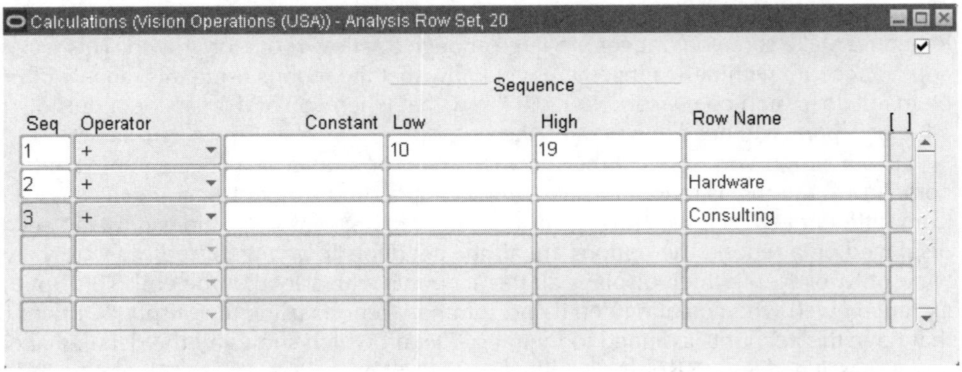

General Ledger Superuser | Reports | Define | Row Set | Define Row | Calculations

FIGURE 6-5   *Adding calculations to rows*

Column Definitions

Column Sets are used to define the Column data across the top of the report. Typically, this is used to define column titles and identify periods you want to appear in each column, and to create variance and calculation columns. As you can see, starting in Figure 6-6, many of the fields in Column Sets will be the same as the fields in Row Sets, allowing for a wide range of financial reporting outside of the traditional income statement and balance sheet formats.

NAME is the unique name of each Column Set created. Being as descriptive as possible will create less confusion when trying to decide which Column Sets to use on predefined Reports or Ad Hoc Reports. Column Sets are often reused on multiple reports. DESCRIPTION is not required but a good practice. Make sure to update the Description as maintenance takes place and Column Sets change.

OVERRIDE SEGMENT can be used to limit a report's data by a specific segment value. Use the Override segment in addition to the Override Value on each Column to override the accounts assigned to the Row Sets. An example would be if the Row Assignments setting selects companies 1–10, select the Company as the Override Segment and then columns can be created for each company that exists between 1 and 10. ENABLE SECURITY will limit access to modify this Column Set, but not to run reports containing this Column Set. The next step is to DEFINE COLUMNS. Many of the fields are the same as the Row Sets, allowing greater design flexibility when creating reports.

Clicking into the Column Details, as seen in Figure 6-7, POSITION is the number of spaces from the left that this column will start to print on the report. You may be thinking, how am I supposed to know where it will look good? Someone at Oracle figured this out as well, and the actual position can be updated when the next step is performed to BUILD COLUMN SET. But since this is a required field, I usually start with a default of 10 for all columns and forget about it. I will change them later, when I create my headings. A word of caution: once you have your report built and are testing, you may have to come back and increase the columns, either here or in the Build

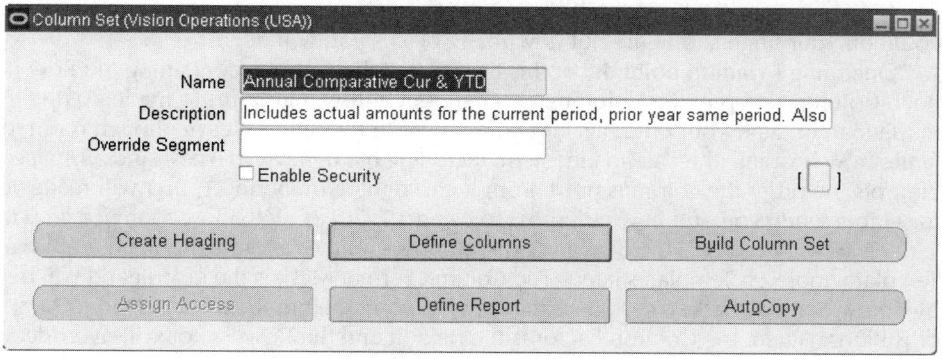

General Ledger Superuser | Reports | Define | Column Set

FIGURE 6-6 *Creating columns for a report*

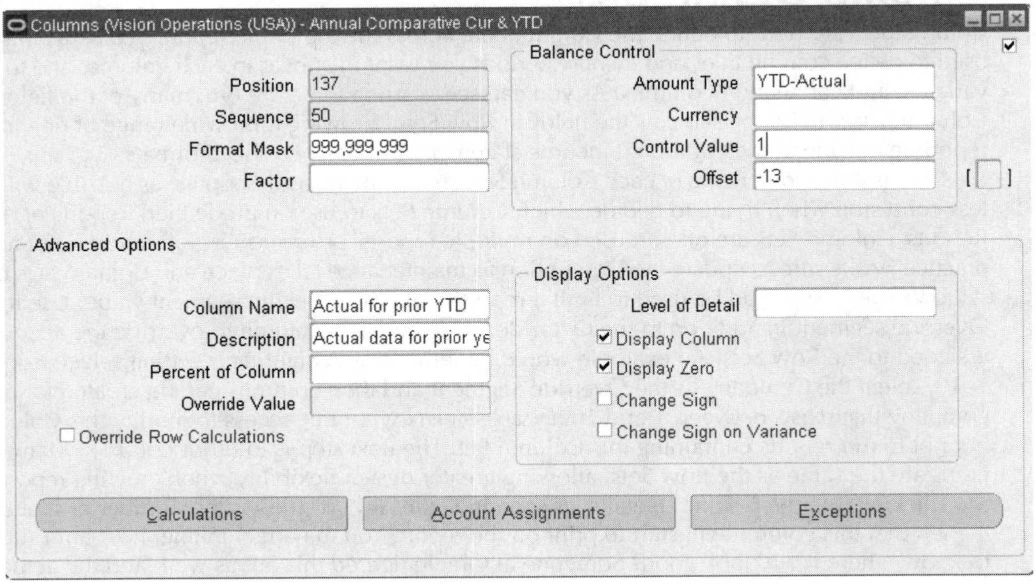

General Ledger Superuser | Reports | Define | Column Set | Define Columns

FIGURE 6-7   *Column details*

Column Sets. If your numbers are coming out as #####, the column is not wide enough for the data in the column. If your gross revenue is 10 million dollars, it is wise to make the column wide enough to accommodate 100 million, including decimal points, commas, and zeros. Yes, you can count on your fingers to figure out how many places you will need.

One thing I want to point out at this time is that the Column containing the Row headings is not a Column set up in the Column Sets at all, but a Row that prints to the left of the first column in the margin. Start your columns far enough over to the right to leave enough room for your largest row heading (the data in Line Item, including the number in INDENT and all spaces). SEQUENCE controls the order the columns print, from left to right. Numbering 1, 2, 3 will make your life miserable when you add new columns, so using 10, 20, 30 will allow room for growth

FORMAT MASK controls the display of the numbers on the output, when you are not using a Template (more on Templates later). The Column Format Mask is the default and will be overridden by a Row Format Mask. FACTOR determines what point the numbers will round to, such as Millions or Billions. Again, the Column Factor is the default and the Row Factor will override it.

BALANCE CONTROL section covers all the information that will control the period of data for this column. AMOUNT TYPE determines what period of financial data will appear (actual or budget, year to date or period to date, and so on). This is a predefined listing that corresponds to balances maintained in the database, so any additional periods will need to be obtained with a calculation. CURRENCY identifies the currency you want to appear on this column, if you have multiple currencies in your General Ledger. The column is the default and any values in the Row will override it.

CONTROL VALUE is used in conjunction with Budgets, Encumbrances, and Currencies. When using an Amount Type of Budget (YTD, PTD, and so on), you need to tell EBS which Budget you want to use for this report. The Control Value is any value you want to assign: 1, 2, 50. Then this

Control Value is added to the REPORT and linked to a Budget, an Encumbrance, a constant period, or a Currency. Since this is assigned at the Report level, it means that a Column Set having a Control Value of 1 can mean two different things on two different reports. It also means that if two Column Sets have a control value of 1, they again can have two different meanings.

Figure 6-8 shows an example of how the CONTROL VALUE of 1 is assigned to the BIS CORPORATE budget—any row or column where the Control Value of 1 is assigned for this report will show the relevant data for this budget. CURRENCIES associates the CONTROL VALUE of 2 with Entered transactions with a Currency of USD, and CONSTANT PERIODS OF INTEREST (POI) selects the thirteenth period of 2002, whereas the numbers for this period will appear on all columns and rows where the CONTROL VALUE of 3 appears. A CONTROL VALUE number is available to be set up only where the actual value appears on either the Row Set or the Column Set associated with this report.

OFFSET determines how many months away from the period a report is run for that report should appear. If you run the report for May-07, and it is PTD information, and you want to show May-06 data, the Offset would be –12, whereas 12 would give you May-08 numbers. Remember to count any adjustment periods, if you have them set up, when determining which month EBS prints based on the offset. One year prior is actually –13 when one adjustment period is set up.

ADVANCED OPTIONS allow some advanced features to be set up, such as COLUMN NAME, which is used the same as ROW NAMES in calculations. DESCRIPTION will default in on the Build Column Sets as the column title that will print on the report. I like to be as consistent as possible between Column Name and Description. PERCENT OF COLUMN and PERCENT OF ROW work in tandem with each other in order to create a Percent of Total column. In the Column, enter the column name or number you are using as the basis for your percentage calculation in the PERCENT OF COLUMN field. In the Row, enter the Row number or Name that is the Total Row (that is, the one that equals 100 percent, usually a calculated row adding all the other rows up) for each row that you want to calculate a percentage on.

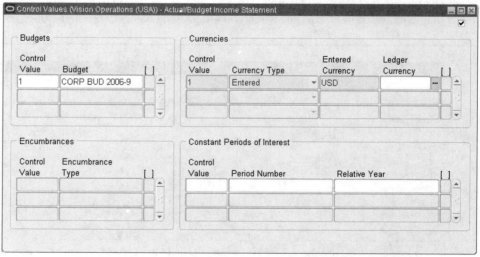

General Ledger Superuser | Reports | Define | Report | Control Values button

FIGURE 6-8 *Assigning a control value to a report*

OVERRIDE VALUE is used to override a specific segment value for that column and is only available when the Override Segment is identified on the Column Set header page. Using this feature allows Financial Statements to be created where one column represents one balancing segment (or company) in an organization. OVERRIDE ROW CALCULATIONS allows Column settings to override the Row settings when the Row settings are the default. These fields are limited to overriding the Row Accounts and/or Calculations, and Activity (DR, CR, or Net).

DISPLAY OPTIONS allow display settings to be created for this column, such as LEVEL OF DETAIL, which works much the same way Level of Detail works on Row and identifies if a Column will appear on a report for a specific function or level. DISPLAY COLUMN allows columns to be created for calculations and not displayed. DISPLAY ZERO determines if a column will show if it has data equaling zero. CHANGE SIGN reverses the sign on the balance of the accounts. CHANGE SIGN ON VARIANCE reverses the sign on variances.

Calculations, shown in Figure 6-9, can be added to reports to create column data where EBS does not provide an AMOUNT TYPE for the calculation required. EBS does provide a large number of amount types, including variances, eliminating the need for many calculations. Column Set Calculations will always override the Row Set Calculations unless you tell the Rows to override the Column calculations. This is important to know when you are troubleshooting FSGs that are not footing correctly. Add the SEQUENCE number, which will determine in what order the calculation is performed.

The same OPERATORS are available in Column Set Calculations that are available in Row Set Calculations. CONSTANT is used to have a constant value in the calculation. Use a constant only when it is truly a constant that will never change; if this number may change from time to time, even infrequently, set up a STAT account for it instead and maintain it there. One "constant" often seen set up is outstanding shares, used in Earnings per Share calculations, but this number does change, though infrequently, and should be in a STAT account so that FSGs are not maintained when the rare changes do happen. Add either a SEQUENCE LOW and HIGH or a COLUMN NAME.

Column Account Assignments work exactly like Row Account Assignments.

Exceptions allow you to flag rows in a given column that meet specific criteria, such as being over a certain dollar value (see Figure 6-10). FLAG allows you to enter the symbol you want to use to flag data. DESCRIPTION explains when you are flagging data. CONDITION includes predefined

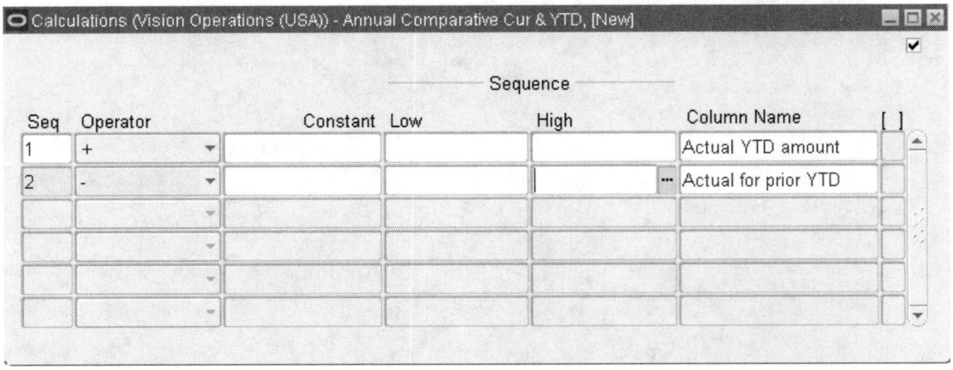

General Ledger Superuser | Reports | Define | Column Sets | Define Columns | Calculations

FIGURE 6-9 *Column calculations*

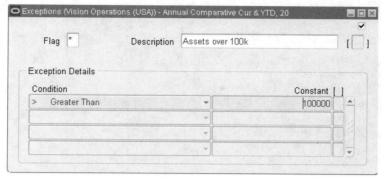

General Ledger Superuser | Reports | Define | Column Set | Define Columns | Exceptions button

FIGURE 6-10   *Exceptions*

conditions you can select from, such as Greater Than, Less Than, Equal To. CONSTANT is the value
you are comparing to the amounts in the row for that column.

Continue creating additional rows for the columns until all the columns have been defined.
Once that is done, you are ready to Build your Column Set. Select Build Column Set from the
main Column Set page.

CAUTION
*If this is an existing report, any formatting you previously did will
be lost once you select this button! If you are modifying an existing
report, you may want to use the Create Headings screen instead.*

As mentioned earlier, Figure 6-11 shows how the BUILD COLUMN SET function allows you to
format the way the headers and spacing on your columns will look on your report. Even if you
decide to use the defaults for the columns and to make no changes, you must still click BUILD YOUR
COLUMN SET and save it. You can also make some changes to the fields that were entered in the
Define Columns form. SEQUENCE, NAME, AMOUNT TYPE, and OFFSET all default in from the Define
Column form but can be modified if needed. None of these fields will show on the report, but
they do affect the way the report behaves.

LEFT MARGIN is the number of spaces allowed for the LINE ITEM on the Row Sets, basically your
row titles. WIDTH is the number of characters for each column. Notice that here, it is not the
number of characters form the left of the page, but the actual characters for each column.
Remember when reviewing the widths to make them at least one wider than the data printing
(including decimals, commas, and brackets for negative numbers) in the column to prevent
problems when running the report.

Notice that on this form, the width is the width of the column, not the number of spaces from
the left margin, as it is on the Define Columns form (POSITION). This makes it much easier to create
your column widths on this form, as opposed to counting how many spaces from the left you
want this column to appear. HEADING will default in from the AMOUNT TYPE for the first row, and the

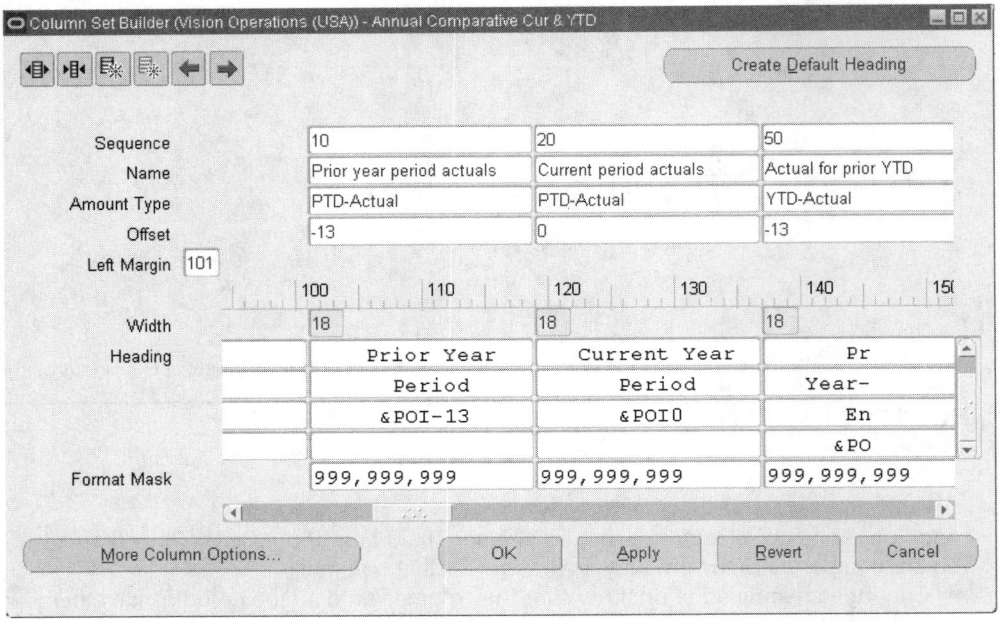

General Ledger Superuser | Reports | Define | Column Set | Build Column Set button

FIGURE 6-11 *Building the column headings*

odd-looking second line (&POI0) actually tells EBS what period this column is for—literally Period Of Interest. The zero at the end tells EBS to put the month and year this report is run for on this column, whereas &POI-1 would be the month prior. All this information can be changed as needed from the defaults. Click CREATE DEFAULT HEADING at any time to get back to the defaults. To save your changes, click APPLY, and to undo the last change that was saved, click REVERT.

MORE COLUMN OPTIONS will allow updates to be made to the column CURRENCY, CONTROL VALUES, OVERRIDE VALUES, PERCENT OF COLUMN, and OVERRIDE ROW CALCULATIONS. Also, the FORMATTING OPTIONS and DESCRIPTION can be maintained. The buttons on the top left of the form allow you to increase or decrease the width of a column, delete or add a column, or move columns left or right.

Figure 6-12 also helps to create headings on the report, same as the Build Column Sets form, but it gives a graphical presentation of how it will look on the report—though it is not necessary to use this feature, it can sometimes help to see what the report will look like for the headings without printing it out. If you do make a change on this form, such as adding a space to center something, it will move all the positions to the right over one, causing them to be off.

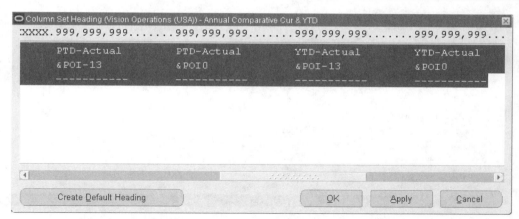

General Ledger Superuser | Reports | Define | Column Set | Create Heading button

FIGURE 6-12 *Column Headings visual view*

Restricting Content

Content Sets are a powerful tool that can limit data on a report, therefore allowing the same Row Set to be used on multiple reports, as well as create multiple reports from a single Row Set and a single Column Set combined into one report. For example, if more than one Sequence is added with account assignments on the Content Set, each sequence will create one report, restricting the data for each page to only the data that falls within the range. Refer to Figure 6-13 to see an example of this. In this way, one Report can be used to create a P&L for each department, creating a separate report for each one. The advantage to creating a report with a Content Set, as opposed to multiple reports and using segment overrides, is that they can all be run at the same time. Also, Content Sets can be added when the report is run, making the same report available to multiple users, who add their own respective Content Sets.

When developing an FSG strategy for your company, there are two different ways Content Sets can be used. First, multiple reports can be created using the same Row and Column Sets, but having different Content Sets. This works well when there are a large number of users who will be running these reports, as it limits the training requirements and controls the data the users will run on a report, but it is more work to set it up. In an organization where Financial Analysts run all the reports and then analyze and disburse the data, it is worth creating core reports with standard Row and Column Sets, and allowing each analyst to add his or her own Content Sets when they are run. I prefer this option when there is a very finite number of users running reports, and they all need the same basic reports with different company or department combinations.

The CONTENT SET is the name of the set, and it is what appears in the list of values when users select a Content Set when submitting an FSG or assign one to a report. Add a DESCRIPTION to further identify why this was set up and how it is to be used, remembering to update the description

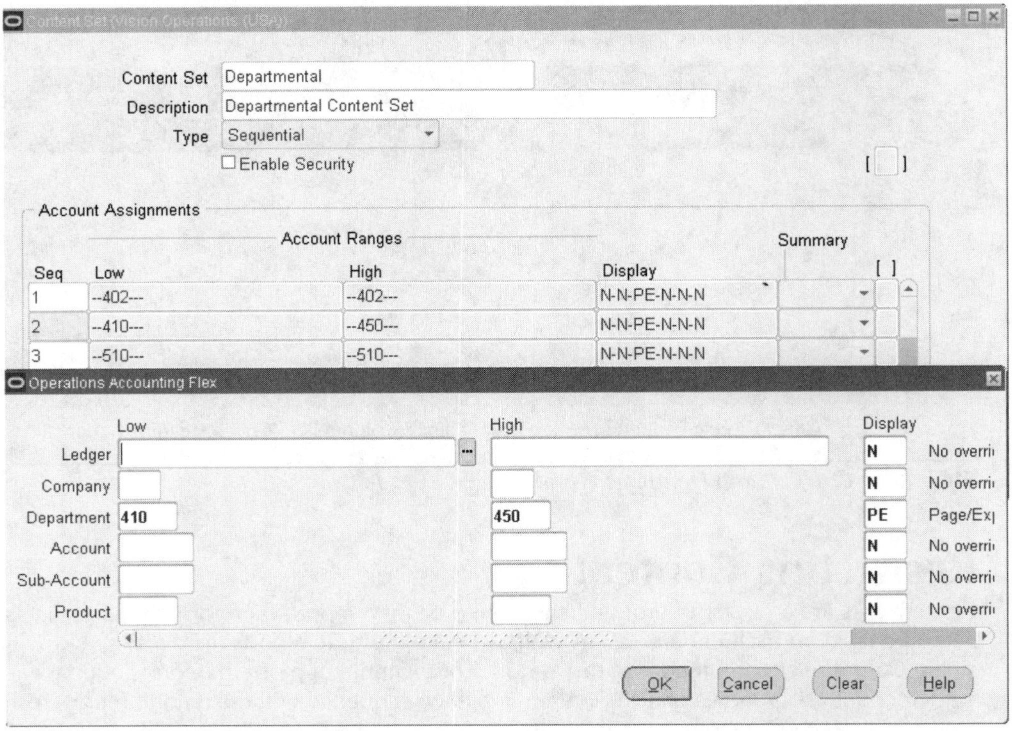

General Ledger Superuser | Reports | Define | Content Set

FIGURE 6-13   *Content sets allow data to be restricted.*

when the Content Set is updated. TYPE will determine how the FSG will run if it is to create multiple output sheets. SEQUENTIAL will run reports one at a time, whereas parallel will run multiple reports at the same time. Selecting SEQUENTIAL can reduce the system resources required to run this report, as only one report will run at a time. Also, if there is one report that requires data from the previous report to be calculated prior to its use, SEQUENTIAL is required so that the calculations are performed and completed prior to the line they are used on.

ACCOUNT ASSIGNMENTS determines the data and pages this report will produce. SEQUENCE is the order the reports will run and publish. ACCOUNT RANGES, LOW and HIGH will determine what value you are overriding or selecting for a given report. Any segments not filled in will be ignored and only the data that is completed will be picked up and used. In this example, the first sheet will be department 402 and the second will be department 410-450.

DISPLAY determines what detail will appear for the override value. There are a few more options than on Row and Column account assignments. CT displays only a total balance for the segment. N uses the Row Set Definition with no override at all. PE expands the range and creates a page for each segment in the range. When using a parent, this will produce a page for each child. PT does not expand Parent Accounts into separate pages but gives a page for each parent. RB shows all the accounts in a range on the same page but does not provide a total for them. RE creates multiple rows for all the segments in the range. RT shows all the accounts in a range on the same page and includes a total at the end.

Ordering Detailed Account Information

Row Orders are used to determine in what order the expanded, or detailed, data within a row will print out on the report. The rows will print out in the order of the SEQUENCE numbers you assigned them, but if you selected any of the data to EXPAND, Row Orders determines the order of the expanded data. In Figure 6-14, ROW ORDER is the name the users will see when selecting a Row Order. DESCRIPTION is a detailed description of what this row order does or when it should be used. Selecting ENABLE SECURITY allows this Row Order to be modified only by users with the proper access, though everyone can use it.

You have two options in creating a Row Order: Rank by Column or Account Display. RANK BY COLUMN allows you to order your rows based on the values in a specific column. Select the Column NAME from the list of values (yes, you see every column in the database). Alternatively, enter the displayed column number you want to ORDER by. For example if the third column on a report is the column you want to use, but there is a hidden column between columns 1 and 2, enter a **4** in the ORDER field. Though selecting this column does make this Row Order usable for multiple reports, it will be incorrect if you add a column to your report. Select the RANK as ASCENDING or DESCENDING. The other option is to sort your data by the account number or the description. Note that both these options are used only to sort data with a specific section, or one defined row on a report where Expand is used.

Setting up the ACCOUNT DISPLAY will also control what fields of the account number are displayed on the report. The SEQUENCE determines the order in which the segments are both displayed and ranked. SEGMENT is the accounting segment you want to sort on or display. It is not required to sort or display all of your segments. ORDER BY gives you the options of which value you want to actually sort on, selecting from VALUE for the segment value, DESCRIPTION for the segment description, and

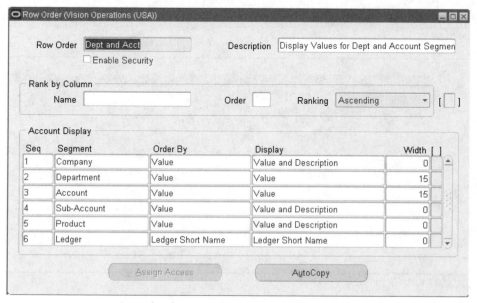

General Ledger Superuser | Reports | Define | Order

FIGURE 6-14 *Row Order*

COLUMN to use the column defined in RANK BY COLUMN. DISPLAY determines if the Value, the Description, or both Value and Description will display on the report, and the WIDTH is how many characters the DISPLAY will have. A WIDTH of zero can be used when you want a specific SEGMENT to be used for ranking the order, but not to have that field displayed when printing. Creating a WIDTH one larger than the segments, when displaying only the segment value, can resolve the problem where the entire segment is not displayed.

Display Options to Control Rows and Columns Displayed on a Report

Display Sets and Display Groups, like Content Sets, can limit data on a report, but instead of using account segments, they use Rows and Columns to limit data. The same report can be used to create an Income Statement with Earnings per Share, and an Income Statement without Earnings per Share, by adding a Display Group. Display Groups identify ranges of rows or columns, and Display Sets combine Display Groups together. Sets can be used either to identify what row or column data to display or exclude from the report. It is important to understand that this option will only exclude the data; the Row and Column headings will still appear on the report.

Display Groups

Display Groups only need to be created if there is a range of rows or columns you do not want to display on a specific report. Figure 6-15 is an example of setting up a Display Group. Give the group a meaningful NAME and DESCRIPTION. Identify either a ROW SET or a COLUMN SET where you do not want to see specific rows or columns. Since the Display Group is limited to either one or the other, you will have to create two Display Groups to restrict the displayed data for both. Identify the FROM and TO SEQUENCES, identifying which Rows or Columns you want to add to the group.

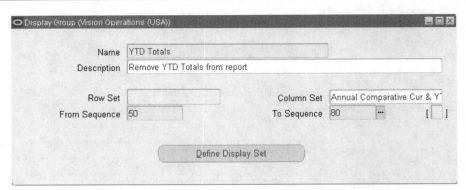

General Ledger Superuser | Reports | Define | Display | Group

FIGURE 6-15 *Display Groups*

Display Sets

Display Sets combine multiple Display Groups into one set for use on a report, as shown in Figure 6-16. Both Display Sets and Groups must be set up to use this feature. Assign a meaningful NAME and DESCRIPTION. Enter a Row and/or Column Set to be excluded (or included) from the report. Though these are not required fields, entering data in them will limit the Display Groups that appear on the list of values. Enter a unique SEQ for each line. DISPLAY determines if the data on this Row or Column Group will be displayed. Since a Display Set is typically created to hide data, this is usually not checked. Any rows or columns not included in a Row or Display Group will by default print on the report. Add either the ROW or COLUMN GROUP you want included in this set. DESCRIPTION is optional and can help explain why this data is being excluded from this specific report.

Putting It All Together

Of all the features just discussed (Row Set, Column Set, Content Set, Order, and Display), only Row Set and Column Set are required to create a report. And these two components take the longest to create and maintain. So adding additional components that allow the same Row or

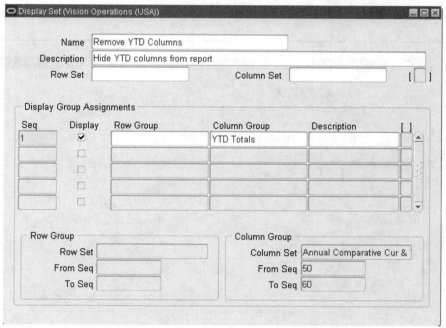

General Ledger Superuser | Reports | Define | Display | Set

FIGURE 6-16   *Display Sets*

Column Sets to be reused on multiple reports can help reduce the amount of maintenance required to keep your FSGs up to date and running smoothly.

We started at Reports, showing how all the pieces fit together—and that is where we will end, as shown in Figure 6-17. Complete the REPORT name and TITLE of the report, adding a DESCRIPTION of what the report will display. Add at a minimum a ROW SET and a COLUMN SET. Optionally add a CONTENT SET, a ROW ORDER, and a DISPLAY SET. The Other Options allow additional flexibility in FSGs so that you can reuse the same components and achieve different report data.

SEGMENT OVERRIDE allows you to override a specific segment of the account combination when running the report. This will override *all* components, including Row and Column Sets. CURRENCY assigns a specific Currency for this report overriding all components' currency settings. The ROUNDING OPTION determines how calculations are done for this report. LEVEL OF DETAIL allows you to assign a Level of Detail to each Row or Column. Entering a Level of Detail will restrict this report to only rows and columns that match. The OUTPUT OPTION determines the default Output for the report and will be overridden, depending on where you actually run the report.

An important thing to remember when creating reports is that many of these options can be added or changed when running reports. Currency, Segment Override, Content Set, Row Order, Display Set, Rounding Options, if Exceptions are used, and Output Options can all be added or changed. So the decision comes into play, do I create multiple reports, selecting different values for these options, which will make it easier for the users, or create one basic report, and train the users how to select the proper options? Both choices have pros and cons.

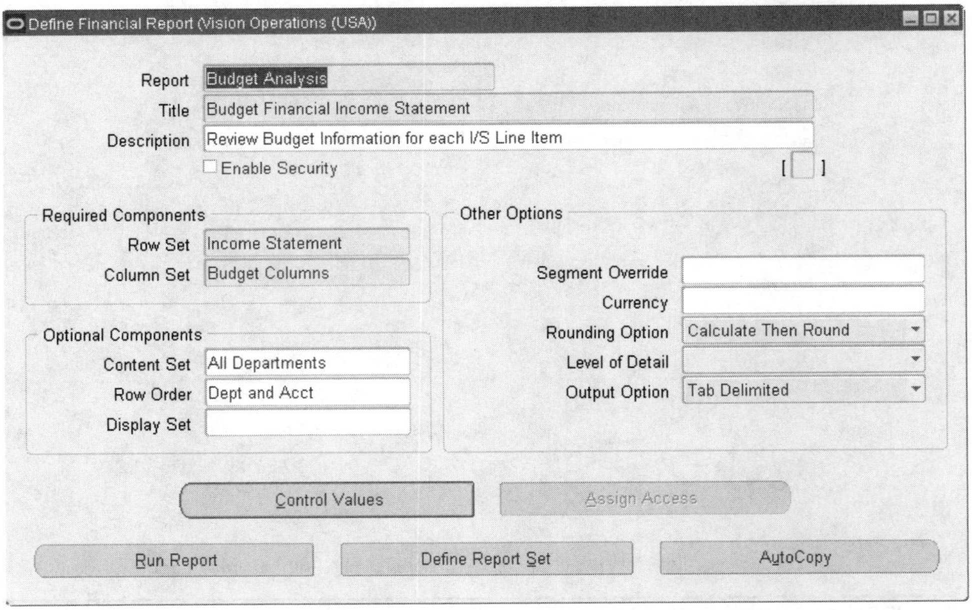

General Ledger Superuser | Reports | Define | Report

FIGURE 6-17 *Report definition, combining all the components*

Report Maintenance

Once a report is created and in use, it never needs to be maintained or new reports created ever again. Right? Not so? So let's learn about a few features that can help with this process.

Copying in the Same Instance

The AutoCopy feature (Figure 6-18) allows any component of an FSG to be copied, either to be modified for a new reporting requirement, or for troubleshooting. When a problem crops up on an established FSG, it sometimes takes a little bit of detective work as well as trial and error to find and resolve it—and of course these problems never happen during the slow time of month, when there is time for a leisurely clone. Usually, the problem will not exist in a test environment but will need to be resolved prior to your getting to go home. Copying the report components, and troubleshooting them in the copy, allows the report to stay intact while another copy has the chaotic changes made to it to try to figure out the problem. This is a safe way of "troubleshooting in production" without danger.

Select the COMPONENT you want to copy from the list. The SOURCE is the existing Row Set or Report or Column Set you want to copy. Its list is restricted by the Component you select. The TARGET is the new name you want to give the Copy; it can be any unique name. Clicking COPY starts the concurrent process. Note that if a Report is copied, it is only the report itself that EBS makes a copy of; the components associated with it are still the original Row and Column Sets. For this reason, it is better to copy the component that is causing the problem, and then copy the report (or create a new one), substituting the copied Row/Column Set with the copied one.

Copying from One Instance to Another

In addition to copying a component to a new one, they can also be copied from one database to another, such as Test to Production. Before this transfer can be made, a database link will need to be set up between the two instances. You will probably need the assistance of your DBA to create this link. Set up the Database Link in the instance you want to transfer the FSGs to, as shown in Figure 6-19. For example, if the FSG resides in Test and you want to move it to Production, set up the Link in Production.

DATABASE NAME is the name of where you are copying the data from, in this case, TEST. Run this SQL: SELECT value FROM v$parameter WHERE UPPER(name) = 'DB_NAME'. DESCRIPTION is a description of the database you are connecting to; it can be any description that makes sense to

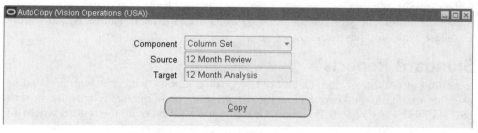

General Ledger Superuser | Reports | Autocopy

FIGURE 6-18   *Copying reports and components*

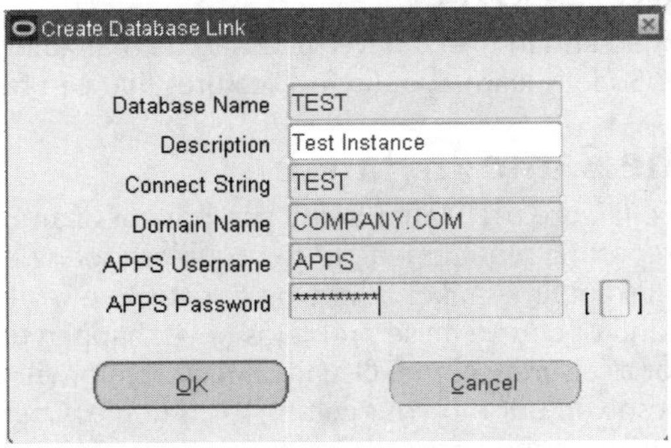

General Ledger Superuser | Setup | System | Database Links

FIGURE 6-19 *Copying reports or components between instances*

the users. CONNECT STRING points to the database from which you want to Copy, again, TEST in this case. This is usually the SID in the TNS Names files on the server. DOMAIN NAME is the domain for the database you want to Copy from. This can be obtained by running this SQL: SELECT value FROM v$parameter WHERE UPPER(name) = 'DB_DOMAIN'.

APPS USERNAME is from the database, and it is not the user name you sign in with to the application. Companies may want to set up a custom user name and password to create this link; just ensure it has the proper privileges, not only to access the data, but to establish the database link. APPS PASSWORD is usually a secure password and the DBA will usually type this in for you.

Once the Database Link is defined, you can run the Concurrent Request FSG Transfer Program to move any component from the linked database to the instance you are in. Any component you transfer over must have a unique name in the instance you are moving it to. This means if you were working on a problem or change to a Row Set that already existed in PROD, where you are moving it to, you must change the name in either test or prod so that it is a unique name.

For COMPONENT TYPE, either select a specific component or select ALL to copy all components. For COMPONENT NAME, you can enter the name you want to transfer, or leave the value blank to transfer all of them. This can be used only if a Specific Component was selected first. SOURCE DB CHART OF ACCOUNTS is the Chart of Accounts the FSGs are coming from. There is no list of values for the Component Name or Source DB Chart of Accounts. Use caution and be sure to type the names *exactly* as they appear, or the program will not transfer the data! TARGET DB CHART OF ACCOUNTS is the Chart of Accounts you want the FSG to copy to. Use the list of values to correctly enter the name. When selecting the SOURCE DATABASE, select from the list of values, which will show the Database Links you have already set up.

Standard Reports

In addition to AutoCopy and Database Links, some reports that come with EBS can be extremely useful to maintain and keep track of the reports and components. Perhaps the most useful is the FSG – Where Used report. This report will provide a listing of all the reports where a specific account string, Row Set, Column Set, Content Set, or some combination of these is used. It is extremely helpful in finding all the reports using a component, prior to modifying it. Other reports include listings of the different components, as well as the entire report, that can be printed out and reviewed. All these reports begin with "FSG."

Running FSG Reports

In R12, FSG reports can only be published with BI (Business Intelligence) Publisher. This was formerly called XML Publisher. There are two options for publishing the reports: either by running a concurrent request that will create a PDF file, or by submitting it from the Report Manager and selecting a template to use. There are some distinct differences between the two options.

Running the report can be done either from the concurrent program called Program – Run Financial Statement Generator or by going to the form Reports | Request | Financial. Once this report runs, a concurrent process call Program – Publish FSG Report is spawned, which takes the FSG output from the request in XML, and overlays the seeded template called FSGXML for formatting and publishing. This template publishes the FSG in Rich Text Format (RTF), a universal format for word processing. Per MetaLink, this template default cannot be changed or modified. When a report is run this way, the data resides in the concurrent manager. That was the technical explanation of what goes on. For the functional users, reports that are run from the concurrent manager or from the report form cannot be stored in the Report Manager but only viewed in PDF with a predefined look. And perhaps the most important thing is that drill-downs cannot be performed on reports run this way.

Report Manager

Running and publishing the report in Oracle's Report Manager has more robust capability, the most important being that any template (seeded or custom) can be used to publish the report, the reports are saved in a Report Repository, where any person with the proper rights can view it, and drill-downs can be enabled for analysis. From the Report Manager Superuser responsibility, you have the ability to create new templates as well as run the report.

Templates

To create a new template or modify an existing one, use the Financial Report Template Editor seen in Figure 6-20. You can either select an existing template or create one from scratch using a specific FSG as a model. Excel is used as the TEMPLATE EDITOR. When saving the template back into EBS, you have the option to ENABLE FSG DRILLDOWNS, which will allow users to see detailed account balances and transactions for rows with account assignments, aiding in analysis. Without this option selected on the template, drill-downs are not available. It is important to know that drill-downs also do not exist on rows with calculations. This Financial Report Template Editor can only be used to create Excel templates for FSG reports. The XML Publisher responsibility can be used to create RTF or other types of templates.

When creating or modifying a template, you will always need to select the REPORT NAME for EBS to use as a guide for the template. You then have the option to CREATE NEW or MODIFY EXISTING templates. Creating a new template will default the columns and rows based on the report that was selected, while MODIFY EXISTING will overlay an existing template and will need modifications to accommodate the Column and Row data on a specific report. Select the LANGUAGE to enable the reports to be run in different languages. Choose Excel Template Editor as the EDITOR and click Create. This will open Excel with the Template.

Once the template is opened in Excel, as seen in Figure 6-21, all the formatting is done similar to formatting an Excel spreadsheet; you can add fonts, column widths and row heights, number formatting, and colors. All data on the template that starts with an ampersand (&) will be replaced with specific data from the FSG itself; for example, &LedgerName will be replaced with the Ledger this report represents, and &40 refers to either the Row or Column number, depending

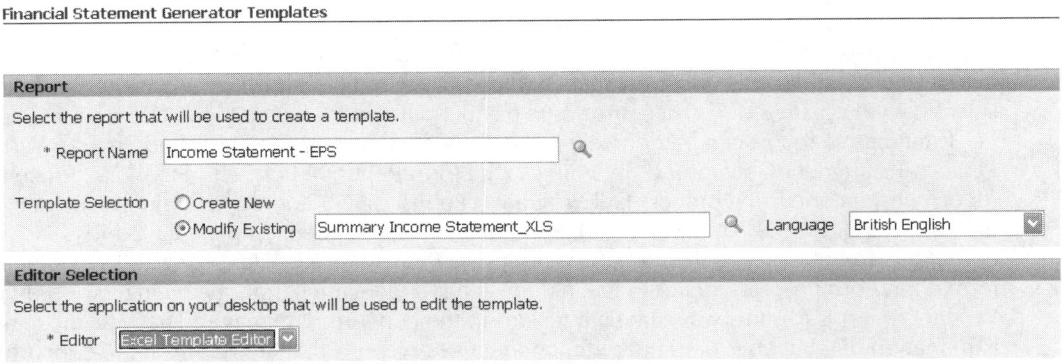

Financial Statement Generator Templates

Report

Select the report that will be used to create a template.

* Report Name Income Statement - EPS 🔍

Template Selection   ○ Create New
                      ⊙ Modify Existing Summary Income Statement_XLS 🔍   Language British English ⬇

Editor Selection

Select the application on your desktop that will be used to edit the template.

* Editor Excel Template Editor ⬇

Report Manager Superuser | Financial Report Template Editor

FIGURE 6-20 *Editing report templates*

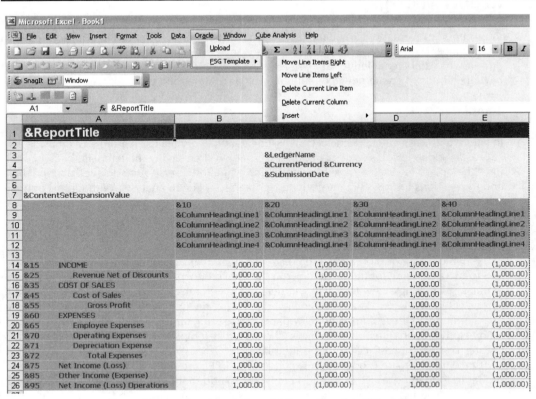

Report Manager Superuser | Financial Report Template Editor | Create

FIGURE 6-21 *Editing template details*

on where it is located. Additional data elements and columns or rows can be added by using the Oracle menu in the Excel toolbar. This menu is loaded when the template is downloaded from EBS. Images can also be saved with the template, to include company logos and other pictures. Images must be in one of the following formats: .PNG, .GIF, .JPEG, or .BMP.

Changes made are not made in EBS at the same time; they need to be uploaded back into EBS to be used. Select Oracle| Upload from the Excel toolbar to get the box shown in Figure 6-22, and assign the TEMPLATE NAME. Add a DESCRIPTION to explain what this template includes so that it can be used on more than one report. Select the LANGUAGE this report will be displayed in.

The next two check boxes are important in uploading and functionality of the template. You must check OVERWRITE EXISTING TEMPLATE if you modified a template and want to save the modification with the same name. You must check ENABLE DRILLDOWN if you want to use the drill-down feature with this template; if it is not checked, the feature will not be available. Select UPLOAD, and close the forms when the upload is completed. Once the report template is saved, it will now default in for the report that was selected when it was created, though it can be overridden when the report is run from the Report Manager. This template is also available to assign to any other FSG, and it usually works well if the report the template was designed from and the other report have the same Row Set.

Running Reports

Running the report from the Report Manager allows it to be saved into the Repository for future reference. First, select the FSG name, period, and other components as you would when running the report from the General Ledger (see Figure 6-23). If you select a currency at this time, the currency must be associated with the Primary Ledger as a Reporting currency.

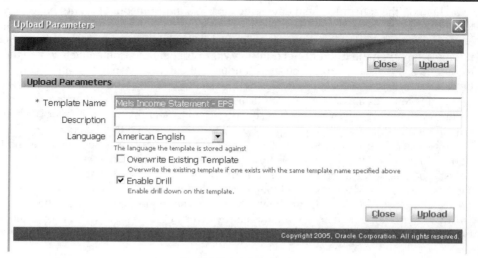

Excel | Oracle | Upload

FIGURE 6-22   *Uploading report templates back into EBS*

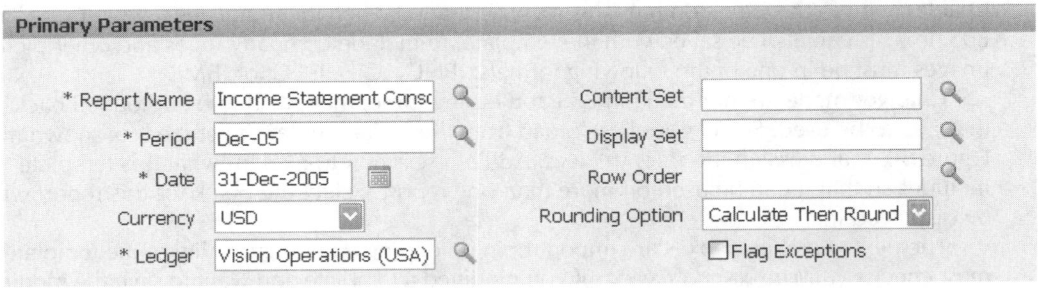

Primary Parameters

* Report Name	Income Statement Conso	Content Set	
* Period	Dec-05	Display Set	
* Date	31-Dec-2005	Row Order	
Currency	USD	Rounding Option	Calculate Then Round
* Ledger	Vision Operations (USA)		☐ Flag Exceptions

Report Manager Superuser | Financial Report Submission

FIGURE 6-23 *Running reports from Report Manager*

Referring to Figure 6-24, select a DEFAULT TEMPLATE from the Repository for this report; once this is completed the first time, this template will default in for future reports until it is changed. The TIMEFRAME field allows a time frame to be added to a report so that the exact date it pertains to is known; this field gets its values from the Calendar set up in General Ledger. By setting up a new calendar (do not associate it to any LEDGER), as well as a Type, you can have daily periods available in the TIMEFRAME field that read "PRE-JAN 01, 08," "PRE-JAN 02, 08," and so on. This will then be appended onto the end of the report name, enabling you to store more than one version of the report in the Report Repository. This can be especially useful during the month end when you want to keep the history of a balance sheet during a close process. This field does not affect the data on the report; it only appends to the end of the name of the report when it is saved.

Selecting Yes for SET AUTO ARCHIVE allows you to enter a date when this report will automatically be archived from the Report Repository. This is useful during the close, to set all preliminary reports to archive on the scheduled final day of the close, so that someone does not have to go into the Report Manager and manually archive them. Select the date for archiving in the next field.

SECURITY can be added to a report based on the Flexfield security set up in the General Ledger for any segment in the Chart of Accounts; it will restrict data in Content Sets where the data is expanded as PE. USER TO VALUE security is unique to the Report Manager; it allows any Value Set to be created and assigned as security, restricting data to only the values included in the Value Sets. Again, this requires a Content Set with PE as the expand option to be effective. User to Value security will always override Flexfield security. The last security option is CUSTOM SECURITY, which will allow a custom PL/SQL package to be written and attached to this report.

AVAILABILITY determines when users can see this report: NOW, on a Specific date and time, or ON HOLD, which prevents them from seeing it until it is reviewed. No matter when it is available, it will still be data as of when the report was run, not the date it is available.

The REVIEWERS field allows additional reviewers to be added to reports that are to be available on a specific date and time, or one that is on hold. The requestor will always be the first reviewer, so any names added here are for additional reviewers. Once a reviewer approves the report, it becomes eligible for viewing (depending on when the specific date and time were set for; it will

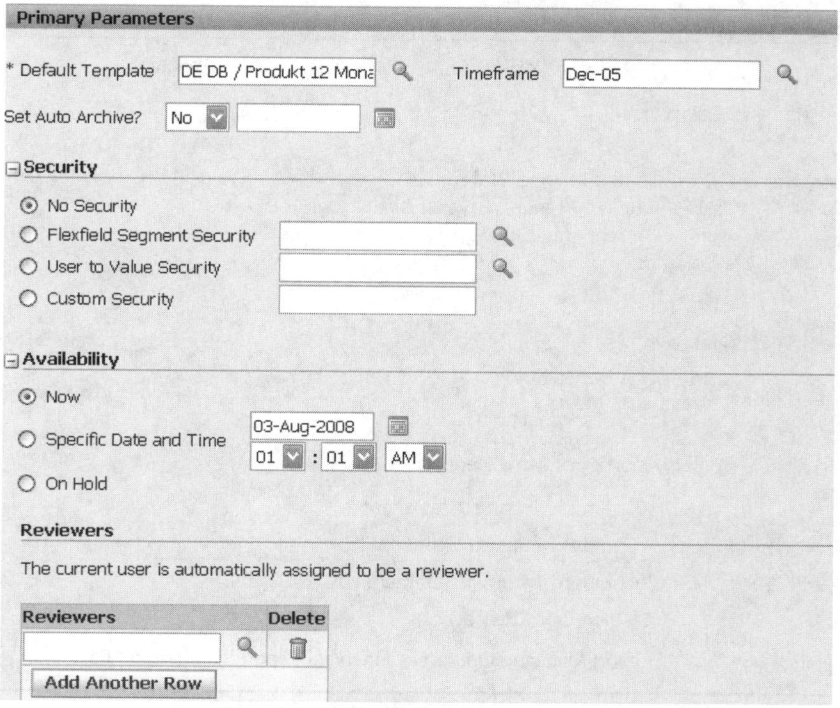

Primary Parameters

* Default Template   DE DB / Produkt 12 Mona   Timeframe   Dec-05

Set Auto Archive?   No

Security

- No Security
- Flexfield Segment Security
- User to Value Security
- Custom Security

Availability

- Now
- Specific Date and Time   03-Aug-2008   01 : 01   AM
- On Hold

Reviewers

The current user is automatically assigned to be a reviewer.

Reviewers	Delete

Add Another Row

Report Manager Superuser | Financial Report Submission | Page 2

FIGURE 6-24   *Selecting report parameters*

not be available prior to that date even if it is reviewed). Reviewers' approvals pertain to *all* of the report, not just the portion that security allows a specific person to review. Next, you can assign a Location where the report will be saved in the Repository, as well as a report name—if the report name is not entered, the actual name of the report will be used. If a report by the name already exists, and a unique TIMEFRAME was not selected, then the new report will save over the old report, which will be lost.

Once the report is submitted, it will run and be saved into the Report Repository. The report can then be viewed from the concurrent request manager, or from the Repository Manager | Repository Management, as shown in Figure 6-25. Select the branch of the tree where the report was saved, and select VIEW next to the report name. If a TIMEFRAME was assigned to a report that was run multiple times, the different report versions will be one level down on the tree. You still VIEW the report from the top level, but once it is published, you can change the TIMEFRAME to get a different version of the report.

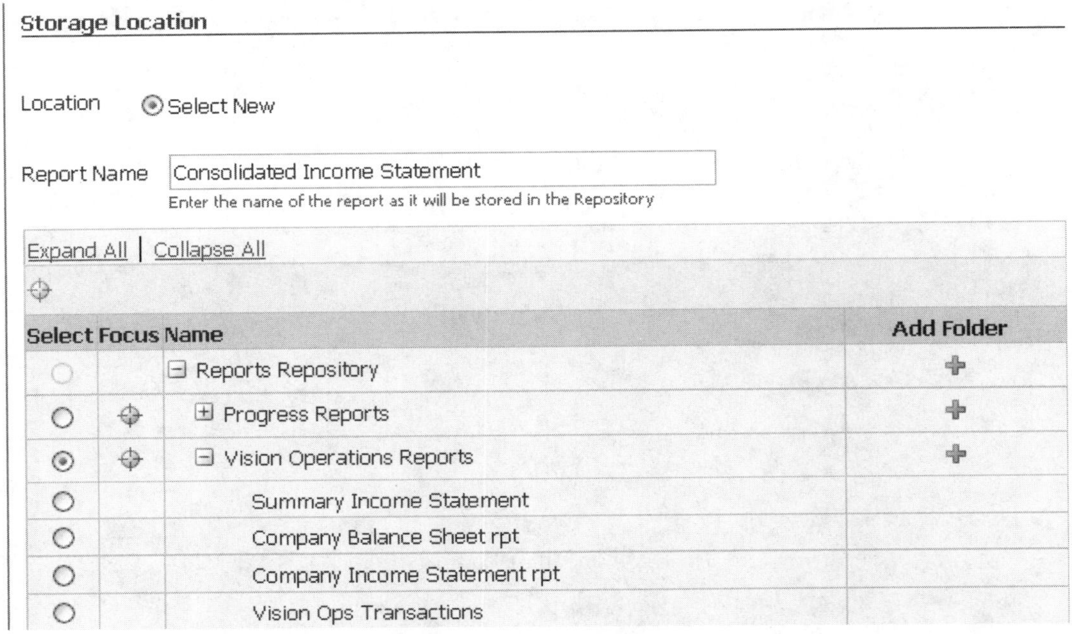

Storage Location

Location ⦿ Select New

Report Name Consolidated Income Statement

Enter the name of the report as it will be stored in the Repository

Expand All | Collapse All

Select	Focus	Name	Add Folder
○		⊟ Reports Repository	✚
○	⊕	⊞ Progress Reports	✚
⦿	⊕	⊟ Vision Operations Reports	✚
○		Summary Income Statement	
○		Company Balance Sheet rpt	
○		Company Income Statement rpt	
○		Vision Ops Transactions	

Report Manager Superuser | Financial Report Submission | Page 3

FIGURE 6-25 *Setting the report to save in the Repository for users to see*

Viewing Reports from the Repository

Once a report is saved and available, it can be viewed by any user with the proper rights in the Repository. FSGs still have drill-down capabilities, but this is a little different in R12 than it had previously been in EBS. In order to use the drill-down feature, you must drill down on a row that has account ranges assigned to it as opposed to a calculation. You can drill down from either an HTML or EXCEL output version of the report. You cannot drill down on TEXT or PDF.

Once in the Drill Account Balances window shown in Figure 6-26, you can change some information prior to obtaining account balances. The PERIOD can be expanded, the BALANCE TYPE changed, as well as the CURRENCY TYPE. The two remaining options will decide how much data is displayed: first, decide if you want to DISPLAY SUMMARY ACCOUNTS, then if ACCOUNTS WITH NO ACTIVITY are to be shown.

All these fields can be left with the defaults; select Go to get the information. From here, double-click the PTD field in blue to drill to the next level. Detailed journal entries are now visible, which can be searched on, or again double-click to see the details of the actual transaction. Note that once you get back to an actual transaction in the subledger, it takes you back to the forms from the HTML screens. During this drill process, you may get prompted to select the responsibility the transaction resides in. This drill feature is a little more cumbersome than the old ADI feature,

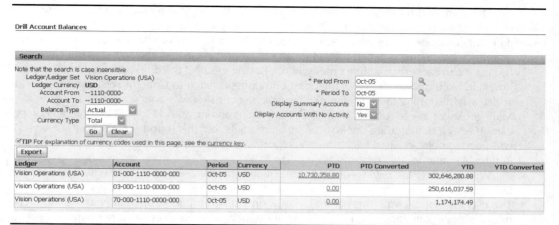

Drill Account Balances

FIGURE 6-26   *Drill-down in Report Repository*

which is no longer available, and has been revised several times since the release of R12. Please keep an eye on MetaLink releases for any changes to its functionality.

A note to system administrators: if you are creating custom responsibilities to add Report Manager to the users' General Ledger or other responsibilities, ensure the following functions are added if they plan on using the drill-down feature shown in Figure 6-26: FSG Drilldown: Launch Page, FSG Drilldown: Select Content Set Rows, FSG Drilldown: Effective Range Selection Page, FSG Drilldown: Balance Inquiry Page, and Account Analysis and Drilldown Mirror. These are the pages used by the drill-down feature seen in Figure 6-27.

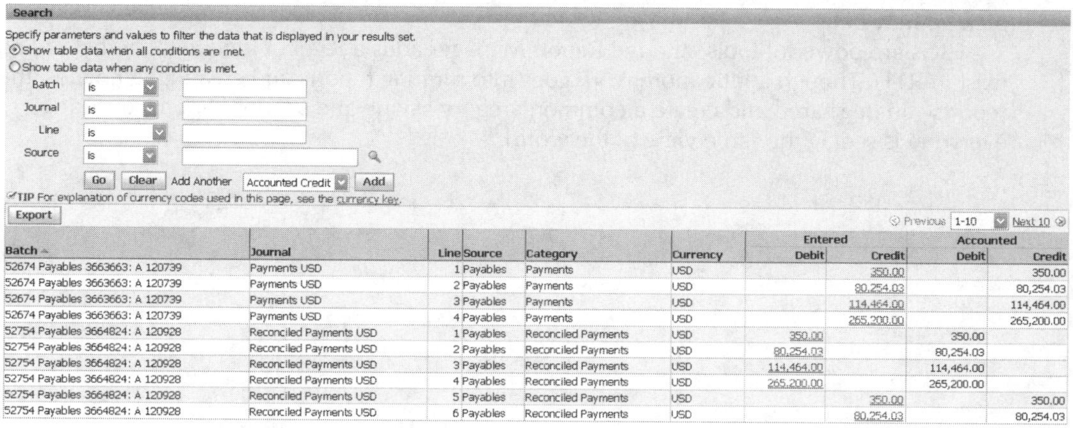

Report Manager Superuser | Repository Manager | View | select HTML or Excel

FIGURE 6-27   *Viewing reports with drill-downs saved to the Repository*

There are two options for running reports in the Report Manager (as well as from the General Ledger Superuser responsibility): either run an existing Report or create an Ad Hoc report where different components are combined but not saved as a report definition to be rerun. The main difference between the two is that when an FSG report is created and saved in the General Ledger, it can be rerun multiple times without having to select the different components, specifically Row and Column Sets. Some of the other components, such as Content Sets, can be overridden or added when running these predefined reports. Select FINANCIAL REPORT SUBMISSION from the Report Manager Superuser to run this type of report. When running an Ad Hoc FSG report, all components can be selected, including the Row and Column Sets, but this report definition is not saved and will need to be re-created each time the report is run. Select the AD HOC FSG SUBMISSION from the Report Manager for this type of FSG report.

When an Ad Hoc FSG is run from the concurrent manager, a REPORT is actually created in the Define Report form. The name of this report is "FSG-AD-HOC" followed by a sequential number. The user cannot override this name. Usually, one of two things happen after an Ad Hoc report is run: it is never run again, or the user finds it useful and wants to create a permanent report out of it. To create a permanent report, find the Ad Hoc report in the Define Reports form, and give it a meaningful name. Reports that are not going to be used again should be deleted, using the Program – Delete Ad Hoc Reports concurrent request. This report will delete all Ad Hoc reports created in this General Ledger responsibility, based on the number of days old you assign as a parameter. (If you assign ten days, all Ad Hoc reports over ten days old will be deleted.) If you want to delete all Ad Hoc reports for all responsibilities at the same time, run this process from the System Administrator responsibility. It is the Report name (FSG-AD-HOC) that makes it eligible to be deleted by this process.

When the reports are run in the Report Manager, they are saved to a Repository and made available for multiple users to view (if they have the proper responsibility). This feature solves the problem of having to run the reports and save them to a network drive for multiple user viewing. An important thing to understand is that once the report is run and saved to the Repository, it is a static report and is not updated for subsequent transactions. The report will need to be rerun to pick up new data.

FSGs are powerful tools, and the Report Manager adds a level of functionality that did not exist in R11*i*. Though a little more work goes into running reports and creating templates, these reports can be shared and create a common area for saving and sharing reports, ensuring everyone is seeing the same view of the world.

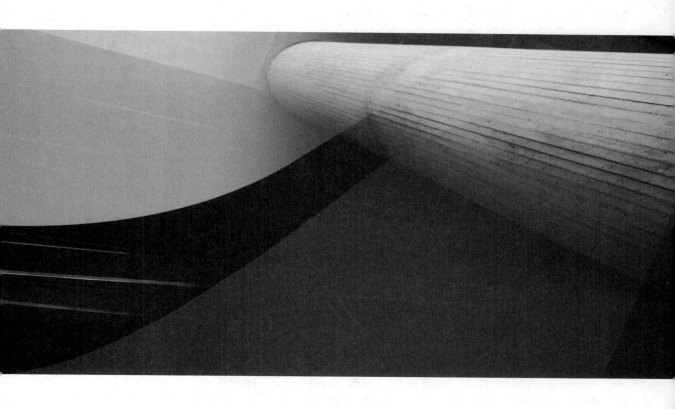

CHAPTER
7

Consolidations

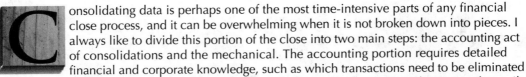 onsolidating data is perhaps one of the most time-intensive parts of any financial close process, and it can be overwhelming when it is not broken down into pieces. I always like to divide this portion of the close into two main steps: the accounting act of consolidations and the mechanical. The accounting portion requires detailed financial and corporate knowledge, such as which transactions need to be eliminated or which entities should incur an expense or revenue for a specific transaction, that cannot be easily programmed into a computer. The mechanical portion of a consolidation—combining the data, getting consolidated reports, repeatable eliminations, and so on—requires less specific knowledge. These can be classified as transactions and tasks that can easily be defined and then created in a repeatable manner.

Thinking about the tasks performed helps to distinguish what can be repeated each month from what requires very specific insight, and it allows the repeatable steps to be defined once and used over and over again. EBS contains a large amount of functionality that can aid in this repeatable work.

Consolidation Considerations

People often think that EBS cannot be used for consolidations if not all the entities being consolidated are using EBS as their financial system, but this is not true. If a financial statement or trial balance is received from a company not using EBS, it can be loaded into EBS and then used for consolidations. This statements can be loaded using Web ADI or via the Journal API directly from the third-party system into the journal interface tables and then imported as a journal entry. If the systems do not have the same Chart of Accounts, a mapping between the non-EBS Chart of Accounts and the Chart of Accounts used in consolidations will need to be maintained. Using Excel to store these mappings can work if you are uploading the journals with ADI, but I have found that creating a custom mapping table in either EBS or the third-party system, which can be used to export and import the data into the journal interface, works more efficiently when designed correctly. These cross-reference tables will need to be maintained on a regular basis. The final option is to set up a ledger with the subsidiary chart of accounts and maintain mappings within EBS.

Ledger Considerations

The way you set up your Ledgers for the different entities using EBS will, to a degree, dictate the mechanical steps required to perform a consolidation. There are three main options. Option 1, and the easiest, is to create one Ledger and multiple balancing segments under that Ledger. In this case, an FSG can be created to generate a consolidated financial statement. This will only work if the 4 Cs are the same: Chart of Accounts, Currency, Calendar, and aCcounting Method. There are legal and business reasons not to have all the balancing segments in one Ledger, so consider this when making the decision.

Option 2 is when there are multiple Ledgers, but they all share the same Chart of Accounts. This will greatly reduce the mapping required to perform a consolidation, but the consolidation process will still need to be run prior to generating consolidated financial statements. Option 3 is where the Charts of Accounts are different, and mapping from one to the other will need to be performed. Once this mapping is created, it can be maintained and reused from month to month. Option 1 has no real setups, other than creating an FSG (see Chapter 6 on FSG). Options 2 and 3 will be outlined next.

Consolidation Hub

Consolidations consist of setups, such as defining the mapping and eliminations, and monthly processing steps, including finalizing subsidiary data, transferring data into the consolidation, and running eliminations. These are all part of the General Ledger functionality and are also known as Global Consolidation System, or GCS. Oracle also provides the Financial Consolidation Hub, which is part of the Enterprise Performance Foundation. This module provides a more in-depth look at consolidations, as well as integration into Corporate Performance Management, General Ledger, Enterprise Planning and Budgeting, and Governance, Risk, and Compliance. The Consolidation Hub provides more robust reporting and upload capabilities, as well as interactive tracking for the consolidation process. Deciding which is used, EBS Consolidations or the Consolidation Hub, really depends on the complexity of your consolidations as well as your reporting needs. EBS Consolidations are relatively fast and easy to set up, whereas the Consolidation Hub requires more extensive setups but also provides more details about the consolidation (steps, integration, and so on). This chapter addresses the General Ledger consolidation solution.

Setups

Prior to using EBS Consolidations, a few setups are required, including identifying each company within the consolidation hierarchy and mapping a different chart of accounts.

Defining the Consolidation Definition and Mapping

The definitions will tell EBS which companies are parents (getting data from somewhere else) and which are children (providing the data to parents); mappings are created to determine how data is moved from one Ledger to another, especially when two different Charts of Accounts are used.

Defining Mappings

The Chart of Accounts Mapping window, shown in Figure 7-1, works in a way that is a bit unusual—you first need to define your mapping prior to defining the consolidation. Mappings are built between Charts of Accounts, not Ledgers, allowing the mappings to be reused in multiple consolidations. This mapping form is also found under Setup | Account | Chart Of Accounts | Mapping. Once you click the MAPPING button, you can define the mapping rules. Be aware that multiple mapping rules can be defined between the same two Charts of Accounts, and these mappings are used not only for consolidations, but also for Secondary Ledgers that have a different Chart of Accounts than the Primary Ledger. The one that will be used is the one assigned to the consolidation. Once the consolidation is set up, however, the mapping rules cannot be changed without creating a new consolidation.

Assign a name to the MAPPING and add a DESCRIPTION. Check ENABLE SECURITY to limit access to this mapping. Enter the TARGET chart of accounts, which is the chart where the data is being mapped into, and select the SOURCE, which is where the data is coming from. If both Ledgers being consolidated have the same Chart of Accounts, the mapping rules still need to be defined, and the TARGET and SOURCE will be the same. Mapping between the same Chart of Accounts can be a simple one-to-one mapping, or more complicated where, for example, an asset account is mapped to an expense account. This may need to be performed for such reasons as a local government requiring the transactions to be accounted differently than the parent located in another country (such as IFRS versus GAAP accounting.). Add EFFECTIVE DATES to know what period this mapping was valid for.

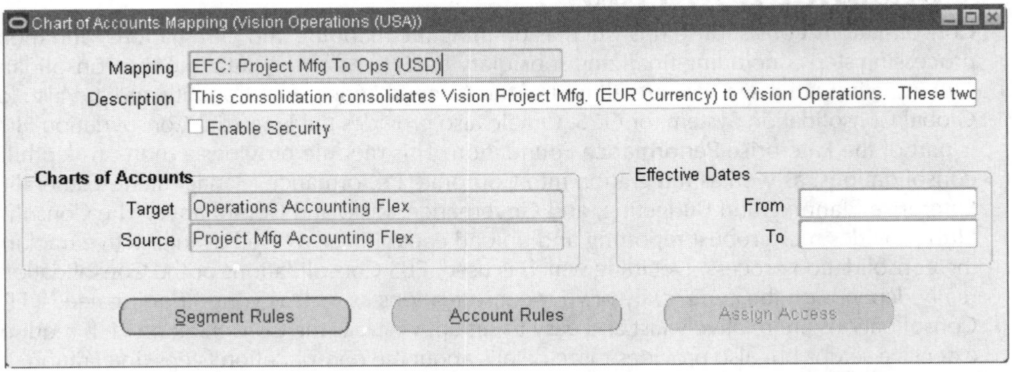

General Ledger Superuser | Consolidation | Define | Consolidation | Mapping button

FIGURE 7-1   *Chart of Accounts mapping definitions*

Segment Rules will define how each individual segment is mapped, whereas Account Rules override the segment rules and assign a specific combination or range of combinations to a specific combination in the parent Ledger. Segment Rules, shown in Figure 7-2, are set up where every segment in the SOURCE and TARGET Charts of Accounts must be mapped with an Action. There are several ACTIONS: NOT ASSIGNED is the default but is not valid for a consolidation. COPY VALUE FROM will assign the value from the SOURCE segment to the TARGET segment with a one-to-one correlation. Ensure all your values in the source segment are set up in the target segment if this one is selected for two different charts of accounts. If you are using the same Chart of Accounts in both the parent and subsidiary Ledgers, and you want to move the account numbers over without changing them, select COPY VALUE FROM for all the segments. ASSIGNing a SINGLE VALUE allows you to assign a defined value for that segment when the data is transferred to your consolidation. For example, if the Sub-Analysis segment has ASSIGN SINGLE VALUE of 000, then all combinations will have the Sub-Analysis of 000 in the consolidated Ledger. USE ROLLUP RULES FROM allows a value or range of values to be combined into one target value. If your Cost Center is set up to Use Rollup Rules From Cost Center, then each cost center in the target Chart of Accounts can be assigned a TRANSFER LEVEL (detail or summary), as well as a rule defining how the data will roll up. If USING is set to Parent, assign the Parent that will make up the TARGET SEGMENT DETAIL VALUE. If DETAIL or PARENT RANGES is selected, then assign the SOURCE LOW and HIGH values for this target range. Once the mapping is saved, it can be used in multiple consolidations or for Ledgers.

Next, Account Assignments, shown in Figure 7-3, can be added to override the Segment rules for specific accounts. Account Assignments can be assigned for a range of account combinations, mapping them directly to a specific new combination in the new Chart of Accounts.

Defining Consolidations

The consolidations are defined next, creating the consolidation relationships among each company. One consolidation definition will need to be created for each relationship, or each combination of a parent and subsidiary company. This means if your organization has one parent company and two child companies, then two consolidation definitions will need to be set up, one for each of the parent/subsidiary relationships.

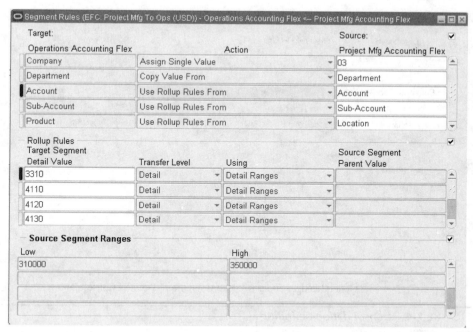

General Ledger Superuser | Consolidation | Define | Consolidation | Mapping button | Segment Rules button

FIGURE 7-2   *Segment rules*

Add the name of the CONSOLIDATION as shown in Figure 7-4, ensuring it is descriptive enough for the users to know who this will consolidate into whom, and a DESCRIPTION. Checking ENABLE SECURITY will allow security to be added to this consolidation setup. Select the PARENT company from the list of values—this is the Ledger you want to consolidate the data into. The CURRENCY can be entered based on the currencies set up on this Ledger. Select the SUBSIDIARY—this is the company you want

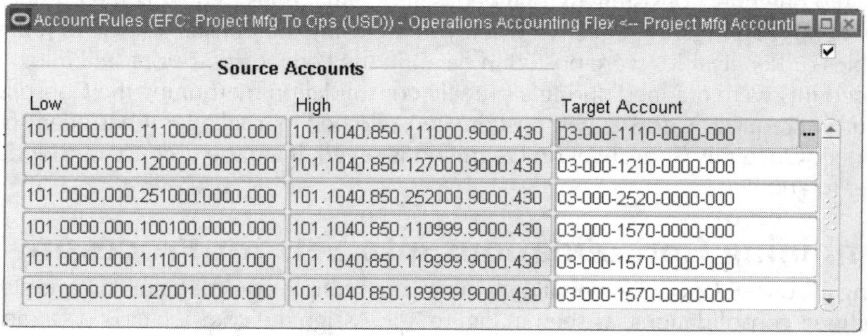

General Ledger Superuser | Consolidation | Define | Consolidation | Mapping button | Account Assignments button

FIGURE 7-3   *Account assignments*

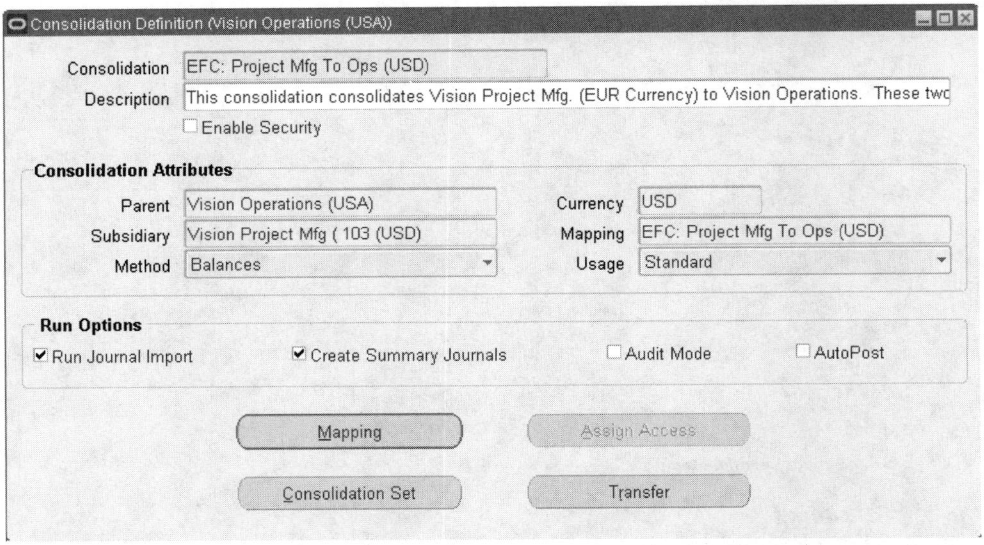

General Ledger Superuser | Consolidation | Define | Consolidation

FIGURE 7-4 *Consolidation definitions*

to transfer the data from. Enter the MAPPING you want to use for this consolidation; make sure you defined the mapping prior to setting up your consolidation. The MAPPING selected must be between the Charts of Accounts assigned to the parent and target on this consolidation.

Next identify the METHOD for moving the data to the consolidation of BALANCES, which will only bring over net debits and net credits for the account, or JOURNAL, which will bring over each journal entry. Select a USAGE of STANDARD or AVERAGE to determine which balance is to be consolidated; only Ledgers that maintain average balances can have a USAGE of AVERAGE. Checking RUN JOURNAL IMPORT will kick off the import process after the consolidation is complete, eliminating the need to run this step manually. CREATE SUMMARY JOURNALS takes all transactions in a specific account and combines them into one line, consisting of total debits and total credits, reducing the number of lines on a journal entry. This is most effective when you are using the transfer METHOD of Journals, and either Payables or Receivables were posted in detail in the Ledger. AUDIT MODE will allow you to see how the accounts were mapped during a specific consolidation by running the Consolidation – Audit concurrent request. AUTOPOST will post the consolidated journal after it has been successfully imported. Once this Consolidation Definition is saved, it can be used to transfer data from one Ledger to another.

Combining Consolidations into Sets for Processing

Adding a Consolidation Set will allow you to run multiple consolidations in one step. Sets combine predefined consolidations, as seen in Figure 7-5. Assign the CONSOLIDATION SET a meaningful name, as this is what the users will select when running the consolidation. Select the PARENT for this Consolidation Set—note that only one parent can be assigned to each consolidation set. Add a DESCRIPTION and a METHOD. It is the combination of the PARENT and the METHOD that determines which consolidations are eligible to add to this set. Assigning RUN OPTIONS at the Consolidation Set level will

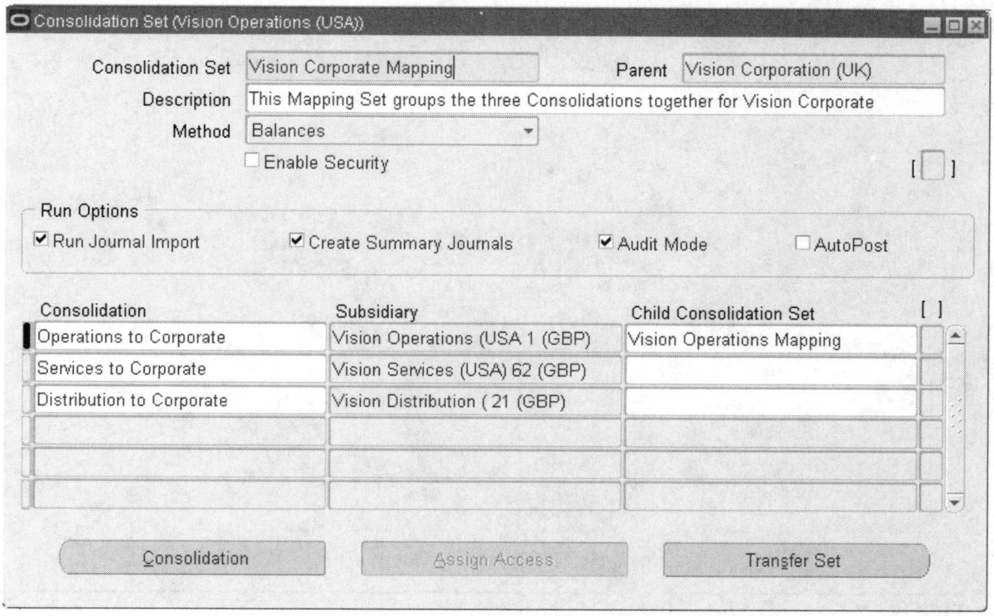

General Ledger Superuser | Consolidation | Define | Consolidation Set

FIGURE 7-5   *Consolidation Sets*

override the options at the consolidation level. From the list of values, select the CONSOLIDATION—only consolidations with the assigned PARENT will appear. A CHILD CONSOLIDATION SET can be added to run another consolidation set at the same time of this one, but it must also have the same PARENT and METHOD to be selected.

Performing Consolidations

Once the setups are complete, the best way to run consolidations is from the Consolidation Workbench. The advantage of doing this is that you can see the status of the consolidation for the selected period, ensuring that data is not imported more than one time without deleting the prior journal entry. Consolidations can be run as many times as needed throughout a period or close cycle, but EBS does not bring in the net change from the last run; it will always bring in either YTD or PTD data for the entire period, as specified during the transfer. If consolidations were already run once, then the consolidating journal entry created and posted will need to be reversed to ensure the balances are not overstated.

In the Consolidation Workbench Find window, seen in Figure 7-6, enter the PARENT and PARENT PERIOD you want to see the status of and select FIND. The two main fields for determining the status of any given consolidation are STATUS, which give the status of the consolidation and (if created) journal entry, and TRANSFERRED BALANCES. An obsolete status will let you know that the data transferred into the parent Ledger is missing at least one journal entry and should be retransferred. Once you have reviewed the status of a consolidation, click TRANSFER to transfer a consolidation according to the predefined setups.

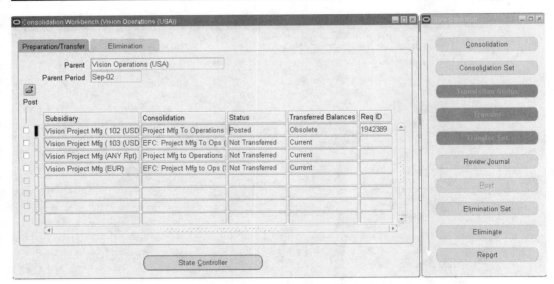

FIGURE 7-6 *Consolidation Workbench*

When creating consolidations and running the transfers, it is possible to transfer data from another EBS instance (if you have production data in more than one instance or have a parent or subsidiary company that runs EBS as well). The setups to use this feature require three steps, and you will need the assistance of your DBA. First, you will need to create a database user name with limited access to the instance you want to consolidate the data into (the parent). This user should be granted access to Execute on gl_ci_remte_invoke_pkg and gl_journal_import_pkg, and to select access on gl_je_batches and fnd_oracle_userid. Once this is created, a database link will need to be defined in EBS for the instance you want to send the data from (the subsidiary).

To create a database link, go to General Ledger| System| Database Link and get the DATABASE NAME by running this SQL on the database you want to copy the FSG from: SELECT value FROM v$parameter WHERE UPPER(name) = 'DB_NAME'. DESCRIPTION is a description of the database you are connecting to. CONNECT STRING points to the database from which you want to copy. DOMAIN NAME is the domain for the database you want to Copy from and can be found by running the SQL SELECT value FROM v$parameter WHERE UPPER(name) = 'DB_DOMAIN'. APPS USER NAME is for the database. This is not the user name you sign in with to the application. APPS PASSWORD is usually a secure password, and the DBA will usually type this in for you.

A parent Ledger mimicking the exact Ledger setups of the other instance will need to be created. This Ledger must have the same currency, calendar, and Chart of Accounts as the other instance. Once this is set up, you can then select TRANSFER, which will allow you to select the DATABASE and RESPONSIBILITY for the remote database (the subsidiary EBS instance). The RESPONSIBILITY is case sensitive, so use caution when entering it. Click VALIDATE to test the connection and then OK and proceed with the transfer. On the parent side, ensure that the parent Ledger is the default Ledger for the data access set assigned to the responsibility you are using.

To run the actual Consolidation, select CONSOLIDATION and refer to Figure 7-7. The CONSOLIDATION will default in from the workbench but can be changed to any valid consolidation for this Ledger.

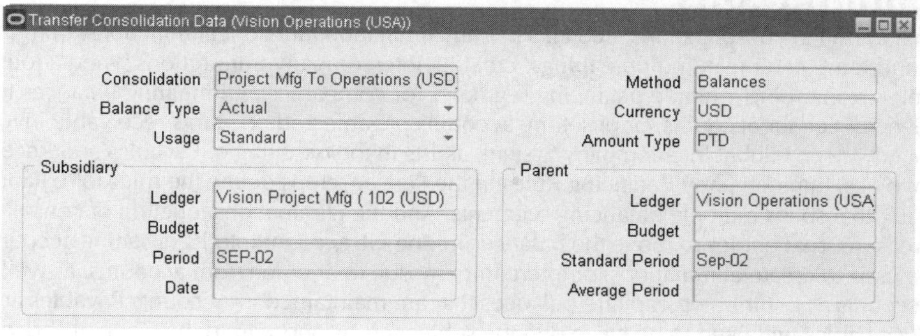

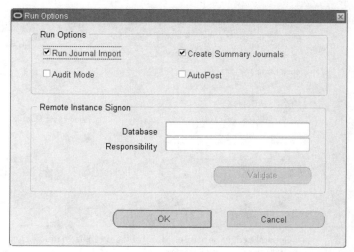

General Ledger Superuser | Consolidation | Workbench | Transfer button

FIGURE 7-7   *Running consolidation transfers*

Information will default in from this consolidation, and the following data changed or added to the defaulted data: BALANCE TYPE can be set to ACTUAL or BUDGET and AMOUNT TYPE is usually set to PTD (Period to Date) for all consolidations except the first one. This will bring over the period to date balances from the subsidiary Ledger. Selecting YTD (year to date) will bring over the year to date balances instead. Bringing in YTD data each month will cause inaccurate balances, as it is not the net change, but the true YTD balances. Also be aware that if the calendars are different in the two Ledgers, the YTD balances that are consolidated will be based on the subsidiary Ledger, not the parent Ledger's calendar periods. Select the PERIOD for both Ledgers that you want to consolidate. Click TRANSFER to begin the transfer process.

The run options shown in Figure 7-8 will allow you to change some of the options, as well as sign in to a remote EBS database if consolidations are to be imported from another instance and a database link exists.

General Ledger Superuser | Consolidation | Workbench | Transfer button | Run Options

FIGURE 7-8   *Consolidation run options*

Eliminations

In addition to consolidations, EBS also has an Elimination function. Eliminations, from an accounting standpoint, can mean multiple things: creating intercompany transactions when a journal is entered spanning multiple balancing segments (or companies), eliminating balances in offsetting General Ledger accounts, or offsetting accounts payable and accounts receivable invoices. AGIS, or Advanced Global Intercompany System, assists in the offsetting of Payables and Receivables invoices. Intracompany Balancing Rules in the Ledger setups define the rules for balancing a journal entry that spans multiple balancing segments. And the Eliminations function of consolidations will create journal entries to move the balances in one GL account into its offsetting account. These can be used to create eliminations for intercompany due to and due from accounts, as well as such accounts as contributed capital. (Balances that are maintained in Accounts Payables and Accounts Receivables will need to be cleared in the subledgers as opposed to the General Ledger, but can also be eliminated during the consolidation process.) The journal entries that are created by the system can process through an intercompany balancing segment as well, isolating the elimination transactions into a separate company.

First create an ELIMINATION SET, shown in Figure 7-9, which combines specific accounts for elimination. All the accounts assigned to a specific set will create one journal entry, which ideally will balance all the debits and credits in these accounts. If the debits and credits do not net to zero, balancing options can be added. Select the LEDGER and assign a name to the ELIMINATION SET, and then add a DESCRIPTION. Assigning an ELIMINATION COMPANY will run all the journals through this company, isolating them. Selecting TRACK ELIMINATION STATUS will allow the status of these eliminations to be tracked on the Consolidation Workbench, and ENABLE SECURITY will allow access to this setup to be restricted. Adding EFFECTIVE DATES will limit the period this elimination can be processed for. EBS will populate the PERIOD LAST RUN for tracking purposes.

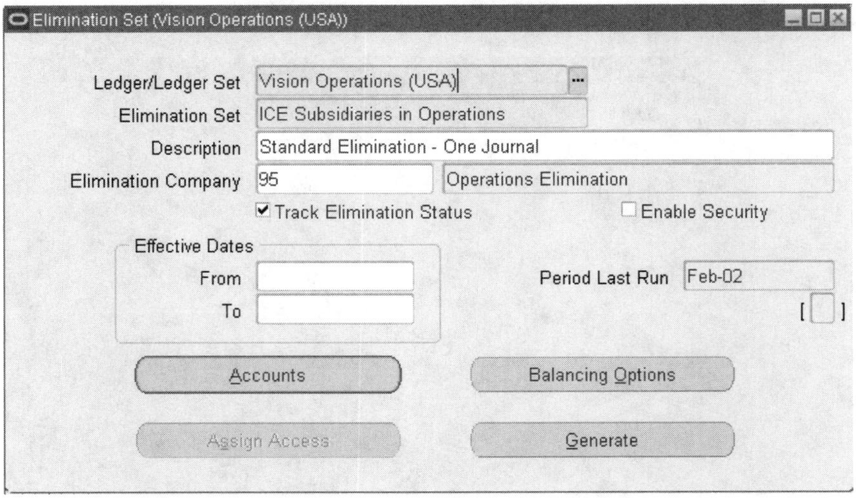

General Ledger Superuser | Consolidation | Elimination | Define

FIGURE 7-9 *Creating automated eliminations*

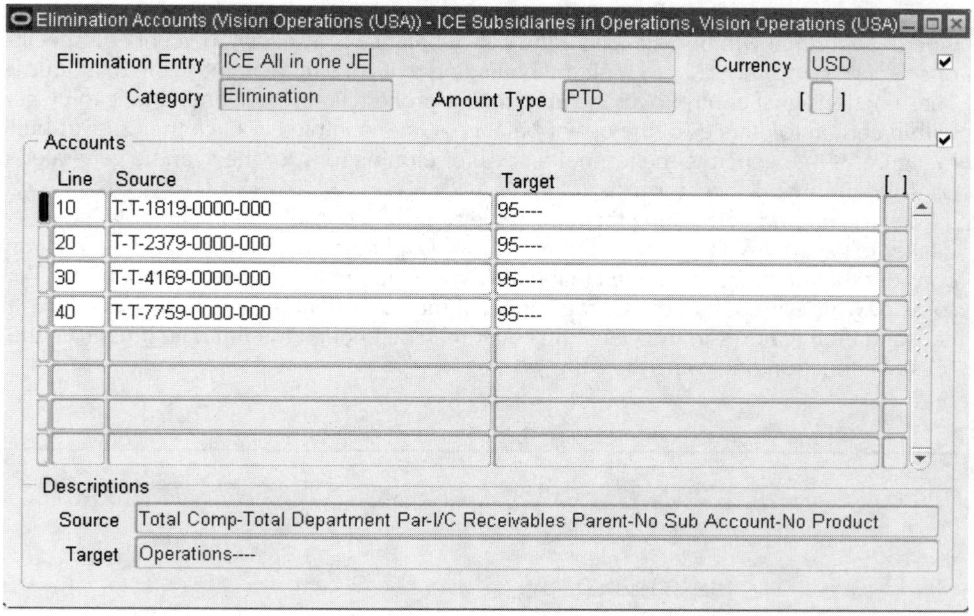

General Ledger Superuser | Consolidation | Elimination | Define | Accounts button

FIGURE 7-10 *Elimination accounts*

Select the ACCOUNTS button to add the elimination accounts for this set, shown in Figure 7-10. Multiple entries can be added to each set, with each entry creating a different journal, and each journal should balance to zero. Add the ELIMINATION ENTRY, which will become the name of this journal entry, and the CURRENCY this journal will balance and be created in. Assign a journal CATEGORY as well as the AMOUNT TYPE to eliminate. Assign a LINE number to the journal and the SOURCE and TARGET accounts.

The SOURCE account is the account that has the transactions you want to eliminate and can be a parent account. Using a parent account will cause all the child accounts assigned to it to be eliminated. Assign a specific TARGET account string or segment. When only a segment is assigned, the rest of the string will come from the SOURCE account from which the balance is being eliminated (if a parent account is assigned as the SOURCE, then the child values will be used from the TARGET string).

There are times that the journal entry created for eliminations will not balance. For example, if account 1819 has a debit of $200, and account 2379, its offset, only has a balance of $150, then the journal entry will be out of balance. EBS can handle this in several different ways. Setting up Balancing Options as shown in Figure 7-11 tells EBS what to do when the journal created is out of balance. Selecting ALLOW OUT OF BALANCE JOURNAL will generate these out-of-balance journals, but unless suspense posting is turned on, these journals cannot be posted. The advantage to using this method is it allows the users to see the out-of-balances and rectify them prior to posting. Select BALANCE WITH NET DIFFERENCE ACCOUNTS to generate the journal, and post any out-of-balances into the accounts assigned in the NET DIFFERENCE ACCOUNTS section. USE THRESHOLD RULES allows the balancing option to be used, but only within certain values. Under the THRESHOLD RULES, enter a CONSTANT AMOUNT as a hard limit for balancing out-of-balance journals, or a PERCENT OF ACCOUNT, where the journal will be balanced if the out-of-balance is a specific percent of a specific account, or select PERCENT OF JOURNAL to limit the balancing to a specific percent of the total journal entry. These options give control over the elimination process, allowing eliminations to be generated within certain tolerances of the out-of-balance. Once completed, click the GENERATE button, shown in Figure 7-9, to generate the journal entries for eliminations, or they can be generated from the consolidation worksheet form.

Setting up and performing the repeatable steps of a consolidation can greatly reduce the time it takes to get preliminary data on a timely basis. Depending on the complexity of the consolidation, consider the functionality of the Financial Consolidation Hub, as well as that of third-party tools, some of which are part of the Oracle family. If the consolidations are fairly basic, then the consolidation features in the General Ledger may be enough to eliminate time from the time-sensitive function of closing the Ledgers.

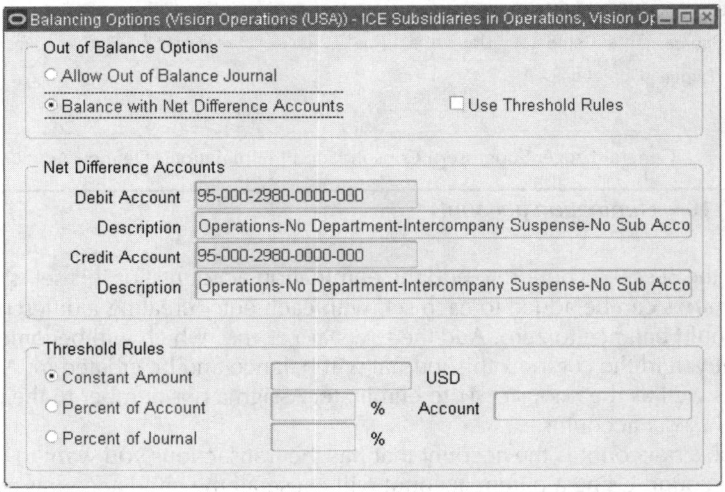

General Ledger Superuser | Consolidation | Elimination | Define | Balancing Options button

FIGURE 7-11 *Balancing options*

CHAPTER
8

Budget Tracking

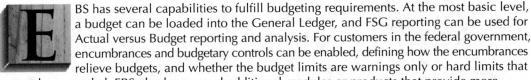

BS has several capabilities to fulfill budgeting requirements. At the most basic level, a budget can be loaded into the General Ledger, and FSG reporting can be used for Actual versus Budget reporting and analysis. For customers in the federal government, encumbrances and budgetary controls can be enabled, defining how the encumbrances relieve budgets, and whether the budget limits are warnings only or hard limits that cannot be exceeded. EBS also has several additional modules or products that provide more advanced budgeting features, including Hyperion and Enterprise Planning and Budgeting.

Hyperion is best known for its ability to combine financial and operational data into a consolidated view of an organization, allowing faster responses to both good and bad deviations from budgets, and to make better forecasts. Enterprise Planning and Budgeting has an Excel integration for more powerful integrated drill-downs to the source EBS transactions; the ability to distribute, monitor, and submit budgets and forecasts with management; comprehensive security; and reporting capabilities. Neither of these productions are part of the General Ledger module of EBS. This chapter will focus on EBS's standard budgeting features and the federal government's model of encumbrances and budgetary controls.

One important step to understanding how EBS can assist with your budgeting process is to bear in mind that EBS is a mechanical tool—it can only report on data that is actually stored inside EBS. This goes for all the budgeting tools in the Oracle family: they can only report on data that they have available, using variable degrees of complexity in the formulas to predict future growth and declines.

As a member of the accounting trade as well as upper management, budgeting has been a part of my life for many years. I find that many people are looking for a tool that will tell them definitively what next year's budget should be. No computer system can do that—it takes knowledge of last year's performance, corporate goals for the next year, an outlook of the current business economy, growth strategies, some hard work, and more than a little bit of luck to get these budgets right. There are volumes written on this process, and none of them are right all of the time.

Neither EBS nor Hyperion nor Enterprise Planning and Budgeting can perform this task in place of a human being. What they can do (with varying degrees of success and ease) is report on actual transactions, provide tools for performing what-if scenarios, and serve as a tracking mechanism to keep all the loose ends of budgeting straight, such as, did John return his budget yet and is Jane on pass 2 or pass 3, and did the CFO agree to only 18 percent growth in revenue next year yet? Understanding what your needs are in these areas will help determine how sophisticated a tool you need for budgeting. Have a great admin who can pull it all together and keep track of who is doing what? Is your executive management team all crackerjacks on Excel? Is the data actually needed to do what-if scenarios even available? Ask the tough questions, and then devise a budgeting process that works for the answers.

Budget Setups

Prior to entering budgets, there are a few setup steps to be completed. Budgets have two components: the budget itself, which controls the periods it is available for, and the budget organization, which controls the accounts associated with it. This allows some flexibility in EBS when creating budgets. Each budget year can be set up as a separate budget, but it is important to understand how this will affect FSG reporting before deciding to create budgets this way. Budgets are associated with Control Values on the FSGs (refer to Chapter 6 for more information on Control Values). This Control Value tells the report which budget should appear on it, so if a new budget is set up for each fiscal year, then the FSG report definitions will need to be modified prior to seeing the new budget information. Using only one master budget across years will avoid the need to perform this maintenance on FSG reports. Budget Organizations actually control the Account Numbers that appear on a budget, such as Balance Sheet and Income Statement accounts, or only Income Statement. The two are combined when inputting budget data to control the periods and accounts. Companies will often set up multiple budget organizations, not only to segregate companies or departments, but also to create both budget and forecast balances.

Traditionally, in accounting, budget numbers are set during a formal budgeting process and approved at some level by management. Forecasts, on the other hand, tend to roll or change on a scheduled basis, based on the new financial outlook as the year progresses. While EBS does not have any functionality called Forecast, there is no reason the budgeting feature cannot be used to maintain forecast balances. Creating these as additional budgets instead allows for Actual vs. Budget vs. Forecast reporting to be performed.

The Budget

To define a budget, enter a name for the BUDGET, and add a DESCRIPTION, as seen in Figure 8-1. Select the LEDGER this budget pertains to; budgets cannot cross over Ledgers. Selecting the STATUS of OPEN will allow budgets to be uploaded and modified, while FROZEN will prevent this budget from being changed. The DATES are informational, letting the users know when a specific budget was CREATED as well as FROZEN. Selecting REQUIRE BUDGET JOURNALS will require balanced journal entries for this budget. Since not all accounts always have budgets created for them, EBS gives the option of entering budgets in an unbalanced entry.

Select the FIRST and LAST period available for this budget. The LAST period selection is limited to the periods set up for this calendar; this should always be set to the last period in a fiscal year; otherwise, it cannot be changed or extended. Budgets do need to have the years opened prior to use. Click OPEN NEXT YEAR to open the first and any future years. The LATEST YEAR OPEN field will tell you what year was last opened; if it is blank, then the first year has not yet been opened. MASTER BUDGETS work with budgetary controls and are not intended for general budget reporting. A master budget uses summary accounts and its own budget entries to ensure that controls are maintained in individual budget accounts at a master level.

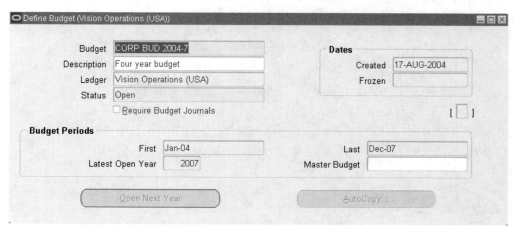

General Ledger Superuser | Budgets | Define | Budget

FIGURE 8-1 *Defining budgets*

The Organization

Budget organizations are the main method for assigning account numbers to a specific budget. These can be set up as one all-inclusive organization, or multiple smaller organizations, such as Human Resources or Information Technology. Since budget organizations can have security enabled, the access to each individual organization can be restricted. These should be set up to be in line with how your company's budgeting process works: does one person consolidate the budgets and enter them into EBS, or are multiple people responsibility for doing this?

A budget can also be set up as a forecast for the same accounts and same period. Referring to Figure 8-2, assign an ORGANIZATION name and a DESCRIPTION, and select the LEDGER from the list; you must have access to the Ledger to select it on this form. If you name your ORGANIZATION "ALL," EBS will automatically assign all accounts assigned to any other organizations to this budget. The ORDERING SEGMENT defaults to ACCOUNT, and the DISPLAY SEQUENCE for the segments can be assigned. EBS will allow the cost center segment to be displayed first, which will sort the budget by department as opposed to balancing segment. This may help with entry and analysis. Select ENABLE SECURITY to restrict access to this budget organization. In addition, PASSWORD SECURITY can be enabled for this budget, requiring a password to either inquire or change the numbers. EFFECTIVE DATES limit the dates this organization can be used. If you named the organization ALL, then ranges do not have to be assigned, as EBS will include every account in this budget organization.

Assigning ranges of accounts to a budget is a two-step process: First a range is defined, telling EBS the range of accounts that should be considered for this budget. Then the individual combinations that fall within this range will be added. When you are creating budgets for the first time, saving

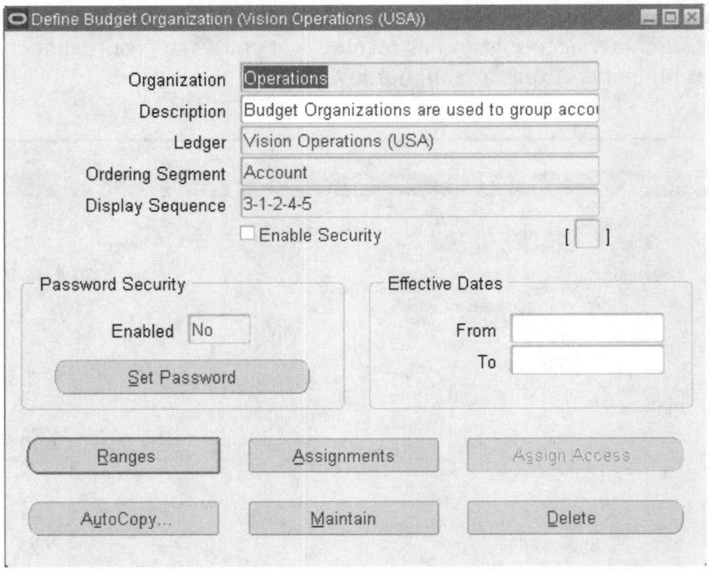

General Ledger Superuser | Budgets | Define | Organization

FIGURE 8-2 *Defining budget organizations*

records on the Account Ranges form seen in Figure 8-3 will automatically start a concurrent request called Program – Maintain Budget Organization. It is important to understand that this is a static addition of accounts—only combinations that are active in EBS when this process is run are added to the budget. As accounts are added after the fact, or disabled, the accounts assigned to a budget organization are not automatically maintained. Prior to starting the budget cycle each year (or updating the current year's budget), the account assigned should be updated. This can be done by clicking the MAINTAIN button on the Budget Organization page. To add a range, enter a LINE number and the LOW and HIGH segments you want included in this budget. Using 000-999 or 000-ZZZ will include every value in that segment. The TYPE can be set to ENTERED, which is required for encumbrances, or CALCULATED to use a mass budget formula to create the budget amount (see Chapter 5). Select the CURRENCY for this range of accounts (you can create budgets for stat balances). Save the record to create the accounts.

After the account combinations have been populated, they can be viewed under the ASSIGNMENTS button seen in Figure 8-2. On this screen, specific accounts can also be deleted from this budget. Select the row and click the DELETE button (the red x). Remember, just because an account was deleted from a budget, if either the combination is not disabled, the budget box on the combination screen is not unchecked, or the range is modified not to include these accounts, the next time the Program – Maintain Budget Organization is run, the accounts will be re-added to the organization. The only way to prevent this is to remove it from the actual range of accounts assigned to the budget. At this point, the budgets are ready for use.

AutoCopy is available for the budgets and is used to copy budget amounts from an existing budget to a new one. This feature can only be used if the budget you are copying the amounts to has not had any years open yet; once a year is opened, then this feature is no longer available. Check and ensure LATEST YEAR OPEN is a blank field. To copy the amounts, click AUTOCOPY and enter the name of the budget you want to copy the amounts from. This feature requires that the person running the AutoCopy has read and write access to the Ledger, and access to all balancing segments and management segment values.

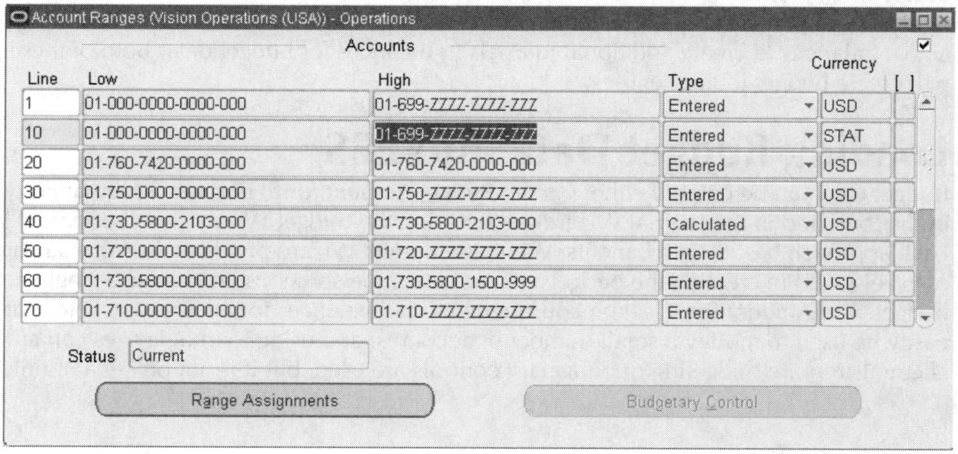

Line	Low	High	Type	Currency
1	01-000-0000-0000-000	01-699-ZZZZ-ZZZZ-ZZZ	Entered	USD
10	01-000-0000-0000-000	01-699-ZZZZ-ZZZZ-ZZZ	Entered	STAT
20	01-760-7420-0000-000	01-760-7420-0000-000	Entered	USD
30	01-750-0000-0000-000	01-750-ZZZZ-ZZZZ-ZZZ	Entered	USD
40	01-730-5800-2103-000	01-730-5800-2103-000	Calculated	USD
50	01-720-0000-0000-000	01-720-ZZZZ-ZZZZ-ZZZ	Entered	USD
60	01-730-5800-0000-000	01-730-5800-1500-999	Entered	USD
70	01-710-0000-0000-000	01-710-ZZZZ-ZZZZ-ZZZ	Entered	USD

Status Current

Range Assignments   Budgetary Control

General Ledger Superuser | Budgets | Define | Organization | Ranges button

FIGURE 8-3 *Assigning accounts to budget organizations*

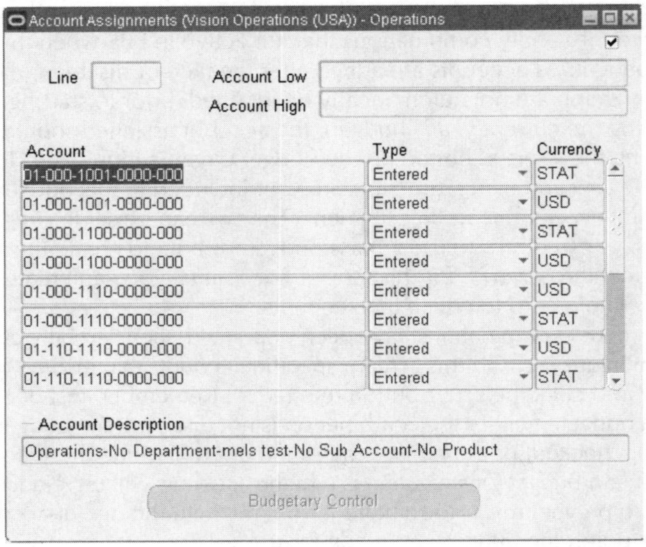

General Ledger Superuser | Budgets | Define | Organization | Assignments button

FIGURE 8-4 *Reviewing combinations assigned to a budget*

Advanced Features

Some Advanced Budgeting features in EBS can help reduce work when creating budgets. Mass Budgets work very much like Mass Allocation journal entries, but they are associated with a specific budget and act on the budget balances. These can be used to create fixed allocations, based on entered budget numbers loaded into this budget. Budget formulas, on the other hand, work similar to recurring journal entries. By entering formulas, you can use both budget and actual balances to create additional journals or balances for budget data. Both of these processes will create budget journal entries.

Loading Budget Data into EBS

Budget data can be entered either via the Budget Amount form, through a Journal Entry (both in the form and in the Journal Wizard), or by using the Budget Wizard, another part of WebADI. Each approach has its own benefits. While the Budget Wizard provides the formula capabilities of Excel to aid in creating the budgets, it can be cumbersome just to change a single account budget. The Amount form is time consuming to load balances for all accounts into, but it can easily be used to modify a small number of accounts; and using Journal Entries can aid if all accounts require budgeting or budgetary controls are used, but it is not practical if only income statement accounts and perhaps a few assets or liabilities are budgeted for, as opposed to all balance sheet accounts.

Budget Amount Form

The budget Amount form shown in Figure 8-5 can be used not only to enter a budget from scratch, but also to make small changes to budgets already loaded in the system via another source. First, select the BUDGET and BUDGET ORGANIZATION to enter or modify the amounts in. The ACCOUNTING PERIODS can be selected for any fiscal year assigned to the budget. There are two modes of entry: Worksheet and Single Row. Both will allow a fiscal year of data to be entered for a specific account, but Worksheet displays more than one account at a time, whereas Single Row will display only one account number and each period in the fiscal year. When querying up the data, either all the accounts assigned to the budget can be queried or only a specific range of accounts at a time. When you first click in the Account field, a list of values appears, allowing the account ranges to be selected. To see all accounts assigned to the budget, click the OK button in the list of values form. A fiscal total for each account is available by clicking Show Totals.

You can speed data entry by selecting Budgeting Rules. Table 8-1 shows the rules that exist and can be applied to either an account or a grouping of accounts.

The Budget Rules will be applied to the account the cursor is on, and you can use the up and down arrows to move through the accounts as rules are created and applied. The OPTIONS button allows for rounding considerations (either to apply the rounding difference to a certain period, or to ignore it) and also allows you to decide if the rule will apply to an adjustment period or not. The Budget rules are saved and can be changed as needed to modify your budget. Once a budget is posted, it will not automatically update for changes to actual or budget balances. Exiting the form or clicking POST will post the budgets to the accounts.

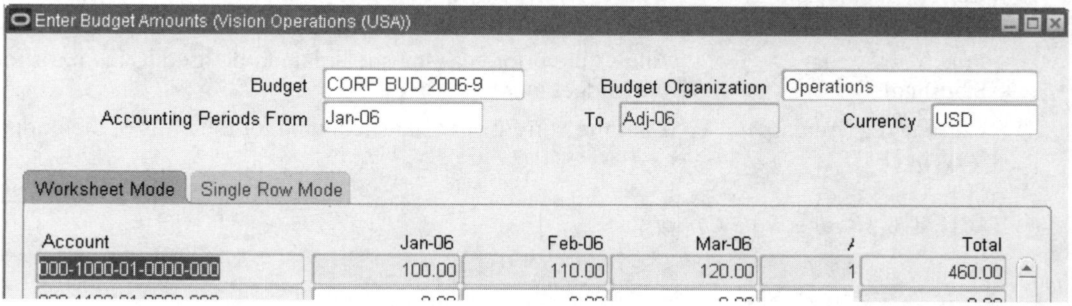

General Ledger Superuser | Budgets | Enter | Amounts

FIGURE 8-5 *Entering budget amounts*

Rule	Description
Divide Evenly	Distributes entered amount evenly over all fiscal periods for a specific account.
Repeat per Period	Repeats the entered amount for each fiscal period for a specific account.
Prior Year Budget Monetary	Allows the budgeted amount for the prior year to be increased by a certain factor. The AMOUNT entered is the percent to increase last year's budget, the BUDGET name determines which budget is the basis for the increase, and the ACCOUNT is the specific account, or amount. A different account can be used for the basis than the account that is being budgeted for (for example, increase salaries 4 percent over last year's budget).
Current Year Budget Monetary	Uses the current year budgeted amounts as a basis for amounts in other accounts. (For example, you can use Hardware as the basis to determine that software revenue should be 75 percent of the hardware revenue.) Ensure you save the data for the accounts that are being used as the basis prior to applying a rule to the amounts.
Prior Year Statistical	Allows prior year budgeted amounts for statistical data to be increased by a certain amount.
Current Year Budget Statistical	Allows current year amounts for statistical data to be used to calculate the budgeted amounts in an account (using current year budgeted head count to drive salary data).
Prior Year Actual Monetary	Uses the prior year actual amounts as a basis for increase for the current year.
Current Year Actual Monetary	Uses the current year balances in an account as the basis for the budget.
Prior Year Actual Statistical	Allows the prior year statistical data to be used as the basis for the budget increase.
Current Year Actual Statistical	Uses the current year statistical data for the basis of the budget.

TABLE 8-1   *Budget Rule Options*

Budget Journals

Budget Journals can be entered either with the Journal Wizard or with the Budget | Journal form. To use the Journal Wizard, select either a seeded or custom Budget template. The Budget template will allow a budget organization to be selected, as well as allow unbalanced entries to be uploaded.

To create a budget journal in the form (Budget | Enter | Journals), the same form appears as to enter a budget, with one additional tab. This tab allows the same data to be entered in a more traditional journal format, with debits and credits, along with descriptions for each period and account. Creating the budgets from this form becomes a two-step process, when the journal will need to be created via the Journal Import process, and then posted. Clicking CREATE JOURNALS will start the Journal Wizard. Once complete, the journal can be posted the same way a regular journal is posted.

Budget Wizard

The Budget Wizard is another feature of WebADI, creating an Excel file with downloaded actual data and budget data, as well as all the features of Excel, to create formulas and what-if scenarios for budget numbers.

After you launch the Budget Wizard, a page appears as shown in Figure 8-6. Select the name of the BUDGET and ORGANIZATION, and assign ACCOUNT FROM and TO values. Unlike the budget organization range assignments, the low and high combinations must be existing combinations. If the range entered here is less than the range on the organization, it will override the organization and return fewer rows. Again, this will only return account combinations that have been assigned to the Budget Organization, so ensure the budget was Maintained prior to using the Budget Wizard. Select the CURRENCY for the periods, and the FROM and TO PERIODS you want to enter. Selecting INCLUDE ACTUAL will return actual data in addition to any budget data that exists so that it can be used for what-if scenarios or budget calculations (for example, what if Revenue increased by 10 percent next year?). Actual data will appear as one tab on the worksheet, whereas budget data will appear on a separate tab. Click CREATE DOCUMENT to start the wizard. A Download box will open and give you the status of your downloaded budget—closing this box will cause the download to abort. Depending on the amount of data and how fast your PC, network, and database are, this can take several minutes.

The spreadsheet seen in Figure 8-7 will have two worksheets: one for actual costs if INCLUDE ACTUAL was selected, and the other for budgets. The full power of Excel is now available for analysis and creating budgets. You can also use this same method to download existing budgets,

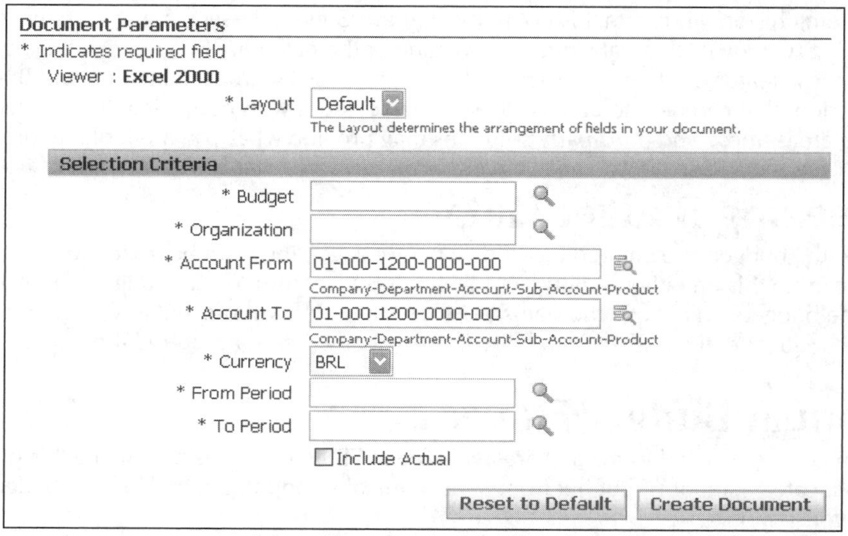

General Ledger Superuser | Budgets | Launch Budget Wizard

FIGURE 8-6 *Launching Budget Wizard*

	A	B	C	D	E	F	G	H	I	J	K	L	M	N	O	P
2		View Context						View Line								
3	Budget							CORP BUD 2004-7								
4	Organization							Operations								
5	Currency							USD								
6	Period Year							2005								
7	Ledger							Vision Operations (USA								
8	Data Access Set							Vision Operations (USA								
10	Upl Co Dpt Acct Sub Prd												Jan-05	Feb-05	Total	Messages
11	* List - Account															
12	01 410 4110 0000 000												4000000	1500000	5500000	
13	01 410 4120 0000 000												200000	200000	400000	
14	01 410 4130 0000 000												600000	700000	1300000	
15	01 410 4140 0000 000												100000	120000	220000	
16	01 410 4150 0000 000												300000	400000	700000	

FIGURE 8-7 *Budget Wizard in Excel*

make modifications, and then upload the modified budget. When uploading a modified budget, you have two BUDGET UPDATE MODES: Add to the existing balances, and Replace, which discards the existing balances and loads the balances in the spreadsheet. To reload the budget, using the Oracle menu on your Excel toolbar, select Oracle | Upload, and select the options for upload. Selecting AUTOMATIC IMPORT OF BUDGET AMOUNTS will start the process that transfers the data from the interface table to the actual accounts. If this is not selected, then the amounts will not appear in the accounts and must be imported separately by selecting Journals | Import | Run.

In general, budgeting is more of an exercise in coordination, consolidation of data, and providing historical data, as well as defining future financial goals. After the budget numbers are created for a period, then it becomes a simple exercise of reporting actual results against them, and explaining any differences. The budgeting features that come with the General Ledger are designed to ease the pain of getting historical information from the General Ledger, consolidating the new budgets, and reporting actual results against the budgets. The hardest part of budgeting, providing historical data that is not tracked in the General Ledger, along with the coordination of tracking who owns that data and what version of the data you are looking at, is not addressed with these features. Oracle has other offerings, such as Enterprise Planning and Budgeting and Hyperion, that can help to address these specific issues with budgeting. If you need a tool for these areas, these and third-party solutions may provide what you are looking for.

Freezing Budget Data

Once the budgets are entered into the General Ledger, they can be frozen to prevent changes. You can do this on either the Budget | Define | Budget form or the Budget | Freeze form. Query up the budget and change the status to Frozen, and this will prevent any updates from being made inadvertently. Budgets can be reopened at any time for required modifications.

Annual Budget Flows

Seeing the setups and forms that are available in EBS for budgets may make this process seem complicated—and it is, but not from a mechanical standpoint. Simply put, a budgeting cycle in EBS consists of

- Opening the next year in the Budget

- Maintaining the Accounts assigned to an Organization

- Using the Budget Wizard to download the budget worksheets

- Updating the sheets with the new budget information

- Uploading the new budget data into EBS

- Freezing budgets to prevent changes

- Creating and running FSG reports for monitoring actual versus budget results

The hard part of budgeting is the nebulous task just listed as updating the sheets with the new budget information. What exactly is that? There are tools outside of the General Ledger and EBS's core budget capability that can assist with this, but in reality, it is as much an art as a process, requiring a gut instinct for the upcoming market conditions for your company.

Forecasting

EBS does not have a feature called forecasting, but forecasts can easily be created as a new budget and loading forecasted amounts into it. This can then be referenced on FSG reports by assigning the forecast instead of the budget to the control value.

Encumbrances and Budgetary Controls

For Public Sector organizations, budgets take on another dimension, called *budgetary controls* and *encumbrances.* EBS provides a strong solution for both. These features allow not only tracking, but also preventing, transactions that are over the budget amounts. Encumbrance is an accounting term that actually changes the point in time that an organization recognizes a financial obligation.

The most common methods of accounting are *cash* and *accrual.* Cash accounting records financial obligations when the cash is either received or paid out. Accrual accounting records financial obligations when the product or service is received. Encumbrance, an additional accounting method, records the obligation when two organizations engage in an agreement to buy. To take these methods back to transactions, Cash records the expenses when a check is cut, accrual when the item or service is received, and encumbrance when a requisition or purchase order is created. Budgetary controls allows tracking against budgets and can create both soft and hard controls when the budgets are reached, either providing a warning or preventing future purchasing from being made.

Setups for Encumbrances and Budgetary Controls

There are several setups that need to be completed before using encumbrances and budgetary controls. Public sector–specific setups will not be addressed in this book, but they include the setup and usage of transaction codes, as well as budgetary account types. The use of these features is usually limited to U.S. federal government agencies.

Encumbrance Types

Encumbrance types are used to classify and track both commitments and obligations through the procurement life cycle. At the simplest levels, an *obligation* is recognized when a requisition is created in EBS, but it turns into a *commitment* when the requisition is turned into a purchase order. EBS comes with encumbrance types already created, which can be disabled, as well as

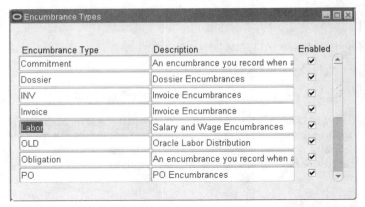

General Ledger Superuser | Setup | Journal | Encumbrances

FIGURE 8-8 *Setting up encumbrance types*

new ones added. In Figure 8-8, the ENCUMBRANCE NAME is what appears on all reports and forms, while the DESCRIPTION helps users understand what this refers to. Uncheck the ENABLED box to disable any seeded or used encumbrance types.

Summary Accounts

Summary accounts can be used for budgetary controls to perform the funds checking at the summary level as opposed to the individual account level, allowing for more flexibility on how a budget is specifically spent, but still keeping the spending within the budgeted amount. Since summary accounts are groupings of accounts where the balances are recorded at the account level and then rolled up and summarized at the summary level, a budget can be entered at the summary level only, and the funds check is performed against that balance for all the individual accounts included in the summary account. An example of how this is used is if the IT department is ultimately responsible for the budgeted computer equipment for the entire organization, but the expenses are recorded on each department's Profit and Loss statements. The IT department can budget one amount and record that at the summary level, and each individual department's expenditure for computer equipment can be recorded at the department level. IT would approve all expenditures and see a global picture of how much of the budget is spent, but it would not have to budget at the individual department level.

Summary accounts are not required for budgetary controls but are an optional way to perform funds checking for multiple accounts against one budget number. This setup step can be skipped if this is not needed for your organization, and if controls are maintained at the individual account levels.

Summary accounts are set up in several steps. First a *rollup group* is defined, which is basically a name for the group of accounts that are to be summarized. This group is then assigned to a parent account in the Key Flexfield Values window. The group is also assigned to a summary account template, which assigns specific budgetary controls to it and determines how the accounts assigned to the parent account are going to roll up.

A rollup group is defined so that it can be assigned to a parent value, turning it into a summary account. Before the rollup group can be added, the Key Accounting Flexfield needs to be queried up: Select General Ledger as the APPLICATION, and the TITLE of your Accounting Flexfield. Enter the SEGMENT name that you want to add the rollup group for and select Find. Here, as seen in Figure 8-9, a CODE for the rollup group needs to be added for EBS to use, and this will default into the NAME, where it can be changed. The NAME is what the users will see on forms and reports. Add a DESCRIPTION for the rollup group, and include the parent account number (here it is COMP) to help track where it is used in the system.

Next, assign the rollup group to a parent value in your Accounting Flexfield. Again, query up your Accounting Flexfield the same way you did when creating the rollup group. Once you find the parent value that you want to assign this group to, add the rollup name in the GROUP field (see Figure 8-10). Notice that this field is only available for population on accounts marked as Parent. Ensure that there are Child Ranges assigned to this parent, and save the record.

Referring to Figure 8-11, create a summary account template by adding a NAME for the summary template and selecting the LEDGER—this will default in if the responsibility only has access to one Ledger. When you click the TEMPLATE, a pop-up box will appear that has each segment of your Accounting Flexfield listed. Here is where EBS is told at what levels the summary accounts and balances will be created and maintained.

Every field in the Accounting Flexfield has the option of D or T, and the segments that have had rollup groups defined will have the rollup groups listed as well. Selecting T will create one summary account for every value in this segment, acting as a total. To use this, you must set up T as a valid value for the segment. Selecting D will create one summary account for each segment value, and selecting the rollup group name determines that these segments will use the parent account(s) it is assigned to as the summary account for all its children. Before you ask, yes, you can have more than one segment assigned a rollup group, and you could have assigned a rollup group to more than one parent. In the example, only the second segment, cost center, will create detailed accounts. If there are ten cost centers, then ten combinations will be created for this summary account template.

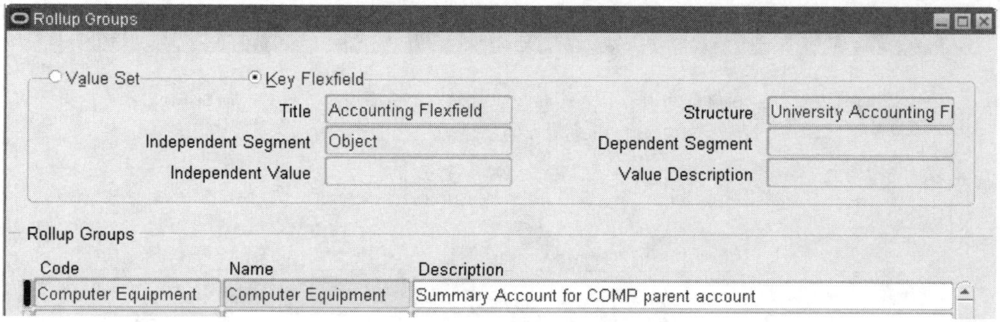

General Ledger Superuser | Setup | Financials | Flexfields | Key | Groups

FIGURE 8-9   *Adding a rollup group for summary accounts*

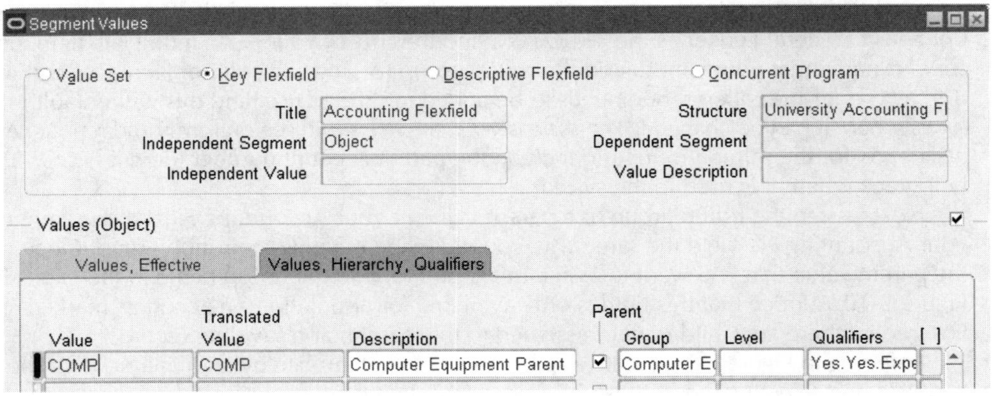

General Ledger Superuser | Setup | Financial | Flexfields | Key | Values

FIGURE 8-10   *Adding a rollup group to a parent account segment*

Add a DESCRIPTION, and assign the EARLIEST PERIOD that this summary account will have balances for. The STATUS will read current after it is saved and the concurrent request Add/Delete Summary Accounts completes, creating all the summary accounts and their balances.

Summary accounts can be used for a number of different processes in EBS besides budgetary control; they can be used in FSG reporting, and mass allocation and recurring journal formulas. At this point, they are ready for use for any of these reasons.

To add budgetary controls to a summary template, click the BUDGETARY CONTROL button. Again, this is seen in Figure 8-11. This is only available if budgetary controls are turned on for this

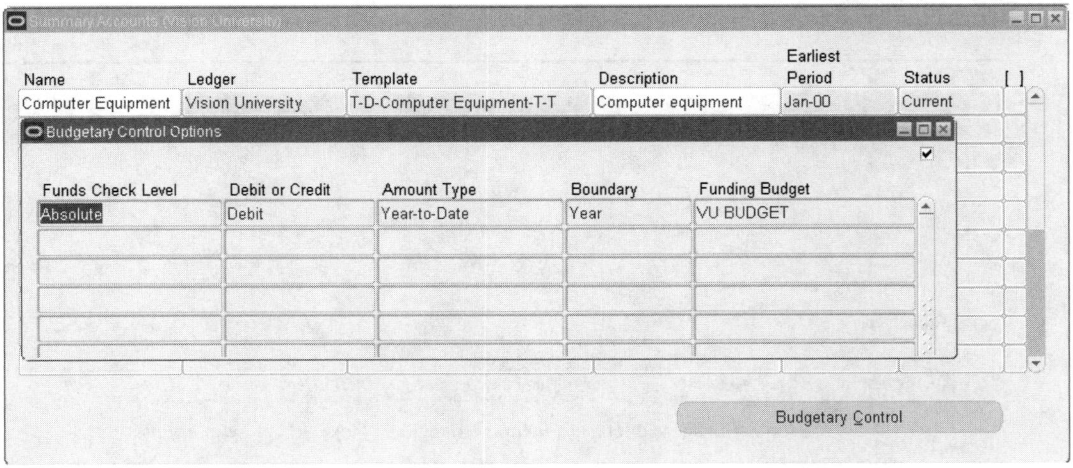

General Ledger Superuser | Setup | Accounts | Summary

FIGURE 8-11   *Summary account templates with budgetary controls*

Ledger. You can define a control as either a hard or a soft control—this determines whether users are stopped if a transaction goes over the budget limit, or only warned and allowed to proceed with the transaction. The FUNDS CHECK LEVEL of ABSOLUTE will cause the transactions to be stopped, whereas ADVISORY will just provide a warning and allow the entry to be made. Available funds are determined by the simple equation of budgeted amount less the actual balances and any encumbrance balances.

The DEBIT OR CREDIT field determines how a transaction will pass this formula. Remember that debits are actually positive balances; if the result is a positive, it will pass if this field is set to DEBIT, and fail if it is set to CREDIT. Negative results will pass when this is set to CREDIT. When designing your summary accounts, ensure that both debit and credit balances are not combined in one template. For this reason, most often templates are set up separately for Assets and Liabilities, Income and Expense accounts.

The AMOUNT TYPE and BOUNDARY will control the availability of funds when transactions take place. AMOUNT TYPE determines what time period the budget balances are included for. If YEAR-TO-DATE is selected, then the entire budget balance from the first month to the month the transaction is entered is available for consideration during funds checking. BOUNDARY dictates if any leftover budget balances can be used in subsequent periods. A selection of QUARTER TO DATE would mean that any underspending in the first two months of the quarter could be spent in the third month, but not any months outside the quarter (as defined in the calendar). Setting these two fields determines when and how any budget balances can be used: current month only or any future month.

Among the boundary options, PERIOD allows any leftover funds from prior periods (as defined in the Amount type) to be used, but no future period funds. QUARTER only considers budget amounts from the quarter, YEAR looks at the entire budgeted amount for the year, and PROJECT works in conjunction with the projects segment of the Accounting Flexfield, allowing budgets to cross years for the same budget. Select the FUNDING BUDGET name for the budget where the budget limits were loaded. This is the budget, not the organization, that is available for selection. The budget must be open, but balances do not have to be loaded into it.

Budgets

Creating budgets for budgetary controls is exactly the same as when not using budgetary controls, with some additional steps. First, on the Budget Organization, the budgetary controls have to be added to each of the account ranges or individual accounts where the controls are needed. Funds checking does not have to be 100 percent across all accounts; it is possible to set up some accounts ranges as Absolute Control, some as Advisory, and others with no control at all. Also, the same budget does not have to be selected for each range, as multiple budgets can be used in the funds checking.

To add budgetary controls to an account range, query up the budget (General Ledger Superuser | Budgets | Define | Organizations). Select RANGES and then the BUDGETARY CONTROLS button for the range. This is set up the same as on a summary template, where the FUNDS CHECK LEVEL is added, and the AMOUNT TYPES and BOUNDARIES defined for how budget amounts are viewed and carried forward. Also, assign the FUNDING BUDGET. Budgetary controls can only be assigned to budget accounts that have a TYPE of Entered (as opposed to Calculated), and they must be in the primary Ledgers currency.

Ensure on the Budget window (General Ledger Superuser | Budgets | Define | Budget) that Budget Journals are required.

Once the budgets are set up, Budget Journals will need to be created for all accounts with budgetary controls turned on. These budget amounts are entered at the individual account levels, not the summary account levels, because you cannot enter a journal against a parent account.

When the budgets are entered, a funds check will need to be performed prior to generating the journal entry to ensure that the budget numbers are not being reduced for Absolute accounts lower than the actual reserved amounts.

Ledgers

For a Ledger to be set up for budgetary controls, the Subledger Accounting should be Encumbrance if the budgets are going to be controlled at the encumbranced levels. Encumbrances record obligations and commitments for an organization prior to an invoice being received, usually at the requisition (obligation) and purchase order (commitment) levels. Tracking your budgetary controls back at this level will prevent items from being ordered in the first place that are over the budgeted amount, as opposed to tracking budgetary controls beginning with the invoice, when the item has usually already been received, and sometimes even consumed.

The ENABLE BUDGETARY CONTROLS setting must also be selected on the Ledger (Setups | Financial | Accounting Setup Manager | Accounting Setups | Advanced Options Region) for funds checking to take place.

Though these options can be changed and updated at any time, the timing of these changes may be critical to achieve your desired results. For example, if you want to start tracing budgetary controls with encumbrances, changing the Subledger Accounting method mid–fiscal year will not only cause the funds available balance to be incorrect (any purchase order or requisition that is already created will not be reduced from the amount available), it will also have an impact on the General Ledger. When encumbrance accounting is used, transactions are recorded not only for entering a requisition or a purchase order, but also for clearing these transactions when the document is closed and moved to the next state. (Requisitions are cleared when the purchase order is approved, and purchase orders are cleared when an invoice is entered against it.) Ensure you try this in tests and understand the impacts prior to turning it on or off after the Ledger has been used.

How New Accounting Segment Values Are Treated with Budgetary Controls

When adding new segment values to the Accounting Flexfield (Setup | Accounting | Key | Values), it is important to understand how they will be treated for funds checking. When summary accounts are used, any new value added and used will automatically be added to the summary accounts, and funds checking will take place at the summary balance level.

When budgetary control amounts are set up at the individual account levels, and an account combination is created via dynamic insertion and used, the budget amount defaults to zero. Transactions against this new account may pass if there is a control set up (see the next section) with a tolerance. If there are no controls, then it will fail the funds checking.

No matter which method is used, the process to Maintain Budget Organizations (Budgets | Define | Organization | Maintain button) is not required when using funds checking; all account combinations added either manually or with dynamic insertion will automatically be created in the budget as well, with a zero budget amount.

Sometimes, an account can be added that does not fall into a range of accounts on the budget, or range of accounts assigned to the summary accounts. A profile option called PSA: DEFAULT FOR MISSING BUDGET controls how budgetary control is handled on these accounts. If the profile is set to NONE, then no funds checking will take place. If it is set to ABSOLUTE, then it will be treated as a zero budget for funds checking.

Adding Controls with Budgetary Control Groups

Budgetary control groups allow additional funds checking options and controls to be added to sources and categories. These include tolerance levels and override amounts. Control groups are required only if these additional control features are needed.

To create a control group as seen in Figure 8-12, assign a GROUP name, and add a DESCRIPTION. The SOURCE and CATEGORY will default to OTHER when you click down in the Budgetary Control Rules section. Other will be the rule that is used for any source and combination not defined. FUNDS CHECK LEVEL determines if it is an ABSOLUTE check, denoting that any transaction that fails the checking cannot be saved, or ADVISORY, which will give a warning only to the users. NONE will actually turn off budgetary controls for this specific journal entry.

The next few fields determine how these funds check levels are enforced. The TOLERANCE % and AMOUNT provide some limits surrounding the amount of funds available. The percent value will allow funds checking to pass up to that percent over the actual budget, whereas AMOUNT provides a hard limit over the balance to which funds checking will pass. When both these fields are set, the lower of the two will be used on each transaction. These tolerances pertain to the amount that the transaction can go over the budget, not the total amount the budget can be exceeded in the system for all transactions. Adding an Amount and a Percent can help keep these overages in check for both large and small transactions. Adding a tolerance of zero will enforce the budget as entered and allow no overages.

The OVERRIDE AMOUNT is designed for use with Absolute funds checking levels; it allows a failed transaction to be overridden and processed. These overrides are per transaction and also need to be available for every budget on a transaction that requires the override. Here is an example of how this works: if a purchase order is created for three different accounts in the distribution, and two of the accounts fail funds reservation, then overrides need to exist for both of the accounts that failed in order for the lines to be overridden and the purchase order booked.

Once a budgetary control group is set up, it needs to be assigned with the profile option BUDGETARY CONTROL GROUP (System Administrator | Setup | Profile | System). If it is not, then no controls will not be used by EBS.

Hierarchy of Setup for Funds Checking

As you can see from the preceding setups, budgetary control guidelines are set up at a variety of different places, with seemingly the same information. There is a hierarchy on how these setups are all used. Summary or individual accounts can either have budgetary controls assigned to them as ABSOLUTE or ADVISORY, or have no budgetary controls assigned to them, making the funds check level equal to NONE. CATEGORY and SOURCES have the option of NONE in addition to ADVISORY and ABSOLUTE. Table 8-2 shows the hierarchy of the controls.

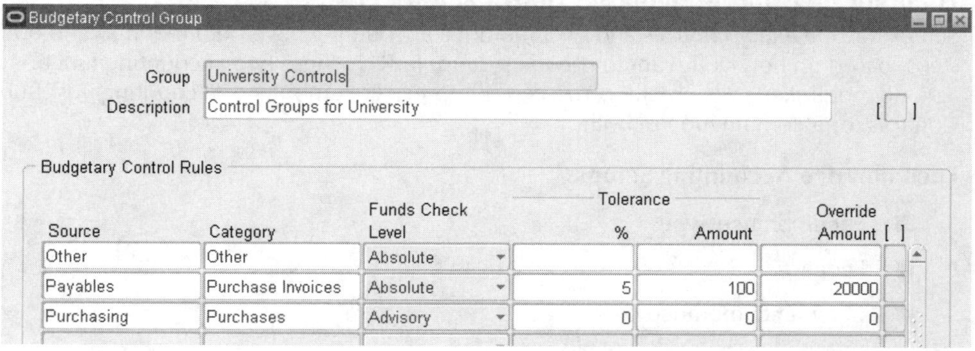

General Ledger Superuser | Budgets | Define | Controls

FIGURE 8-12 *Adding additional controls with control groups*

Journal Source and Category Setting	Summary or Budget Account without Budgetary Controls	Summary or Budget Account Set to Advisory	Summary or Budget Account Set to Absolute
NONE	The account level setting will always prevail when it has no budgetary controls, and no funds checking will take place.	The category setting will override the account setting, making the funds checking None.	An account setting of ABSOLUTE will override any other setting, requiring absolute funds checking for all transactions against this account.
ADVISORY	Same as above.	Since both are the same setting, the funds check level will be ADVISORY.	Same as above.
ABSOLUTE	Same as above.	An ABSOLUTE setting at any level will override any other level, in this case, making the funds change level ABSOLUTE.	Same as above.

TABLE 8-2   *Funds Checking Level Defaults and Hierarchies When the Setups Are in Conflict*

Opening the Encumbrance Year

The last setup needed for budgetary controls with encumbrances is that the year needs to be opened. This is completed in the same place as any period (General Ledger Superuser | Setup | Open/Close). Under the ENCUMBRANCE YEAR section, click OPEN NEXT YEAR. This needs to be done prior to using any encumbrance years. The LATEST YEAR OPEN will show which year has already been open. The first encumbrance year is opened when a Ledger is saved, so it does not require being opened manually.

Encumbrance and Budgetary Control Setup Recap

Setups for budgetary controls and encumbrance accounting have both required and optional steps, based on how you want to use the system. In R12, these two accounting functions are actually not linked to each other. You can set up just Encumbrance Accounting, just Budgetary Controls, or a combination of both.

Encumbrance Accounting Setups

- Encumbrance Types
- Ledger
- Open Encumbrance year

Budgetary Control Setups, Account Basis

- Summary Accounts – Optional

- Budgets – Required, Budgetary Controls on budget accounts – Required
- Ledger – Required
- Control Groups – Optional

Budgetary Control Setup, Encumbrance Basis

- Encumbrance Types – Required
- Summary Accounts – Optional
- Budgets – Required, Budgetary Controls on budget accounts – Required
- Ledger – Required
- Control Groups – Optional
- Open Encumbrance year – Required

Using Encumbrances and Budgetary Controls

Once encumbrances and budgetary controls are set up and turned on, using them becomes fairly simple, but there are a few additional things you need to know.

Creating Encumbrance Entries

Encumbrance journal entries will all originate from the subledgers. They can be created for Requisitions, Purchase Orders, or both. In Payables or Purchasing, these setups are completed in the Financial Options on the ENCUMBRANCE tab (Payables Superuser | Setup | Options | Financial Options or Purchasing Superuser | Setup | Organizations | Financial Options). Select USE REQUISITION ENCUMBRANCES to create encumbrance entries for requisitions, and select if funds should be reserved at completion (recommended for budgetary controls). If encumbrance entries are needed for purchase orders as well, select USE PO ENCUMBRANCE.

Ensuring that SLA has encumbrance transactions included in them (EBS comes with seeded encumbrance SLA setups) makes these entries available for journal entries when the Create Accounting process is run. Once these two setups are complete, encumbrance entries will be created for requisitions and purchase orders.

Performing Funds Checking on Manual Journal Entries

Entering a journal entry for budgetary controlled accounts is the same as entering a journal entry without budgetary controls, but the CHECK FUNDS, RESERVE FUNDS, and VIEW RESULTS buttons are now available on the journal entry screen as seen in Figure 8-13.

Select the CHECK FUNDS button to confirm there is enough budget reserve for the accounts on the journal entry without reserving the funds, leaving them available for other transactions. RESERVE FUNDS will also check if there is enough budget reserve for each line of the journal entry, but it will reserve the funds if the journal passes a successful funds check; this will prevent any other transaction (in Payables and Purchasing as well as the General Ledger) from reserving the funds prior to this journal being posted. Posting will always confirm that there are available funds for any journal where Reserve Funds has not been completed successfully. Once Funds Reservation has take place, the journal entry cannot be changed or deleted without first unreserving the funds.

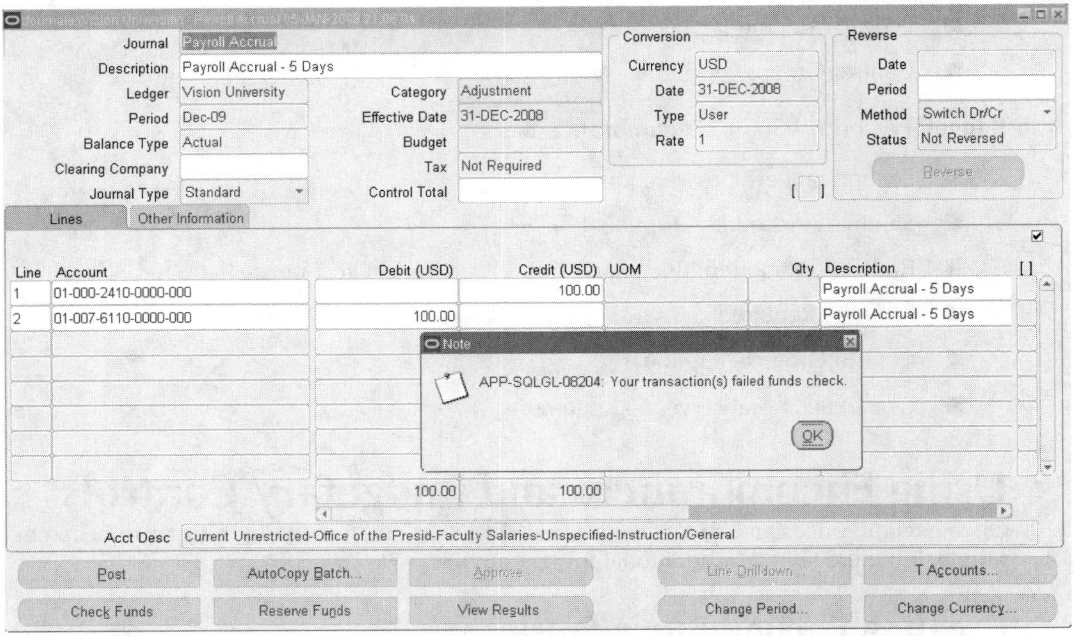

General Ledger Superuser | Journal | Enter

FIGURE 8-13   *Entering journal entries manually with budgetary controls turned on*

Clicking the VIEW REPORT, shown in Figure 8-14, after funds checking has been completed (either successfully or unsuccessfully) will show the results of the check, including a Result Message for why it passed or failed, and the previous funds and current funds available.

Funds Inquiry

At any time, you can review the funds available and reserved in the Inquiry Funds window. The LEDGER and BUDGET will usually default in, depending on the access for the responsibility you are in. AMOUNT TYPE can be set at different levels to present different time periods for the data; changing these can actually change the data on this screen. For example, if you select PERIOD TO DATE, it will only represent the period to date funds, whereas YEAR TO DATE will take the entire year into consideration. To see all encumbrances, leave ALL in the ENCUMBRANCE TYPE. Select the PERIOD, and decide if you want to see ALL ACCOUNT LEVELS, or only a SUMMARY or DETAIL account.

Referring to Figure 8-15, enter the ACCOUNT or account ranges to see the related fields. BUDGET is the amount entered against an individual account or the detail accounts if it is a summary account, and ENCUMBRANCE shows any encumbrance entries against the account, broken down below for commitments, obligations, and other encumbrances. ACTUAL reflects journal entries, excluding those created for encumbrances. The FUNDS AVAILABLE field reflects the actual budget balance available for future transactions.

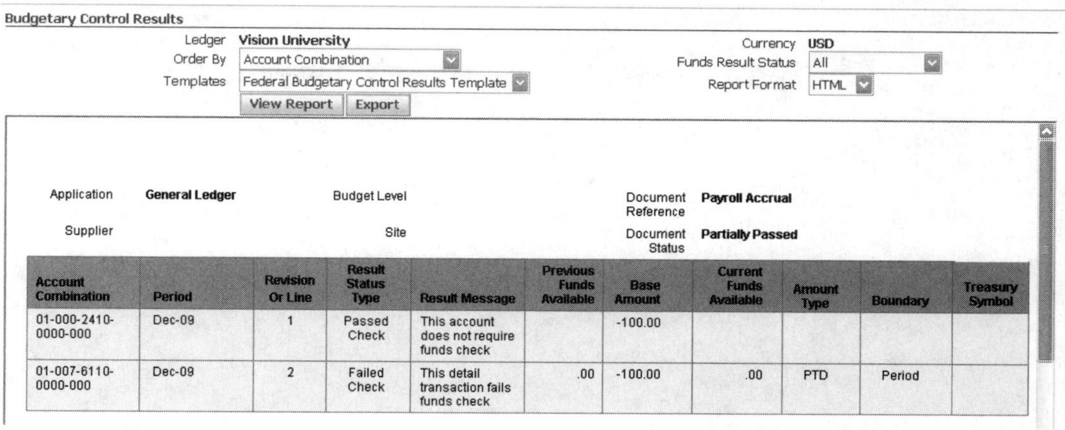

Budgetary Control Results

Ledger	**Vision University**	
Order By	Account Combination	
Templates	Federal Budgetary Control Results Template	

Currency	**USD**	
Funds Result Status	All	
Report Format	HTML	

View Report   Export

Application	**General Ledger**		Budget Level				Document Reference	**Payroll Accrual**			
Supplier			Site				Document Status	**Partially Passed**			

Account Combination	Period	Revision Or Line	Result Status Type	Result Message	Previous Funds Available	Base Amount	Current Funds Available	Amount Type	Boundary	Treasury Symbol
01-000-2410-0000-000	Dec-09	1	Passed Check	This account does not require funds check		-100.00				
01-007-6110-0000-000	Dec-09	2	Failed Check	This detail transaction fails funds check	.00	-100.00	.00	PTD	Period	

General Ledger Superuser | Journal | Enter | Funds Check or Reserve Funds | View Results

FIGURE 8-14   *Reviewing fund check results*

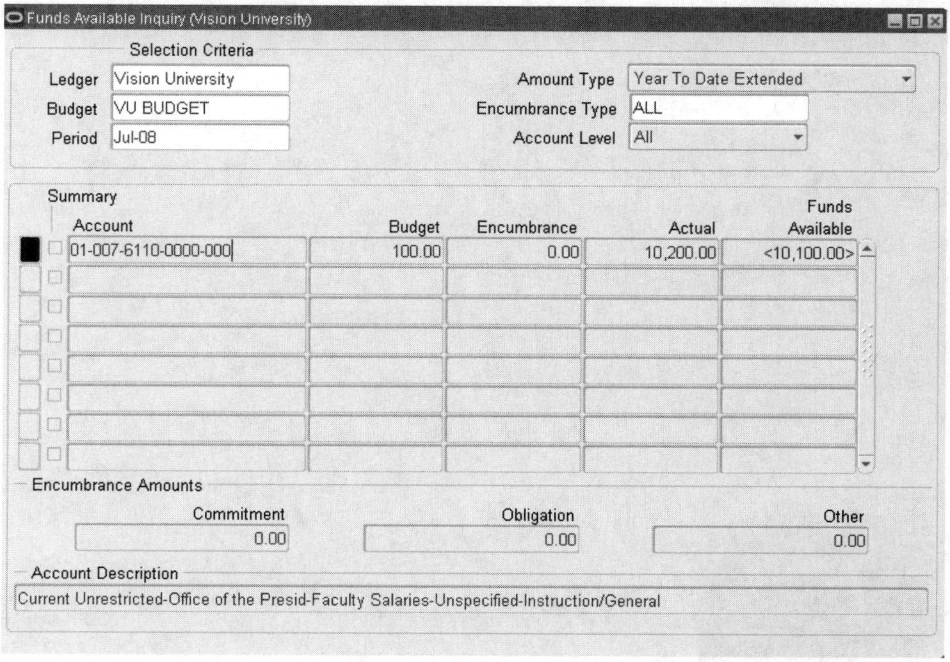

Funds Available Inquiry (Vision University)

Selection Criteria

Ledger	Vision University	
Budget	VU BUDGET	
Period	Jul-08	

Amount Type	Year To Date Extended	
Encumbrance Type	ALL	
Account Level	All	

Summary

Account	Budget	Encumbrance	Actual	Funds Available
01-007-6110-0000-000	100.00	0.00	10,200.00	<10,100.00>

Encumbrance Amounts

Commitment	Obligation	Other
0.00	0.00	0.00

Account Description

Current Unrestricted-Office of the Presid-Faculty Salaries-Unspecified-Instruction/General

General Ledger Superuser | Inquiry | Funds

FIGURE 8-15   *Viewing available funds*

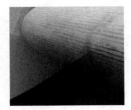

CHAPTER
9

Currencies

o matter how you slice it, foreign currency accounting is just plain complicated. In EBS, there are several tools that can comply with these guidelines and regulations, but it still requires an understanding of the basic rules to use them. This book was not created to explain accounting concepts nor to analyze how these fit into complex regulations, but you must understand some of the basics for currencies prior to understanding the setups in EBS.

Types of Currency Transactions

EBS, like most comprehensive accounting systems, handles currencies at three levels. When a Ledger is set up, it is assigned a *functional currency.* All transactions entered in a currency other than the functional currency are foreign currency transactions. EBS also allows for *reporting currencies* on Ledgers, which will track balances in a currency other than the functional currency, allowing for reporting in both currencies. Finally, any foreign currency balances will need to be revalued from time to time, using more current conversion rates.

Foreign Currency Transactions

Foreign currency transactions happen when transactions are recorded in a currency other than the functional currency. For example, if the functional currency is US Dollars in a Ledger, and an invoice is received for payment in Canadian Dollars, it is entered as a foreign currency transaction. This invoice will be recorded and tracked in Canadian Dollars, and conversion rates will need to be entered at the time of the transaction so that it can be converted to US Dollars for the journal entry in the General Ledger. These rates can either default in from rates loaded into EBS, or the user can supply the rate. A second conversion rate will be assigned to the invoice when it is settled, and it is the difference between the invoice rate and the settlement rate that will create a foreign currency gain or loss on the transaction.

Translations

Translations apply when you keep track of balances in the General Ledger for all accounts in two (or more) different currencies, the functional currency and a foreign reporting currency. EBS can create these balances at different levels, depending on how the Ledger was set up. At the highest level, called the *balance level,* EBS uses a process called *translations* to convert balances at a given time to another currency. This is a separate process that needs to be run to create the foreign currency balances, and it can only use a Period Average or Period End Rate for these conversions (called Historical Rates in EBS). If the option of *Journal* was selected, then the foreign currency balances are built in the General Ledger each time a journal entry is posted. Because the balances are built journal by journal, and journals can only be for a specific day, Daily Rates can be used to create the balances. The final option is called *Subledger,* which actually creates all transactions in the Subledger Accounting process in a foreign currency. This last option allows all reports available in the subledger to be run in both the functional currency and the reporting currency.

Two rules govern how translations are created and accounted for. The first method, called Equity, translates nonmonetary accounts, which are noncash accounts such as Inventory, Fixed Assets, Depreciation, and Cost of Goods Sold, at period end rates; the default rates and rules are shown in Table 9-1. When translations are created, gains and losses are generated in the translated currency to make up for the inevitable out-of-balances of not translating all the transactions and balances at the same rate. Typically, these gains and losses are recorded as an income or expense.

Type of Balance	Rate and Rule
Monetary Assets and Liabilities (such as Cash)	Period End rate on the Year to Date rule
Non-Monetary Assets and Liabilities (such as Fixed Assets)	Period End rate on the Year to Date rule
Equity	Historical rates for the Period to Date rule
Monetary Revenue and Expenses (such as Income)	Period End rate using Year to Date rule
Nonmonetary Revenue and Expenses (such as Cost of Goods Sold and Depreciation)	Period End rate using Year to Date rule

TABLE 9-1   *General Guideline of Translation Rules—Equity Method*

The second method, called Temporal, translates these same nonmonetary balances at historical rates, as defined in the EBS Rates Manager. When using the Temporal method, the foreign currency gains and losses are booked to Equity as opposed to the income statement. Table 9-2 show these rates and rules.

Default Rules for the Balances Used When Translating

When translations are completed, either the Period to Date or the Year to Date rule can be used. Period to Date takes the Period Average rate in EBS and multiplies it against the Period to Date balance in the Ledger. For the Year to Date rule, a Period End rate is used instead, which is then multiplied against the year to date balance in the Ledger. This number is then reduced by the beginning translated balance to come up with a new balance. In EBS, the rule for Assets and Liabilities is always Year to Date and cannot be changed. Both Equity and Income or Expense accounts can use either method but will default to Period to Date.

Type of Balance	Rate and Balance
Monetary Assets and Liabilities (such as Cash)	Period End rate on the Year to Date balances
Nonmonetary Assets and Liabilities (such as Fixed Assets)	Historical rate
Equity	Historical rate
Monetary Revenue and Expenses (such as Income)	Period End rate using Year to Date rule
Nonmonetary Revenue and Expenses (such as Cost of Goods Sold and Depreciation)	Historical rate

TABLE 9-2   *General Guidelines of Translations Rules—Temporal Method*

For translations, both the Equity and Income and Expense defaults can be changed. In System Administrator | Profile | System, set the GL TRANSLATION: REVENUE/EXPENSE TRANSLATION rule and the GL: OWNERS EQUITY TRANSLATION rule. FOR FORM REVALUATIONS rules, only the Income and Expense accounts can be changed, and that is set with GL: INCOME STATEMENT ACCOUNTS REVALUATION rule.

Revaluations

Revaluations allow for any given account balance or group of accounts to be revalued at a specified rate in EBS. Unlike translations, revaluations create journal entries for posting as opposed to generating a balance, and they can be run for a range of accounts instead of being limited to the entire trial balance. While EBS allows revaluations to be performed on any account, they typically are performed on balance sheet accounts that will be settled at a later date, such as Accounts Payables or Accounts Receivables. The revaluation process will revalue these balances using a more appropriate rate (often the period end rate for the period) to accurately reflect the current reality of paying or receiving these open transactions.

An example of when to revalue an account is if a Payables invoice is still unpaid and over 60 days old. If the exchange rate between the functional and translated currencies has had a large fluctuation up or down, the account should be revalued to reflect the true cash outlay for payment at this point in time. Revaluation journal entries are usually reversed on the first of the next period, when the balances are again evaluated for revaluation.

The other profile option for revaluations, besides the GL: INCOME STATEMENT ACCOUNTS REVALUATION rule, is called GL REVALUATION: USE PRIMARY BOOK CURRENCY INSTEAD OF ENTERED CURRENCY. Setting YES here will always use the functional currency to create the revaluations, no matter what currency the transaction was entered in. Selecting NO will use the entered currency instead. If the transaction is going to be settled in the transaction currency, then this profile should be set to NO to more accurately reflect the settlement value.

Currency Setups

In order to create transactions in a foreign currency or to report in multiple currencies, a few setups are required.

Currencies

The setups required for currencies depend on what you are doing. First, ensure the currencies you want to use are enabled on your system. Go to the currency window (General Ledger Superuser | Setup | Currencies | Define) and you will see that many currencies are predefined, but most will not be enabled. Check ENABLE to begin using one of these currencies. If the currency you need is not included on this form, it can be added. Here are the fields you can modify or add for a new currency: CODE is the three-digit code used for this currency (such as USD), and NAME is the actual name it goes by. DESCRIPTION is a description of the currency, and EBS often defaults the NAME into this field, but it can be overridden. An ISSUING TERRITORY can be assigned to the currency, as can the SYMBOL, which EBS will then use on forms and reports that have currency symbols on them. PRECISION allows you to define how many decimal places will be used for transactions in this currency, whereas EXTENDED PRECISION defines the number of decimal places for calculations in such modules as Inventory. Enter a MINIMUM ACCOUNTABLE UNIT for the smallest allowed unit in this currency.

When working with the Euro, there are some additional setups that can be performed to create the connections between the base currencies for the country and the Euro. This triangulation rule is set up as CURRENCY DERIVATION in EBS. To use this feature, set up the Euro as the EURO CURRENCY TYPE, and all the other countries as EURO DERIVED TYPE. This will then allow a FACTOR and an EFFECTIVE date to be added. All transactions in currencies set up as EURO DERIVED will have the transactional translations derived from the exchange rate for the Euro to the currencies entered. In this way, the Euro becomes the base for the exchange. An example is that if a transaction is entered in FRANCS, and FRANCS is set up with a CURRENCY DERIVATION, then it will convert FRANCS into EURO, and EURO into USD using the rates set up under the EURO. Once the currencies are set up, foreign currency journals can be entered. If a currency set up as EURO DERIVED is selected, then the Rate Type will default to EMU Fixed and cannot be changed by the users in the journals form.

Rates

Once the currencies are set up, users can begin to enter foreign currency transactions by supplying the conversion rates, but EBS will not default these rates until they are set up. You have four options available for entering conversion rates on a transaction: USER, PERIOD END, PERIOD AVERAGE, and a DAILY RATE. User will require the person entering the journal entry or any other transaction to supply the exchange rate. This option works best for currencies that are used extremely infrequently by an organization, and there are very few controls around the rates entered. PERIOD END and PERIOD AVERAGE are most commonly used for translations based on balances, whereas DAILY is used for foreign currency transactions as well as journal- and subledger-based translations.

The rates used as PERIOD END and PERIOD AVERAGE are assigned when the Ledger is set up, and can be found in the CURRENCY TRANSLATION OPTIONS section. EBS will take the rates from the last day of the month if there are rates set up for more than one day. DAILY RATES are usually set up for each business day of the month and will default the rate in on foreign currency transactions when selected.

EBS comes with a limited number of Rate Types, and additional ones can be added if they are needed. There are two forms for adding Rate Types: use the Currency Rate Manager when a triangulation is needed (General Ledger Superuser | Setup | Currencies | Currency Rates Manager | Rate Types). The form under Rates | Types does not allow this functionality to be set up.

The Daily Rates Manager shown in Figure 9-1 can be used to enter dates for either a specific date or a range of dates, between two currencies. Only the actual conversion rate needs to be entered, and EBS will calculate the INVERSE RATE. Inverse Rates are the reverse exchange; for example, if you enter a rate of 1.1 between USD and CAD, the INVERSE RATE for CAD to USD is 0.9090. There are three options for entering rates into EBS; two are on this form and can be used without any additional programming.

You can enter rates on the form itself by clicking CREATE DAILY RATES; this is a good option if your organization uses only one or two foreign currencies. If it uses more currencies, Web ADI has a worksheet that has all the same fields as the form but allows the conversion rates to be entered into a Excel spreadsheet and uploaded for faster data entry. This is an especially good option if you have a service that the rates can be downloaded from. For large organizations transacting in multiple countries that are required to track a large amount of conversions, an application programming interface (API) exists where these rates can be directly imported into an interface table, then into EBS for use.

Files can often be obtained from a subscription service for these exchange rates. The cost of writing this interface as well as that of the subscription service should be evaluated against the cost and accuracy of a person entering them manually. Once the rates are loaded into EBS, they will default in when a user selects SPOT or CORPORATE when making a journal entry or other transactions in any module, based on the DATE provided in the Conversion section of the journal or transaction.

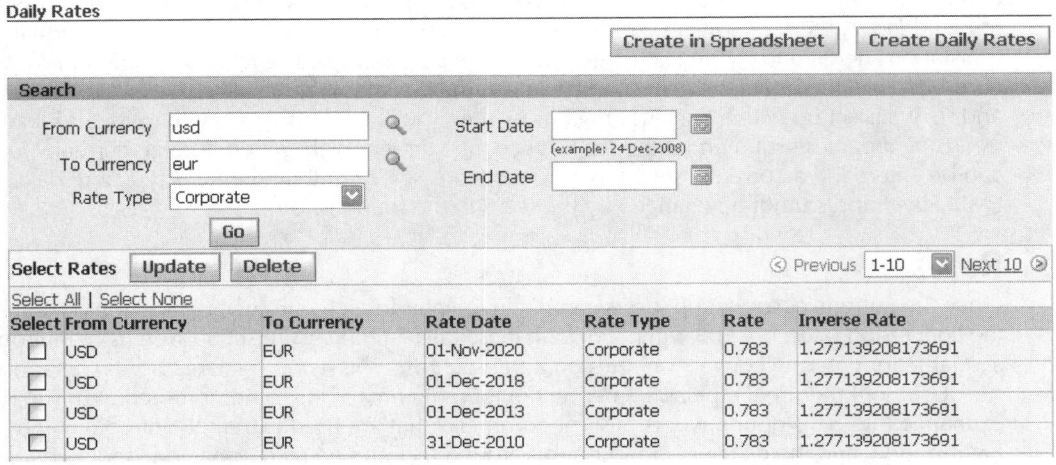

Daily Rates

| | | | | | Create in Spreadsheet | | Create Daily Rates |

Search

From Currency	usd	🔍		Start Date		📅
To Currency	eur	🔍			(example: 24-Dec-2008)	
Rate Type	Corporate	▾		End Date		📅

Go

Select Rates | **Update** | **Delete** | ◁ Previous | 1-10 ▾ | Next 10 ▷

Select All | Select None

Select	From Currency	To Currency	Rate Date	Rate Type	Rate	Inverse Rate
☐	USD	EUR	01-Nov-2020	Corporate	0.783	1.277139208173691
☐	USD	EUR	01-Dec-2018	Corporate	0.783	1.277139208173691
☐	USD	EUR	01-Dec-2013	Corporate	0.783	1.277139208173691
☐	USD	EUR	31-Dec-2010	Corporate	0.783	1.277139208173691

General Ledger Superuser | Setup | Currencies | Currency Rate Manager | Daily Rates

FIGURE 9-1 *Entering and maintaining currencies*

Historical rates can also be entered in the HISTORICAL tab of the Currency Rates Manager. Historical rates are used during translations for specific accounts (see Tables 9-1 and 9-2), and during revaluations; they usually refer to a rate at a specific point in time in the past. Historical rates are most accepted for use in Equity, where the balances are always converted at the point in time when they were recorded, such as a Fiscal Year End for a prior year's retained earnings. Since this is not a transaction that will be changing in the future but one that is fixed in the past, a historical rate is assigned.

Running a Translation for Balance Level Reporting Currencies

Translations only need to be run when the REPORTING CURRENCIES CURRENCY CONVERSION LEVEL is set to BALANCE. If it is set to JOURNAL, translations happen when the journal is posted, and if it is set to SUBLEDGER, then they happen during the accounting process.

General Ledger balances will need the first period translated separately from future translations. Remember the rules that EBS uses to translate balances: either the period to date balance is translated and added on to the prior period's translated values, or the year to date balance is translated and then reduced by the prior period year to date translated balance to come up with the current period translation.

This initialization process is completed by running the concurrent request Reporting Currency – Create Opening Balance Journals in Reporting Currencies. This process will create foreign currency balances for the period designated in the request through to the first period in the General Ledger where the period status is neither opened nor future enabled. It is important to understand what periods this process will create the balances for. Ensure you go back far enough to accommodate any foreign currency reporting needs for historical data, such as annual comparisons on financial statements. Once this process is run, it cannot be rerun for an earlier period. It is a good idea to select the first period of a fiscal year to ensure the year to date and quarter to date balances are correct in the tables.

Monthly translations can be run from either the translation form or the concurrent request called Translations. In the translation form shown in Figure 9-2, select the LEDGER/LEDGER SET to perform the translation for. USAGE determines if the Standard or Average balances will be translated, or both at the same time. When dealing with currencies, Budgets can be entered for a functional currency and then translated for reporting purposes by selecting the BALANCE TYPE of Budget. Select the TARGET CURRENCY for this translation run. The selection here is not limited to currencies that are set up as reporting currencies under the Ledger.

Running a Translation for a currency that is not set up in the Ledger will create a Balance Level reporting currency automatically, assigning the default name that appears in REPORTING CURRENCY (this cannot be changed here but can be modified in the Accounting Manager after it is saved). Select the PERIOD for this translation, ensuring that the rates needed are set up. EBS will give a warning if there are no rates for the target currency and period selected. The BALANCING SEGMENT section determines if ALL segments will be translated at the same time, or only a specific value. There are some rules surrounding a new currency the first time translations is run. Just as when journals are created for a new install to create the initial balances in a reporting currency, new balancing segments require an initial balance to be created. Running the Translation for that currency alone will perform this process, but a currency that has not been initialized will not create any translations when ALL is selected.

If BUDGET was selected as the BALANCE TYPE, enter both the SOURCE and TARGET budget names. These can be the same budget. For budgets translations only, PERIOD END and PERIOD AVERAGE rates can be selected. For actual balances, the rate types set up in the Ledger will be used.

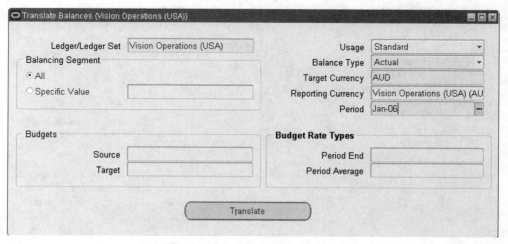

General Ledger Superuser | Currency | Translation

FIGURE 9-2   *Translations*

Performing Revaluations

Revaluations are typically used to update foreign currency balances that will be cleared or settled at a future date to the current exchange rates. An example of this is Accounts Payable. If you have an invoice that is over 60 days old, and the exchange rate has had a material change, you will want to revalue this balance to the current exchange rate. Revaluations, when run, create journal entries that can be reversed in the next period. Defined revaluations can be rerun for different periods, reusing the same definition multiple times.

Defining Revaluations

To revalue balances, assign a REVALUATION name and a DESCRIPTION to the revaluation, as shown in Figure 9-3. Selecting AUTOPOST REVALUATION will cause the journal entry to be posted automatically when the revaluation is run. ENABLE SECURITY allows this form to be secured with a definition access set. Under CURRENCY OPTIONS, determine if this will apply to all reporting currencies, or only a SINGLE CURRENCY. A specific DAILY RATE defined in the rates table can be selected, or a ONE-TIME RATE entered for this definition. Once a revaluation is defined, it can be updated prior to running it, allowing the one-time rate to be modified for each period it is run for.

Assign the accounts where UNREALIZED GAIN and LOSS will be recorded, and select the account or range of accounts that this revaluation will pertain to. Parent accounts can be used in both the balancing segment and the natural account, and EBS will show that they are used when you check the EXPAND check boxes. These are display-only fields and cannot be updated.

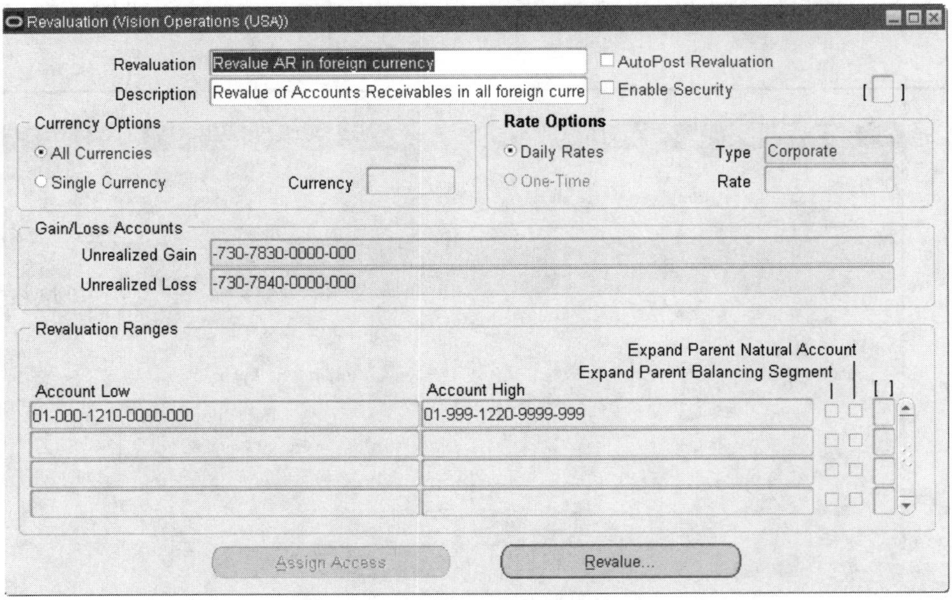

General Ledger Superuser | Currency | Revaluation

FIGURE 9-3 *Revaluations*

Running Revaluations

You can run revaluations by either clicking the REVALUE button or running the concurrent request Program – Revalue Balances. When running the revaluation, select the LEDGER or LEDGER SETS it should be run for and the REVALUATION definition (which you just made). Enter the PERIOD, which determines which balances will be revalued. The EFFECTIVE DATE will default in according to the period entered and will become the effective date of the journal entry. Note that if the effective date is changed outside of the period entered, EBS will change it back to the default date for the period. (For prior periods, the default is the last day of the month; for future periods, the default is the first day of the month; and for the current period, the default is the system date.) The RATE DATE is only considered if DAILY RATE was selected, and the rates are entered for each day. Then the rate for the date entered in the RATE DATE will be used for the revaluation.

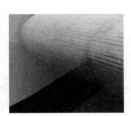

CHAPTER
10

Reporting, Inquiry, and Integration

E BS comes with a large number of predefined concurrent processes. These can be broken down into three main categories: Reports, Listings, and Processes.

Reports are predefined reports that can be used by any organization to view data entered into EBS. In the General Ledger, this includes such things as Journal Entries and Trial Balances. In general, these are reports written in PL-SQL and either output using Oracle's Reports 6*i* program or used to create XML and be published by the BI Publisher, which overlays a formatting template. EBS does not come with any predefined balance sheets or income statements, as these are unique to each organization that uses EBS. The FSG feature is used to create these reports and is described in Chapter 6.

Listings are reports as well but usually relate to setup data as opposed to transactional data. These can be used to review, confirm, or document the setups in your system. Both Reports and Listings can be run at any time without any fear of updating data in the system, as they are only reporting on the data in the system.

Processes (also called Programs) require a little more caution when running. These concurrent requests will actually update or generate data in some way in the database. Many can be reversed, but there are some that cannot. When in doubt, it is always better to run Processes in a test instance first when unsure of the results.

Requests are run from the Concurrent Request Manager and can be printed as well as viewed within the manager. There is a profile that controls the method a report is viewed in called VIEWER: TEXT. This can be set to BROWSER to use your browser to view any report output. The advantages to using this feature are that you can see all pages of the report at the same time, as opposed to one page at a time, and the report can be saved as a text file for future reference or to open up in Excel. There are also profiles that control the default printing options. The profile PRINTER sets the default printer associated with each request and can be set at the user level, and CONCURRENT: REPORT COPIES determines how many default copies will print for each request (setting this to zero will print no copies). All three of these profiles can be set for the entire system (System Administrator | Profile | System), or they can be set by individual users under Edit | Preferences | Profiles and is available from the seeded responsibilities and, when set, will only affect the user who sets it.

Grouping Requests to Run Together

When submitting a request, you can choose either a Single Request or a Request Set. A majority of the requests that come with EBS are Single Requests, which run one process at a time. Some request groups are available out of the box, but they are usually started not from the Request Manager, but from a form, such as Deprecation in Fixed Assets. Request Groups are simply a grouping of reports that are always run at the same time, saving steps when processing the request.

To define a request group, go to the Request Set form as shown in Figure 10-1, and assign a name to the SET. The SET CODE is the system name for this set and is not seen by the users. Select the APPLICATION the reports are associated with, and add a DESCRIPTION. The OWNER will default to your user name but can be changed if you are creating this on behalf of another user. The ACTIVE DATES assign the first and last date that this set can be used. RUN OPTIONS determines whether the reports can PRINT TOGETHER after the entire request set or print as they complete when this option is not checked.

ALLOW INCOMPATABILITY determines if certain processes can run at the same time as this request set. There are specific processes of EBS that, from a database integrity or system resource standpoint, should not run at the same time. One of the most apparent examples of this is Fixed Asset Depreciation and the process to add assets to the system, the Mass Additions process. You cannot add assets at the same time you are running deprecations, because the asset being added may be missed in the depreciation process, so these two processes are incompatible with each other, and EBS will ensure that if one is running, the other will stay in a Pending status until it is completed. Request Sets actually disable this feature of EBS for all the processes within the request. Checking ALLOW INCOMPATABILITY allows the system administrator to set up incompatibilities for this specific request set, with itself, other request sets, and other individual processes.

Click DEFINE STAGES to move on to the next step. Enter a DISPLAY SEQUENCE, which will determine the order the stages in this request will be run. Each stage can have multiple requests assigned to it. The benefit to using multiple stages as opposed to only one stage with all the requests assigned to it is twofold. First, stages can be set up to process the reports in the request in sequence (one report at a time) as opposed to in parallel (all stages run at the same time), which will limit the system resources it will take to complete these requests. Parallel will have them all kick off at the same time, potentially limiting the requests other users can process until it is completed. Second, sometimes a request will build on the prior stage for information that is required for the next stage to complete. If you are creating a request set to run depreciation and create journal entries in fixed assets, deprecation will need to complete before the process of creating journal entries can start. Assign a STAGE name and DESCRIPTION, as well as a STAGE CODE, or internal name, for each stage. For each stage, select THE RETURN VALUE OF THIS STAGE AFFECTS THE SET OUTCOME if you want the request set to stop if it encounters an error, or leave it unselected if you want the set to proceed and complete the rest of the stages. This can be seen in Figure 10-2.

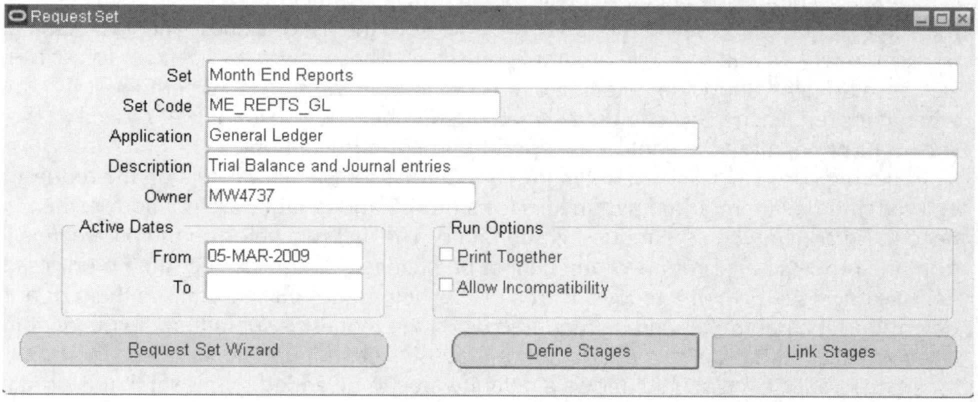

General Ledger Superuser | Other | Report | Set

FIGURE 10-1 *Creating a grouping of reports to run at the same time (Request Set)*

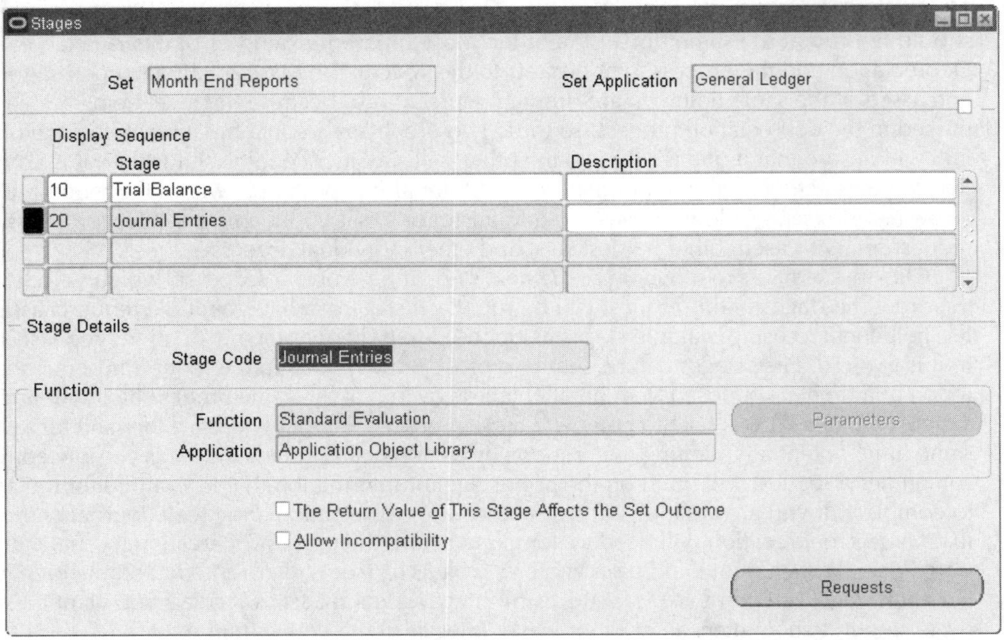

General Ledger Superuser | Other | Report | Set | Define Stages

FIGURE 10-2 *Defining stages for request sets*

Next is to define the actual REQUESTS for each STAGE by clicking REQUESTS. Assign a SEQUENCE to the actual request, and select the PROGRAM name from the list of values. The APPLICATION and the DESCRIPTION will default from the program you select. The ALLOW STAGE FUNCTION TO USE THIS PROGRAM'S RESULTS setting will allow the outcome of this program in the stage to determine if it passes or fails when checked. Each stage can be assigned the number of COPIES to output as well as the PRINTER it should print on, allowing control by report for the printing options.

Clicking PARAMETERS, shown in Figure 10-3, allows for the parameters on the request to be entered. If there are required parameters for a report, and defaults are not added, then they will need to be added when the request is submitted. The first two fields on the parameters form are from the process being run itself and cannot be changed. These are the same prompts that are completed or seen when a request is run. DISPLAY determines if users can see them or not. MODIFY determines if a parameter can be modified when the request is submitted. If you want to set up a request set that has defaulted parameters that users cannot update, uncheck this box.

The SHARED PARAMETER field allows a default value to be added to this set that is used by all reports in this set—you have to set the default value one time and then assign a consistent name under SHARED PARAMETER for all the reports and prompts you want to default this parameter in. Some of the DEFAULT TYPES and VALUES will already be populated—these are from the report itself and usually should not be changed. To add a default, select the TYPE from the list of values and populate in the DEFAULT for that field. Unlike when running reports, you have no lists to select from for the

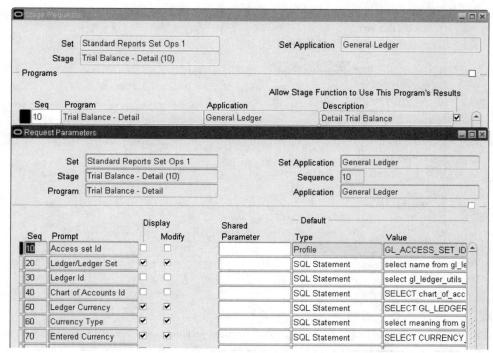

FIGURE 10-3 *Adding parameters to a request set*

VALUES. Luckily, this only needs to be set up once. The easiest way to populate these fields is to actually do it on a single request and copy the information into this form. That way, it is accurate. Once this is completed, the work can be saved and the request set run.

Running Reports

You run a request from the Process Manager (View | Requests | submit a new Request), where you first select Single Request or Request Set. Referring to Figure 10-4, select the NAME from the list of values. EBS does offer security on the requests that a specific responsibility can run. Request Groups are set up in System Administrator and are used to grant access to run a request, or remove a request. Most requests have both required and not-required parameters, which will help narrow down data this report will select—click in the PARAMETERS field to enter these values. Not all fields will be required; white fields are optional, whereas yellow fields are required.

When running a report or process, you have options as to when it can be run as well as where and if it is printed. The default for running is AS SOON AS POSSIBLE. To change this to a future date or time, or to set up this request as a recurring request that will run on given dates and times, click SCHEDULE. To run this request once at a later time, select ONCE and enter the RUN AT date and time.

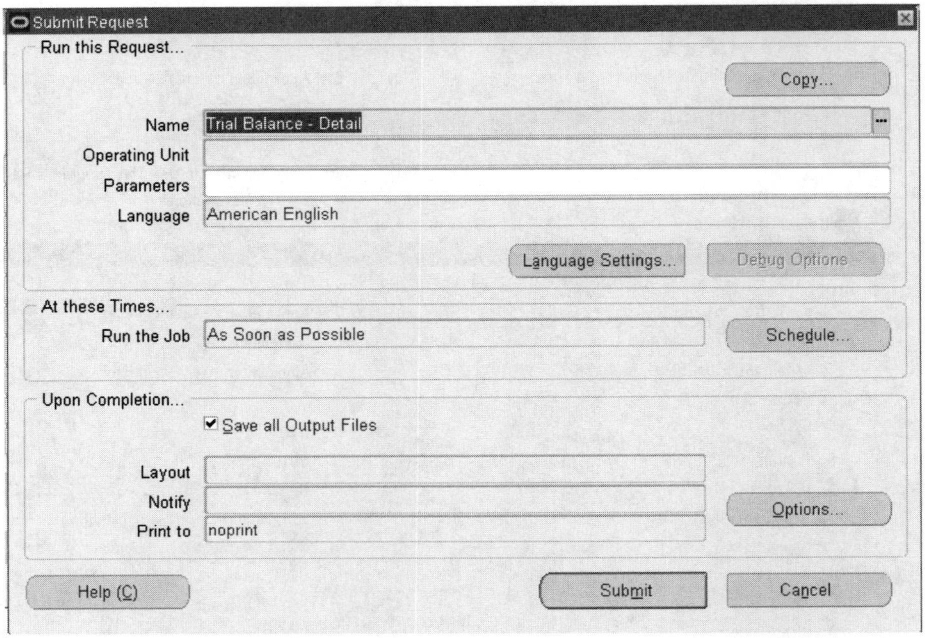

General Ledger Superuser | View | Requests | Submit a new request | Single Request

FIGURE 10-4 *Submitting a request in the Concurrent Manager*

You can schedule a request to run on a regular basis by setting it up to run PERIODICALLY or ON SPECIFIC DAYS. To run it periodically, select that option and enter a START AT date and time (this defaults to now) and optionally an END AT date and time. If you don't enter an end date, this request will run forever until someone cancels the request.

Select the frequency by entering the time interval as a number, and selecting from Month, Week, Day, Hour, or Minute. Select the APPLY INTERVAL as FROM THE START OF THE PRIOR RUN to start the timer for the frequency when the process gets started, whereas COMPLETION will start that countdown from the end of the prior process. Many reports and processes have date parameters; checking INCREMENT DATE PARAMETER EACH RUN will automatically increase these parameters each time the request is run. Select SAVE THIS SCHEDULE to assign it a name and make it possible to use it on multiple requests. When selecting ON SPECIFIC DAYS, you can either specify a specific calendar day of the month, the last calendar day of the month, no matter what the date is, or specific days of the week.

The other request OPTIONS include sending a notification to a specific person once this request is completed, and setting the printer and copies that this report will print to. The printer and copies will default from your personal profiles if they are set, and the system profiles if they are not. These can be changed for any individual requests in the Printer section of the page.

From the Submit Request window, clicking COPY to select a request that was previously run and rerun it, either with the same PARAMETERS or by modifying them. This is a nice feature that reduces the data you need to enter when running a commonly used request. Often users will rerun the same reports over and over again, and this avoids the repetitiveness of reentering all the information over and over; just change the fields to get the information you need (often dates or accounts).

Once a report is completed, it can be reprinted as many times as needed. With the mouse on the Request, select Tools | Reprint. Select the PRINTER and COPIES and click APPLY. Be aware that most companies purge their concurrent requests on a regular basis (the interval can be select by that company), so processed requests are not available forever.

Additional options are available in the Concurrent Manager for managing your requests. When a report is in the status of Pending or Scheduled, it is safe to cancel the request by clicking CANCEL REQUEST. For requests that are in the Pending status, canceling will stop the report from processing. For requests that are in the Scheduled status, canceling will stop all future or scheduled runs of this report. Use extreme caution in canceling requests that are actually running. If the request is just a report, canceling it is not a problem. But if the request updates any data, canceling can sometimes cause a problem with the process being run, requiring technical assistance to resolve it. A request may not have rollback features properly written in, causing some or all updated data to remain in the database. This problem often arises with the Depreciation process in Assets; canceling this at certain points requires an update to the database to rerun the process.

Another feature is holding a process. This is very helpful if a request is started that uses a lot of system resources and is holding up other requests. The process can be placed on hold by the person who submitted it or the system administrator with the HOLD REQUEST button, allowing other processes to complete; then it can be restarted when there is less activity going on. This is also particularly helpful if a long-running report is preventing another report to process because of a conflict.

Conflicts are set up for all concurrent requests, letting the system know that two or more specific processes, either update processes or a report and an update process, are going to use the exact same data to run. Updating the same data with two separate processes can cause data inconsistencies, and updating the exact data you are trying to report on basically confuses EBS, because it does not know if a specific record should be updated or reported first. You can tell if two reports are in conflict when running by highlighting your request and going to Tools | Manager. If the process is in conflict with any other process running in the system, the Conflict Resolution Manager will appear under the Concurrent Manager section. Once the process in conflict is completed, this will resolve and your process will run.

In the manager, click VIEW DETAILS to review specific details about a request, such as the Parameters or the Schedule it is set to run on. Though not 100 percent accurate, the details will also display Date and Time started and Date and Time completed—this helps users review how long requests are taking to run, and can be helpful in determining if perhaps this request should not be run during the day, or if the time has substantially increased. In such a case, inform the DBA so that the reasons can be determined (for example, if the time to run an FSG is increasing each month, the Program Optimizer may need to be run).

Programs That Update Data

Table 10-1 lists all the programs that will cause updates to EBS, as well as a short description of what each actually does.

Concurrent Request Name – Programs	Description
AutoAllocation Launcher	Generates Allocation journal entries.
Close Process – Create Balance Sheet Closing Journals	Uses Journal Import to create Balance Sheet journal entries for year end.
Close Process – Create Income Statement Closing Journals	Uses Journal Import to create Income Statement journal entries for year end.
Consolidation – Restore Unconsolidated Status to Batches	When a consolidation is performed, batches are marked as consolidated and stored in several control tables. If the consolidation errors out during processing, these statuses are not reset. Running this report will reverse all the updates for the specific request (using the request number for the consolidation that failed), making the batches available for consolidation and updating all the consolidation tables.
Open Period	Opens periods across Ledger Sets with one process.
Periods – Close Period	Closes periods across Ledger Sets with one process.
Periods – Gapless Close Periods	Closes periods and applies sequencing to journals, ensuring the numbering is gapless.
Periods – Permanently Close Period	Closes periods permanently, such that they cannot be reopened.
Program – Automatic Reversal	Generates reversing journal entries for a given period based on the journal category setups and flags in the reverse period section of the journal entry.
Program – Prepare Journal Batches for Management Segment Upgrade	Used to add the Management Segment Qualifier to an existing Chart of Accounts that has already been used. This process will kick off the Process Journal Batches for Management Segment Upgrade.
Program – Revalue Balance	Runs Revaluations and creates journal entries for posting.
Program – Complete Management Segment Upgrade	Finalizes the adding of a Management Segment to a Chart of Accounts.
Program – Creates Journals	Creates journal entries for Purchasing and Payables transactions that have passed the funds checking—this is only used with Encumbrance Accounting.
Program – Daily Rates Import and Calculations	This program has two functions, as the name implies: it can be used to import data via the Rates interface for currency conversions, and it is kicked off automatically when daily rates are saved, causing the Contra rates to be calculated and populated in EBS.

TABLE 10-1 *Reports That Update Data*

Concurrent Request Name – Programs	Description
Program – Delete Ad Hoc Reports	Deletes ad hoc FSG reports from the EBS database.
Program – Delete Budget Organization	Deletes a Budget Organization from the database; this cannot be rolled back once it is started, nor can the budget organization be recovered.
Program – Delete Journal Import Data	Deletes unimported data from the Journal Import interface tables, based on Source, Request ID, and Ledger. This is especially useful if WebADI is used to upload journal entries. It is *never* recommended for submodule journal entries, as these cannot be re-created; if the R12 function is used to roll back journals with problems for the subledgers, then there is no danger of that happening.
Program – FSG Transfer	Transfers FSG components between databases.
Program – General Ledger Flexfield	EBS runs this report when the Accounting Flexfield is created, or values added to it, to update the GL Flexfield and keep the two Flexfields in synch.
Program – Generate Upgrade for Balances Entered in Ledger Currency	Postupgrade program used to populate the Entered Currency fields in General Ledger. This program should only be run as part of an upgrade.
Program – Import Journals	Process used by EBS to import data from subledgers, third-party systems that populate the journal interface tables, consolidations, etc. This can be kicked off from either a form or another process, or else run manually.
Program – Incremental Add/Delete Summary Templates	Used for Ledgers with Summary accounts Enabled to update the summary template and balances when a new account is added or deleted.
Program – Inherit Segment Value Attributes	Updates account combinations to have the same attributes as the segment values. This includes end dates, enabled status, and posting status.
Program – Maintain Authorized Users for Journal Approval Reassignment	Running this process restricts the reassignment of Journal Approvals to only people who are authorized to approval journal entries.
Program – Maintain Budget Organizations	Adds specific account combinations to a budget based on the account ranges assigned to the budget. This needs to be run periodically to ensure all individual account combinations are assigned to the budget.
Program – Maintain Summary Templates	Ensures that the posting process is efficient and that all balances are maintained for the summary accounts, based on any new accounts that have been added.

TABLE 10-1   *Reports That Update Data* (continued)

Concurrent Request Name – Programs	Description
Program – Optimizer	Optimizes General Ledger performance for such process as FSG reports by creating or dropping database indexes for new or deleted segment values, based on which values are marked for indexing in the Flexfield.
Program – Track Budgetary Debit/Credit Accounts as Balance Sheet Accounts	Creates beginning balances for income and expense accounts that are under budgetary controls. This works similar to the 11.5.10 process of creating carry-forward balances.
Reconciliation – Automatic Reconciliation	Reconciles transactions for a specific account based on the defined criteria.
Reporting Currency – Create Opening Balance Journals in Reporting currency	Creates opening translation balances for converted balances, based on the period status.
Setup Flattening Program for Table Validated Sets	If the accounting Flexfield was set up with one or more segments that are validated by a table in EBS, this process needs to be run when the Flexfield structure is set up or changed, any time the Parent/Child hierarchy is changed, or whenever a new segment value is added. The process will move any information that is relevant to the Chart of Accounts from the value set to the General Ledger Hierarchy and the security tables; not running this under these circumstances may cause inaccurate data on some reports and features.
Translation	Creates balance-level transactions in Reporting Currencies.
XBRL – Load Taxonomy	Used to load the XBRL codes into EBS.
XBRL – Remove Taxonomy	Used to remove the XBRL codes from EBS.

TABLE 10-1   *Reports That Update Data* (continued)

Listings of Setup Data

EBS comes with many report listings that can aid in reviewing and understanding setups that are done in the system. Some of these reports, such as Chart of Accounts – Segment Values Listing, may be able to replace manual spreadsheets or listings in accounting, so familiarizing yourself with what is available can help to streamline work. These reports are listed in Table 10-2.

Concurrent Request Name (Listing)	Description
Accounting Setup Manager Post – Update Diagnostic Report	This report should be run after the Ledger setups are completed, after an upgrade, or whenever the setups have changed. It will look for inconsistent or invalid setups in the Ledgers. When an inconsistency or invalid setup is found, determine if the setup is correct for your company needs prior to making the change, especially during an upgrade, where the report was clean prior to the upgrade. Some items that show up on this report are critical, while others are more a flag that you are not doing things Oracle's recommended way, not always a bad thing for your scenarios and needs.
Budget – Frozen Budgets Accounts Listing	Lists all budgets, and identifies them as frozen or not, along with the account ranges that are assigned to the budget.
Budget – Hierarchy Listing	Lists all the master and budget relationships that are defined in your system.
Budget – Organization Listing	Lists all account combinations assigned to a specific budget organization, and specific details, such as budgetary control information for each account.
Budget – Organization Range Listing	Lists the range of account combinations assigned to a specific budget.
Chart of Accounts – Account Hierarchy	Lists summary accounts with the rollup combinations; can be run for all templates or a specific template. This is not for parent-child relationships, which can be found on the Chart of Accounts—Rollup Detail Listing report.
Chart of Accounts – Detail Listing	Lists all combinations for each natural account, and includes such information as Account type and the Enabled flag.
Chart of Accounts – Inactive Accounts Listing	Includes any account combination that has been disabled or end dated.
Chart of Accounts – Mapping Rules	Details of a specific mapping rule and how the account segments are being mapped for either consolidations or Subledger Accounting.

TABLE 10-2 *Setup Listings*

Concurrent Request Name (Listing)	Description
Chart of Accounts – Rollup Detail Listing	Detailed listing of parent-child relationships. This report shows every child account that is assigned to a parent. This report does not show the ranges assigned to the parent; see the Chart of Accounts – Rollup Range listing for this information.
Chart of Accounts – Rollup Range Listing	Listing of Parent-Child relationships, but based on ranges assigned to parents, as opposed to each individual value that falls within the range. See the Chart of Accounts – Rollup Detail listing for individual values.
Chart of Accounts – Segment Values Listing	Lists all segment values, with such details as Posting Allowed and Parent Flag, for a specific segment of the Chart of Accounts.
Chart of Accounts – Suspense Accounts Listing	Lists the suspense account combinations assigned to specific Journal Sources and Categories.
Currency – Daily Conversion Rates Listing	Lists conversion rates and the reciprocal rate for any two currencies for a given time period.
Currency – Historical Rates Listing	Lists all historical rates entered for a given time period, for all currencies and accounts.
FSG Detail and Summary Listings	FSG reports can sometimes be tricky to maintain and review for accuracy. EBS provides summary and detail listings of many of the components (Column, Content, Report, Report Sets, Row Order, Row Sets). These reports are convenient not only to troubleshoot problems or review for accuracy, but also to use as backups for change control.
FSG – Where Used	The goal of all FSGs is to write as few components as possible, and to use each one multiple times with different reports. But it is imperative to ensure you know where a component is used prior to making any changes; the change needed for one specific report may not be valid for another report using the same component. This listing will show all the different FSG Reports using a specific row set or column set (or any component).

TABLE 10-2 *Setup Listings* (continued)

Concurrent Request Name (Listing)	Description
Other – Data Access Set Listing	Lists which segment values a specific data access has access to by Ledger or Ledger Set.
Other – Definition Access by User	By User, lists types of Privileges (Use, View, or Modify) that user has to a specific Definition Type (this is all the screens where Security Enable is available—mostly in the Setup area).
Other – Definition Access Set Listing	Lists the Privileges (Use, View, or Modify) specific Definition Access Sets offer, by both Type and Specific Definition Name (or each individual setup, like within Calendars, which specific calendar can it access?). It does not list which users have access to these Definition Access Sets.
Other – Ledger Set Listing	Lists all the Ledgers or Ledger Sets assigned to a specific Ledger set.
Other – MassAllocation Formula Listing	Listing of all the lines in a specific MassAllocation, or all MassAllocations.
Other – Recurring Formula Listing	Listing of all the lines in a specific Recurring Formula, or all Recurring Formulas.
Other – Transaction Code Listing	Listing of Transaction Codes, usually used with budgetary controls, and their associated debit and credit accounts.
Other – Units of Measure Listing	Lists the specific units of measure that are associated with an account for statistical journal entries.
Other – Calendar Validation Report	This report is run every time a change is made to a calendar; it lists any calendar violations, such as missing periods or missing dates.

TABLE 10-2   *Setup Listings* (continued)

Transactional Reports

The last grouping of reports, shown in Table 10-3, are more transactional in nature, providing information not on the setups, but on the actual transactions in the system.

Concurrent Request Name (Reports)	Description
Account Analysis – 132 and 180 Char	Detailed account information, including beginning and ending balances and details for the journal lines. The 180 Char version provides more room in some of the columns.
Account Analysis – Average Balance Audit	Shows the account activity and details utilized in creating average balances.
Account Analysis – Contra Account	Provides similar data by account as the Account Analysis (180 Char), but it also shows the offset to the journal entry for each account.
Budget – Journals by Account	Lists all the budget journals for a specified year and account number.
Budget – Master/Detail	Lists the available funds for all detail accounts assigned to a master budget.
Budget – Summary/Detail	Shows the detail accounts and their balances for a specific summary account.
Budget – Unbudgeted Master/Detail Accounts	Reports all the detail budget accounts where the sums do not equal the master budget account.
Budgetary Control Results report	Lists all the transactions against a specific budget account for a period, identifying their Funds Check status.
Consolidation – Audit	Available when the Audit mode option is used for consolidations, this report shows the actual account mappings used for consolidated transactions.
Consolidation – Disabled Parent Accounts	Available when the Audit mode option is used for consolidations, this will report on any account on the parent Ledger that a child Ledger tried to map a balance or transaction to.
Consolidation – Journals	When performing consolidations at the transaction level, this report can be run from a parent to see the original journals from a child Ledger, along with the account it was posted to in the parent Ledger.
Consolidation – Unmapped Subsidiary Accounts	Once a consolidation is performed, this report lists all the journals in the child Ledgers that were not consolidated because they were not mapped. This report includes only journals for accounts that were assigned to the consolidation that had a balance.
General Ledger – 132 and 180 Char	Detailed report of account combinations, balances, and journal-level transactions.
General Ledger – Entered Currency	Shows both foreign and functional currency journals in the currency they were entered, including currency and translation data.

TABLE 10-3   *Transactional Reports*

Concurrent Request Name (Reports)	Description
Journals – 132 and 180 Char	Detailed journal entry listings by period as well as batch.
Journals – Batch Summary	At the batch level (excludes detailed line data), lists batch information.
Journals – Check	Detailed listing of journals for a period or batch, and is in a good format for reviewing manual journal entries for accuracy.
Journals – Day Book	Detailed listing of journals for a period or batch, sorted by Date.
Journals – Document Number	High-level journal information for a specific document sequence.
Journals – Enter Currency – 132 and 180 Char	Summary journal information showing journal details in both the entered and accounted currencies.
Journals – Entry	Detailed journal report.
Journals – Extended	Detailed journal report.
Journals – Line	Detailed journal report.
Journals – Tax	Detailed report used to validate the Tax added to journal lines.
Journals – Voucher	Detailed journal report.
Program – Publish FSG report	Publishes an FSG by overlaying a default template. Usually, this is spawned after the FSG report completes.
Program – Run Financial Statement Generator	Runs an FSG report without using the form. Includes the same options and overrides as the FSG form.
Publish RX Reports	RX reports is an old version of reports still used in some places; like XML, it requires a two-step process to run the report and then publish it. This is most commonly seen in Assets.
Reconciliation – Reconciled Transactions	Detailed report of reconciled transactions in an account.
Reconciliation – Unreconciled Transactions	Detailed report of unreconciled transactions in an account.
Trial Balance	Summary-level balance data, summarizing by the Natural Account Segment.
Trial Balance – Additional Segment Detail	Most trial balances only allow one page break to be identified when the report is run; this allows for two.

TABLE 10-3   *Transactional Reports* (continued)

Concurrent Request Name (Reports)	Description
Trial Balance – Average	Trial balance showing both average and standard balances.
Trial Balance – Budget	Trial balance report for budget balances.
Trial Balance – Detail	Trial balance showing balances for each account combination.
Trial Balance – Encumbrance	Trial balance report by encumbrance type.
Trial Balance – Expanded	Summary-level trial balance by natural account, but showing beginning balance, total debits and credits for the period, and ending balance.
Trial Balance – Translation	Trail balance for a reporting currency, available after the balances have been translated.
XML Report Publisher	Used to publish a report whose output is set to XML. Assigns a default template to the report for viewing. Use the Report Manager to select a template other than the default one that comes with EBS.

TABLE 10-3   *Transactional Reports* (continued)

Integration

Tracking the information from the EBS standard subledgers, in past releases, required in-depth knowledge of the integrated system and unique organization setups. Now, the responsibility called Integration Repository assists with this. This responsibility contains detailed information on all the integration points between, and within, each module. This information used to be scattered in multiple MetaLink notes and Users Manuals, combined with the actual setups in your system. It provides a technical overview of how Oracle works, as shown in Figure 10-5.

From a functional standpoint, there is still no easy way within EBS to see the relationships of transactions from a specific subledger to the setups. It requires specific knowledge about the setup process. For each subledger, an overview of the journals created in the General Ledger, as well the subledger-specific transaction, is found next. The specific setups that guide these are different in every system and can be found in the Subledger Accounting Setups. What follows is a discussion of the more common subledgers with their respective sources.

Purchasing

Purchasing generates only two transactions in the General Ledger: Receiving and Accruals. Receiving journals reflect any receipt, both for inventory and expense items, made during the period. EBS performs two types of accruals for receipts: perpetual and reversing. Usually, perpetual is used for transactions received into inventory, and reversing for expensed items. When an inventory item is received, it will debit inventory and credit an accrual account. This accrual is then relieved when the invoice is matched to the purchase order. For reversing accruals, running the Period End Accrual process during the close cycle will create a reversing journal entry for all receipts against purchase orders that have not yet been matched to an invoice. This journal entry then needs to be reversed when the next General Ledger period is opened.

Financials
- Assets
- Cash Management
- Collections
- Credit Management
- E-Business Tax
- European Localizations
- Federal Financials
- Financials Common Modules
- General Ledger
- Internet Expenses
- Payables
  - Asset
  - **Journal Entry**
  - Payables Invoice
  - Supplier
  - Supplier Contact
  - Supplier Payment
  - Supplier Site
- Property Manager
- Public Sector Applications
- Receivables
- Subledger Accounting
- Trading Community
- Treasury

Full Description

Executes the concurrent program to transfer data from Payables to General Ledger's GL_INTERFACE table.

Source Information

Parameters

Name	Type	Required	Displayed	Description
selection_type	FND_NUMBER	Yes	No	Transfer Selection Type (1-Batch Transfer)
set_of_books_id	AP_SRS_SOB_INFO	Yes	Yes	Ledger Id
include_reporting_sob	AP_SRS_MRC_INFO	Yes	Yes	Transfer Reporting SOB(Yes/No)
batch_name	XLA_CHAR15	Yes	Yes	Transfer Batch Name
from_date	FND_STANDARD_DATE	Yes	Yes	Transfer Date From
to_date	FND_STANDARD_DATE_REQUIRED	Yes	Yes	Transfer Date To
accounting_method	AP_SRS_ACCT_METHOD	Yes	No	Accounting Method associated with a Ledger
document_class	FND_CHAR240	Yes	No	Document Class
journal_category	AP_JE_CATEGORIES	Yes	Yes	Sub Ledger Category
Validate_Account	AP_SRS_YES_NO_MAND	Yes	Yes	Validate Accounts
gl_transfer_mode	AP_GL_TRANSFER_MODE	Yes	Yes	Transfer To GL Interface
submit_journal_import	AP_SRS_SUBMIT_JOURNAL_IMP	Yes	Yes	Submit Journal Import
summary_journal_entry	AP_SRS_JE_SUMMARY	Yes	No	Summarize Journal Entires
process_days	FND_NUMBER	Yes	No	Process days per commit cycle
debug_flag	XLA_CHAR15	Yes	No	Debug Flag
Trace Option	AP_SRS_YES_NO_MAND	Yes	No	Trace Option

Open Interface Tables/Views

Name	Direction	Status	Description
GL_INTERFACE	Outbound	Active	GL_INTERFACE is used to import journal entry batches through Journal Import.

FIGURE 10-5 *Integration Repository*

Payables

Payables records three main types of transactions: invoices and payments in all systems, reconciled payments where this feature is used, and cross-currency transactions. Invoices will create the liability and offset for payment using the Purchase Invoice category. Payments will relieve the liability and record cash. Reconciled payments are created when Payables is set up to account for payments when the payment is cleared. In this case, the actual payment will record into a cash clearing account; it relieves cash only when the payment clears via the treasury module. Cross-Currency is actually the currency gain or loss calculated from the time a foreign currency invoice is entered to the time of payment.

Assets

Assets generate a large number of journal entries, the two main ones being Depreciation and Retirement transactions, including gains and losses. Assets will also generate clearing transactions for asset additions, Construction in Progress journals, and adjustments for asset cost or depreciation, as well as asset transfers.

Receivables

Receivables creates invoice, receipt, and currency journal entries, but they are broken down into the different types of transactions Receivables uses. For invoices, EBS has not only sales invoices, but credit memos, debit memos, chargebacks, and adjustment transactions. Receivables treats all credit memos as a two-step process and entry: the creation of the credit memo and the application of the credit memo. Receipts are broken down into Miscellaneous (cash received for noninvoiced transactions) and Trade receipts relating to invoices. EBS again posts all Trade receipts to a clearing account prior to being applied to an invoice, even if this is all done in Receivables at the same time. If a receipt is left as unapplied or On Account with a customer, it will leave the balance in these clearing accounts until it is applied. Cross-Currency journals are created for foreign currency invoices and receipts, recording the gain or loss on the transaction.

Inventory

Inventory in general will record material transactions and work in process transactions, to track both the movement of inventory and the burdening. The source for these transactions can include work orders, miscellaneous issues and receipts, and shipments for cost of goods sold transactions. Cycle counting and physical inventories also generate journal entries. When a cost update is performed on standard costs, a journal entry is made for the differences in inventory.

Other EBS Subledgers

Other less-used modules, such as Projects and Payroll, also generate journal entries in the General Ledger.

Inquiry and Research

All forms where transactions are processed can be used both for data entry and for inquiry purposes. There are a few that are for inquiry only; they can be useful when researching transactions or balances in the General Ledger. Though the drill-down feature on an FSG is a powerful tool for researching a balance in the Ledger, sometime more detail is required. The account analysis and drill-down feature, shown in Figure 10-6, can be very useful.

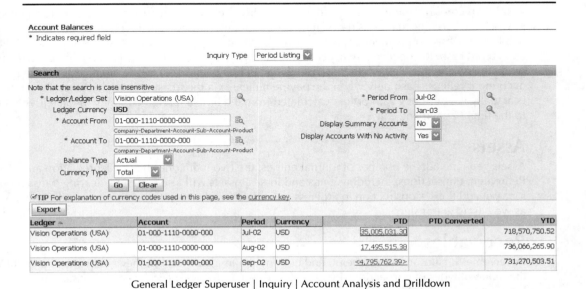

General Ledger Superuser | Inquiry | Account Analysis and Drilldown

FIGURE 10-6   *Researching balances*

This feature shows detailed transactions and allows drill-down to the subledger transactions, as well as trend data for a specific account or range of accounts. And it can easily be exported to Excel using the EXPORT button. When drilling down to display the transaction-level information, the web forms will display a Java logo and appear to stop. But the detailed transactional information from the submodule will appear back in the main non-HTML forms, showing detailed information for that transaction. The Account Inquiry window gives similar information in a slightly different format (General Ledger Superuser | Inquiry | Account). Journal Inquiry, Account Inquiry, and Account Analysis and Drilldown are the three main features for inquiring into specific accounts and transactions. These, in combination with the drill-down feature of FSG reports, as well as the Account Analysis and Trial Balance reports, provide a solid assortment of ways to research balances and transactions. This drill-down screen, which is actually the Subledger Accounting forms and information, can also be accessed from Journal Entry, Journal Inquiry, and Account Inquiry.

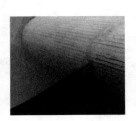

CHAPTER
11

Monthly Processing

onth end, from an accountant's standpoint, is the most hectic time of the month and requires processes to be in place, as well as a good understanding of how your accounting system can help out, in order to meet the deadlines imposed by the business and by government agencies. Like consolidations, month end actually has two components: mechanical, reproducible processes and the intellectual, analytical side. Bill Gates introduced the idea of a digital nervous system back in 1999, where accurate, immediate information is brought to the fingertips of knowledge workers, who collaborate and develop insights based on this information. Month end processing is the ultimate digital nervous system, where many of the repetitive tasks are taken over by the accounting software being used, allowing the accountants to become knowledge workers as opposed to number crunchers—after all, isn't that the reason the very first computers were conceived? To crunch the numbers? (Think Abacus, often considered the world's first computer.) In order to effectively use EBS as a true number crunching system, the process of closing the subledgers, reconciliations, and reporting needs to be understood and utilized.

Subledgers

The first part of any ERP close actually starts in the subledgers. The focus of this chapter is not the mechanical steps to closing these modules, but a general understanding of how to close them—mechanical steps to each subledger will be included in the books on those modules. There are two basic steps to closing each subledger, and the order in which they are closed is also important. The first step is moving all the data from the subledgers to the General Ledger, and then the second step, physically closing the periods to prevent additional transactions, can be completed. Reconciliations also need to be performed to ensure that all transactions are accounted for in the General Ledger.

To close modules such as Payables, Receivables, Inventory, or Purchasing, transactions must be in the proper state to transfer them to the General Ledger and then successfully transferred. There is a specific order required when closing the modules to prevent errors or stray transactions. Each subledger has its own requirements as to when a transaction is ready to create accounting; for example, Payables requires that the invoices be validated prior to creating accounting. When running the Create Accounting process, the mode in which it is run will determine what happens to the accounting transactions. If it is set as Final, they will automatically transfer over to the General Ledger, whereas Draft only creates the accounting and does not transfer it to the General Ledger in the same request. Running the Transfer to General Ledger process after accounting for all transactions will ensure any transactions that were accounted as Draft are sent over. The last mode the Create Accounting process can be run in is Final Post, which not only transfers the entries to the General Ledger but posts them as well.

Once the transactions have all been accounted and transferred to the General Ledger, confirm there are no outstanding items by running the Subledger Accounting Period Close Exception report; this will list any accounting problems and allow them to be reviewed and resolved. After all the transactions are resolved and transferred to the General Ledger, the period can be closed.

In most subledgers, there are several close statuses: Preliminary Close allows a module to be closed for transactions without having to transfer all the transactions to the General Ledger. This status is used when a transaction has a problem that is preventing it from being posted to the General Ledger. Set the period to Preliminary Closed to prevent any additional transactions while the problem is resolved. Also, this can be used during the short period the subledger is reconciled to the General Ledger, waiting to close until after the balances tie. This status is not available in every subledger.

Another status is Closed. This status prevents transactions from being posted to this period, but it also requires that all transactions be accounted and transferred to the General Ledger. This does allow, in a majority of the modules, a period to be reopened at a future date for problem resolution or additional transactions, but be aware that Assets and Inventory (Cost Periods) do not allow any period to be reopened once it is closed.

Permanently Closed is similar to Closed in that transactions cannot be entered and all transactions must be accounted and transferred to the General Ledger, but, as the name implies, it is a permanent state and the period cannot be reopened. Though this sounds like a good control, there is no going back once a period is permanently closed, and that may be a problem for unexpected events. Using the Close status and locking down the actual open/close function in EBS is a much safer route.

Subledger Closing Order

Following the flow of transactions aids in understanding the order in which the subledgers should be closed.

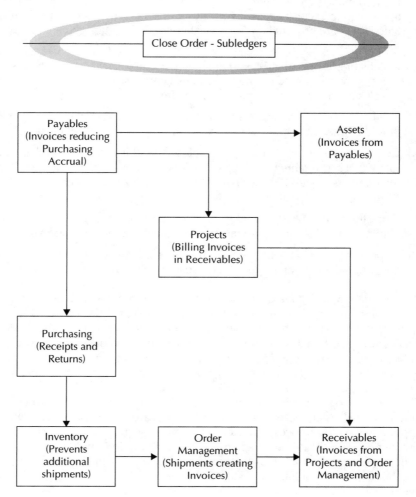

1. Payables is the first subledger to be closed. Specific Payables transactions (matching invoices to received purchase orders) affect the transactions that are selected for accruing orders that have been received but not yet invoiced, which is created from the Purchasing subledger.

2. Purchasing gets closed next, preventing any additional receipts or returns to vendors, which can affect inventory balances and the Purchasing accruals.

3. Inventory is closed after Purchasing, ensuring no additional shipments are created that can generate Receivables invoices and cost of goods sold transactions.

4. Projects can be closed any time after Payables and Inventory and before Receivables. Projects receives cost (expense) transactions from Payables, and sends bills (customer invoices) to Receivables.

5. Order Management does not actually generate any accounting transactions, though the information created in this module determines how a lot of the transactions are accounted for, such as cost of goods sold as well as revenue and customer invoicing. Since there are no actual transactions here in Order Management, there is no period to close.

6. Receivables is closed after both the Inventory subledger (creates shipments, which triggers invoices based on the order management setups) and Projects (creates invoices) are closed, ensuring transactions coming from them are processed.

7. The last common subledger is Fixed Assets, which is only dependent on Payables being closed to prevent additional invoices being entered and creating assets.

8. General Ledger is the last step in the close, and this can be opened and closed as many times as required during a close process. Closing the period while still analyzing the numbers creates a static environment to analyze, instead of one that is constantly changing from journal entries.

9. Once the General Ledger is closed (or in a preliminary state), consolidations and eliminations can be run, creating consolidated reporting for analysis.

10. Depending on what Ledger revaluations need to take place (in the parent or child Ledger), balances can be reevaluated either before or after the consolidation.

Many of the modules have diagnostics that can be run before and during the close process to assist in finding any problems that may exist. For example, the General Ledger Close diagnostics give important information about the statuses of the subledger periods, and the Receivables Close diagnostics will report on any unposted items, giving detailed database-level information. Oracle regularly comes out with new diagnostic scripts, and monitoring MetaLink will keep you informed of any new releases. You can find the diagnostics available by performing an advanced search on the product Oracle Diagnostics Pack for R12.

After the subledgers have all been closed and balanced to the General Ledger, mass allocations, as well as adjusting and recurring entries, are made in the General Ledger. Up to this point in the close process, the steps are largely mechanical. Using such EBS tools as scheduling processes, AutoPost, Diagnostics, accurate and informative FSGs, and AutoReverse can help to reduce the actual steps a person has to take, allowing him or her to spend more time on the human part of the close, such as research and explaining large variances, hopefully positive ones.

Opening and Closing Periods in the General Ledger

Periods in the General Ledger have four statuses: Future-Entry, Open, Closed, and Permanently Closed. Future-Entry allows transactions to be entered or generated, but not posted. Open allows transactions to be entered and posted. Closed does not allow transactions to be entered, imported, or posted, but a transaction can be reopened at a future date. Permanently closed works the same as closed, but it can *never* be reopened—I advise using this with extreme caution, unless you like to pay for technical consultants to resolve the problems that it inevitably causes.

You can open Ledgers and their corresponding Reporting currencies either as a group combined into a Ledger Set or as individual Ledgers. You can open Ledgers individually using the Open/Close window. To open the next period, as seen in Figure 11-1, click OPEN PERIOD and identify the TARGE PERIOD you want to open. In R12, periods cannot be opened by changing the status next to the period name.

This process does a few things in EBS: it sets the Future-Entry status on the number of periods that are set in the Ledger setups, creates balances in the tables for these future periods, and moves balances from Income and Expense accounts to Retained Earnings if this is the first period of the fiscal year. It can also generate all recurring entries if this option was selected. Opening periods kick off a concurrent request and can take several minutes to process, especially if this is the first period of a year. Check and ensure the period is open prior to trying to use it. In order to see the change in a period that was just opened, you must requery this form; it does not update automatically.

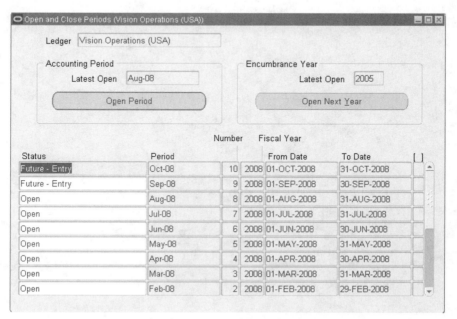

General Ledger Superuser | Setups | Open/Close

FIGURE 11-1 *Maintaining General Ledger periods*

To change the STATUS of an existing period, usually used to close periods, select from the list of values. Future-Entry is not available on this list. Changing the status on a period to anything other than Open never starts a request; it is changed as soon as the record is saved. Note that closing a period never checks to ensure all the journals for that period are posted; this must be done manually in the Journals | Post form—only unposted journals will appear here. If you are using Encumbrances, the encumbrance years will need to be opened each year with the OPEN NEXT YEAR button.

To open or close a period for a Ledger Set, you have several concurrent processes available. To open a period for a Ledger Set, run the process called Open Period from the concurrent manager, and select a LEDGER or LEDGER SET to process, as well as the PERIOD you want to open. There are three processes for closing periods: Periods – Close Period, Periods – Gapless Close Period, and Periods – Permanently Close Period. The first and last work the same as in the form, with the exception that you can run them for a Ledger Set as opposed to only one Ledger at a time. The Gapless Close Period ensures that when Reporting Sequences are used, the sequential numbers assigned are gapless and can only be performed from the concurrent request. All these requests can be run for a Ledger as well as a Ledger Set.

PART

II

Subledger Accounting: Concepts and Setups

CHAPTER
12

Subledger Accounting

ubledger Accounting (SLA) is a new concept that is introduced in R12, sometimes referred to as the Financial Services Accounting Hub or Accounting Methods, which incorporates all the accounting rules, as well as the application of these rules, to subledger transactions. Setups for accounting can be found within the Subledger Accounting menus in each subledger and are module specific. They are utilized by the system when the Create Accounting process is run or when performing accounting inquires on transactions within a subledger or in the General Ledger.

It is important to understand that this is a service, if you will, provided to the subledgers, not an actual module itself with its own responsibility. Prior to its introduction, each subledger had its own method of accounting for transactions. Payables used the Payables Accounting process to generate liability accounts and journal entries, whereas Receivables would use AutoAccounting. Subledger Accounting was designed to be a service that replaces all the different methods of creating accounting transactions with one common process. To date, Subledger Accounting (SLA) works with the following modules: Assets, Cash Management, Contract Commitment, Core Banking, Cost Management, Federal Financials, Financial Common Modules, Institutional Banking, Loans, Inventory, Payables, Payroll, Process Manufacturing, Projects, Property Manager, Purchasing, Receivables, and Trade Management. It is Oracle's direction that SLA is here to stay beyond R12 and into Fusion.

To put it simply, SLA takes transactions (invoices, payments, inventory receipts) and turns them into events that can be accounted for based on the setups assigned to the event. Besides consistency among the different subledgers, perhaps the biggest advantage with using SLA is flexibility. Changes to account processes are easier to make, without programming, and SLA can also represent transactions in multiple ways for different Ledger reporting requirements, such as GAAP or local requirements outside the U.S.

As it seems with all things, the more functionality there is, the more it takes to understand how it works! SLA is no exception. While the old accounting modules varied from subledger to subledger, they were fairly easy to follow and understand. Besides being new, SLA is necessarily complicated and technical. It is this complexity that allows Ledgers to be accounted for in multiple ways at the touch of a button. And as always, taking the time to understand some of the basics will help better understand how the system works and where it goes wrong.

These setups are broken down into two chapters: read Chapter 13 to gain a very detailed and technical overview of information most users will not need to know, while Chapter 14 explains the setups that are most commonly modified and are directly related to creating the accounting entries themselves.

SLA Upgrade Considerations

During an upgrade, the switch to SLA is not mandatory (you can upgrade and still use the old accounting methods that are already set up), but these accounting methods cannot be modified after the upgrade. Any future changes would have to be made using SLA. Implementing SLA during an upgrade is a big decision, which should be determined by how well your current accounting methods upgrade and work from a system standpoint, as well as how well these existing rules meet your current and near-future business needs.

You have some processes available to you that assist with upgrading current data in your system from its current accounting format to SLA. The first is the SLA Pre-Upgrade Program. This program is available via Patch 5233248 and needs to be applied to your 11*i* instance and run prior to the upgrade, if your business needs require it. When the upgrade to R12 is made, it will upgrade transactions in the subledgers to the new SLA tables according to what the current period is in the General Ledger, including all transactions for the current fiscal year, as well as six months of the prior fiscal year. Running the SLA Pre-Upgrade Program can change this to be a longer or shorter period of time, depending on your specific business and system requirements. Converting transactions to SLA is necessary for two reasons: so that General Ledger drill-downs will work for these transactions, and so that any converted transactions can be canceled or reversed after the upgrade. The SLA Pre-Upgrade Program allows you to set either more or fewer periods to be converted to SLA; it does not do the actual conversion but just tags the transaction periods as needing to be converted. It is important to understand that although this program can be run multiple times, it does not undo the periods it has already marked for conversion. Thus if you run it for 20 months, and then you decide that it takes too long to upgrade and want to reduce the period to 18 months, the earliest two months will not be untagged by rerunning the program.

Not all subledgers that are converting to SLA use this strict, date-sensitive upgrade. For example, the Global Accounting Engine will upgrade all transactions, no matter what. There is an impact to the upgrade if the time period is increased: first, the more transactions the upgrade has to convert, the longer it will take, and second, it will take more disk space to process and store the transactions. After the upgrade is complete and the initial transactions are converted, it is still possible to convert additional transactions to SLA. Oracle recommends that you convert as much as possible during the upgrade itself, when the system is not competing for resources, as opposed to using this postupgrade process, which happens in the context of a live system. It was more intended as a fix for minor transaction issues than as an upgrade step.

Defining Subledger Accounting Step-by-Step

Subledger Accounting is broken down into several components, each containing defaults that can be copied and modified if it does not meet your organization's needs. Since EBS does come with a large number of preseeded SLA setups, reviewing them closely prior to creating one from scratch or modifying an existing one will help prevent some long nights and frustration (and maybe even a few gray hairs!). To use any existing setup as a starting point, it will need to be copied prior to making any modifications.

When creating or modifying each step in the SLA setups, they must be completed in order, from the bottom up. The high-level steps, in order of completion, are as follows:

- Subledger Applications
- Account Methods Builder Steps:
    - Events
    - Sources

- Journal Entry Setups:
  - Journal Line Types
  - Journal Descriptions
  - Mapping Sets
  - Account Deviation Rules
  - Supporting References
- Methods and Definitions
- Subledger Accounting Options in the Ledgers

Chapter 13 will cover the process through Journal Descriptions. Most companies will never change or add to any of this information. Chapter 14 will begin with Mapping Sets, where you begin creating the actual rules for Subledger Accounting and is probably where most organizations will begin making modifications in SLA.

CHAPTER
13

Subledger Accounting
Seeded Setups

any Subledger Accounting (SLA) setups will never require modifications in most organizations. These setups are seeded for the EBS subledgers, requiring modification only for third-party systems to use SLA or for extremely unusual business cases. This chapter outlines these seeded setups.

Defining Subledger Applications (Seeded for EBS Subledgers)

Prior to using SLA for any subledger, the Application must first be registered. This happens automatically for all EBS subledgers, as shown in Figure 13-1, and therefore only needs to be performed if SLA will be used to create accounting for non-EBS transactions. The APPLICATION NAME must be a name registered on the responsibility prior to selecting it here (System Administrator | Application | Register). This setup has built-in security for the seeded subledgers, as do all SLA setups, so only the setups for the application this responsibility is registered to can be seen.

The DRILLDOWN OPTIONS tell EBS what packaged procedures will be used to drill down from the General Ledger to the subledger to obtain more details on journal entries. Neither the APPLICATION NAME nor the DRILLDOWN PROCEDURES can be changed for EBS subledgers. Selecting USE SECURITY will allow security to be added when viewing business events in SLA. Transactions themselves are secured by Data Access Sets, Security Rules, and Responsibilities. SLA, on the other hand, inherently allows any transaction in a subledger such as Payables to be viewed, as opposed to only the entries this responsibility has access to, which is controlled with the profile MO: Security Profile (System Administrator | Profile | System). When USE SECURITY is checked, the Data Access Set will be utilized to determine which transactions can be seen in SLA. The JOURNAL SOURCE will default to the APPLICATION NAME. The THIRD PARTY CONTROL ACCOUNT TYPE works in conjunction with the qualifier on the accounting Flexfield, preventing manual journal entries from being made to specific account values. (This is used when adding values to the chart of accounts in General

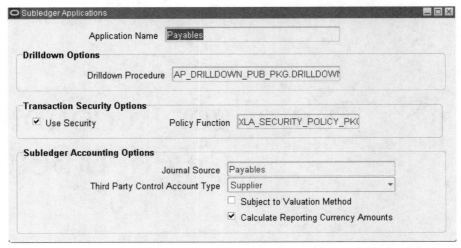

Payables Manager | Setup | Accounting Setups | Subledger Accounting Setup | Subledger Applications

FIGURE 13-1 *Registering a subledger application*

Ledger Superuser | Setup | Financial | Flexfields | Key | Values). When an account is set up to have a control of Supplier, then any transactions from a subledger with the Control Type of Supplier can post to that account, and manual transactions or other modules cannot. These TYPES can be set to SUPPLIER, CUSTOMER, ALL for both, or NONE.

Valuation methods refers to when SLA creates an accounting transaction based on specific rules. One of the main premises of SLA is that multiple valuations methods can be created for a single transaction, for example, one for GAAP and one for local non-U.S. reporting. Selecting SUBJECT TO VALUATION METHOD will enable this subledger to create more than one accounting for each transaction. (Of course, each SLA will need to be defined and assigned to the Ledger first! It is not quite as simple as checking this box.) Selecting CALCULATE REPORTING CURRENCY AMOUNTS will generate subledger transactions in any reporting currencies associated with the Primary Ledger. This does not pertain to transactions in foreign currencies or to Secondary Ledger currencies. When this is selected, if the accounting process for reporting currencies fails, because of currency rates that are not set up, the entire accounting process is rolled back and no journals are created for any currency.

Building the Accounting Methods

Accounting methods consists of several setup steps, including events, sources, journal entry setups, and methods and applications. These setups first identify how a transaction is classified, and then how the classification will be processed.

Defining Subledger Accounting Events (Seeded for EBS Events)

Any accounting system, no matter what it is tracking, ultimately comes down to generating accounting events, or accountable transactions. EBS is no different. Not all transactions in a system generate accounting transactions; for example, entering a supplier into Payables is not an accountable event, but creating an invoice against that supplier is. And invoices can be accounted at different points of time. For example, if you are running a cash basis accounting system, the accounting event does not take place until the invoice is paid. For accrual accounting, there actually are two accounting events: one when the invoice is entered, and the other when the invoice is paid. It is these accounting events, or Event Types, that are the basis for Subledger Accounting.

EBS comes with a large number of seeded events, and modifications are not usually required. In Payables, there are two main event codes, also called ENTITY CODES: AP Invoices and AP Payments. Invoices include such transactions, or Event Classes, as Credit Memos, Debit Memos, and Invoices, while Payments include Payments, Reconciled Payments, and Refunds. Underneath each of the Event Classes are Event Types, such as Invoice Adjustments and Invoice Cancellations under Invoices. When setting up events, an Event Type is associated with an Event Class, which is in turn assigned to the Event Code. It is the individual Event Types and Classes that will ultimately have accounting setups assigned to them. A Class can include several Event Types; for example, the Class of Invoices includes adjustments, as well as valid and cancelled invoices, as all these events will be accounted for with the same rules.

Creating Entities in the Event Modeler

The Event Modeler, shown in Figure 13-2, allows for ENTITY CODES to be entered and associated with identifiers, which simply tell EBS which unique identification number in the database is used for this type of event. An identifier for invoices would be Invoice_ID. Selecting GAPLESS EVENT PROCESSING will hold all accounting transactions where a gap in the event numbering exists. Event numbers are assigned to transactions when they are saved and identified as accountable. EBS will create the accounting for events in the order of the event numbering. When gaps exist, either because a prior event is missing or because it is incomplete, this flag prevents the accounting process from continuing and allows the gaps to be resolved.

The Event Numbers are assigned to each event relating to a transaction as the transactions are created; for example, if an invoice is saved and then canceled, the invoice is event number 1 and the cancellation is event number 2. Event 2, or the cancellation, should not be accounted until the invoice has been accounted for; GAPLESS EVENT PROCESSING prevents this from happening if Event 1 is either missing or incomplete due to an error. Once an Entity, or accounting event, is created and saved, Event Classes, shown in Figure 13-3, are associated with it, and Event Codes are associated with each class. EBS does require that transactions be accounted in a specific order; for instance, an invoice must be accounted prior to the payment on that same invoice. This is where the PREDECESSORS setting comes into play—it lets EBS know what event classes need to be accounted prior to the current one. Often, since all the common accounting events come seeded in EBS, no changes or additions are required to these Event setups.

Adding Process Categories (Seeded)

Process Categories come predefined in EBS and cannot be added to or modified. These categories are logical groupings of Event Classes that can be used when running the Create Accounting program. They are important for two reasons: first, as mentioned earlier, accounting events are created using

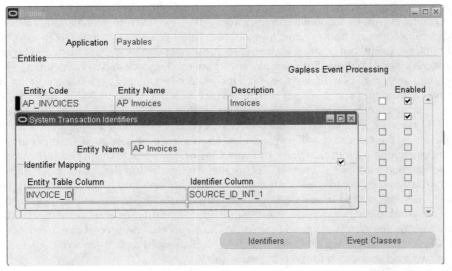

Payables Manager | Setup | Accounting Setups | Subledger Accounting Setup | Accounting Methods Builder | Events | Event Model | Identifiers button

FIGURE 13-2 *Events and their identifiers*

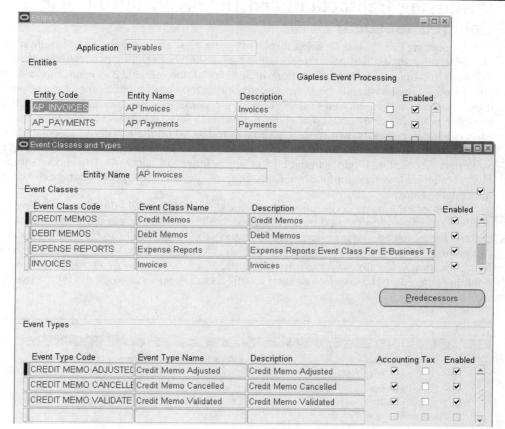

Payables Manager | Setup | Accounting Setups | Subledger Accounting Setup | Accounting Methods Builder |
Events | Event Model | Event Classes button

FIGURE 13-3   *Reviewing event setups for classes and types*

required predecessors. These are almost never a problem; EBS assigns the event numbers in the order
the transactions are created in EBS, and it will process the accounting correctly. Every once in a great
while, these numbers get out of order. A common scenario for this to happen is when an invoice is
entered, it is paid, and then the payment is voided as well as the invoice, and the Create Accounting
process is not run after each step. EBS must account for the invoice first, the payment second, and the
void payment next, followed by the cancellation of the invoice. If the create accounting program
does not pick up these transactions in this order, the one that is out of order where the predecessors
are not complete will not account. Rerunning the Create Accounting program for just invoices, then
just payments, often resolves this problem. The other reason is that you may want to account only the
invoices to obtain specific reports, where the accounting for the payments is not required, and it is
these Process Category groupings that allow this.

Identifying Transactions and Their Associated Database Columns (Seeded)

The Accounting Event Class Options shown in Figure 13-4 allow the defined accounting event classes to be assigned additional information that is used both during processing and when inquiring into the accounting transactions in SLA. For all the seeded EBS events, this window is already populated (as are all the Event screens during the installation). Some of the important information set up here includes DEFAULT JOURNAL CATEGORIES, and the informational fields that are available when inquiring on a created journal. When a journal entry is created from a subledger, each event can create its own specific journal entry, based on the categories associated with the event. These are defined here with the initial installs but can be overwritten when setting up the Subledger Accounting Options in the Ledger setups (refer to Chapter 4). The Ledger setups will always override the Accounting Event Class Options, but it is the Options that are the defaults for the Ledger setups.

The other information controlled here is the default data available when inquiring on an accounting transaction created by SLA. Notice that the Accounting Event Class Options are defined for the BALANCE TYPES of ACTUAL, BUDGET, and ENCUMBRANCE and can be different for each one, or the same for any combination of these balances. The TRANSACTION VIEW is a database view that identifies what fields are available for viewing the SLA associated with a transaction, and the columns entered on the User Transaction Identifiers tab specify each column with a user-friendly

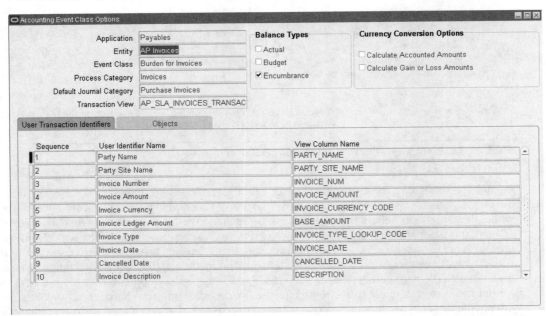

Payables Manager | Setup | Accounting Setups | Subledger Accounting Setup | Accounting Methods Builder | Events | Accounting Event Class Options

FIGURE 13-4 *Reviewing event options*

name. This is the information that appears on any transaction in the subledger when you go to Tools | View Accounting Events | View Journal Entries button.

The Objects tab will identify the source of the data for this accounting event, which can be either Table or View names. These main sources for the transactions are defined in the section of the window called TRANSACTION OBJECTS and are set up at both the header and line levels. REFERENCE OBJECTS are also set up here and refer to primary and secondary tables where additional information related to a transaction is stored. When Project Costing is being used, then the table that stores project information onto an invoice associated with a project would be a Primary Reference Object; it is additional information needed to create accounting for the event. The Join conditions between the Reference and Transaction Objects are also defined here.

Subledger Sources (Seeded for EBS Subledgers)

At this point in the setups, the program called Create and Assign Sources needs to be run. This can be run in either Validate Only mode or Validate and Create mode. The validation will confirm that all the Events setup data is consistent, not only with itself, but with data defined in the database. Once they have been validated, a Source will be created for all the Transaction and Reference Objects. This will create all the information on the Setup | Accounting Methods Builder | Sources | Sources screen, based on the Reference Objects. To put it simply, a source is created for every reference object, and then each source is associated on the source assignments form to an event type, with any Key Flexfields, Descriptive Flexfields, and Value Sets associated with each column.

Accounting Assignments get associated with Event Types next (Setup | Accounting Setups | Accounting Methods Builder | Sources | Accounting Attribute Assignments). Accounting Attributes are predefined for EBS subledgers. Each Accounting Attribute can be assigned to multiple sources and multiple event types. For example, the accounting attribute for Accounted Amount is assigned to Invoices, Credit Memos, and Debit Memos. This is because the event will determine if the accounted amount relates to an Invoice or a Debit Memo. Accounted amounts for Invoices can also have multiple sources under each Event Class. Under Invoice, it can have a source of FEDERAL ANTICIPATED AMOUNT or INVOICE DISTRIBUTION LEDGER AMOUNT. It will have a default, but depending on the transaction, that could represent either of these numbers. The link between accounting attributes and sources is also set up under the line types (see the later section "Journal Line Types"), but defaults from here.

Validating Event Class Options (Seeded for EBS Subledgers)

Once the Accounting Event Class Options are completed, they need to be validated by either clicking VALIDATE ASSIGNMENTS or running the concurrent request called VALIDATE APPLICATIONS ACCOUNTING DEFINITIONS, which will validate more than one class at a time. Ensure any violations on this report are resolved before moving on to the next step. To see details on any violations, ensure it is run with the profile options set as follows: FND: DEBUG LOG ENABLED = YES, FND: DEBUG LOG MODULE = %, FND: DEBUG LOG LEVEL = STATEMENT (System Administrator | Profile | System). This will give detailed error messages in the log file for what needs to be corrected.

The Events and Sources described here will not need to be set up in a majority of the EBS installations; using the defaults will be more than adequate. Understanding how they work, on the other hand, can help when troubleshooting SLA problems, both in dealing with errors and in understanding why SLA actually did what it did. The next section will describe the journal entry setups; most customizations will be made here for SLA, but again, there are a large number of seeded setups to start from.

Reviewing and Modifying Journal Entry Setups (Seeded)

The journal entry setups consist of both line types and descriptions, assigning default information, conditions, and options to event classes.

Journal Line Types

Journal line types, shown in Figure 13-5, are used to define different options for each line as well as the conditions under which it will be called, and additional, overriding information for Accounting Attributes. In order to change any of the information on the seeded journal line types, you should first copy and then modify the seeded one. You can do this by clicking COPY and then adding the LINE TYPE CODE as well as a new name.

It is the combination of the APPLICATION, EVENT CLASS, and ACCOUNTING CLASS that makes a unique journal line. ACCOUNTING and ROUNDING CLASSES are defined as Subledger Accounting Lookups (Payables Manager | Setup | Lookups | Subledger Accounting Lookups) and can be added as needed. The ROUNDING CLASS is used when transactions are entered in foreign currencies and there

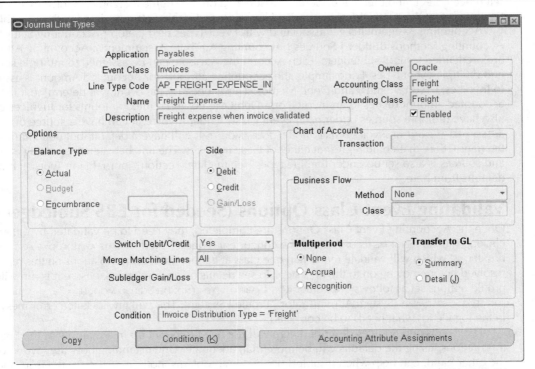

Payables Manager | Setup | Accounting Setups | Subledger Accounting Setup | Accounting Methods Builder | Journal Entry Setups | Journal Line Types

FIGURE 13-5   *Journal line type modifications*

is a rounding on the currency conversion that causes the journal entry to be out of balance (for example, a rounded, converted transaction may come out to be 0.008, which will round to 0.01). The LINE TYPE CODE is a unique code that identifies this journal line type to the system, whereas the NAME is what the users will see in the application.

Under the Options region, determine what Balance Types this will pertain to: ACTUAL, BUDGET, or ENCUMBRANCE. There are three options in the Side region: GAIN/LOSS is grayed out and used exclusively by SLA when a Gain or Loss is created on a transaction. For reference, a gain will always represent a credit, whereas any loss will be a debit. When this is selected, the SUBLEDGER GAIN/LOSS field becomes available for update. Setting this to YES tells SLA that the Gain or Loss is calculated by the Primary Ledger, and that it should not be converted to a reporting currency. If NO is selected, then SLA will calculate the gains and losses. For all other transactions, select the side that is most common for the transaction, either DEBIT or CREDIT. The SWITCH DEBIT/CREDIT setting determines how balances entered for whatever the Side is not set for are handled. If YES is selected, a Credit entered on a transaction whose default Side is DEBIT will result in a Credit, as opposed to a negative Debit. This field also determines how a negative Debit entered by a user would be handled; in this case, it would become a Credit.

The TRANSACTION Chart of Accounts is only used when a Secondary Ledger is selected for setting up journal line types, and the Secondary Ledger has a different accounting Flexfield than the Primary Ledger, and, therefore, for the transaction as well. Since the LEDGER is a unique identifier when creating a line type, and it is related to what is called the Accounting Chart of Accounts, you would enter the Chart of Accounts from the transaction itself. This is the same as the Chart of Accounts assigned to the Primary Ledger.

The Business Flow is a way of adapting some accounting attributes from a prior SLA transaction associated to this transaction. If NONE is select, this feature is not used. When selecting PRIOR ENTRY, it can identify the Accounting Class of the prior Entry. Or optionally select SAME ENTRY to use data from this transaction, but for a different SLA event. The fields that can be carried forward when PRIOR ENTRY is selected are Currency Code, Conversion Rate Type, Conversion Date, Conversion Rate, Party Type, Party Identifier, Party Site Identifier, and Encumbrance types.

Use MERGE MATCHING LINES to summarize lines on the same subledger transaction, based on specific criteria. When set to Yes or all, it means that all lines with the same data in these fields will be merged: Accounting Class, Rounding Class, Transaction Rounding, Reference, Switch Side Flag, Gain or Loss Flag, Business Flow Class Code, Multiperiod Option, Currency, Conversion Rate Type, Conversion Date, Conversion Rate, Third Party, Third Party Site, Third Party Type, Accounting Flexfield, Description, Reconciliation Reference, Gain/Loss Reference, Encumbrance Type. When SWITCH DEBIT/CREDIT is set to YES, the negative amounts are represented as the opposite side as opposed to a negative amount. Set MULTIPERIOD to determine if this line type will create ACCRUALS across periods, enable RECOGNITION of revenue, or not allow multiperiod transactions. For example, MULTIPERIOD is commonly used to recognize revenue or record a prepaid expense in a future period. TRANSFER TO GL determines if the journal lines are transferred to the General Ledger with the same DETAIL that exists in the Subledger, or if they will create SUMMARY lines, one for each unique account combination.

Click the CONDITIONS button to enter the specific criteria for when this line type will get used. For example, for the Freight Invoice lines, this gets used when the SOURCE of the transaction is invoice distribution type and the VALUE is set to freight. If the line was entered as TAX or LINE, this journal line type will not get called. Again, EBS comes seeded with all the standard transactions as journal line types, but you can copy them by clicking COPY and modify them if necessary.

The Accounting Attribute assignments on the journal line types will default in from the attributes that were associated with the Event Class when it was created.

Journal Descriptions (Seeded)

Journal Entry Descriptions will default description information in on the Subledger Journal Entry screen. This screen, seen later in Figure 13-7, is different than the Journal | Entry screen in the General Ledger and can be accessed either from the subledger transaction itself, by selecting Tools | View Accounting Events, or by clicking DRILLDOWN and selecting View Journal Entry from either the Journal Entry or Account Analysis window. Journal entry descriptions are associated with journal line definitions. Again, these come seeded in EBS, but they can be added or modified by copying.

To view the Journal Entry Description setup window, refer to Figure 13-6. The APPLICATION will default in based on what module you are in. The JOURNAL DESCRIPTION CODE is an assigned system name, whereas the JOURNAL DESCRIPTION NAME is what the users see in the applications. To restrict this description to a specific Chart of Accounts, enter the TRANSACTION CHART OF ACCOUNTS. The PRIORITY determines what order the transactions are evaluated for to see which condition they agree with, and then the DESCRIPTION DETAILS will be added to that line. EBS does not evaluate all the conditions, but it starts with PRIORITY 1, continues until it reaches a condition that the transaction matches, and then stops. This means two things: First, if there are two entries with the same conditions, the one with the lowest priority will always be selected and the second one never used. Second, these should be written in order of usage, making the most commonly met condition the lowest priority number to reduce processing time. Only the PRIORITY number needs to be entered on this screen, as the DESCRIPTION defaults in when the DETAILS are added by clicking the DETAILS button. Details can be as simple as Invoice Number, or more complicated to give more complete information.

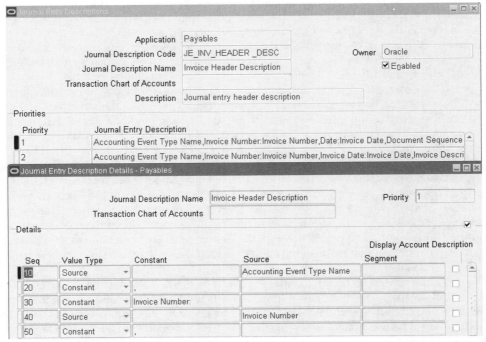

Payables Manager | Setup | Accounting Setups | Subledger Accounting Setup | Accounting Methods Builder | Journal Entry Setups | Journal Entry Descriptions

FIGURE 13-6 *Accounting attributes*

Each SEQUENCE, or section, of the description, can have a VALUE TYPE of CONSTANT, which will print whatever is in the CONSTANT field, or of SOURCE, which will select transaction-based information, such as Invoice Number. Conditions work the same for journal entry descriptions as they do for journal line types, where specific conditions need to be met for this description to be used. Select the SOURCE of the condition, such as Invoice Number, and select one of the available OPERATORS from the list of values. A good example of how to find an invoice header is to set the SOURCE to INVOICE NUMBER and the OPERATOR to IS NOT NULL. This will select all events that have invoice numbers (as opposed to Payments, which do not).

In the example of journal descriptions being used in Figure 13-7, the DESCRIPTION on the Header defaulted in from the journal entry description reviewed earlier. The Accounting Event Type Name is INVOICE VALIDATED, INVOICE NUMBER and INVOICE DATE show, and there was no INVOICE DESCRIPTION. Again, this information only shows in drilldowns in the General Ledger or when viewing accounting events from subledgers, not the actual journal entry window in the General Ledger; it is part of SLA and not the GL.

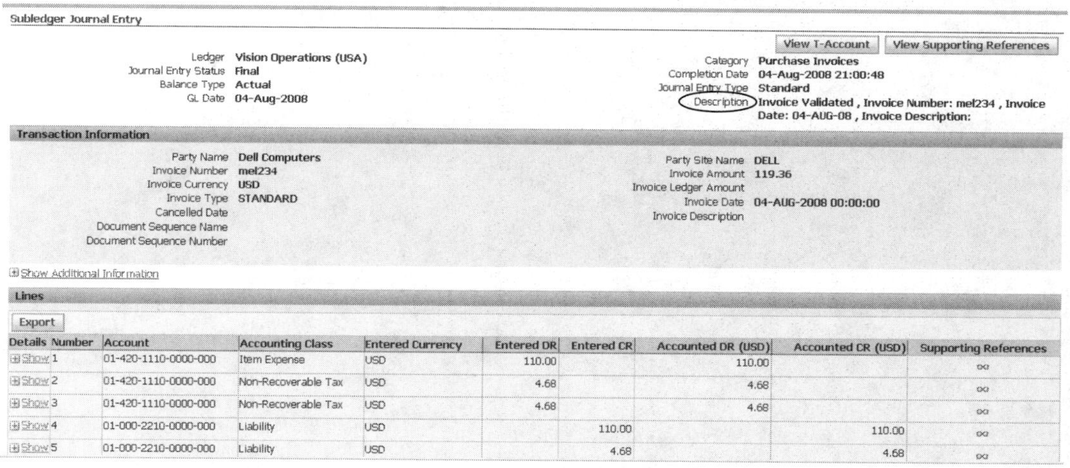

Payables Manager | Invoice | Entry | Query up an accounted invoice| Tools | View Accounting Events | View Journal Entry

FIGURE 13-7 *Example of journal descriptions when querying on an accounting transaction*

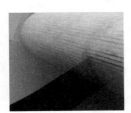

CHAPTER
14

Subledger Accounting
Modified Setups

n general, most organizations will begin any subledger accounting modifications with the Mapping Sets, which can take values passed from the transactions being accounted and map them to specific accounts or values. These values can then, in turn, be used when creating the account numbers. Whereas Chapter 13 was background information for most companies, the information presented in this chapter will help you understand exactly how an account number is derived for the subledger accounting entries.

Mapping Sets

Mapping sets, defined next in the subledger accounting setups, in the simplest terms are mappings that derive accounting information from Lookup Types or Value Sets that are associated with a transaction. For example, AR transactions can have the natural account derived based on the risk level that has been assigned to the customer, tracking high risk in one account number and low risk in another. A second example would be to map the Primary Ledger account numbers to Secondary Ledger numbers. Most likely these mappings will be built from scratch. For the first example, where a Value Set is being mapped to a segment in the Chart of Accounts, the Value Set must be set up prior to being used in the Mapping Sets.

Value Sets Set Up for Use in Mapping Sets

A *Value Set* is a set of defaults or values that can be created in EBS for reference by SLA, reports or used in Descriptive Flexfields. The huge advantage of using Value Sets is that they are easily maintainable without programming intervention. Once a Value Set is defined, it can be used in multiple places. EBS comes with a large number of predefined Value Sets available for use, so look to see if what you need already exists prior to creating one. Once the Value Set is saved, it can also be assigned to a Descriptive or Key Flexfield, such as the segments in the Chart of Accounts, and it can then be populated when entering a transaction, either manually or with a default, and becomes available for use by SLA for mapping

To set up a Value Set, referring to Figure 14-1, assign a VALUE SET NAME, which will be used when attaching the Value Set to a Flexfield or Mapping Set. Add a DESCRIPTION next to describe the data being stored. The LIST TYPE determines how the List of Values will display in windows: LIST OF VALUES is usually used in EBS when there are between 10 and 200 results. LONG LIST OF VALUES is used for large lists and will prompt users to reduce the list prior to display. The final option, POPLIST, is used with very short lists and does not allow the list to be reduced in a search page. While all three of these options will display the same data, how the user requests the data being displayed is different. The SECURITY TYPE determines if there is NO SECURITY, if security for the Value Set is assigned at the parent level (HIERARCHICAL) and cascades down to all the child values, or if security is to be assigned for each child individually (NON-HIERARCHICAL). These security types only pertain to Value Sets when they are assigned to a Flexfield. The Format Validation region dictates the MAXIMUM SIZE of the values in the fields, and if character or numeric values are allowed. Selecting NUMBERS ONLY or UPPERCASE ONLY allows control over the types of values set up in this Value Set, and RIGHT-JUSTIFY and ZERO-FILL NUMBERS will allow a user to enter a 1 and have EBS default it to look like 0001; this option only works for numeric values. MIN and MAX values limit the values that can be associated with this Value Set.

While EBS allows values to be predefined for each Value Set (Setup | Flexfields | Validation | Values), it also allows unvalidated data to be entered. This is controlled with the VALIDATION TYPE. Selecting NONE will allow the users to enter any unvalidated string of characters into the field. This

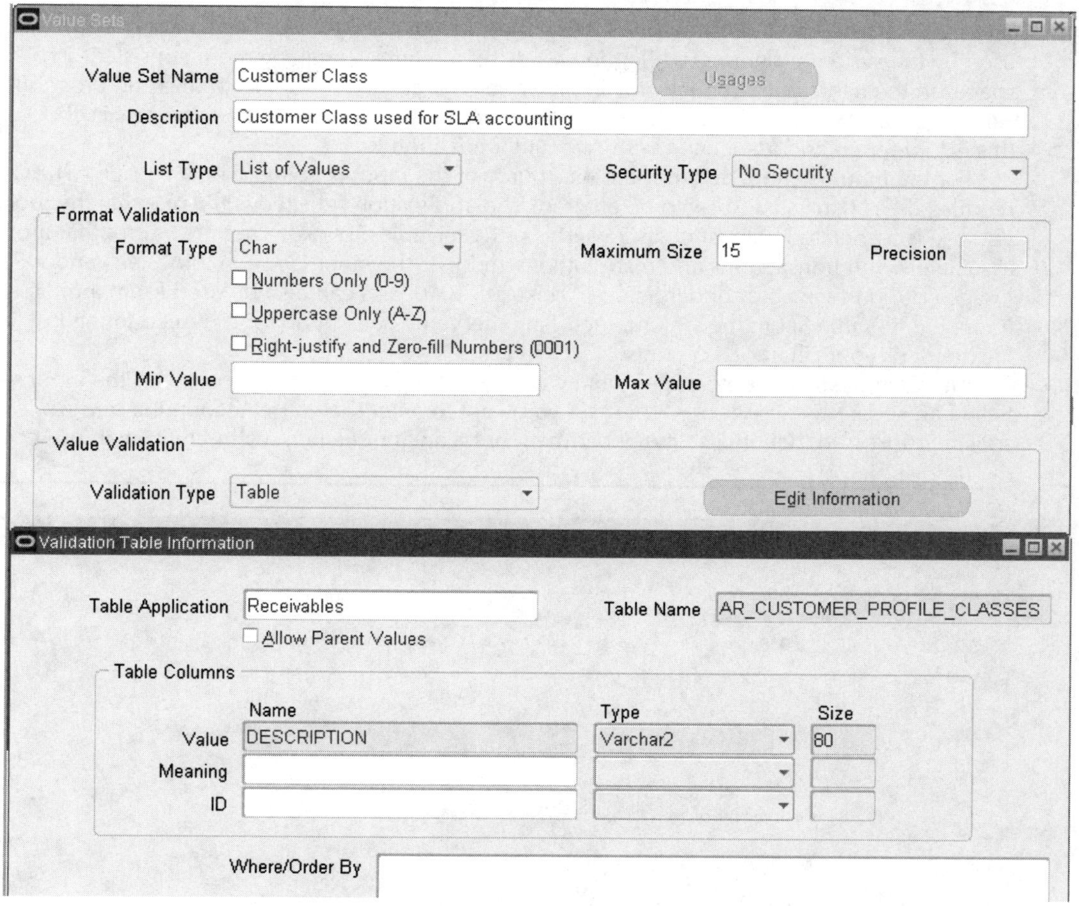

Payables Manager | Setup | Flexfields | Validation | Sets

FIGURE 14-1 *Setting up Value Sets for use in Mapping Sets or in Descriptive Flexfields*

means that a predefined list of values is not maintained. INDEPENDENT allows any active value setup in this Value Set to be added. DEPENDENT values work similar to Independent Value Sets, except that the list of values in the depending field is narrowed down to values entered in a prior field. This option is only available when multiple value sets will be used with one flexfield. An example would be limiting the departments allowed against a specific company or balancing segment. PAIR allows high and low values to be added within the field, whereas SPECIAL builds a multisegment value, as if for an item number being added to the Value Set. TABLE will select data from any table in the Oracle database and is most often used to populate information that is already stored there. TRANSLATABLE INDEPENDENT and DEPENDENT validation types allow the data in the Value Set to be translated if multiple languages is turned on. Once the Value Set is set up and values are populated (Setup | Flexfield | Validation | Values), this information is now available to use in a Mapping Set.

Creating Mapping Sets

To set up a Mapping Set as shown in Figure 14-2, assign a MAPPING SET CODE and a NAME; the CODE is used by the system programs, while the NAME is seen by users; making them consistent (replacing spaces in the name with underscores in the code) will assist in troubleshooting and programming. Add a DESCRIPTION to explain why this code is set up or used. Ensure the ENABLED box is checked if this is to be used and associated with Account Derivation Rules.

For the Input section, determine if the source of the input is going to be a LOOKUP TYPE, which requires the LOOKUP APPLICATION to be entered. The application selected is the one that the lookup you use is associated with, such as Payables or Receivables. LOOKUP TYPES are values that are associated with transactions and many other windows; they include such things as Vendor Site Usage (found in Payables under Setup | Lookups). VALUE SETS can also be used for mapping, and include any Value Set in the system, including the Value Sets set up for the Accounting Key Flexfield, or your Chart of Accounts.

The Output section determines what values will be passed into SLA based on the input values. Select an ACCOUNTING CHART OF ACCOUNTS if you want to enter the entire accounting FLEXFIELD, or a specific SEGMENT to identify just the department or balancing segment within that Chart of Accounts.

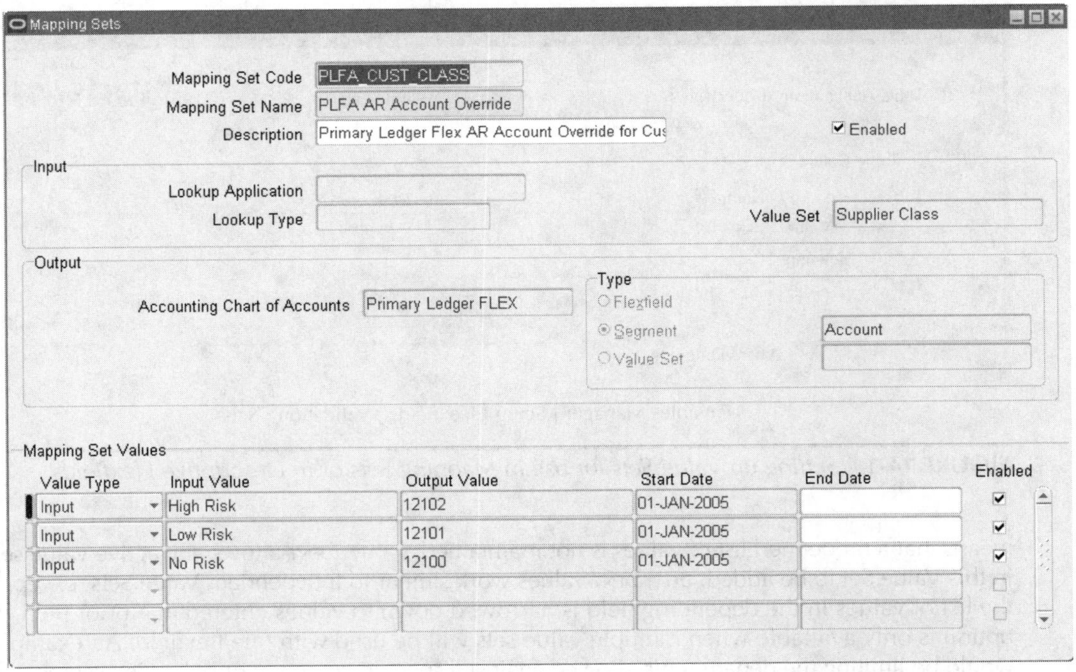

Payables Manager | Setup | Accounting Setups | Subledger Accounting Setup | Accounting Methods Builder | Journal Entry Setups | Mapping Sets

FIGURE 14-2   *Creating Mapping Sets*

If you want to use a VALUE SET as an output, then the ACCOUNTING CHART OF ACCOUNTS should not be populated. Since segments within a Chart of Accounts are actually value sets, either of these options can be used. The option you select depends on the following: If a specific value set is assigned to multiple Charts of Accounts, creating a Mapping Set for the segment will make it available to all the Charts of Accounts that use it, whereas selecting it as a segment against a specific Chart of Accounts limits the usage to that Chart of Accounts only.

Under the Mapping Set Values section, map the INPUTS to the OUTPUT VALUES and assign effective START and END dates. Uncheck ENABLED to remove date tracking from this Mapping Set and make it disabled the moment the box is unchecked and saved; then date tracking cannot be used to process a transaction prior to a specific date using the old value. An ENABLED box is best used when a Mapping Set is wrong and you want to discontinue use immediately for all transactions, no matter what the effective date is on the transactions. For changes in accounting policies or mappings, it is best to use the START DATE and END DATE for consistent accounting during those periods. The other option for Mapping Set Values is VALUE TYPE, which can be set to INPUT, to use the input values in the Lookups or the Value Set, or DEFAULT, which will default a specific value into the Mapping Set.

Account Derivation Rules for Building the Account Strings

Account Derivation Rules are used to build the accounting string based on rules and conditions. Unlike Mapping Sets, which map the data, Account Derivation Rules determine when the Mapping Sets are used. Rules, once they are created and enabled, are shared and can be used by any application that has a common Reference Object on the Accounting Event Class Options (Setup | Accounting Setups | Subledger Accounting Setup | Accounting Methods Builder | Events | Accounting Event Class Options). The rule defined for the example that follows, and in Figure 14-3, determines how the natural account for the distribution is to be derived from an invoice entered into Payables. This rule is for the natural account only, and would then be combined in a second rule to build the rest of the string. In English, it states:

- When the natural account on an invoice is 57100, replace it with 17110.

- When the natural account on an invoice is 57200, replace it with 17120.

- When the natural account on an invoice is 57300, replace it with 17130.

If the natural account is not any of these values, check if the PO Number field is populated:

- When it is not, use the account number from the Invoice Distribution.

- When it is, use the account number from the purchase order it is matched to.

This rule is designed to do two main things: First, ensure that any assets that are miscoded to depreciation (57X00) are posted to the correct asset account. Second, ensure that the coding used is what was entered in AP for non–purchase order–matched invoices, and from the Purchase Order for any invoice matched to a PO.

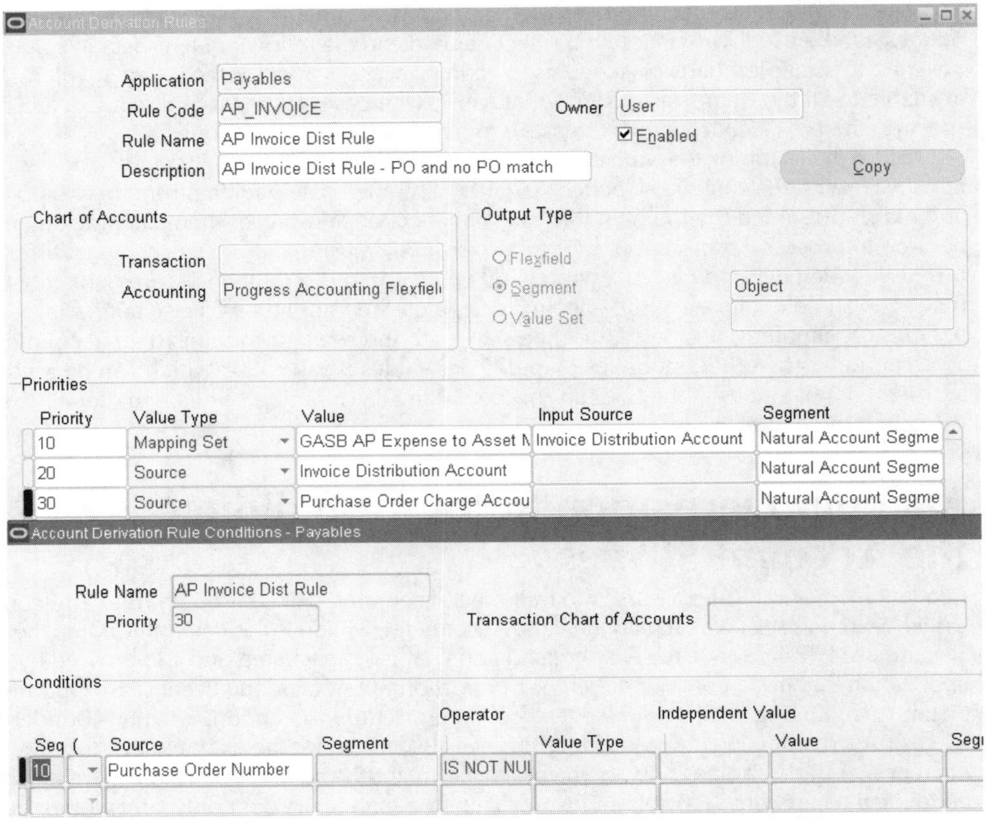

Payables Manager | Setup | Accounting Setups | Subledger Accounting Setup | Accounts Method Builder | Journal Entry Setups | Account Derivation Rules

FIGURE 14-3 *Account Derivation Rules for building account numbers*

Here are the field-by-field instructions to create this rule. First, open the Account Derivation window and a Find screen appears; from here, you will copy an existing rule by using the COPY button or create a new rule using the NEW button on the Find screen. Remember, you cannot change any seeded rule or saved rules. The APPLICATION will default in from your responsibility's application and cannot be changed; if you need to create a rule for cash receipts in Receivables, then you need to use a Receivables responsibility that is assigned to the Receivables application (System Administrator | Security | Responsibility | Define). The RULE CODE is the internal name for the rule, while the RULE NAME is what appears on many of the windows. Both of these fields must have unique values. The OWNER will default to USER for any rule modified or created, while ORACLE will denote a seeded rule. Select ENABLED if you want to have this rule active. The COPY button will allow you to copy a saved or seeded rule for modifications, but remember, this is a copy, and you are not actually modifying the rule—you will need to go back and call any upstream setups (setups that use this rule) to call the new, modified rule instead of the old one.

Entering a TRANSACTION or ACCOUNTING Chart of Accounts will decide what type of rule this is, and work together with the output type. Once one or both of these are entered, the output type of FLEXFIELD or SEGMENT is available. VALUE SET can only be selected when there is no Chart of Accounts populated. The TRANSACTION Chart of Accounts relates to the Chart of Accounts the transaction was entered in, which is one associated with the Primary Ledger. The ACCOUNTING Chart of Accounts refers to the chart that the subledger accounting will be related to, which can be the same as the TRANSACTION for a Primary Ledger rule, or a different Chart of Accounts, such as one assigned to a Secondary Ledger. This most often comes into play when transactions are being accounted for in two different ways, one associated with the Primary Ledger and the other associated with a Secondary Ledger that has a different Chart of Accounts. When either Chart of Accounts is assigned, the Account Derivation Rule will be limited to transactions with that TRANSACTION Chart of Accounts associated with it.

The Output Type section determines what the output of this rule will be: FLEXFIELD can only be used with a Chart of Accounts and refers to the entire accounting string. SEGMENT refers to a segment with a specific qualifier in a Chart of Accounts (when one is selected) or all Charts of Accounts assigned that qualifier. The qualifier can refer to Balancing Segments, Natural Accounts, Cost Centers, Intercompany, or Management Segments. If you select this option and enter a qualifier that is not required, such as Management Segment, when a Chart of Accounts is used that does not have this segment, this rule will be ignored. When a Chart of Accounts *is* entered, then this field will show the actual segments of that Chart of Accounts as the list of values. VALUE SET refers to any Value Set in the system, including the Value Sets used in each segment of the Chart of Accounts. When either SEGMENT or VALUE SET is selected, then the types must be identified in the field next to the option. At this point, you should realize that the same Output Type can be selected many different ways:

- With a Chart of Accounts and a flexfield
- With a Chart of Accounts and a segment
- With only a flexfield
- With only a segment
- With only a value set

The type you use determines how many transactions can utilize this Derivation Rule. Either a Flexfield or Segment with the Chart of Accounts is most restrictive, whereas Segment or Value Set alone are the least restrictive, allowing this Derivation Rule to be used for multiple Charts of Accounts.

The Priorities section determines what order the Derivation Rules will be evaluated in; these settings do not determine which rule best meets the transactions, nor do they return more than one value. Once the condition associated with a rule is met, EBS will no longer look at the remaining rules. This makes the PRIORITY of the rules very important for two reasons: first, if your conditions associated with the first priority are all-encompassing, then EBS will never make it to the second rule. On the other hand, if the first evaluated condition is one that comes up less than 10 percent of the time, it will slow down processing for the other 90 percent of the transactions as they are evaluated for a rule they will never meet.

Let's look at the preceding example. If the purchase order field being populated was evaluated prior to the actual account number, the account number rules will never be reached, since all invoices either are matched to a purchase order or the purchase order number field is blank. This AP to Asset Mapping Set currently reads that all invoices are first evaluated for the depreciation account numbers, and if they pass that rule, then the Derivation Rule will determine if the invoices are matched to a PO. Next, we put non–purchase order invoices first, since they make up most of the transactions at this company. When the invoice is matched to a PO, then the rule uses the purchase order account number. By changing the order for this rule to where the PO match is evaluated *before* the distribution account, it actually changes the business rule that would now read:

- If the PO number is not populated, use the distribution on the invoice.

- If the PO number is populated, use the distribution on the purchase order.

- When the natural account on an invoice is 57100, replace it with 17110.

- When the natural account on an invoice is 57200, replace it with 17120.

- When the natural account on an invoice is 57300, replace it with 17130.

Since all invoices either have a purchase order populated or do not have this field populated, the final three rules that check for the natural account will never be evaluated or used.

The PRIORITY is the order in which the rules are evaluated. The lowest value is evaluated first. The VALUE TYPE determines what is used to evaluate this rule. The selections in the VALUE TYPE are determined by the Chart of Accounts and Output Type that were selected. Using an Output Type of SEGMENT without a chart of account will limit the VALUE TYPE options to Account Derivation Rule and Source. When a transactional Chart of Accounts is entered, two additional values are available: mapping set and constant.

Source allows any source setup in Subledger Accounting (Setup | Subledger Accounting Setup | Accounting Methods Builder | Sources) to be selected. Selecting Account Derivation Rule will allow you to select any rule that is defined in the system. This means that any Account Derivation Rule can be reused multiple times. Mapping Set will allow any mapping rules that were defined to be selected, whereas Constant allows a constant value to be entered.

Once the VALUE TYPE is entered, the actual VALUE can be selected from the list of values. INPUT VALUES can be added only when the VALUE TYPE is set to Mapping Set, and allows an input value for the mapping set to be selected. SEGMENT is available when the OUTPUT TYPE is set to Segment and allows the segment for the output to be selected.

The Account Derivation Rule Conditions, defined by clicking the CONDITION button, determine when the rule will be used. When no conditions are added, then this rule is always used. Adding these conditions allows transactions to be evaluated to determine when a specific rule is applied. All the conditions added to a specific rule must be met in order for the rule to be used.

Conditions will be evaluated based on the SEQ, with the lowest number being evaluated first. Next, select the SOURCE for the data being evaluated. These sources are not only the sources defined in SLA, but also key flexfields, such as a Chart of Accounts. The source selected will determine if a segment can be added—only sources that are key flexfields will allow a SEGMENT to be selected. Next, enter the OPERATOR for the evaluation. For the VALUE TYPE, select if the data is a constant or coming from the SOURCE entered in the previous field, then add the INDEPENDENT VALUE,

VALUE, or SEGMENT, depending on the SOURCE entered. The final option here is to determine if the next condition you add is going to be an "and" condition, requiring that both conditions be met, or an "or" condition, allowing either condition to be met.

Once all the derivation rules and conditions are created, additional information can be added to the journal entries.

Adding Reference Data

Supporting References is an optional setup that allows additional data to be stored on each accounting entry. Journal Entry Descriptions can create a large amount of information that is stored with the actual journal but can also get long and cumbersome to read. Adding Supporting References to the entries provides additional information in the SLA inquiry windows, but not on the actual journal.

To create a new Reference, as shown in Figure 14-4, select CREATE and add a CODE for the system to use, which must be in uppercase with no spaces. Also add a NAME, which is what the users will see when adding this reference to other forms. Add a DESCRIPTION to provide useful information as to why this was created and when it should be used. Select ENABLED if this reference is active. Click ADD DETAIL and assign a DETAIL CODE, using all uppercase and no spaces, and a DETAIL NAME. You can add up to four sources to each detail you create for additional information, and more than one detail can be added to each reference. Click ASSIGN SOURCES. To narrow down the data, enter an APPLICATION NAME, and either an EVENT CLASS NAME or a SOURCE NAME, and select GO. This will give a list of the sources that are available to add to the entries; select up to four sources before clicking APPLY to save.

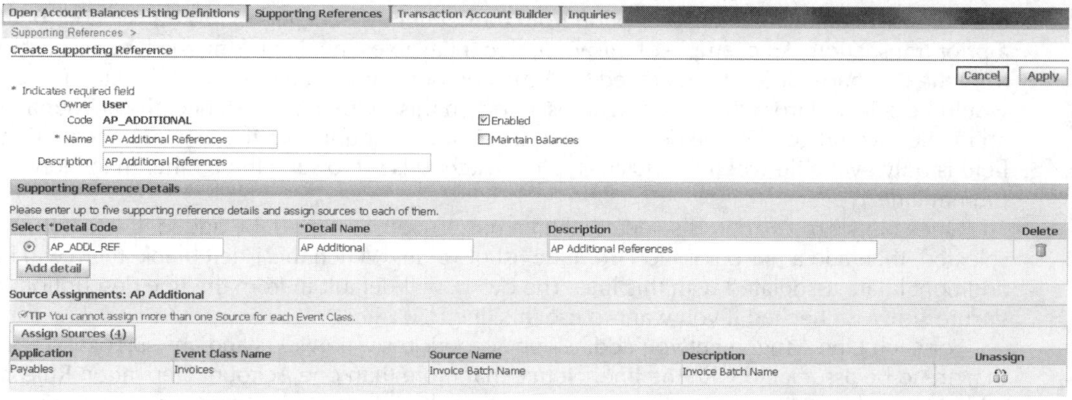

Payables Manager | Setup | Accounting Setups | Subledger Accounting Setup | Accounts Method Builder | Journal Entry Setups | Supporting References

FIGURE 14-4   *Adding supporting reference data to a rule*

Putting All the Data Together

Prior to now, there were some links among each of the setups described in Chapter 13 and this chapter, but all the different setups have not yet been tied together to create one subledger accounting rule. This begins with the next step, Journal Line Definitions.

Journal Line Definitions

So far, we have covered how to define an Application, which has Event Classes and Types that get associated with Journal Lines and Line Descriptions. Then Account Derivation rules determine how account numbers are built, using multiple sources, including Mapping Sets. Journal Line Definitions ties all these elements together, with the Event Class and Event Types being the lowest common denominator.

As shown in Figure 14-5, the APPLICATION will default in based on the responsibility. Select an EVENT CLASS and an EVENT TYPE from the lists, remembering that these selections will restrict the additional fields. For example, if you select Invoices | All, then only Line Assignments that are associated with Invoices can be selected. Add a unique system name in the DEFINITION CODE, and a user-friendly name in the DEFINITION NAME. OWNER will default to ORACLE for all seeded definitions, and to USER for all new or copied ones. Add a meaningful DESCRIPTION to best describe when this is used and what it does, and select ENABLED to allow this Journal Lines Definitions to be used.

When using the Budgetary Controls feature in a Ledger, all transactions require setups for Budgetary Controls; this causes the Create Accounting program to select only Journal Line Definitions that are set up with BUDGETARY CONTROL selected. Adding either a TRANSACTION or ACCOUNTING Chart of Accounts will limit when this definition is used, and also which Account Derivation rules are available.

Select the JOURNAL LINE TYPES that are to be associated with this rule. For the Journal Line Type selected, if the Business Flow Method was set up as Entry or Prior, you can select to INHERIT DESCRIPTION. Basically, this means if the Journal Line type was set up with a Business Flow Method of Prior, it will take the Line Description from transactions associated to this transaction, but from a prior transaction. An example of this would be a Payables invoice taking the line description from the Purchase Order it is matched to. A method of Same would mean that the Line Description would be selected from the offsetting transaction on this journal; for instance, the accounting for an invoice would get the line description for a liability account from the expense accounting. This field is only available when the Business Flow Method is set to something other than None on the Journal Line Type.

Once INHERIT DESCRIPTION is selected, then a LINE DESCRIPTION cannot be added. If it is not selected, then add a LINE DESCRIPTION from the list of values. When this is left blank, there will be no additional data associated with this line. The OWNER will default in from the line description itself. Ensure ACTIVE is checked if you want to use this line.

For each Line Assignment you add, assign ACCOUNT DERIVATION RULES and any SUPPORTING REFERENCES that are to be associated with the line. Notice that more than one Account Derivation Rule can be added to the line type; this is another way to use multiple rules to build your account number. As discussed, when building the Account Derivation Rules, you can call one rule within another rule to override the natural account or any other segment, especially when the conditions are not the

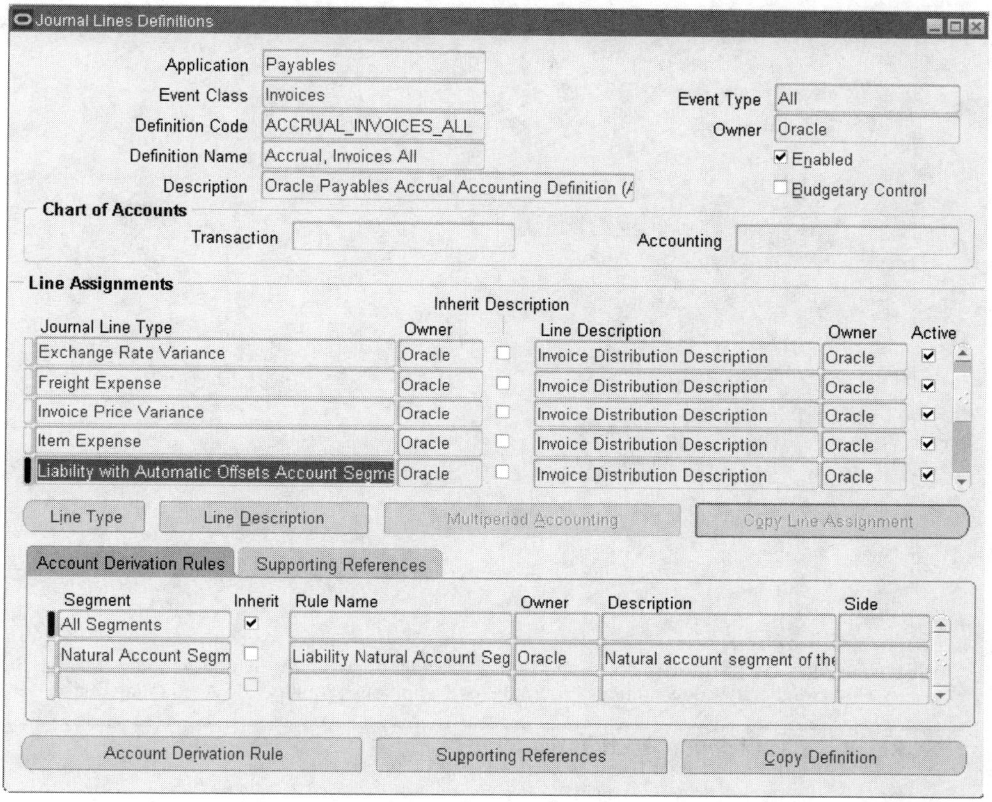

FIGURE 14-5   *Journal Lines Definitions*

same. The example here where two rules are called does the exact same thing: the Natural Account Segment rule will override the natural account assigned in the All Segments rule. The LINE TYPE and LINE DESCRIPTION buttons are used to view or set up new entries on those windows, not to add a Line Type or Line Description to the Journal Line Definitions.

To create a Journal Line Definition that spans multiple accounting periods, Multiperiod Accounting must be set up, as seen in Figure 14-6. The MULTIPERIOD ACCOUNTING button is only available when the Journal Line Type selected was set up with Multiperiod set to Accrual or Recognition, and when it has the attributes Multiperiod, Multiperiod Start Date, and Multiperiod

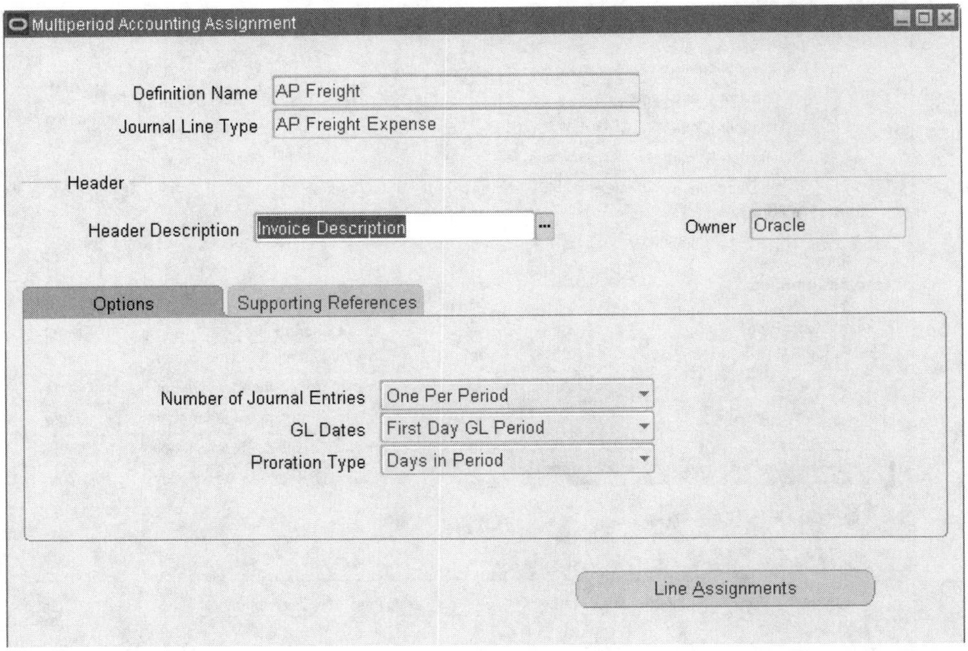

Payables Manager | Setup | Accounting Setups | Subledger Accounting Setup | Accounts Method Builder | Methods And Definitions | Journal Line Definitions | Multiperiod Accounting button

FIGURE 14-6 *Multiperiod Accounting setups*

End Date assigned to it. Multiperiod transactions allow for journal entries and accounting that span over more than one period. For example, if a prepayment for services is entered into Payables that is to be recognized over a span of three months, you can set up SLA to create the proper journal entries in each month for you without having to create journals in General Ledger manually. Once the transaction is entered as a multiperiod transaction, it will then be accounted by the Journal Line Assignments where the conditions select the transaction.

When the Create Accounting process is run, it will create any current period transactions based on the Multiperiod setups, and then the Complete Multiperiod Accounting process is run each month to generate the additional accounting, including reversals of accruals, based on the setups completed here. The DEFINITION NAME and JOURNAL LINE TYPE will default in from the previous page. Select a HEADER DESCRIPTION from the list that will be assigned to the SLA entry description at the header level. The Options section determines exactly how these entries will be generated. NUMBER OF JOURNAL ENTRIES determines if ONE journal is created for the transaction, or if ONE PER PERIOD is generated, using the Multiperiod Start and End dates from the transaction. The GL DATES setting determines what day of the month the multiperiod journal will be effective. Options are the FIRST day of the month, LAST day of the month, or ORIGINATING day, which uses the effective day of the transaction for all future months.

The PRORATION TYPE, which is only allowed when the NUMBER OF JOURNAL ENTRIES is set to ONE PER PERIOD, determines not only how the last month is prorated, but also how the actual accrual is calculated, as shown in Table 14-1.

Click LINE ASSIGNMENTS; this window will default the data based on the Account Derivation rules. If the INHERIT DESCRIPTION field is checked, it can be unchecked here to allow additional Line Assignments and Account Derivation Rules to be added. The default Journal Line Types and Derivation Rules will be used on the entries that reverse the initial accruals. Additional lines will be used to create the next accrual transaction. With the cursor on the Journal Line Type, arrow down to enter a new TYPE and add a LINE DESCRIPTION for that type. The OWNERS will default in for both these. Click the SEGMENT under the Account Derivation rules to add different rules to the newly added Journal Line Type.

Prorate Basis	Accrual Definition	Accrual Calculation
360 Days	Partial months are based on a 360-day period.	Total accrual / 360 * number of days
Days in Period	Partial months are based on the number of days in the month.	Total days in month / days to accrue for that month * total accrual
First Period	Accrue an equal amount for each month, starting with the first month.	Total accrual / number of months
Total Days in period	Accrual is based on the actual days in each month as well as the total days in the accrual.	Days in the month / total number of days for the accrual * total accrual

TABLE 14-1 *Accrual Prorate Conventions*

Recap of Setups So Far

Though SLA setups need to be created in a specific order, the flow of the setups from step to step can get confusing. The following flowchart shows how the data from each setup step is used to build and create the next series of steps.

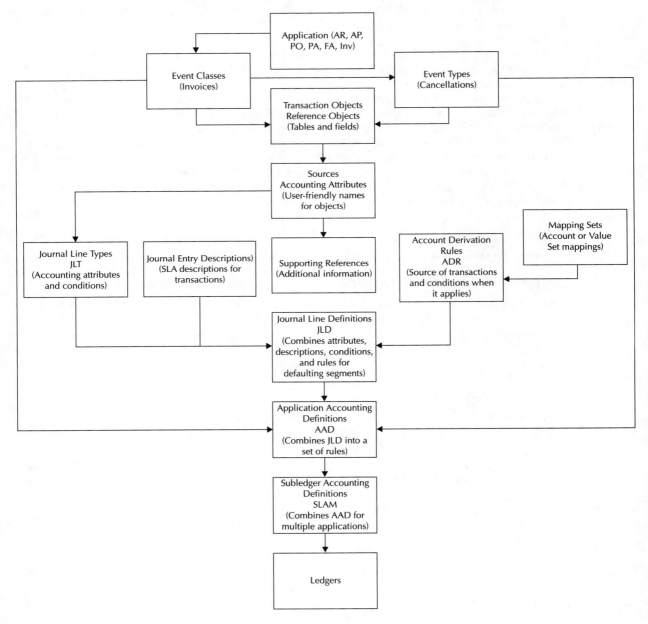

Application Accounting Definitions

Up to this point, many of the setups have related to specific Event Classes and Types. There is no restriction on setting up more than one process, such as an Account Derivation Rule, per event class. This has allowed seeded rules, customizations of these rules by copying them, and creating multiple rules for different accounting practices. The next three steps are where you combine these rules and limit what each Ledger can use to create entries. Application Accounting Definitions, shown in Figure 14-7, will group Event Classes and assign Journal Line Definitions to them, and the Subledger Accounting Methods combine one Application Accounting Definition for each subledger, which then gets assigned to a Ledger.

Application Accounting Definitions do come seeded for EBS for all the seeded events. There are a few basic definitions, such as Accrual and Cash in Payables, that can either be copied or used as is. If you have created one or more Journal Line Definitions, you will need to either copy and modify a seeded rule or create a rule from scratch. Ensure, if creating one from scratch, that

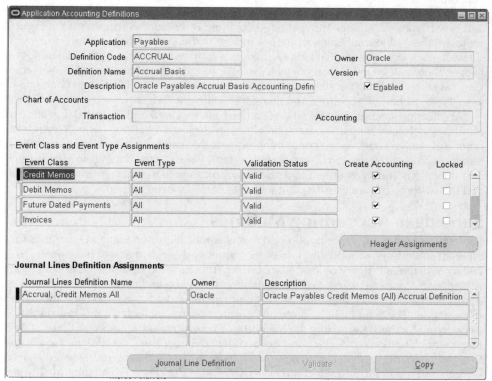

Payables Manager | Setup | Accounting Setups | Subledger Accounting Setup| Accounts Method Builder | Methods And Definitions | Application Accounting Definitions

FIGURE 14-7 *Setting up the accounting definitions*

all the event classes for the subledger you are working on are included in the definition, otherwise a specific event class will not generate any accounting entries. As always, the APPLICATION will default from your responsibility. Create a DEFINITION CODE for the system and a DEFINITION NAME for users to see; again, keeping these consistent with the exception of spaces can make things easier when modifying or troubleshooting down the road. Add a DESCRIPTION that describes this definition and where it is used. The OWNER will default to USER for all copied or new definitions.

Enter a TRANSACTION or ACCOUNTING Chart of Accounts to limit this definition when assigning it to Ledgers. When entering EVENT CLASSES and EVENT TYPES, including all the valid events for the subledger you are in is important—if an event is not added, it will not be accounted! Application Accounting Definitions require validation prior to use; the VALIDATION STATUS will show the status of each Event Class and Type. All Accounting Events do not have to Create Accounting transactions in the General Ledger; checking the CREATE ACCOUNTING box will ensure that they do, while unchecking it will create SLA transactions that are not reflected in the General Ledger. A common example of when this is used might be for Tax Fixed Asset books; you may want to see the accounting but not create entries in the General Ledger. Selecting LOCKED makes this definition so it cannot be modified. Selecting the HEADER ASSIGNMENTS button allows Header Descriptions, as well as Supporting References and Accounting Attributes, to be assigned to this SLA entry for this Event.

Next assign Journal Lines Definitions to each event. Only definitions where the Event Class and Event Types match this Application Accounting Definition will appear. If the Event Type is set to ALL, then all Journal Line Definitions for any of the Event Types for this Event Class will also show. If more than one Journal Line Definition is assigned, and they both create lines for the same Ledger, there will be more than one entry in SLA and, if Create Accounting is selected, in the General Ledger. It is appropriate to assign more than one Journal Line when each line pertains to a different Chart of Accounts, and therefore a different Ledger.

Application Accounting Definitions can be both exported and imported, a feature that is especially helpful during an upgrade or when developing and testing definitions in test. These processes, called Loaders, are concurrent requests that can be run: EXPORT APPLICATION ACCOUNTING DEFINITIONS and IMPORT APPLICATION ACCOUNTING DEFINITIONS. As with all things in EBS, exporting any customizations and saving them in a safe location can help to reduce frustration after an upgrade and the customized processes are lost and unexpectedly need to be re-created.

Subledger Accounting Methods

Subledger Accounting Methods allows different Application Accounting Definitions for the different subledgers, or modules, into one comprehensive rule that will be assigned to each Ledger, whether a Primary or Secondary Ledger. There should be at least one definition for each subledger that you are using, and that definition should be inclusive of all events that you want to account. Referring to Figure 14-8, add a system name under the METHOD CODE and a user-friendly METHOD NAME. The OWNER will be User, and ensure ENABLED is selected if this is an active Subledger Accounting Method. Restricting the method to a TRANSACTION or ACCOUNTING Chart of Accounts will restrict the definitions to Application Accounting Definitions that are assigned to the specific Chart of Accounts, or assigned to none, and therefore applicable to any. Select the APPLICATION you want to add a rule for, and select the NAME of the rule. The OWNER will default in. The START DATE is required, and there can be no overlap in definition assignments. For example, you can assign two rules for Payables, but *only* if their effective dates do not overlap. Once the rule is no longer used, add an END DATE.

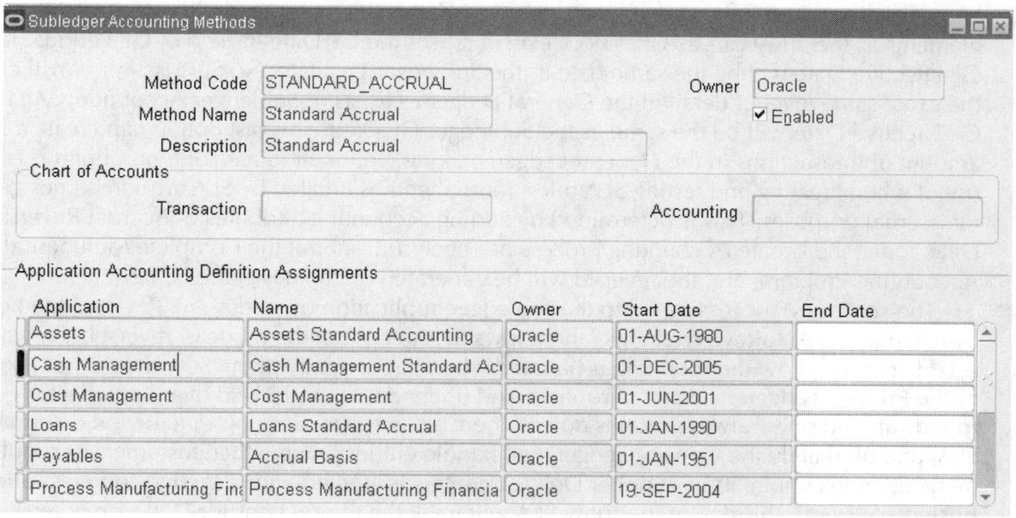

Payables Manager | Setup | Accounting Setups | Subledger Accounting Setup | Accounts Method Builder |
Methods And Definitions | Subledger Accounting Methods

FIGURE 14-8 *Creating Subledger Accounting Methods*

Ledger Setups

Once the Subledger Accounting Methods are created, they need to be associated to the Ledgers that will be using them.

Assigning Subledger Accounting Methods to a Ledger

The association between Accounting Methods and Ledgers is created in the Accounting Setup window from any responsibility (General Ledger | Setup | Financial | Accounting Setup Manager | Accounting Setups | Primary or Secondary Ledger | Subledger Accounting Options). There are two options that can be modified here: Accounting and System. Accounting controls how the Create Accounting process will default and work for each module, and System determines how many resources will be used.

Creating Ledger Accounting Options

To set up the Accounting Options for a specific module, select the yellow pencil next to the name under Accounting Options, and the windows shown in Figure 14-9 will appear. There are several options on how data will create the GENERAL LEDGER JOURNAL ENTRY SUMMARIZIATION. The first option, SUMMARIZE BY GL PERIOD, is the default when Daily Balancing is turned off for the Ledger. This option will summarize all entries by GL Period, General Ledger Journal Category, GL Account, Entered Currency, Balance Type, and side of transaction (i.e., Debit or Credit), and the GL effective date for the journal entry will default to the last day of the accounting period. Summarize by GL Date becomes the default if the Ledger is set up to use daily balancing. This will group on the same elements as the Summarize by GL Period, except it uses the GL Date instead of GL Period. Here, the GL Effective Date will be the same date as the Subledger GL Date. No Summarization will create the exact same level of detail in the General Ledger as exists in Subledger Accounting. Again, the GL Effective Date will be the same as the Subledger GL Date. This last option can create a large amount of transactions in the General Ledger, making it difficult to read at times, but it is extremely useful when creating and testing SLA rules. Journal entries created by SLA are sometimes generated for accrual purposes. This is determined by adding accounting attributes of Accrual Reversal GL Date. Once the Create Accounting process has been run, submit the Complete Multiperiod Accounting Program, and the reversal will be generated on the designated date.

The Reversal Method assigned to the subledger application overrides any Reversal Methods assigned in the AutoReverse setups, and allows SLA to control the mode of reversal. The Rounding Rule determines how the rounding is handled when the currency of the SLA entry is not the same as the Primary Ledger. Nearest will round 4 and under down, and 5 and over up, whereas up always rounds up and down always rounds down. The Third Party Merge Accounting Option determines how SLA, and ultimately the General Ledger, will handle entries when either customers or suppliers are merged. For example, if the supplier Dell Computers is merged with a second supplier called Dell Business Systems, this determines how SLA will track the transactions for Dell Computers: if None is selected, then nothing will happen. Selecting Replace Third Party will change the name seen in SLA to the new supplier: Dell Business Systems. Transfer of the Third-party Control Account Balance will ensure that any existing journal entries will be reversed and rebooked against the new control account, usually a liability account for the new supplier, for all transactions after the date of

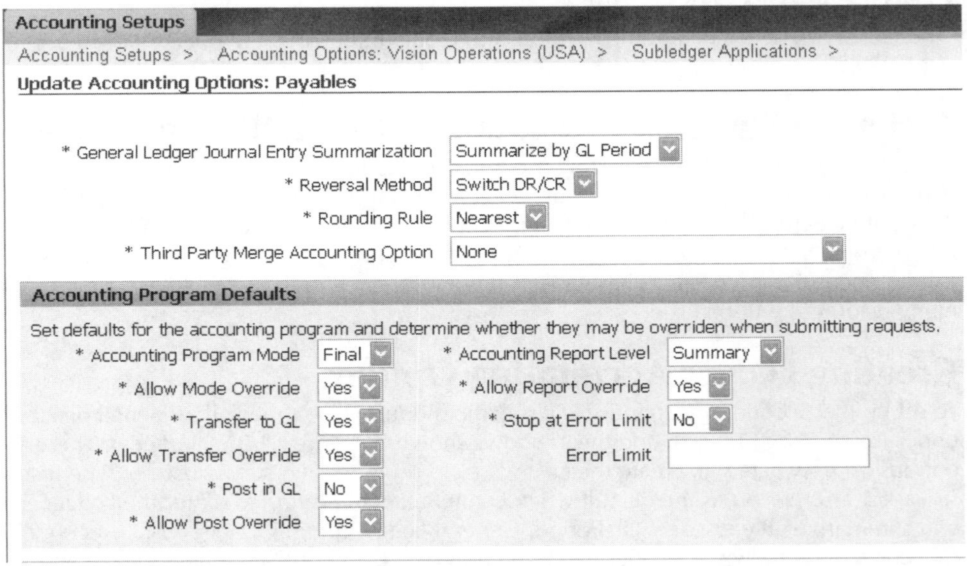

General Ledger | Setup | Financial | Accounting Setup Manager | Accounting Setups | Primary Ledger | Subledger Accounting Options

FIGURE 14-9 *Adding Subledger Accounting Options to a Ledger*

the merge. This is helpful if the suppliers being merged were assigned to two different liability accounts. A separate accounting program used for this option, Create Accounting for Third Party Merge program, will create these additional transfer journal entries.

Under the Accounting Program Defaults, additional options are available to control the Create Accounting process for this subledger. Select the default for the ACCOUNTING PROGRAM MODE as FINAL, which will create the journal entries, or DRAFT, which creates the accounting entries for review and does not transfer them to the General Ledger. ALLOW MODE OVERRIDE will determine if the users can change this default when submitting the program. This may be a control point that the organization wants to restrict. TRANSFER TO GL can be set to YES when the Accounting Program Mode is set to Final, which will prevent the transactions from having to be transferred separately.

Again, the ALLOW TRANSFER OVERRIDE setting determines if users can change this setting when they submit the Create Accounting process. POST IN GL determines if these journal entries are automatically posted; it should only be used when TRANSFER TO GL is set to YES and ACCOUNTING PROGRAM MODE is creating the entries in Final mode. ALLOW POST OVERRIDE controls if the users can change this setting.

Every time that the Create Accounting program is run, a report is produced for the entries created or in error. Setting the ACCOUNTING REPORT LEVEL to summary will not print out details of the accounting entries created without errors; it will list just a summary, but it will provide details of any errors that occurred during the process for troubleshooting purposes. ALLOW REPORT OVERRIDE determines if the users can change this option from summary to detail. SLA's creation of account combinations will inevitably create invalid combinations at some point, especially during the creation of the rules and testing. Setting STOP AT ERROR LIMIT to YES will prevent SLA from continuing to the end of all the records, stopping instead once it has hit the number of errors identified in ERROR LIMIT. This is particularly useful when testing SLA setups.

Next, you can identify what Journal Entry Categories will be assigned to entries from each specific Event Classes, as seen in Figure 14-10. Select the CATEGORY from the list of values to assign it.

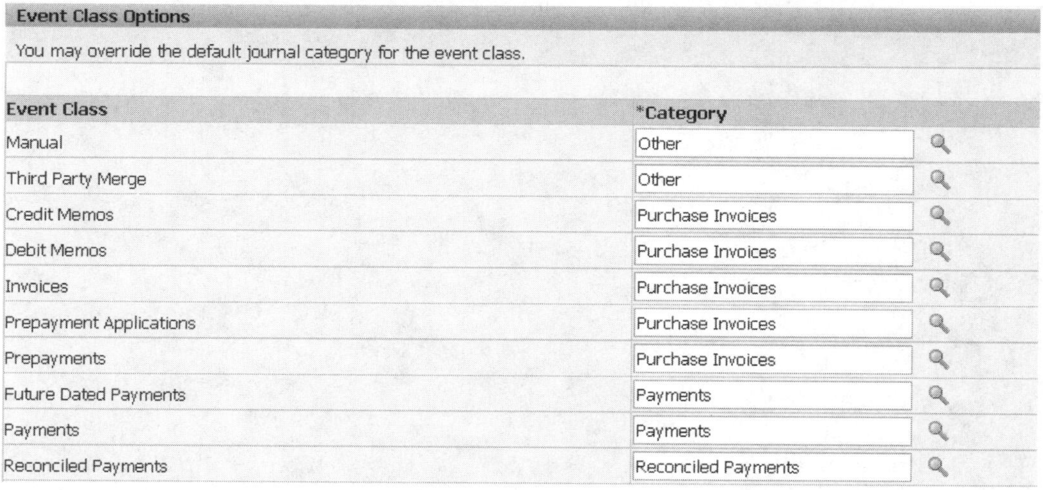

Event Class Options

You may override the default journal category for the event class.

Event Class	*Category	
Manual	Other	🔍
Third Party Merge	Other	🔍
Credit Memos	Purchase Invoices	🔍
Debit Memos	Purchase Invoices	🔍
Invoices	Purchase Invoices	🔍
Prepayment Applications	Purchase Invoices	🔍
Prepayments	Purchase Invoices	🔍
Future Dated Payments	Payments	🔍
Payments	Payments	🔍
Reconciled Payments	Reconciled Payments	🔍

General Ledger | Setup | Financial | Accounting Setup Manager | Accounting Setups | Primary Ledger | Subledger Accounting Options

FIGURE 14-10 *Changing journal categories for events*

The SLS System Options are designed to improve performance during the Create Accounting Process. Working with your DBA, you can assign a specific number of parallel processes to be used. The more processors assigned, the faster the request will run, but at a cost—this will prevent these resources from being used by the rest of the system. You can also assign the Processing Unit Size, which is the number of units, or transactions, that will be processed before releasing the workers and committing. This can be assigned as a default for all events or at a different level for each event.

At this point, the Subledger Accounting setups are complete and ready for use.

Glossary

BS has its own set of terms and language, which I call Oracle-ese. The most commonly used terms in this book can be found here.

Accounting Flexfield The definition of the segments that make up the chart of accounts.

Accounting Methods Also known as Subledger Accounting, provides rules for how subledger transactions are accounted and represented in the General Ledger.

Advanced Global Intercompany System (AGIS) A service in R12 that tracks and controls intercompany transactions.

budgetary controls Controls put in place surrounding a budget, presenting either a warning or a hard prevention on any transactions created over the budget limits. Usually used with encumbrances, the controls can be set up on all or specific accounts.

Budget Wizard Part of WebADI, this allows budget and actual data to be downloaded into Excel, changed, and then uploaded into EBS.

Concurrent (Processing) Manager A method used in EBS to run reports and processes.

Cross-Validation Rules (CVRs) A set of defined rules in EBS that control the account combinations that can be created.

Descriptive Flexfields Also called DFF, these are fields denoted with [] on windows, or the CONTEXT VALUE field on web windows, that can be enabled to track data specific to your company.

Dynamic Insertion The ability to create account combinations on the fly in EBS, based on rules defined in the Cross-Validation Rules.

encumbrance The accounting practice of recording of obligations prior to paying them out. An encumbrance will be recorded when a purchase order or requisition is booked, whereas accrual accounting will record this obligation when the product is received. Encumbrances are usually used in the federal government.

Enterprise Performance Foundation A set of predefined tables and dimensions used by Management and Planning applications in EBS such as the Consolidation Hub. The data and tables are tightly integrated with EBS data but also allow data from other systems to be loaded and used.

Financial Consolidation Hub Advanced consolidation processes and workbenches.

GCS (Global Consolidation System) Groupings of setups and processes used by EBS to perform a consolidation of multiple Ledgers.

General Ledger Key Flexfields The EBS name for the segments in a chart of accounts.

GL Ledger Flexfield A copy of the General Ledger Key Flexfield, it is utilized by EBS when running Mass Allocations, FSGs, and other processes to improve processing time. This is automatically updated when changes are made to the General Ledger Key Flexfield and should never be manually maintained.

intracompany   Set of transactions that cross the balancing segment of the Accounting Flexfield, where the balancing segments are all assigned to the same Legal Entity and Ledger.

intercompany   Set of transactions that cross balancing segments that are assigned to different Legal Entities within the same Ledger.

Journal Wizard   Also called Web ADI, this is a direct link between Excel and various windows in EBS, allowing for faster data entry. Journal Wizard refers specifically to the journal entry feature of Web ADI.

Ledger   Defined by the commonality of the 4 C's—Chart of Accounts, Calendar, Currency, and aCcounting Methods. Along with other setups, EBS will segregate all data in a Ledger from other Ledgers. The 4C's are the main drivers when determining if a company should have one or more Ledgers set up in their system.

legal entity   Literally, the entity responsible for paying obligations, including invoices and payroll, or performing any transaction.

MOAC (Multiple Organization Access Control)   Allows multiple operating units to be accessed from one responsibility in the Subledgers.

operating unit   Also known as an Org in EBS, this segregates data in submodules such as Receivables and Payables. MOAC allows operating units to be grouped for centralized access. This is not to be confused with an Inventory Org, which is one level lower and only pertains to inventory transactions.

parent account   A grouping of child accounts used in reporting and processing. Unlike summary accounts, parent accounts do not have actual balances.

Processing (Concurrent) Manager   A method used in EBS to run reports and processes.

Profile Option   A variable that is set in System Administration for any of the system levels, or at a user level from any responsibility with access to personal profiles. The system profiles can be set at the Site, Application, or Responsibility level, controlling certain features of the system.

reconciliation accounts   Accounts that are set up allowing the system to automatically reconcile transactions. This feature is most commonly used for clearing accounts.

Report Manager   A report repository to share and store reports.

responsibility   A grouping of windows, functions, and reports that can be assigned to specific users or roles (which then get assigned to users). Also, many system profiles are set at the Responsibility level, changing the data that is accessed (such as when a Ledger is assigned) or how the system behaves (such as when Sequential Numbering is set).

Revaluation   This revalues translated balances in the Ledger based on more current conversion rates.

seeded   Set of data that gets installed with the base EBS database and is accessible for all companies for use. Some seed data can be disabled if it is not going to be used, while other data is required to stay active for the system to function properly.

segment qualifier   Additional attributes added to a Flexfield to provide additional functionality.

subledger   Subledgers refer to non–General Ledger modules that are available from EBS, such as Payables and Receivables.

Subledger Accounting (SLA)   Also known as Accounting Methods, provides rules for how subledger transactions are accounted and represented in the General Ledger.

summary accounts   Accounts combining multiple detail accounts, where the balance of the detail accounts is maintained in the summary account.

translations   A process that converts balances in the functional currency of a Ledger to a Reporting currency.

Value Set   Value Sets are lists of data that are both used by EBS's programs and selected and entered by users. They can be as important as valid General Ledger account numbers, and as trivial as a designation for a supplier. Value Sets can be added not only for custom data, like your Accounting Flexfield, but also to restrict data allowed in Descriptive Flexfields. These are also a good way to track data that may change for custom reporting so that the users, not just the programmers, will have access to make updates.

Web ADI   An Excel-to-Oracle interface that allows faster data entry. Integrators for this feature are constantly being added by Oracle.

XML (Extended Markup Language)   A programming language used by Oracle to create reports using Excel, Word, or PDF templates.

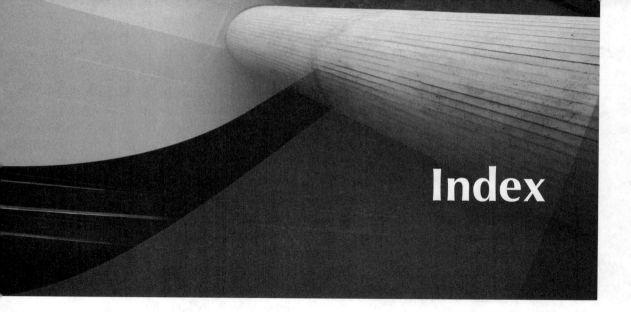

Index

data *(continued)*
    reports updating EBS, 209–212
    resolving conflicts in concurrent report
        requests, 209
    rounding financial statement, 130–131
    tracking subledger integration of, 218–219
    transferring from Secondary to Primary
        Ledger, 84–85
    validating event setup data, 241
    workflow for SLA setups, 260
Data Access Sets
    about, 28
    setting up, 86–87
dates for Report Manager, 154–155
Definition Access Sets
    setting up, 30–32
    table of, 28–30
deleting Journal Wizard entries, 118
dependent validation, 42
Depreciation transactions, 219
Descriptive Flexfields (DFF)
    adding custom fields, 55–56
    importing data from, 107
    using, 26
diagnostics for month-end closing, 226
disabled accounts, 49, 50
display groups and sets (FSG), 146–147
Document Sequences, 88–89
drilling down data
    defining subledger procedures for, 236
    displaying as transactions, 220
    viewing detail in Report Repository,
        156–157
Dynamic Insertion
    allowing for Accounting Flexfield
        segments, 38
    creating account combinations
        automatically, 49
    using, 26

E

EBS. *See* Oracle E-Business Suite
editing
    imported journal entries, 107–108
    report templates, 151–153
eliminations, 168–170
employee hierarchies, 66–67
encumbrance journals, 120
encumbrance year, 188

encumbrances and budgetary controls, 181–189
    about, 181
    checking encumbrance funds, 189–190
    creating encumbrance entries, 189
    hierarchy of funds checking levels, 187–189
    reviewing funds available, 190–191
    summary accounts, 182–185
    summary setup steps for, 188–189
    types of encumbrances, 181–182
Enterprise Planning and Budgeting, 172
enterprise resource planning (ERP) system, 4
entities. *See* Legal Entities
Equity translations, 194–195
errors
    account setup, 54–55
    correcting imported journal entries, 107–108
    creating CVR account combinations, 53
    resolving Journal Wizard data loading, 115
Event Classes
    changing journal categories for, 265
    defining, 238, 239
Event Modeler, 237–238
events
    about Subledger Accounting
        application, 237
    associating with unique ID numbers,
        237–238
    defining Event Classes for, 238, 239
    reviewing options for, 240–241
    validating setup data for, 241
Excel
    editing report templates in, 151–153
    entering transactions with Web ADI, 114–117
    using data in Budget Wizard, 179–180
    viewing Journal Wizard in, 117

F

fields. *See also* Accounting Flexfield;
    Descriptive Flexfields
    adding custom DFF, 55–56
    Journal Wizard, 115–116
files
    attaching data, 113–114
    uploading journals from text, 117–118
Financial Report Template Editor, 151, 152
Financial Statement Generator (FSG), 128–158
    about, 128–129
    Ad Hoc reports, 158
    columns for, 137–143

S

GET YOUR FREE SUBSCRIPTION TO *ORACLE MAGAZINE*

Oracle Magazine is essential gear for today's information technology professionals. Stay informed and increase your productivity with every issue of *Oracle Magazine*. Inside each free bimonthly issue you'll get:

- Up-to-date information on Oracle Database, Oracle Application Server, Web development, enterprise grid computing, database technology, and business trends
- Third-party news and announcements
- Technical articles on Oracle and partner products, technologies, and operating environments
- Development and administration tips
- Real-world customer stories

If there are other Oracle users at your location who would like to receive their own subscription to *Oracle Magazine*, please photocopy this form and pass it along.

Three easy ways to subscribe:

① **Web**
Visit our Web site at **oracle.com/oraclemagazine**
You'll find a subscription form there, plus much more

② **Fax**
Complete the questionnaire on the back of this card and fax the questionnaire side only to **+1.847.763.9638**

③ **Mail**
Complete the questionnaire on the back of this card and mail it to **P.O. Box 1263, Skokie, IL 60076-8263**

ORACLE

Want your own FREE subscription?

To receive a free subscription to *Oracle Magazine*, you must fill out the entire card, sign it, and date it (incomplete cards cannot be processed or acknowledged). You can also fax your application to +1.847.763.9638. Or subscribe at our Web site at oracle.com/oraclemagazine

○ **Yes, please send me a FREE subscription** *Oracle Magazine*.   ○ No.

○ From time to time, Oracle Publishing allows our partners exclusive access to our e-mail addresses for special promotions and announcements. To be included in this program, please check this circle. If you do not wish to be included, you will only receive notices about your subscription via e-mail.

○ Oracle Publishing allows sharing of our postal mailing list with selected third parties. If you prefer your mailing address not to be included in this program, please check this circle.

If at any time you would like to be removed from either mailing list, please contact Customer Service at +1.847.763.9635 or send an e-mail to oracle@halldata.com. If you opt in to the sharing of information, Oracle may also provide you with e-mail related to Oracle products, services, and events. If you want to completely unsubscribe from any e-mail communication from Oracle, please send an e-mail to: unsubscribe@oracle-mail.com with the following in the subject line: REMOVE [your e-mail address]. For complete information on Oracle Publishing's privacy practices, please visit oracle.com/html/privacy/html

X _____   _____
signature (required)   date

name _____   title _____

company _____   e-mail address _____

street/p.o. box _____

city/state/zip or postal code _____   telephone _____

country _____   fax _____

Would you like to receive your free subscription in digital format instead of print if it becomes available? ○ Yes ○ No

---

YOU MUST ANSWER ALL 10 QUESTIONS BELOW.

① WHAT IS THE PRIMARY BUSINESS ACTIVITY OF YOUR FIRM AT THIS LOCATION? (check one only)

- ☐ 01 Aerospace and Defense Manufacturing
- ☐ 02 Application Service Provider
- ☐ 03 Automotive Manufacturing
- ☐ 04 Chemicals
- ☐ 05 Media and Entertainment
- ☐ 06 Construction/Engineering
- ☐ 07 Consumer Sector/Consumer Packaged Goods
- ☐ 08 Education
- ☐ 09 Financial Services/Insurance
- ☐ 10 Health Care
- ☐ 11 High Technology Manufacturing, OEM
- ☐ 12 Industrial Manufacturing
- ☐ 13 Independent Software Vendor
- ☐ 14 Life Sciences (biotech, pharmaceuticals)
- ☐ 15 Natural Resources
- ☐ 16 Oil and Gas
- ☐ 17 Professional Services
- ☐ 18 Public Sector (government)
- ☐ 19 Research
- ☐ 20 Retail/Wholesale/Distribution
- ☐ 21 Systems Integrator, VAR/VAD
- ☐ 22 Telecommunications
- ☐ 23 Travel and Transportation
- ☐ 24 Utilities (electric, gas, sanitation, water)
- ☐ 98 Other Business and Services _____

② WHICH OF THE FOLLOWING BEST DESCRIBES YOUR PRIMARY JOB FUNCTION? (check one only)

CORPORATE MANAGEMENT/STAFF
- ☐ 01 Executive Management (President, Chair, CEO, CFO, Owner, Partner, Principal)
- ☐ 02 Finance/Administrative Management (VP/Director/ Manager/Controller, Purchasing, Administration)
- ☐ 03 Sales/Marketing Management (VP/Director/Manager)
- ☐ 04 Computer Systems/Operations Management (CIO/VP/Director/Manager MIS/IS/IT, Ops)

IS/IT STAFF
- ☐ 05 Application Development/Programming Management
- ☐ 06 Application Development/Programming Staff
- ☐ 07 Consulting
- ☐ 08 DBA/Systems Administrator
- ☐ 09 Education/Training
- ☐ 10 Technical Support Director/Manager
- ☐ 11 Other Technical Management/Staff
- ☐ 98 Other

③ WHAT IS YOUR CURRENT PRIMARY OPERATING PLATFORM (check all that apply)

- ☐ 01 Digital Equipment Corp UNIX/VAX/VMS
- ☐ 02 HP UNIX
- ☐ 03 IBM AIX
- ☐ 04 IBM UNIX
- ☐ 05 Linux (Red Hat)
- ☐ 06 Linux (SUSE)
- ☐ 07 Linux (Oracle Enterprise)
- ☐ 08 Linux (other)
- ☐ 09 Macintosh
- ☐ 10 MVS
- ☐ 11 Netware
- ☐ 12 Network Computing
- ☐ 13 SCO UNIX
- ☐ 14 Sun Solaris/SunOS
- ☐ 15 Windows
- ☐ 16 Other UNIX
- ☐ 98 Other
- ☐ 99 None of the Above

④ DO YOU EVALUATE, SPECIFY, RECOMMEND, OR AUTHORIZE THE PURCHASE OF ANY OF THE FOLLOWING? (check all that apply)

- ☐ 01 Hardware
- ☐ 02 Business Applications (ERP, CRM, etc.)
- ☐ 03 Application Development Tools
- ☐ 04 Database Products
- ☐ 05 Internet or Intranet Products
- ☐ 06 Other Software
- ☐ 07 Middleware Products
- ☐ 99 None of the Above

⑤ IN YOUR JOB, DO YOU USE OR PLAN TO PURCHASE ANY OF THE FOLLOWING PRODUCTS? (check all that apply)

SOFTWARE
- ☐ 01 CAD/CAE/CAM
- ☐ 02 Collaboration Software
- ☐ 03 Communications
- ☐ 04 Database Management
- ☐ 05 File Management
- ☐ 06 Finance
- ☐ 07 Java
- ☐ 08 Multimedia Authoring
- ☐ 09 Networking
- ☐ 10 Programming
- ☐ 11 Project Management
- ☐ 12 Scientific and Engineering
- ☐ 13 Systems Management
- ☐ 14 Workflow

HARDWARE
- ☐ 15 Macintosh
- ☐ 16 Mainframe
- ☐ 17 Massively Parallel Processing
- ☐ 18 Minicomputer
- ☐ 19 Intel x86(32)
- ☐ 20 Intel x86(64)
- ☐ 21 Network Computer
- ☐ 22 Symmetric Multiprocessing
- ☐ 23 Workstation Services

SERVICES
- ☐ 24 Consulting
- ☐ 25 Education/Training
- ☐ 26 Maintenance
- ☐ 27 Online Database
- ☐ 28 Support
- ☐ 29 Technology-Based Training
- ☐ 30 Other
- ☐ 99 None of the Above

⑥ WHAT IS YOUR COMPANY'S SIZE? (check one only)

- ☐ 01 More than 25,000 Employees
- ☐ 02 10,001 to 25,000 Employees
- ☐ 03 5,001 to 10,000 Employees
- ☐ 04 1,001 to 5,000 Employees
- ☐ 05 101 to 1,000 Employees
- ☐ 06 Fewer than 100 Employees

⑦ DURING THE NEXT 12 MONTHS, HOW MUCH DO YOU ANTICIPATE YOUR ORGANIZATION WILL SPEND ON COMPUTER HARDWARE, SOFTWARE, PERIPHERALS, AND SERVICES FOR YOUR LOCATION? (check one only)

- ☐ 01 Less than $10,000
- ☐ 02 $10,000 to $49,999
- ☐ 03 $50,000 to $99,999
- ☐ 04 $100,000 to $499,999
- ☐ 05 $500,000 to $999,999
- ☐ 06 $1,000,000 and Over

⑧ WHAT IS YOUR COMPANY'S YEARLY SALES REVENUE? (check one only)

- ☐ 01 $500, 000, 000 and above
- ☐ 02 $100, 000, 000 to $500, 000, 000
- ☐ 03 $50, 000, 000 to $100, 000, 000
- ☐ 04 $5, 000, 000 to $50, 000, 000
- ☐ 05 $1, 000, 000 to $5, 000, 000

⑨ WHAT LANGUAGES AND FRAMEWORKS DO YOU USE? (check all that apply)

- ☐ 01 Ajax
- ☐ 02 C
- ☐ 03 C++
- ☐ 04 C#
- ☐ 05 Hibernate
- ☐ 06 J++/J#
- ☐ 07 Java
- ☐ 08 JSP
- ☐ 09 .NET
- ☐ 10 Perl
- ☐ 11 PHP
- ☐ 12 PL/SQL
- ☐ 13 Python
- ☐ 14 Ruby/Rails
- ☐ 15 Spring
- ☐ 16 Struts
- ☐ 17 SQL
- ☐ 18 Visual Basic
- ☐ 98 Other

⑩ WHAT ORACLE PRODUCTS ARE IN USE AT YOUR SITE? (check all that apply)

ORACLE DATABASE
- ☐ 01 Oracle Database 11*g*
- ☐ 02 Oracle Database 10*g*
- ☐ 03 Oracle9*i* Database
- ☐ 04 Oracle Embedded Database (Oracle Lite, Times Ten, Berkeley DB)
- ☐ 05 Other Oracle Database Release

ORACLE FUSION MIDDLEWARE
- ☐ 06 Oracle Application Server
- ☐ 07 Oracle Portal
- ☐ 08 Oracle Enterprise Manager
- ☐ 09 Oracle BPEL Process Manager
- ☐ 10 Oracle Identity Management
- ☐ 11 Oracle SOA Suite
- ☐ 12 Oracle Data Hubs

ORACLE DEVELOPMENT TOOLS
- ☐ 13 Oracle JDeveloper
- ☐ 14 Oracle Forms
- ☐ 15 Oracle Reports
- ☐ 16 Oracle Designer
- ☐ 17 Oracle Discoverer
- ☐ 18 Oracle BI Beans
- ☐ 19 Oracle Warehouse Builder
- ☐ 20 Oracle WebCenter
- ☐ 21 Oracle Application Express

ORACLE APPLICATIONS
- ☐ 22 Oracle E-Business Suite
- ☐ 23 PeopleSoft Enterprise
- ☐ 24 JD Edwards EnterpriseOne
- ☐ 25 JD Edwards World
- ☐ 26 Oracle Fusion
- ☐ 27 Hyperion
- ☐ 28 Siebel CRM

ORACLE SERVICES
- ☐ 28 Oracle E-Business Suite On Demand
- ☐ 29 Oracle Technology On Demand
- ☐ 30 Siebel CRM On Demand
- ☐ 31 Oracle Consulting
- ☐ 32 Oracle Education
- ☐ 33 Oracle Support
- ☐ 98 Other
- ☐ 99 None of the Above

08014Q04